PHILIP JENKINS

PEDOPHILES AND PRIESTS

Anatomy of a Contemporary Crisis

OXFORD
UNIVERSITY PRESS

OXFORD
UNIVERSITY PRESS

Oxford   New York
Athens   Auckland   Bangkok   Bogotá   Buenos Aires
Calcutta   Cape Town   Chennai   Dar es Salaam   Delhi   Florence   Hong Kong
Istanbul   Karachi   Kuala Lumpur   Madrid   Melbourne   Mexico City   Mumbai
Nairobi   Paris   São Paulo   Shanghai   Singapore   Taipei
Tokyo   Toronto   Warsaw

and associated companies in
Berlin   Ibadan

First published in 1996 by Oxford University Press, Inc.
198 Madison Avenue, new York, New York 10016

First issued as an Oxford University Press paperback, 2001

Oxford is a registered trademark of Oxford University Press, Inc.

Library of Congress Cataloging-in-Publication Data
Jenkins, Philip, 1952–
Pedophiles and priests : anatomy of a contemporary crisis / Philip Jenkins
p. cm.   Includes index.
ISBN 0-19-509565-0; 0-19-514597-6 (pbk.)
1. Child sexual abuse by clergy—United States.   2. Catholic
Church—United States—Clergy—Sexual behavior.   I. Title.
BX1912.9.J46   1996
362.7'6—dc20   95-45625

2 4 6 8 9 7 5 3

Printed in the United States of America
on acid free paper

Preface to the Paperback Edition

Though the issue of sexual abuse by clergy has remained very much alive since *Pedophiles and Priests* was completed in 1995, I believe that people no longer give quite so much credit to the most extreme charges against priests, and specifically Catholic priests. In retrospect, the turning point here was the shamefully irresponsible attack on Cardinal Joseph Bernardin, when the media trumpeted quite heinous charges without any serious attempt at verification. Since then, the media have generally become more cautious about seeing sexual misconduct as a distinctive problem of the Roman Catholic Church, and no longer automatically accept the extravagant figures sometimes put forward about the numbers of "pedophile priests." It was interesting that the controversial television series *Nothing Sacred* (ABC, 1997–98), which portrayed the lives of contemporary Catholic priests, made virtually no reference to abuse issues: the omission would have been unthinkable a couple of years earlier. One factor here has been the work of activist groups like the Catholic League for Religious and Civil Rights in challenging blatantly anti-Catholic statements as they arise. Pruning away the anti-Catholic rhetoric has allowed us to gain a better sense of the problem as it exists, among both Catholic and non-Catholic (and indeed, non-Christian) clergy.

This change of attitude makes it easier to look at the scandals that have continued to emerge and assess them on their merits, rather than as elements of a general "Catholic Crisis." Certainly, some of the recent cases have been harrowing enough. In the Catholic Church itself, perhaps the most gruesome incident was the trial of Dallas priest Rudolph Kos, who was sentenced to life imprisonment in 1998 for a series of assaults on altar boys during the 1980s. This case resulted in an astonishing civil judgment of $120 million against Kos and his diocese. There have also been disturbing echoes from older cases. In 1993, at the height of the "pedophile priest" crisis, the Connecticut diocese of Bridgeport had been one of many hit by charges that senior church officials were unsympathetic to victim complaints. Prominent among these officials was the then-bishop, Edward M. Egan, who in 2000 rose to the top of the American hierarchy as Archbishop of New York. Memories of the earlier conflict resulted in protests by victim families against Egan's elevation. Also traumatic has been the protracted sex and money scandal that overwhelmed the California diocese of Santa Rosa in 1999–2000.

Another striking development since the mid-1990s has been the continuing spread of the American "crisis" to other nations, both in the Roman Catholic Church and other denominations. Canada has experienced repeated controversies, particularly over the sexual and physical maltreatment of native children in church-run boarding schools over several decades—in this case, all the nation's major denominations were deeply involved. By 2000, the Anglican Church of Canada was so hard-hit by liability suits that it had to cut back heavily on programs, and faced potential ruin. In both Ireland and Great Britain, clergy abuse continues to be as hotly debated as it was in the United States in the early 1990s, with devastating consequences for the prestige of the churches, and their claims to moral authority. As in the United States as well, the media tend to lump together cases of grotesque exploitation with far milder instances of consensual adult behavior, so that horrifying stories of clergy distributing child pornography are presented alongside news of priests or ministers being exposed as homosexual. Mixing such very different cases together contributes to creating a general public impression that something must be deeply wrong with organized religion, whether Roman Catholic or Anglican. Sadly, too, debates in the British Isles often draw on the very high (and flawed) estimates of "pedophile priests" that used to circulate in North America.

Reflecting continuing concern about sexual misconduct by clergy, the volume of literature continues to expand rapidly. Major contributions include collections of essays such as Anson Shupe's *Wolves Within the Fold* and Thomas G. Plante's *Bless Me Father For I Have Sinned*. Richard Sipe's *Sex, Priests and Power* was a significant historical and psychological study of the "crisis," and I wish I had been able to draw on it in the earlier edition of my own book. One important case study is Mike Echols's *Brother Tony's Boys,* which discusses the Tony Leyva case to which I referred in chapter 1: this gains significance in showing how extreme abuse can occur in religious traditions far removed from Catholicism. My own book *Moral Panic* provides more background about the whole idea of child abuse and molestation, and how the concept changed over time. While not excusing some of the decisions that various dioceses made about responding to abuse problems in the 1960s and 1970s, the material I present may go some way to explaining just what church administrators were thinking at the time.

Some particularly important books have come from outside the United States, reflecting the international spread of interest since the 1980s. From Canada comes *Boys Don't Cry* by Darcy Henton and David McCann, while in Ireland the continuing debate is reflected in the collection of victim testimonies published in Iseult O'Doherty's *Stolen Childhood*. In the Philippines, Earl K. Wilkinson's tireless campaigns against abuse by clergy are reflected in his book *People, Priests and Pedophiles*. If I were to undertake this project anew, I would unquestionably address its global dimension.

While I stand by all the views expressed in this book, I would like to make a clarification of fact arising from my discussion on the James Porter case (p. 134 below). Contrary to my statement there, the order of "Servants of the Paraclete" was not in fact adjudged guilty of negligence, and the case in fact resulted in a settlement with the plaintiffs. Also, I was mistaken in referring to the Paraclete house in Jemez Springs, New Mexico, as a "treatment facility," which it was not for most of its history: Fathers Porter and Holley thus received their treatment from other specialists not directly connected to the Servants. I am grateful to Mr. Alan Konrad for this correction, which I am happy to note here.

University Park, Pennsylvania
October 2000

Contents

PEDOPHILES
AND PRIESTS

I

The Construction of
Problems and Panics

Recognizing a Problem

In 1985, Gilbert Gauthe, a Roman Catholic priest from rural Louisiana, was tried on multiple counts of child molestation. Over the next two years, the story was widely reported as a glaring instance of the serious and predatory nature of child sexual abuse and an illustration that the behavior could affect virtually any individual in any community. At first, there was little suggestion in the media that Gauthe was typical of a large section of the clergy in general, or of Catholic clergy in particular. Matters changed radically over the next decade, so that by 1992 and 1993 it was difficult to find a mainstream periodical or news program that had not covered the phenomenon of "clergy sexual abuse," often repeatedly and in detail. This is a model example of a social problem that undergoes mushroom growth, receiving virtually no attention from media or policy makers before about 1984–1985, yet becoming a major focus of public concern within a few years.

The issue has had a major impact on religious life and practice in North America, especially because the Catholic church is the denomination of perhaps of a quarter of Americans, some sixty million individuals. In the view that has commonly prevailed since about 1989, clergy abuse is a serious problem both in terms of the number of perpetrators involved and the frequency with which they molest children or young people, and thus the potential number of victims is very large. Moreover, victims who are abused are gravely affected or traumatized for the rest of their lives. Although "pedophile priests" are disturbed and dangerous individuals, they could not wreak the harm they do were it not for the institutional context that ignores or connives at their activities. According to the general portrayal of the problem, the churches historically failed to understand either the seriousness or persistence of the behavior and continually overestimated the chance that an abusive priest could reform his behavior. The Catholic church in particular had been more concerned with protecting the reputation of the institution and the clerical profession than in

3

safeguarding real or potential child victims. In consequence, abusive priests were placed in circumstances where they had enormous opportunities to molest, though with little chance of being caught or punished, a combination of circumstances that offered a near-perfect criminogenic environment. The problem of abusive clergy centers on the misdeeds of the institutions in which they serve, and the rhetoric employed to denounce ecclesiastical authorities suggests extensive malfeasance or even complicity. The images presented of the Catholic church are of extreme and unhealthy secrecy and official cynicism.

The abuse issue is said to present that church with its gravest moral crisis in centuries. Journalists have written of an "ecclesiastical Watergate," a "meltdown," the "S. and L. disaster of the Catholic church," the greatest threat facing that church since the Reformation. In response, critics have urged far-reaching reforms in order to curb the danger to the young. Within the Catholic church, demands have included an end to mandatory celibacy, the ordination of women to the priesthood, and limitations on the sanctity of the confessional. Other churches have been forced to recognize the abuse problem as a crucial issue in the training and selection of clergy, and programs of training and counseling have proliferated.

The importance of the issue is beyond question, but it is by no means obvious how it came to be perceived as a problem or, once it was recognized, how the problem came to be defined in those particular terms rather than others. The answer may seem self-evident. If there is a Catholic priest like James Porter, who forcibly molested dozens or hundreds of small children in several states over many years, then clearly he as an individual represents a social danger to be confronted and dealt with. If we find accounts of some other individuals who fit a comparable pattern, then we inevitably begin to generalize and perceive that these separate instances represent components of some larger issue. But the exact nature of the problem as eventually formulated is not predetermined by the original observations, and many alternative interpretations are conceivable or even likely.

The Process of Social Construction

There is a classic definition of a social problem as "a condition which is defined by a considerable number of persons as a deviation from some social norm which they cherish."[1] In this view, the problem may have at its heart an objective condition that can be observed, examined, and quantified, but the exact interpretation will depend on subjective factors, the perception that the condition is harmful, threatening, and worthy of attention. This subjective definition may or may not reflect a rational or balanced assessment of the given problem, and other observers might think that it places far too much or too little emphasis on a particular aspect of the issue. The problem is defined less by rational criteria than by a complex rhetorical and political process that is commonly described as "social construction." This depends on the ideologies and assumptions of a particular society at a given historical moment, and the rhetorical work of the various interest groups and individuals who make and establish claims about issues. A "constructionist" scholar seeks to identify the constituencies involved in the debate, to analyze the motivations and interests of those groups or individuals who portray an issue as singularly threatening and worthy of intervention, and the rhetorical devices that are employed in this process.[2]

In recent scholarship on social problems, there have been "constructionist" studies of the origin and development of many public fears, ranging from drugs, child abuse, and AIDS to serial murder, Satanism, and domestic violence.[3] The claims-makers studied have been quite varied, including individual activists, bureaucratic agencies, private pressure groups, charities, and religious organizations, and the gains received from successful problem construction are equally diverse. For example, feminist groups who succeed in projecting their particular interpretation of sexual violence profit in many ways: in the reinforcement and dissemination of their ideological position, in the reshaping of bureaucratic agencies to further women's interests, and perhaps in an increase of resources for agencies like rape crisis centers.[4] Religious fundamentalists profit just as broadly from promoting their view of a perceived danger from the occult or Satanism. However, claims-making activity does not occur in a vacuum, in that even the most dedicated and eloquent activists can achieve little unless external events or underlying changes in social attitudes assist by creating a public mood receptive to the views advanced. The advocacy and reception of social problems can usefully be compared to a bazaar or marketplace in which numerous activists compete to win public attention for their particular wares.[5] Successful salesmanship depends on the changing tastes and demands of the potential consumers no less than on the packaging of the product itself.

To say that a social problem is constructed does not mean that it is not founded upon perceptions that might have some validity, for instance, that activities such as driving while intoxicated cause real harm to individuals and society. To describe the child-abuse problem or the drug problem as constructed phenomena does not mean that a social theorist naively challenges the existence of child molestation or drug abuse, or denies that they can have devastating consequences. It is rare for a constructionist study to deny the whole existence of any objective basis to a putative problem, though this can occur, as in the case of the "ritual child abuse" affair.[6] However, it is still necessary to question why some behaviors rather than others come to be seen as so uniquely harmful in certain societies and historical periods rather than others: why the question of child abuse should have been so fundamentally reformulated during the 1970s and 1980s; why the drug problem was seen as a national menace during the 1980s; and why, by the early 1990s, clergy abuse was perceived as so ubiquitous and pernicious a threat. Analyzing a social problem offers rich opportunities for understanding the fears, concerns, and prejudices of the society that comes to view a given issue as uniquely dangerous.

Nor does the constructionist literature assume that sinister or covert agendas lie behind these processes or that problems are somehow artificial dangers designed to divert public attention from "real" issues. If the media are to report on any question, they must attempt to give it some meaning, to place it in a frame of reference that will be familiar to the assumed audience. To quote Stuart Hall, "If the world is not to be represented as a jumble of random and chaotic events, then they must be identified (i.e., named, defined, related to other events known to the audience), and assigned to a social context (i.e., placed within a frame of meanings familiar to the audience). This process—identification and contextualization—is one of the most important through which events are 'made to mean' by the media."[7] The importance attached to a particular event will vary according to circumstances and timing, and the event can be placed in a number of different contexts or frames. "Framings" are "cultural combinations and constructions that put selected phenomena into comprehensible and consumable focus. Frames . . . are systems of selection, presentation, and accentuation: they are patterned mechanisms of cognition and interpretation that package social experience for producers and purchasers of the frames."[8] In the case of clergy abuse, the individual misdeeds of clergy like Gilbert Gauthe and James Porter have been viewed through a highly selective cultural frame, which emphasizes certain aspects of the cases to the exclusion of others and concentrates on these instances rather than others that could equally well have been chosen.

Alternative Views

The vast majority of people would agree that the actions of a Porter or a Gauthe are wrong, but there is little consensus as to whether they should be seen as a symptom of individual pathology or if they could plausibly be linked to broader social issues. And if the crimes are in fact a component of a wider social problem, exactly what sort of problem do they represent? How, in short, should the cases be framed?

According to their ideological perspectives and their own interests, different individuals would emphasize varying elements of the story to produce radically divergent conclusions, together with the appropriate policy consequences. One observer stresses the individual and developmental factors that shaped the "pedophile priests" and sees them as isolated deviants. Another emphasizes the structural factors within the Catholic priesthood that led them to commit their acts, factors such as mandatory celibacy, the seminary training process, and the belief structure that places so high a premium on the individual priest that a community is reluctant to believe anything amiss about his character. A third person concentrates on the bureaucratic structures of the church that permitted them to continue their careers of abuse unchecked, while yet another commentator sees the case as a manifestation of patriarchal value systems. Depending on one's approach, the cases can be used rhetorically to call for severe criminal and civil penalties against the offending priests and their superiors or for more thoroughgoing structural changes; for a limited reform of the organization of the Catholic priesthood or for the radical overthrow of male and "patriarchal" dominance within the Catholic church.

In the case of clergy abuse, the dominant construction not only suggests the locus of the problem (the Catholic church) but also places the blame on a patriarchal clerical elite anxious to defend the virtually hopeless cause of mandatory celibacy. The central theme is one of organizational deviancy, so that if the church's policies and procedures could be reformed, the problem would be reduced or eliminated. However, even if we suppose that Catholic ministers are disproportionately involved in abuse, it is not inevitable that the problem would have been typified in this way. In other circumstances, the blame for "pedophile priests" could have been laid upon a wholly different cast of villains.

Perhaps the issue might have given an invaluable platform to ecclesiastical conservatives to denounce moral laxity in society at large, the breakdown of clerical discipline under the influence of theological liberalism, and the infiltration of homosexuals into the priesthood. Far from causing a crisis for church prestige, clergy abuse could in these circumstances have provided a rallying point for traditionalists, and it is easy to imagine a pedophilia scandal leading to a purge of homosexual priests. Conservative interpretations could blame the changing sexual standards of the wider society and the prevalence of pornography. We might even suppose a prochurch reaction that would have assailed the excessive litigiousness of contemporary society, and attacked the lawyers and therapists active in exposing the abuse. There certainly were church activists who wished to promote such formulations of the problem, but they enjoyed little success.

Constructing "Pedophile Priests"

From a constructionist perspective, a large gulf separates the objective and verifiable basis at the heart of the clergy-abuse issue from the subjective definition that is so generally accepted. What can be stated with certainty is that since the early 1980s there have been hundreds and probably thousands of cases in which clergy of various denominations have been accused of sexual involvement with minors, and that in a number of instances the charges have been validated by either a criminal conviction or a decision in civil court. The behavior has unquestionably occurred, but beyond that, much is uncertain.

The vigorous process of construction that has been under way in this area is illustrated by the alliterative term "pedophile priests," which is so regularly employed in news stories. Both the words in question are open to controversy because they place a special construction upon the behavior: taken as a whole, the term makes the problem more serious, more dangerous, and more Catholic than it would otherwise appear. To speak of "priests" severely limits the phenomenon of abuse by clergy because the word is commonly understood to refer to Catholic priests, as opposed to the pastors or preachers of other denominations (though *priests* conceivably also implies Episcopal or Orthodox ministers). *Pedophile* requires interpretation as well because it is used here beyond its strict clinical meaning. A pedophile is a man sexually attracted to children below the age of puberty, but the vast majority of recorded instances of clergy "abuse" or misconduct involve an interest in teenagers of either gender, often boys of fifteen or sixteen. The difference may seem trivial, but most psychological opinion holds that pedophiles are far more difficult to treat or control than offenders who direct their attention to older targets. Nor is it possible to speak of a younger child's giving genuine consent to a sexual act, so that the conduct necessarily implies the use of force or grave deception. To speak of a "pedophile priest" implies that the victims are younger and more defenseless than they commonly are and that the offenders are severely compulsive and virtually incurable. The very term most commonly used to describe this problem has powerful rhetorical connotations in its own right, even before a given writer or journalist has begun to select and describe cases to illustrate the phenomenon.

The term *priest pedophilia* is a rhetorical device that attempts to fit a new issue into the framework of a previously established problem. In Best's terms, new issue (*x*) is significant because it is in reality a part of known problem (*y*), and therefore

requires the package of responses and reactions that have already been felt appropriate for problem (y).[9] One form of behavior is stigmatized by linking it ("mapping
together") with another phenomenon that is perceived as far more dangerous, in this
instance using *pedophilia* as a generic term for sexual conduct with minors. This
process of escalation has been described as part of a "signification spiral," a "self-
amplifying sequence within the area of signification: the activity or event with
which the signification deals is *escalated*—made to seem more threatening—within
the course of the signification itself."[10] The activity is thus pushed beyond even the
most liberal threshold of social tolerance, into a region that demands condemnation
and official intervention.

1950's Red Scare

The Catholic Dimension

The construction of the problem has gone through three successive stages, which
can be summarized by the following sentences:

• Many clergy are active in the sexual abuse of children.
• Many Catholic priests are active in sexual abuse.
• The structure of Catholicism makes priests more likely to abuse children.

Each of these statements is open to debate, but a daring leap of logic occurs in the
transition from the first sentence to the second. In reality, it is not obvious that public
attention should be focused so absolutely on the Roman Catholic dimension normally attributed to the question.

This Catholic interpretation is pervasive. In the mass media, a news report will
generally describe a number of examples involving Catholic priests and draw on
experts to analyze exactly what characteristics of that church or its priestly representatives so regularly lead them into sexual misconduct. In the mid-1980s, the
pioneering official report on clergy abuse, "The Problem of Sexual Molestation by
Roman Catholic Clergy," specifically concerned Catholic priests, and this provided
a framework for much of the reporting over the next few years. Among the books on
this topic, the two best-known surveys are respectively subtitled "Catholic Priests
and the Sexual Abuse of Children"[11] and "Children, Sexual Abuse and the Catholic
Church,"[12] and Catholic clergy are the subjects of case studies like Sennott's *Broken
Covenant* (1992) and Harris's *Unholy Orders* (1991). In reality, Catholic clergy are
not necessarily represented in the sexual abuse phenomenon at a rate higher than or
even equal to their numbers in the clerical profession as a whole.

Partially, the apparently high number of cases involving Catholic clergy is an
inevitable consequence of the very size of that denomination; more than fifty thousand priests are currently active in the United States, not counting thousands of
other religious. To put this in context, the number of Catholic *clergy* is larger than
the total membership of many denominations in this country. If we assume for the
sake of argument that the proportion of criminal or sexually disturbed individuals is
likely to be constant in any group of adult males, regardless of celibacy rules, then
there will be many more scandals involving Catholic priests than Episcopal or Presbyterian clergy, precisely because this group is more numerous to begin with. In
fact, the difference is even larger than it initially appears because so many of the

scandals involve events that occurred many years ago, in the 1960s and 1970s, and we would need to compare the total number of clergy that had served in each denomination over that lengthy time period. Because the Catholic priesthood had a particularly high rate of turnover during the 1970s, this gives a very large population in which potentially troubled individuals might be found, at least 150,000 individuals in the United States.

It would be desirable to measure the rate of reported sexual misconduct in the Catholic church relative to other religious groups, but we simply do not have quantitative evidence, and many obstacles stand in the way of effective comparison. Misconduct in the Catholic church is so well known partly because it has been subject to quantification and measurement more frequently and consistently than is true for any other denomination. Some of the most important surveys long predated the recognition of an "abuse problem"; they were undertaken on the assumption that a notionally celibate group would be expected to have a high rate of sexual deviancy, and they provided ammunition for polemical critiques of church policies.[13] Neither the assumption nor the polemical agenda invalidates the findings, but they do explain why statistics are available for this group rather than for other denominations. Because no one assumed in the 1970s that pedophilia or homosexuality was likely to be found among a married population such as Baptist or Methodist clergy, no pressure group or activist took the trouble to investigate the phenomenon.

Similar problems beset the much-cited estimate that in the decade after 1982, about four hundred Catholic clergy in North America were accused of sexual misconduct with minors (see Chapter 5 for a discussion of this statistic). Even if the figure is precisely accurate, it cannot provide a basis for comparison with other denominations because the researcher involved, Jason Berry, happened to be examining Catholic cases to the exclusion of others.[14] Even if he had pursued other stories, he would have been able to count only cases that came to the attention of the courts, and this would not in itself provide an accurate measure of the rate of misbehavior. A cyclical process was at work here, in that a proliferation of cases involving Catholic clergy encouraged other individuals to report incidents involving the Catholic church and to begin litigation, which in turn encouraged future complaints. Because the abuse issue had by the late 1980s shifted so decisively to the question of "pedophile priests," it is scarcely surprising that this concern should have been reflected in litigation. In assessing misconduct in other denominations, we not only have no reliable statistics but also lack the estimates and informed guesses that are so prevalent in the Catholic context.

There are structural and organizational reasons that the Catholic church should have produced a disproportionately high level of *reported* scandals. This is a centralized hierarchical organization with a solid bureaucratic tradition dating back many centuries, and there are national agencies such as that of the apostolic delegate whose functions include the recording and tabulation of formal accusations against priests. Moreover, parish clergy are firmly subordinate to episcopal authorities, who have traditionally observed and recorded their behavior. At the diocesan level, each Catholic priest has a detailed dossier that records official complaints, and in recent years these have provided the source for many legal actions, often based on events that occurred decades previously. As one instance of clergy abuse comes to light in an area, it is now a natural tactic for attorneys to subpoena diocesan archives, which can be used to expose and litigate hitherto unsuspected cases, to create a network effect. The fact that the church kept such records has probably been the largest single element in inflating the number of Catholic clergy who have come to the attention of the courts.

It is useful here to compare the experience of some of the larger Protestant denominations such as the Baptist groups, who heavily prize congregational autonomy and have a traditional loathing of regional or national structures beyond a loose federalism (Baptists are the second-largest religious group in the United States, with some thirty-five to forty million members divided among many denominations). Baptist ministers are "called" and employed by specific congregations and ordained by the clergy of neighboring churches rather than being assigned by the dictates of church superiors. The relationship is that of a freelance professional to a client rather than an employee to a multinational corporation. If a Baptist minister engages in misconduct, litigation will be directed against the congregation involved and its insurers, but it is not feasible to sue the national denomination or its regional branch. Nor will a legal "fishing expedition" elicit the names of colleagues who have been similarly accused over the years. A scandal in a Baptist church will remain strictly localized, except in those rare instances where the pastor concerned had achieved celebrity for political or other achievements. Accurately or otherwise, it is more difficult to assert that sexual misdeeds in this context reflect a systemic problem. In terms of structure, American churches follow a rough spectrum of degrees of central organization and control, with Catholics at one extreme and Baptists at the other, and other groups lying between: Lutherans, Methodists, and Episcopalians leaning more toward the centralized structure, Presbyterians and Pentecostal churches favoring a congregational polity. And that fact does much to determine the apparent incidence of abuse in the various denominations.

Sexual misconduct is more likely to be publicized in a Catholic setting. Because higher rates of reporting are assumed to reflect a higher incidence of the behavior itself, commentators then seek explanations for the particular tendency of Catholic priests to "fall from grace," and they usually cite celibacy. However, consideration of other religious groups produces ideological or organizational factors that seem likely to lead to misconduct or abuse in those settings. One of the more egregious molestation cases of the 1980s concerned a Pentecostal minister named Tony Leyva, who had abused perhaps a hundred boys in various southern states over a period of several years.[15] Fundamentalist evangelists attract veneration and trust from the faithful, and they operate in an intellectual environment which believes firmly in diabolical forces that try to disrupt the efforts of any effective preacher, so that scandals can readily be dismissed as, literally, the work of the devil and his earthly agents. Independent preachers are subject to few or no controls from a denomination or hierarchy, and the highly mobile nature of itinerant ministers makes it unlikely that they will remain in any one area long enough to generate enough complaints to merit investigation. Taken together, factors of opportunity and ideology make this form of religious life quite as attractive to a hypothetical pedophile as the Catholic priesthood.

Unconstructed Cases

The Leyva case is not mentioned in any of the books or analytical articles on clergy abuse, which is noteworthy because in so many ways Leyva's career resembled that of the internationally notorious former parish priest James Porter. Both were accused of having molested about a hundred minors over many years, both received lengthy sentences, and in a sense the Leyva story may have been "worse" than Porter's in that there were accomplices in his sexual activities. Leyva's case also had the potential for celebrity in that it received some (short-lived) coverage in such leading newspapers as the *New York Times*. It has since been forgotten because it does not fit within the cultural frame that dominates public discourse, and that emphasizes the Catholic role to the virtual exclusion of others. There is no cultural home for the "pedophile pastor," and the story is not constructed as part of a problem. In short, it has acquired no true meaning.

Similar points occur if we consider a Catholic-related abuse story that occurred before the process of construction was under way. In 1982, for example, the *Chicago Tribune* reported on an innovative lawsuit filed against the local archdiocese in consequence of the actions of a priest named Robert Mayer, in which the victim's parents demanded $1 million in punitive damages.[16] The story recounted the specific allegations in some detail, but the tone of coverage was strikingly neutral. The headline, "Suit charges moral misconduct by Arlington Heights priest," conspicuously did not include any of the potent words that would have been employed a decade later, words such as *abuse*, *molestation*, and *pedophile*, and does not even emphasize the sexual nature of the charges: it was "*moral* misconduct." Nor, in contrast with later stories, is there any attempt to contextualize the incident. There are no interviews with experts assessing the scale of abuse by priests, no estimates of the number of priests practicing homosexuality, no comments on the flaws in the church's disciplinary structures. The facts are reported simply, and the story is left unconstructed, "meaningless" except in its relevance to those directly involved with the litigation. (Later events would make this a highly significant case; see Chapter 3.)

The difference between the Mayer and Leyva affairs is that abuse cases involving Catholic priests came to be quite elaborately constructed and those against Protestant clergy did not. This is not to imply that the post-1985 media exhibited any conscious bias against the Catholic church or its hierarchy. As with so many other problems, it is difficult for the media to offer a truly balanced account of any given issue because even a relatively objective journalist has preconceptions that limit both the authorities who will be approached for their opinions and the questions they will be asked. In the case of clergy abuse, the media consensus held that this was chiefly a Catholic issue, and a reporter therefore needed expert opinion on the difficulties facing the Catholic clergy. The act of framing the question in this way was just as significant as the specific answers received. In addition, commentators approached for their knowledge of Catholic circumstances inevitably tend to be most familiar with Catholic cases, to which they refer inquiring journalists. Quite conceivably, they had not even heard of Tony Leyva. In consequence, stories about clergy abuse developed a familiar and predictable shape that varied chiefly in the specific Catholic priests whose misdeeds were reported.

This process of selectivity also conditioned attitudes to the relative newsworthiness of particular stories. Little public recognition was achieved by the numerous cases involving non-Catholic clergy that came to light in those years, although they otherwise included virtually all the elements of the familiar cases. They also possessed many of the features that customarily mark a case as newsworthy: the prominence of the individual accused, the organized nature of the abuse, and the peculiarly violent exploitation of the child victims. Some of the Episcopal ministers accused in those years were distinguished leaders of that denomination, and yet the Episcopal church's cases had virtually no impact in the mainstream media. There is no Catholic case comparable to that of three brothers, all Baptist ministers, all facing simultaneous charges of child molestation, although this case too enjoyed only local notoriety.[17]

The point is illustrated by a scandal that occurred in a rural Baptist church in Washtenaw County, Michigan, during the fall of 1992, when an associate pastor and a bus driver were accused of raping small boys who attended the Sunday school.[18] There was every reason to assume that the story would attract national attention, occurring as it did at the peak of media interest in the Porter case, a time when clergy abuse was being addressed in most newsmagazines and television news programs. The setting was rural, but no more so than the Gauthe case, and the affair was picked up almost immediately in the large media market of Detroit, just as the Porter case was taken up by the *Boston Globe*. And as in the Porter story, the alleged abuse included acts of forcible sexual violence against very young children. However, the story soon disappeared from view, even in the Detroit press, and it was never cited outside the state. It is inconceivable that the same oblivion would have befallen a comparable case involving a Catholic priest at that time.

Differences in media attitudes and the process of litigation mean that it is effectively impossible to compare the incidence of abuse across denominations. At the same time, it is not difficult to find numerous scandals and court cases from the whole range of the denominational spectrum, which often involve highly placed members of the group concerned. As one Episcopal clergywoman has remarked, "Unfortunately, pedophilia is ecumenical"—a view quite contrary to the image of the "pedophile priest."[19]

The Book

Estimates about the prevalence of child sexual abuse vary widely, but there is no doubt that the behavior itself is common, and that at least some priests and religious are involved. Occasional investigations and scandals are inevitable, and a handful of genuine instances of clergy sex abuse can be found in any decade of this century. What has been different about the past decade has been the high volume of reported cases and the enormous public attention that these have attracted. Because it is unlikely that pedophile behavior itself has increased so dramatically, the question must be asked why public perceptions have changed so radically. Why should so many cases have come to light during the 1980s rather than in an earlier historical epoch, and why should they have formed the basis of a "pedophile crisis"? Why, similarly, should public attention have come to focus so decisively on the Catholic aspects of the problem? What explains the distinctive construction of the clergy-abuse problem in the past decade?

The chapters of this book informally fall into three sections. Chapters 2 through 5, describe the generation of the clergy-abuse problem and the means by which the media came to accept one particular construction of the issue. Chapters 6 through 9, identify the major claims-makers and interest groups whose agendas shaped this construction, and asks why the issue was formulated in the way it was. Finally, chapter 10 explores the significance of the findings both for the nature of social problems and for the current state of organized religion in North America.

Problem construction is a cumulative or incremental process in which each issue is to some extent built upon its predecessors in the context of a steadily developing fund of socially available knowledge. The construction of clergy sex abuse was a complex process involving a number of separate stages, which initially seemed to have little connection with one another. There were long-term changes in social conditions and attitudes that made the problem possible, broadly from the mid-1960s onward; more immediate developments in the churches, the media, and the legal environment between about 1975 and 1985 that made a controversy probable; and a set of specific events and controversies in the mid-1980s that detonated the eventual crisis. Even at that point, however, it was not inevitable that the problem would have been constructed in precisely the manner that it was if not for the specific endeavors of the various claims-makers identified here.

Modern perceptions of clergy abuse should also be placed in the much longer historical context of anti-Catholic and anticlerical imagery and rhetoric. For centuries these traditions played a crucial part in the history, culture, and political discourse of the United States and other Western nations. Chapter 2, "The Anti-Catholic Tradition," shows the extent to which polemics consistently drew on sexual imagery, denouncing the hypocrisy of the supposedly celibate priests who in reality seduced women and molested altar boys. The rhetoric of sexual hypocrisy was a component of political attacks upon the church, and was most marked when governments or rival religious groups wished to discredit a powerful church establishment.

The term *anti-Catholic* should not be used without proper definition, and attacks on the church hierarchy should often be more properly described as anticlerical. The difficulties of defining anti-Catholic sentiment are illustrated by the analogous concept of anti-Semitism. If a newspaper accurately describes the dishonest or criminal activities of an individual who is Jewish, that would not of itself be anti-Semitic. It would however be grossly anti-semitic if the paper repeatedly described the criminal activities of Jews without noting the similar role of other ethnic groups, and further proposed that this form of criminality was peculiarly characteristic of Jews or arose from features of Jewish religion or ethnicity. The classification would be placed beyond doubt if the account contextualized this particular wrongdoing with real or imaginary instances of Jewish misdeeds through the centuries. Similarly, it is not anti-Catholic to remark that Bishop A or Cardinal B is dishonest or criminal or that a particular priest has committed acts of child molestation. It is more questionable to describe these actions as characteristic of a large body of Catholics or to assert that the behavior arises from ideas and practices fundamental to Catholicism, especially when similar activities by other groups are not similarly highlighted. By these standards, much of the analysis of the "pedophile crisis" from 1985 onward can legitimately be described as anti-Catholic.

The recrudescence of anti-Catholic imagery offers a powerful argument to Catholic conservatives, who can minimize reporting of the pedophile problem as a simple manifestation of religious prejudice. However, the numerous cases that came to light following 1984–1985 made clear that the conduct of church authorities toward sexually exploitative clergy had been questionable, if not grossly irresponsible. The Gauthe case was characteristic, if not exactly typical, in that a priest who molested children in one parish had been repeatedly reassigned to new locations after his predilections became known, without warning the families in the new area of any potential dangers. When cases did arise, the attitude of Catholic authorities to victims and parents was occasionally hostile and arrogant, and it showed that the avoidance of scandal was a consideration that far outweighed the interests of victims.

Chapter 3, "Discovering Clergy Abuse," describes how the Gauthe case provided a template for the media and activist groups seeking to contextualize the perceived epidemic of molestation. In the decade following 1984, several hundred Catholic clergy were accused of sexual abuse, and dioceses in all parts of the country experienced local scandals. By far the most notorious concerned James Porter, most of whose activities had occurred in Massachusetts during the 1960s, but whose prosecution and trial during 1992 and 1993 became a national scandal. In those years, news reporting of clergy abuse reached an unprecedented peak, and the Catholic aspects came to dominate absolutely. The media agreed that the problem had become a "crisis" for the church, a word connoting acute strain or disorder, and a turning point after which it would be very difficult to return to the status quo. The terminology of "crisis" demands action: in the language of the card table, it is a forcing bid. Under intense pressure, church authorities sought desperately to formulate policies that would prevent future disasters.

The fact that offending clergy could be so quietly reshuffled prior to the early 1980s demonstrates that certain structural changes were necessary before clerical misconduct could be constructed as a systemic problem. Before 1984 there was a conspicuous lack of public agencies with the desire or ability to intervene officially in cases, and police and prosecutors were usually reluctant to offend so powerful a constituent as the local Catholic church. Civil suits were difficult because church activities were generally thought to be protected by doctrines of charitable immunity. The media similarly suffered from strong constraints about reporting clerical sex scandals, for the church was a powerful and well-connected group with access to unusually strong defenses against criticism. Apart from the customary legal devices of slander and libel suits, the church could count on a large public following that was likely to view criticism as the outcome of religious bigotry and that had the powerful potential to organize letter-writing campaigns and advertising boycotts. Moreover, sexual charges against Catholic clergy had so long and disreputable a history that their use stigmatizes any group that uses them.

The Gauthe case was the most celebrated of a series of prosecutions and civil lawsuits that demonstrated that ecclesiastical authorities could no longer count upon the traditional protections. There now began a snowball effect of the kind described above, so that litigation and media reporting created expectations about the likelihood of detecting new cases in the Catholic context. In contrast to their earlier attitudes, law enforcement agencies came to appreciate that political capital might actually be gained by showing themselves tough on offending clergy, and a failure to act could lead to disastrous political consequences. At the same time, civil lawsuits against the church showed that it was remarkably easy to establish liability for decisions involving erring priests because of the organizational factors outlined above. By the end of the decade, there was an embarrassing but inevitable crescendo of scandals involving Catholic priests.

The media had once been reluctant to report church scandals, but the abuse stories reflected a swift and dramatic reversal of attitude. Chapter 4, "The Media and the Crisis," shows how both print and visual media not only reported the individual incidents but also offered far-reaching interpretations of the scale of the crisis and its origins in the structure of the Catholic church. At the height of concern during 1992 and 1993, television news programs in particular were regularly presenting aggressive stories about the wrongdoing of the Catholic church in sexual matters, and the images and terminology of this reporting echoed the anticlerical rhetoric of earlier decades. It is superficially tempting to believe that the pedophile issue legitimized the outpouring of a vast reserve of latent anti-Catholic sentiment among journalists and producers, and the sensationalistic tone of coverage undoubtedly owed something to the development of "tabloid" standards throughout the news media.

There might be some truth in these explanations, and a radical change in media attitudes to the Catholic church can be observed between about 1976 and 1981. However, the major reason for the tone of later coverage is more complex and more surprising. In fact, the hostile imagery in the mainstream media from the mid-1980s onward resulted from the precedents set by Catholic newspapers and Catholic commentators, who excoriated the policies of the church hierarchy. It was the Catholic press, above all the liberal *National Catholic Reporter* (*NCR*), that broke ground for other media outlets in drawing attention to clergy sex scandals, in presenting the cases as part of a systemic problem, and by stressing the institutional context of the offenses. As early as 1985, it was *NCR* that pioneered the term "pedophile priests." Over the next decade, media coverage was heavily influenced by reliance on a relatively narrow group of commentators and experts, most of whom were chiefly concerned with the Catholic aspects of the case, individuals like Jason Berry, Andrew Greeley, Thomas Doyle, Eugene Kennedy, and Richard Sipe (Doyle and Greeley are both Catholic priests, as were Kennedy and Sipe formerly).

Media coverage of the pedophile problem consistently presented the issue so that it appeared as harmful and threatening as possible, and it emphasized the contributory role of church authorities and institutions. Chapter 5, "Pedophilia and Child Abuse," examines the means by which this characterization was achieved and suggests that the picture presented was both inaccurate and anachronistic. There were several major problems with the conventional media construction. Definitions of the behavior were seriously flawed, so as to exaggerate the role of "pedophile" victimization of small children as opposed to older teenagers, and loose definitions provided the basis for gross exaggeration of the known or estimated scale of clergy misconduct. Often, activists cited the worst manifestations of abuse by clergy, such as the predatory and forcible molestation by a James Porter, and concluded misleadingly that this behavior was practiced by thousands of priests. In reality, activity of this sort characterized only a tiny minority, but exaggeration was rhetorically and politically valuable for the various claims-makers.

The conventional view of church behavior also ignores the radical change in attitudes toward child sexual abuse that had occurred during the late 1970s and early 1980s. Prior to this point, professional and scholarly opinions generally underplayed the significance and harmfulness of "sex abuse," and the term itself acquired its present meaning only about 1977 or so. This perspective makes it easier to understand why church authorities were so prepared to exercise tolerance toward priests found to be sexually involved with minors: the behavior was not then thought to be harmful or "abusive." In fact, their attitude was well in tune with the best educated opinion of the time, and it is perhaps harsh to evaluate it by the much more rigorous standards of recent years. In questions of child abuse and child sexuality, a quite revolutionary gulf separates us from the thought of the 1970s and before.

The second part of the book describes the different constituencies active in recognizing and delineating the emerging problem. Chapter 6, "Conflict in the Churches," sets the issue against the background of the bitter controversies within the Catholic church. Traditionalist and conservative groups publicized the pedophile issue and perhaps exaggerated its severity in order to counter what they regarded as homosexual subversion of the church. This was part of a common rhetorical strategy of stigmatizing homosexuality by association with pedophilia. Also significant was the cultural and political work of dissident Catholics from the ecclesiastical left who were engaged in a continuing battle with the church hierarchy over numerous issues: sexual ethics, academic freedom, and the role and status of women. This "Catholic civil war" was reaching its height in 1986 and 1987, at precisely the time that abuse cases were beginning to proliferate. The abuse issue illustrated a number of evils denounced by the dissidents, including the closed and secretive workings of the church hierarchy, the neglect or contempt of the laity, and the pernicious effects of mandatory celibacy; as so often in past centuries, anticlerical rhetoric was used to undermine the privileged position of the clergy. Within the church, pedophile charges found a ready audience predisposed to take up an issue that could be used to promote specific views and policy agendas. Increasingly, the solutions proposed to the clergy-abuse problem were diametrically opposed to those sought by the issue's early conservative backers.

Liberal activists asserted that the conditions permitting priestly sexual misconduct were tolerated by a cynical church hierarchy, which in turn echoed the dictates of a despotic Vatican bureaucracy. Obviously, these claims-makers could not be described as "anti-Catholic" because by their own standards they wanted nothing more than the healthy and positive reconstruction of the American Catholic church, but their rhetoric had the potential of appealing to latent hostility to the church in the population at large and specifically in the media. Once these criticisms had been made and validated by their Catholic origin, this legitimized still more severe public attacks that borrowed extensively from the traditional Protestant demonology.

The "abuse crisis" could not have erupted so quickly if there was not a preexisting public demand or expectation about the likely veracity of such charges. The atmosphere of belief and acceptance had been created by the general concern over child abuse during the previous decade, but specific grievances about the churches were enhanced by the growing gulf between traditional religious values and changing social patterns. Chapter 7, "Sins of the Fathers: The Feminist Response," shows how the Catholic church in particular was portrayed during the 1980s as the leading opponent of social advancement for women. In response to this, feminist social and religious thought developed a fundamental critique of churches as patriarchal structures that consciously or otherwise promoted and condoned the sexual abuse of women and children. A "theology of abuse" was largely formulated before public attention was directed toward actual instances of molestation by clergy, but these acts naturally reinforced the feminist view.

Feminist activists stood to profit from the abuse issue in ideological terms and also in the practical sense of advancing women's interests within churches. In fact, feminists advanced beyond the mainstream construction of "clergy abuse" in their assertion that sexual exploitation should be defined more broadly than simple priestly pedophilia. In this perception, the problem is one of "clergy exploitation" directed against adult women as much as children, and this occurs in all denominations. It reflects not the peculiar circumstances of Catholic discipline but the patriarchal values that characterize any male-dominated institution, and the solutions are political rather than organizational.

There was little novelty in the fact that the American Catholic church was subject to attacks from a wide array of factions and interest groups, both internal and external. What made this situation so serious was that the church was now operating in a novel legal environment that greatly enhanced the probability of litigation, especially over matters involving the abuse or maltreatment of children. Chapter 8, "The Legal Environment," describes the changes in the legal profession and the courts during the 1970s and early 1980s that created a "litigation explosion." The legal environment was the largest single factor encouraging the reporting and exposure of cases, and the changes in this area go far toward explaining why a crisis erupted in these years rather than at any earlier point. Once legal action was undertaken, plaintiffs and lawyers soon found that the organization and traditions of the Catholic church made it especially vulnerable, and the number of lawsuits began an inevitable upward spiral.

The legal setting also created interest groups that became active in making and promoting claims about the abuse problem, including attorneys and also the therapists and psychologists who regularly examined complainants and testified in trials. Chapter 9, "Defending Therapy," notes that the clergy-abuse issue arose at an opportune time for medical professionals. During the 1980s the burgeoning issue of child sexual abuse had placed a heavy premium on the expertise of therapists and others working with children and seeking to elicit their testimony for courtroom use. However, the therapeutic community had advanced increasingly ambitious claims about the capacity of professionals to explore memories of abuse, and in the early 1990s a forceful public backlash threatened to destroy the gains of status and reputation that had been acquired in recent years. The media frequently reported stories of child abuse claims that resulted either from the incompetence and ideological slant of therapists or from the cynical greed of plaintiffs and their families. Such accounts reinforced the impression that false abuse allegations could serve as a devastating weapon, notably in marital conflicts and child-custody litigation. Controversy focused on the two related areas of ritual child abuse and the recovery of early memories allegedly suppressed by the patient, and in both matters therapeutic claims met skepticism and derision. However, the clergy-abuse issue offered renewed proof of the widespread and harmful nature of sexual abuse, and the potential for therapists to assist in treatment, even using the much-maligned technique of assisting the recovery of traumatic memories. Therapists should therefore be seen as yet another component of the diverse coalition advocating the reality and seriousness of the problem.

A problem represents a perceived "deviation from a social norm," and analyzing a problem tells us about both the nature of the deviation and the public expectations that it is believed to violate. In other words, by telling us what is wrong with society, problems tell us about the way society is meant to be. As norms and expectations develop over time, so do the potential bases for problems, and a period of radical alteration in social attitudes is likely to be manifested in a rich crop of either new problems or new formulations of older issues. Chapter 10, "Meanings and Directions," suggests that the clergy-abuse affair illustrates the conflicts that have arisen in the past two decades over changing gender roles, new concepts of childhood, and the attack on "patriarchal" authority figures of all kinds. The new environment has caused particular strains in different churches, not merely within Catholicism, and has caused radical shifts in the religious values of American society. These broad changes in values and attitudes prepared the way for public acceptance of the clergy-abuse phenomenon, and shaped perceptions of the nature and scale of the problem. The affair thus tells us much about the nature and function of scandals in a religious setting, and the distinctive rhetoric employed in constructing these issues.

Finally, Part III, chapter 10 considers the likely consequences of the abuse crisis and notes that the effects on the Catholic church might be so far-reaching as to cause the serious discussion of internal changes that would have been inconceivable a decade ago.

In summary, this book does not deny either that sexual abuse by clergy is prevalent and harmful or that ecclesiastical authorities have made persistent errors in dealing with the issue. However, the sins and crimes of a number of priests have been built into a problem with implications that extend far beyond the original behavior. Understanding the diverse meanings of clergy abuse allows us to observe the work of social and cultural construction at its most intense and its most successful.

2

The Anti-Catholic Tradition

In 1993, *A Gospel of Shame* offered a historical context for the recent "pedophile crisis" in the Catholic church. Authors Elinor Burkett and Frank Bruni discuss the Borgia popes of the Renaissance and some of the legendary Roman orgies of that time, at which "children were passed freely among bishops and priests celebrating Catholicism's latest triumph with a sexual bacchanalia."[1] Although such references can be difficult to trace in conventional history, the book finds an abundance of "veiled references in historical texts or in the works of novelists mirroring reality," in revealing fiction like Diderot's *La Religieuse* (The Nun; 1760). *Gospel of Shame* presents an exceedingly dark view of Catholic history, suggesting that in every era distinctively Catholic doctrines were the product of a cynical *raison d'état* and were imposed by naked repressive force. Describing the reluctance of civil authorities to intervene in sexual scandals, the authors recall past eras of papal tyranny and oppression, when "popes sent crusaders to deal with unruly civil leaders, when inquisitors led even the mighty to the torture chamber and the stake."[2]

That such an account could be published as historical in the 1990s is startling evidence of the legitimization of traditional anti-Catholic imagery by the abuse scandals of recent years. The problem does not lie in the specific instances given: the Borgias fell as far short of the papal ideal as their bitterest foes could imagine, and it would not be difficult to find Catholic authorities active in religious repression, any less than their Protestant or Muslim contemporaries. What is surprising here is the overt nature of the stereotyping, and the degree to which the critique is directed against the fundamental beliefs and practices of one particular religious system. It may be true that "priests had been molesting children for centuries, even before Christopher Columbus landed in this hemisphere,"[3] just as it is probably correct that carpenters or shepherds can be found committing acts of abuse in most historical periods. What makes priests different is the suggestion that there is something distinctive about their profession that makes them liable to sexual deviancy, just as popes and bishops are especially likely to be manipulative bullies. Like many writers and journalists of the last decade, the authors of *A Gospel of Shame* seem unaware that their accounts of Catholic misdeeds are uncannily parallel to allegations made over many centuries and fit neatly into a lengthy polemical tradition that has generated an abundance of spurious and extravagant charges.

From a historical perspective, the contemporary abuse problem is reminiscent of images that have been used to stigmatize priests and religious over the centuries.[4] The idea of the supposedly celibate priest as sexual exploiter can be found throughout the medieval and early modern centuries, and it played a prominent role in the culture and politics of the English-speaking world in the eighteenth and nineteenth centuries. Exploring the cultural roots of the clergy-abuse theme thus requires a survey of a lengthy prehistory that includes the intertwined but not necessarily identical themes of anticlerical and anti-Catholic hostility. This is certainly not to assert that modern instances of molestation by clergy are similarly fictitious but that ancient stereotypes contributed to the specific construction of "priest pedophilia."

Anticlericals and Anti-Catholics

At least since the early Middle Ages, a lively anticlerical tradition has existed within the Christian church, and this arose from both economic and religious grievances.[5] Before the nineteenth century, the clergy in most societies possessed considerable power over the secular activities of their congregations, and drew most of their incomes from some form of taxation of the laity. Anticlericalism was enhanced by popular religious sentiments urging more direct lay access to the Bible and spiritual truths, ideas that found expression in heretical movements such as the Lollards, Hussites, and Waldensians, but hostility to the church hierarchy was also a powerful force within the Catholic laity. It was inevitable that lay movements would emerge to resist or challenge clerical authority, and equally likely that these dissidents would emphasize the behaviors by which the clergy were flouting the moral laws they affected to teach. Anti-clerical rhetoric thus challenged the ostentatious wealth and worldly power of the clergy, as well as their real or alleged sexual peccadilloes.

During the sixteenth century, the anticlerical tradition became intertwined with issues of national identity and political loyalty. The events of the Reformation began a period of several centuries in which the conflict between Catholic and Protestant was the dominant political fact in Europe. In a Protestant nation such as England, Catholics were regarded by most of the Protestant majority as an alien and seditious presence. In reaction, England evolved a complex and generally believed set of anti-Catholic and "antipapist" beliefs, which together composed a systematic ideology. In what is normally regarded as a thoroughly pragmatic and antitheoretical culture, anti-popery provided an intellectual context for many aspects of politics and belief.

Catholics were viewed as an alien fifth column, representing powerful foreign interests inimical to Protestant England: seminary priests and Jesuits trained on the Continent were feared as political agents of the Spanish empire or other Catholic powers. Persecution was intermittent, reaching new heights when the public was enraged by economic failures or when the government feared some foreign policy disaster. At these times—the 1580s, the 1640s, the 1670s—repression could be severe, with dozens of priests and laypersons being subjected to the savage penalties of hanging, drawing, and quartering. Between 1535 and 1683, some 350 Catholics were martyred in England and Wales, including 270 clergy, and the act of saying Mass *ipso facto* constituted treason. This fear of Catholic conspiracy was central to English history for centuries, and virtually every mass social movement in England from the sixteenth century to the eighteenth included anti-Catholicism as part of its "platform." Without the popish-plot fears of the 1670s, there could not have been the constitutional revolution that ultimately enshrined "English liberties," and which had an enormous influence on American political thought.[6]

National ideology constructed the Catholic church as the ultimate Other, the imagined hostile force against which English culture defined its own identity. The Other epitomized the exact opposite of what was correct and good, and this concept of inversion pervades the Protestant view of "popery." In contrast to the scriptural foundations claimed by English Protestantism, the Catholic church ignored the Bible and indeed represented the satanic forces portrayed in the book of Revelation. Not until the nineteenth century did a substantial number of English and American Protestants dare to question the orthodoxy that the papacy was the Antichrist and the Whore of Babylon. In political terms, English democratic and libertarian theory emerged as an explicit challenge to the autocratic dictatorship of the Catholic church. Catholics obeyed a secretive hierarchy that sought authoritarian power through plotting and covert manipulation. The whole system was bound up with poverty, ignorance, and arbitrary government—or, as the Whig song termed it, a Catholic king would bring in "the Mass, wooden shoes, and no jury." Contrary English principles were celebrated annually in those twin November rites of approved bigotry, the burning in effigy of Catholic conspirator Guy Fawkes and the cremation of figures of the pope on the anniversary of the accession of Queen Elizabeth. In both, it was customary for participants to masquerade as Catholic cardinals, priests, popes, and nuns.

A Catholic was alien, and essentially untrustworthy. While appearing to be a loyal subject, even the best-intentioned Catholic was un-English in his baffling and cowardly subservience to the clergy and his taste for emotional ("unmanly") and foreign imagery and devotional practices. Catholics suffered from "enthusiasm," a term that then meant not so much dedication or commitment as unhealthy and neurotic fanaticism. English Protestantism attributed to the Catholic priest most of the features that adhered to the Jew in Continental mythologies: the priest was a cynical cosmopolitan who could never offer true loyalty to any one nation; his religious ideas constituted gross superstition, and provided a spurious supernatural justification for fraud, deception, and manipulation; his beliefs, values, and practices contradicted at every point those of "manly" Protestants.[7] The stereotype was permeated with themes of gender subversion and inversion, from the dubious claims to celibacy to the vulgar emotionalism of Catholic religious practice.[8]

These themes are summarized by the tirade of Henry Spencer Ashbee, an English writer best known for providing the most thorough available bibliographical account of pornographic literature. In 1877 he argued that every reflecting mind must find it difficult to understand how, in the present nineteenth century, a system so false, prurient and polluted (as the Roman Catholic Church) can still be believed in, can find devotees ready to lay down their lives in its support, and even make converts of men of knowledge, experience and bright parts. For whether we consider the absurd miracles which are even today being palmed off upon the credulous, the blunders, crimes and follies of the infallible popes; the vices and hypocrisy of many of the clergy, both regular and secular; the duplicity, lax teaching, infamous doctrines, and dishonest commercial dealings of the Jesuits; the scandalous quarrels which have taken place between the different orders, and the irregularities and licentiousness which have at all times distinguished monastic institutions, both male and female; their useless asceticism, puerile macerations, and their flagellations, at once absurd, cruel and indecent; the gross oppression and horrid cruelties of the Inquisition; the terrible system of auricular confession and the abuse which has been made of it; the coarse, scurrilous, abusive and licentious discourses. . . .

[the full sentence continues for several additional pages][9]

The American Inheritance

The English anti-Catholic tradition had a potent influence on the American colonies, all the greater when reinforced by the comparable traditions of immigrant groups from other Protestant nations: Scotch-Irish Presbyterians, Dutch and German Reformed, German and Scandinavian Lutherans, Swiss Anabaptists. Anti-Catholic sentiment was overt in colonial politics, enhanced by local conflicts like the political insurgency of the 1680s. As in England, Catholic influence appeared to be synonymous with domestic tyranny and foreign encroachment. Several colonies granted religious tolerance to all except Catholics, and the almost infallibly tolerant Puritan Roger Williams wrote of the "Romish wolf gorging herself with huge bowls of the blood of saints." Catholics were executed in New York as late as 1741 for allegedly supporting a slave rebellion; and the rebellious colonists of the 1770s had as one of their major grievances the English support of the Catholic church in Lower Canada. Fear of clerical influence on secular politics was a dominant theme in Virginia and other colonies in the decades before the Revolution.[10]

The vigor of the American anti-Catholic tradition in the nineteenth century has been described in such classic works as Ray Allen Billington's *The Protestant Crusade*. Ethnic controversies were first and foremost religious, and the Nativists of the 1840s and Know-Nothing Party of the 1850s achieved national visibility by exploiting anti-Catholic fears.[11] This Nativist tradition contributed much, if indirectly, to the later emergence and success of the Republican Party. Between the 1830s and 1850s, anti-Catholic pamphleteering and journalism reached new heights in the United States, with titles such as Samuel F. B. Morse's *Foreign Conspiracy Against the Liberty of the United States* (1835) and William C. Brownlee's *Popery: An Enemy to Civil and Religious Liberty and Dangerous to Our Republic* (1836). These tracts repeatedly demonstrated the sinister characteristics of the Catholic church by lengthy historical accounts of papal atrocities, invariably including the Borgia popes and the Inquisition, and a catalog of sexual misdeeds.

Anti-Catholic hostility grew steadily with the enormous immigration movement at the end of the century. In the 1880s the famous Republican phrase denounced the supposed constituents of the Democratic Party: Catholic urban immigrants, the liquor interests, and the unreconstructed Confederates, or more succinctly, "Rum, Romanism, and Rebellion." The American Protective Association (APA) of the 1890s kept alive the rhetoric against "papist deviltry" with a strong element of anti-immigrant bigotry.[12] At its height, it had seventy weekly publications nationwide, and the lurid charges presented in propaganda sheets like *The Menace* were enough "to make any boy wonder if the priest kept beautiful young girls tied up in the confessional booths and if there was really an arsenal in the church basement." In the 1920s, anti-Catholicism was the major impetus behind the revived Ku Klux Klan in northern states such as Indiana and Pennsylvania, and national membership swelled to some five million.[13] The movement reached new heights with the 1928 presidential candidacy of the Catholic Al Smith. John Higham aptly described anti-Catholicism as "the most luxuriant, tenacious tradition of paranoiac agitation in American history," and for much of that history, anti-Catholic rhetoric had considerably more incendiary potential than anti-Semitism.[14]

In both Great Britain and North America, the anticlerical tradition was immeasurably strengthened by the growth of Anglo-Catholicism or Ritualism, which grew out of the Oxford Movement of the 1830s. This movement tried to revive Catholic devotional practices within the Anglican church, customs such as making the sign of the cross, wearing vestments and crucifixes, using incense, praying for the dead, invoking Mary and the saints, and confession. Some Ritualists pursued this to the extent of importing doctrines and practices like transubstantiation, celibacy, and monasticism. In the United States, Catholicizing movements affected not only the Episcopal church but also other Protestant bodies, including the Reformed and the Lutheran. From the 1840s onward, conversions to the Roman church became increasingly common, suggesting that the Ritualists had indeed been a subversive papal Trojan horse.

In the United States and Great Britain, the "Catholic Revival" was bitterly opposed by Evangelical and Protestant pressure groups, whose rhetoric is richly informative about the foundations of popular anti-Catholicism and its relationship to appropriate gender roles. Protestantism in this view was a virile religion, the rational worship of the Father and the Son, with an austere refusal to indulge in "womanly" or "childish" images. In contrast, Catholicism was emotional, irrational, effeminate—a stereotype epitomized by the apparently divine honors paid to the Virgin Mary. Its rituals were childish in their theatricality and playacting, their emphasis on toy-like statues, on incense and brilliant colors. Controversy focused on issues of dress, especially the ornate robes and vestments affected by "high" or ritualist clergy. In the United States, one controversial incident of the period was the "Fond du Lac circus" of 1900, in which a group of elaborately robed Episcopal clergy were photographed at an ordination in Wisconsin. In Protestant circles, the ecclesiastical robes implied authoritarianism, ostentatious wealth, theatricality, and all the flamboyant trappings of "popery," and the flowing nature of the clothing implied effeminacy and secret homosexuality.

The Sexual Component

The sexual allegations against the Ritualists continued a tradition at least as old as the Middle Ages when priests were depicted as hypocritical predators who inverted accepted moral standards. Episcopal control over parish clergy was rarely strong, and well into the later Middle Ages it was common for priests to form some sort of domestic arrangement with women. Technically, this meant that the priests were living in a sinful state, which could easily be portrayed by reformers as gross lasciviousness. Centuries of commentary on this theme are epitomized by the tract of the English reformer Simon Fish, whose *Supplication for the Beggars* (1528) attacked the allegedly celibate clergy for their misdeeds: "Yea, and what do they more? Truly nothing but apply themselves, by all the sleights they may, to have to do with every man's wife, every man's daughter, and every man's maid that cuckoldry and bawdry should reign over all your subjects, that no man should know his own child."[15]

Anticlericalism was a powerful ideology in virtually all Christian nations, and the sexual component was overwhelming. Priests were denounced as "fornicators" who raped virgins and seduced married women; in Germany, to visit a prostitute was "to act like a bishop"; the German word for *bastard* is *Pfaffenkind*, "priest's child." Nuns were said to engage in lesbianism and to satisfy the sexual needs of male clergy.[16] The clergy who affected the highest spiritual aspirations were the friars, and they were the group most reviled for seduction and vice.[17] The image of the predatory priest, friar, and monk is familiar from writers such as Chaucer and Boccaccio.

Following the Reformation, clerical celibacy became one of the core issues dividing Catholic Christendom from the Protestant tradition, and this ensured that sexual themes would emerge forcefully in the vast anti-Catholic literature that can be traced over the next four centuries. By professing celibacy, Catholic clergy were laying a claim to a moral status superior to that of their Protestant counterparts, and it was rhetorically essential to discredit this boast. There was also widespread popular skepticism about the ability of the clergy as a group to maintain this discipline. Sexual allegations against clergy have often provided the ideological foundation for government action against the church they represent, and the use of these themes in anticlerical propaganda is exemplified by the experience of societies as diverse as Tudor England, Revolutionary France, Nazi Germany, and Republican Spain.

There were several components of the stereotype. "Celibate" priests were nothing of the sort, and their freedom from marriage only granted them the opportunity to seduce women at random. In Rousseau's *Émile*, a sinful priest is defined as one who sleeps with single women, for as all the world knows, "*un prêtre en bonne règle ne doit faire des enfants qu'aux femmes mariées.*" Seductions occurred in the confessional, another regular element of the fantasy, and the same confessional provided easy absolution for sinful priests. An age-old tradition is summarized in Mark Twain's *Letters from the Earth*:

> The confessional's chief amusement has been seduction—in all the ages of the church. *Père* Hyacinthe testifies that of a hundred priests confessed by him, ninety-nine had used the confessional effectively for the seduction of married women and young girls.

One priest confessed that of nine hundred women and young girls whom he had served as father confessor in his time, none had escaped his lecherous embrace but the elderly and the homely. The official list of questions which the priest is required to ask will overmasteringly excite any woman who is not a paralytic."[18]

The APA of the 1890s endlessly recited the abuses of the confessional, and the deeds of the "libidinous rapist priest with lust in his heart" (the obvious pun on "rapist" and "papist" is familiar in this era).[19]

Anticlerical speculation was excited by the existence of cloistered groups of celibate religious, both men and women, especially when both were known to use flagellation and associated forms of physical penance. At least from the eighteenth century onward, there were authors who assumed that such penitential exercises offered sadomasochistic sexual pleasure. Views of the convent as an arena of sadistic bullying found their literary monument in Diderot's *La Réligieuse*, but there were many more explicit fantasies. Numerous folk legends told of offspring born to nuns and then murdered and of the secret tunnels that linked rectories and convents.[20] Between about 1830 and 1860 the twin themes of political subversion and sexual exploitation created a whole genre of quasi pornography in the United States, that exposed the secret cemeteries, the hidden tunnels, and the clandestine life of the confessional.[21] As late as the 1930s the secular Republican government of Spain ordered the excavation of convent cellars to find the purported graveyards of the murdered children.

Puritan Pornography

These fears and myths tell us as much about the critics as they do about the clergy or the religious practices they were attacking, and Richard Hofstadter argued that "anti-Catholicism has always been the pornography of the Puritan." Catholic atrocities supply the opportunity not merely to catalog sexually explicit behavior but to deplore it in the name of morality.[22] Of Henry Spencer Ashbee's anti-Roman tirades, Stephen Marcus writes that his

> obsession with the sins of Rome is the counterpart and analogue of his interest in pornography. What he experiences with direct sexual pleasure in pornography he experiences with the added pleasure of moral indignation in relation to Rome. For Roman Catholicism is a pornographer's paradise, and there is, as they say, evidence to back up every charge. All priests are lechers, satyrs and pimps, all nuns are concubines or lesbians or both. The confessional is the locus of meeting of lubricity and piety.[23]

This combination of salacious interest with ostensible moralism also characterized the pornography of the French Enlightenment. In 1791 the Marquis de Sade's *Justine* depicted a savage and depraved group of reclusive monks whose chief pleasure is found in the rape and sexual torture of girls and women of all ages. Sade employs these fictional characters, products of his own fantasies, as propaganda tools to support the anticlerical policies of the Revolution. He notes that "as for the monks of St Mary in the Wood, suppression of the religious orders will expose the atrocious crimes of that horrible crew."[24] In England, anti-Catholic pornography was a flourishing genre throughout the nineteenth century, with titles such as *Atrocious Acts of*

Catholic Priests, The Seducing Cardinal, Nunnery Tales, and *A Peep at Popes and Popery.*[25] American publishers offered *Female Convents: Secrets of Nunneries Disclosed.*[26] A lively visual tradition offered similar themes in paintings and prints, regularly depicting sexual intercourse between priests and penitents, monks and nuns, or nuns masturbating with dildoes.[27]

In the eighteenth and nineteenth centuries attacks on the Catholic church gave publishers an opportunity to sell openly works that would assuredly have been censored if they had not been disguised as religious polemic.[28] In their attacks on the high-church Ritualist Movement, Protestant tracts were both prurient and near-pornographic in tone, with a content that was both sadomasochistic and homoerotic.[29]

This was especially true of the thriving genre of "confessions" by real and purported defectors from the Catholic church, commonly "escaped nuns."[30] In the 1830s one purported memoir of such a life in a Québec convent caused protests and riots throughout North America. According to the delusional woman who named herself "Maria Monk," nuns were little more than the exploited sex-slaves of priests and bishops, and flagellation was a weapon both to enforce discipline and to excite sexual urges. On occasion, monastic irregularities reached the point of murder:

> [The Mother Superior] gave me another piece of information which excited other feelings in me. . . . Infants were sometimes born in the Convent, but they were always baptized, and immediately strangled. This secured their everlasting happiness; for the baptism purifies them from all sinfulness, and being sent out of the world before they had time to do any wrong, they were at once admitted into Heaven. . . . How different did a Convent now appear from what I supposed it to be![31]

The success of Maria Monk's diatribe is illustrated by the repeated use of her ideas by Protestant mobs in the civil disturbances of those years, when demonstrators attempted to break into convents to free imprisoned nuns and excavate the corpses of murdered babies.[32] Forty years later, Catholic Québec produced another antipopery activist in the apostate priest Charles Chiniquy, who played a prominent role in North American religious controversy for several decades until his death in 1899.[33] His scurrilous 1875 tract, *The Priest, the Woman and the Confessional,* described the sexual exploitation of women parishioners by lustful priests, and the book had gone into fifty editions in two languages by 1892. In the 1890s one of the regular lecturers of the APA was Margaret Shepherd, and described her convent life as one long round of "grotesque ceremonies, orgies of sex and sadism" at the hands of "licentious and lecherous priests . . . seeking to lure young and innocent girls into sin."[34]

Homosexuals and Pedophiles

Catholic clergy were denounced as homosexuals and pederasts, again on the assumption that celibacy must be a hypocritical cover for sinister sexual activity, and these charges are found very widely in Continental Europe no less than in North America and Britain, and also in Asia and Africa. To argue that such charges were central to anticlerical propaganda is not of course to deny that clerical

homosexuality has an authentic history, or that homoerotic and pedophile subcultures have long existed in clerical contexts. However, this factual basis of
cleri-cal homosexuality has also been systematically exaggerated and employed
for political ends, usually by suggesting that the behavior is characteristic of most
or all clergy.

John Boswell has written extensively on gay subcultures among the clergy of medieval Europe, and David Greenberg argues that "the more the church suppressed
priestly marriage, the stronger must have been the homosexual drive it aroused
within its ranks."[35] The eleventh-century saint Peter Damian wrote *Book of Gomor-
rah,* denouncing clerical homosexuality and pederasty, and providing penalties for
"a cleric or monk who seduces youths or young boys or is found kissing or in any
impure situations."[36] Court records from many parts of Europe indicate the frequency of scandals and prosecutions involving priests and young boys during the
Renaissance and early modern eras.[37] "The intimate living arrangements of the all-
male clerical world and the opportunities that educational and religious duties
afforded for privacy and emotional intimacy, while not themselves 'causes' of
homosexuality, may have contributed substantially to its expression."[38] Pope Julius
III (1550–1556) was perhaps the best-documented case of an active homosexual at
the head of the church, the target of his affections being a fifteen year old boy whom
he raised to the rank of cardinal.

Victorian literary evidence suggests the powerful attractions of the Catholic clerical structure for men of homosexual inclinations, either overt or clandestine, and
homosexuals were well represented in the Oxford Movement and among the prominent converts to the Roman Catholic church (for modern parallels, see chapter 6). In
the late nineteenth century, British "Uranian" or homoerotic writers often chose ecclesiastical settings for their tales, and many either became clergy or assumed clerical
personae. Among the homoerotic writers who feigned the clothing and titles of
priests were Montague Summers, Frederick Rolfe ("Baron Corvo"), and Richard
Charles Jackson.

One authentic clerical pederast was John Francis Bloxam, author of a short story
entitled "The Priest and the Acolyte."[39] The story was set in a traditional Catholic context, with confession, priestly vestments, and the Mass, the spiritual beauty of which
reflects the loving relationship between the twenty-eight-year old priest and the "little
acolyte" Wilfred, a "child" of fourteen. The tale concludes, "On the steps of the altar
was stretched the long ascetic frame of the young priest, robed in the sacred vestments; close beside him, with his curly head pillowed on the gorgeous embroideries
that covered his breast, lay the beautiful boy in scarlet and lace. Their arms were
round each other; a strange hush lay like a shroud over all." The story's publication in
1894 contributed to the antihomosexual scare that culminated in the trial of Oscar
Wilde, and the work was employed by the prosecution to discredit Wilde. A pederas-
tic theme is overt in Bloxam's work, but a fascination with the physical beauty of
boys recurs in the work of other clergy 0and pseudoclergy, including Gerald Manley
Hopkins and Frederick Rolfe. Rolfe, for instance, addressed the beauty of the young
Saint William of Norwich in a sonnet, and sought the same characteristics in the Ital-
ian boys whom he photographed in nude poses. [40]

The Sins of the Fathers

Real or imagined instances of clerical homosexuality were immensely beneficial for anticlerical propagandists. In Great Britain, for instance, there were two well-publicized scandals involving Anglican bishops being prosecuted for homosexual activities, in 1640 and 1822. Both incidents were kept alive into the present century by repeated citation in anticlerical and antireligious books and tracts, customarily with lurid illustrations of the offenses, so that they attained the status of legend or folktale. In 1823 both stories were recounted in a "monumental" work entitled *Crimes of the Clergy,* which "contained a number of specific and detailed accusations of pederasty, sodomy and rape."[41] In the English context, the sexual rhetoric had a strongly populist and antielite element and was especially applied against higher clergy, who were likely to have spent a large part of their careers in the celibate atmosphere of the older universities. From the eighteenth century to the present day, a populist tradition has criticized the clergy for their supposed pedophilic predilections, and this was a familiar theme in pornography as well as in vulgar squibs, jokes, and limericks. One typical example tells of the parson whose "secret desire / was a boy in the choir / with a bottom like jelly on springs"; another concerns the bishop who "buggered three maids while confirming them."[42]

Portraying clergy as pedophiles was polemically more effective than merely suggesting effeminacy or homosexuality. Emphasizing the defenseless and credulous nature of children magnified the harm of the offense and the unscrupulous nature of the offender and thus compounded the violation of chastity. It also had a powerful symbolic significance in implying that the seducing priest was metaphorically betraying his proper paternal role: the priest is a "Father" to his flock, who are expected to "become as little children." There is a substantial Freudian literature on the concept of the priest as betraying or abusive father, and Norman Cohn suggested that in medieval Christianity, "life tends to be seen as a mortal struggle waged by good fathers and good children against bad fathers and bad children," with the role of bad father epitomized by the evil Jew and the lascivious priest. "The Jew and the cleric could also themselves very easily be seen as father figures. . . . Jew and cleric alike became father-figures of a most terrifying kind."[43]

Sexual contact transformed virtuous paternalism into the most malevolent form of oppression. This imagery explains the popularity of clerical sexual exploitation in anticolonial literature, where it becomes a metaphor for the deceptive paternalism of the Europeans. The theme appears in the nineteenth-century Peruvian novel *Aves sin mido* (Birds Without Nests)[44] and more recently in major African fiction such as Mongo Beti's *The Poor Christ of Bomba,* wherein the symbolic corruption is aggravated by the image of venereal disease.[45] Pedophilia was a difficult topic to discuss in the above-ground literature of nineteenth-century Europe and North America , but the same themes of betrayal and child exploitation appear in somewhat disguised forms. In the United States, the popular anti-Catholic novel *Rosamund* (1846) uses a colonial setting to describe how Catholic priests in Cuba captured black boys in order to transform them into sausage meat. The book also notes that "filthy concubinage is inseparable from the Confessional."[46]

The concept of Catholics inverting accepted norms and standards could hardly be expressed more absolutely than in the image of cannibalism. As David Brion Davis remarks of the conspiracy and anti-Catholic literature in the United States in those years, "This obsession with details of sadism, which reached pathological proportions in much of the literature, showed a furious determination to purge the enemy of every admirable quality."[47] It is inexcusable for the authors of *A Gospel of Shame* to treat works from this tradition as historically accurate, as they do in the case of *La Réligieuse* and *Aves sin nido*.[48]

The German "Pedophile Crisis"

The enduring power of the pedophile theme is suggested by the fact that this was the propaganda device utilized by the Nazis in their attempt to break the power of the German Catholic church, especially in the realm of education and social services. An anticlerical campaign reached its apogee with a series of show trials of monks, priests, and nuns, which were intended to prove that ecclesiastical authorities were unworthy to be trusted with the nation's children. More than a thousand clergy were arrested, and in one incident alone several hundred Franciscan friars were tried for sexual offenses allegedly committed against the children and teenage boys under care in their institutions.[49] The prosecutions were facilitated by an expansion of concepts of criminal liability. If any physical contact excited sexual feelings in a child, however disturbed, the burden of proof was placed on the accused cleric to show that he had no improper intent. Moreover, the courts permitted an inordinate relaxation of traditional restraints about accepting the evidence of child witnesses, despite the abundant and skeptical legal literature on the *Psychologie der Kinderaussagen*.[50] By late 1937, sixty-four priests and several hundred religious had been convicted.[51] However, there continued to be many acquittals, even under these exceptionally difficult circumstances, and the campaign probably backfired by enhancing public sympathy for the church and discrediting the party press.[52]

The German clergy-abuse cases were heavily exploited for propaganda purposes, and the graphic evidence was so widely publicized that the daily newspapers were transformed into "pornographic special editions" during 1936 and 1937.[53] *Völkischer Beobachter* remarked in April 1937,

> The German people and especially its young folk know how to judge of people who convert the sacristy into a brothel and whose perversion does not even shrink before the most sacred action of the Catholic church, the Communion. . . . [W]hat parents conscious of their responsibility could now take the responsibility of entrusting their boys and girls to an organization, over a thousand members of which are sexual criminals?[54]

The Nazi papers stressed the familiar anti-Catholic themes of the evils of celibacy and the secretive nature of Catholic authority. Himmler's *Der Schwarze Korps* commented that in the religious houses

> not one crime is lacking from perjury through incest to sexual murder. . . . Behind the walls of monasteries and in the ranks of the Roman brotherhood what else may have been enacted that is not publicly known and has not been expiated through this world's

courts? What may not the church have succeeded in hushing up? All this is the expression and consequence of a system that has elevated into a principle that which is against nature and of an organization that has withdrawn itself from public control.[55]

The Decline of Anti-Catholicism?

From the 1930s to the 1980s overt anti-Catholicism and anticlericalism ceased to be a major political force in most Western nations, in part because religious conflicts were largely supplanted by the ideological struggles of the political Left and Right. The Catholic church was a staunch ally against communism, and Catholic ethnic groups in the United States achieved a substantial degree of assimilation in those years. In the mainstream politics of the 1950s, religious polemic made its main appearance through liberal attacks on perceived Catholic efforts to breach the wall of separation between church and state.[56] Paul Blanshard's *American Freedom and Catholic Power* (1949) catalogued ecclesiastical inroads into secular government in matters like censorship, public education, and foreign policy.[57]

Lingering hostility flared once more with the presidential candidacy of John F. Kennedy in 1960, and Protestant clerics of impeccable respectability warned of the threat posed by the "Senator from Rome."[58] However, Kennedy's tactful handling of the issue was strongly supported by the mass media, who also provided adulatory coverage of the current pope, John XXIII, and religious rivalry played little role in the campaign. Ironically, the Kennedy presidency also marked the beginning of a period of general decline in the power of the Catholic church to influence secular politics, which defused many potential grievances. This decline was manifested in the collapse of urban political machines based on traditional white ethnic groups and the election of black mayors in most major cities in the 1970s and 1980s. Social policy also reflected ideas anathema to Catholic thought, with the U.S. Supreme Court's striking down laws against imposed school prayer (1962), contraception (1965), pornography (1966), and abortion (1973). This left the Catholic church looking like a distinctly fragile paper tiger. The political consensus of the next two decades suggested that anti-Catholicism was virtually extinct as a serious force, a conclusion reinforced by the ecumenical developments of the midcentury. In the media, the chief continuing manifestations of anti-Catholic sentiment concerned improper interference by the hierarchy in social debate, above all in matters like abortion; but this was very mild in comparison with past decades.

Four centuries of ideological development could scarcely be abandoned overnight, however, even if the tradition was not visible in mainstream culture. In the 1980s virtually all the traditional components of the nineteenth-century conspiracy mythology reappeared with full force in ornate American legends about Satanic cults, whose leaders were said to infiltrate legitimate society just as their Jesuit predecessors had done in the 1840s.[59] Several of the recent local cases of Satanic and ritual abuse involve charges of Black Mass rituals before the altars of Catholic or Episcopal churches, and rumors accused clergy of many denominations of leading cults or abuse rings.[60] Satanists, like Catholic priests, were said to abuse women and children in front of holy pictures, with the assurance that divine forgiveness would be instantly forthcoming. The imagined orgies of devilworship were indistinguishable from those described by Margaret Shepherd and the APA tracts of the 1890s, and as in the convents of Maria Monk's day, women were said to bear children who were promptly murdered and buried in secrecy.[61] Antisatanic theorists searched for the graveyards of murdered babies with all the futile zeal of their Nativist predecessors, and even the charge of hidden tunnels reappeared in the McMartin school case.[62] All the charges were false, but the wide credence they received owed much to the underlying power of the antipopery ideology. And as we will see, the ritual abuse idea would gain renewed strength from the recent clergy abuse cases.[63]

Overt anti-Catholicism also survived in the writing of extreme evangelicals and fundamentalists, for whom ecumenical approaches to Rome were deeply dangerous. In 1962, at the opening of the Second Vatican Council, Presbyterian Lorraine Boettner published the first of many editions of a comprehensive polemic against the Catholic church, in which he warned, for example, that "forced celibacy and auricular confession are by their very nature conducive to sex perversion. . . . [T]he monasteries and convents sometimes became cesspools of iniquity."[64] Boettner's book is a source for dozens of books and tracts by later fundamentalists, including Jimmy Swaggart.[65] Nor was the traditional concept of the pope as Antichrist extinct in the 1980s; the idea appears in somewhat restrained form in the influential books of Hal Lindsey.[66] The papacy is the occult force behind the "New World Order," alternatively known as "Babylon."[67] In 1990 there was controversy in the Chicago area about the circulation of tracts directed against the pope and the Catholic clergy, works that originated with evangelist Tony Alamo. Among other familiar canards, Alamo's group asserts Vatican control of the FBI, CIA, IRS, and the United Nations, as well as most public institutions and media outlets.[68]

Equally aggressive is fundamentalist Jack Chick, whose widely disseminated tracts and comics continued to promulgate allegations of Catholic conspiracy and sexual hypocrisy, and who maintains in circulation the nineteenth-century exposés of Charles Chiniquy (who is also cited by Boettner). Chick publications circulate the memoirs of purported modern-day defectors from the church, which faithfully reproduce the ancient charges, including the babies begotten by priests on nuns and subsequently murdered, and Jesuits are quite literally depicted as Satanist adepts. Clerical homosexuality, of course, runs "throughout the system from priests to - Cardinals." Pamphlets and cartoons preserve the APA mythology that attributed the assassination of President Lincoln to Jesuit agents.[69] The Chick enterprise can be regarded as idiosyncratic, but it does represent the views of a fundamentalist fringe.

Anti-Catholic charges also enjoyed a subterranean continuity through jokes, legends, and urban rumor, genres that are rarely reflected in print. However, the themes do appear quite regularly in the ostentatiously tasteless context of the satirical *National Lampoon*. In 1974, for example, an article that indulged both Jewish and Catholic stereotypes depicted a taxidriver taking two young boys to Saint Patrick's Cathedral, where they would experience oral sex and sodomy with priests.[70] The taxidriver presumes that the priests were acting as pimps on behalf of Cardinal Spellman. When one boy starts crying, the priest calms him by "saying it was a privilege, an honor, that the kid was too young to understand how important it was for him, but that he should trust the church and he would always be taken care of . . . [that]

his parents are proud of him and that he was going to get a scholarship to Notre Dame."

Recounting the painful experiences of one boy, the priest notes that the boy "would always be invited to the special parties for the bishops and the cardinals and sometimes things got a little out of hand." The boy is imagined becoming a homosexual adult, perhaps a male prostitute, and suffering from venereal disease. Of course, the *National Lampoon* piece was at once a parade of stereotypes and a parody of those stereotypes, but the item reproduced with remarkable fidelity all the age-old clichés. The author expected these images to be sufficiently familiar to an audience to be amusing, although the overt expression of these stories had not been permissible in the mainstream media for decades.

The continuity in the stereotype of the lascivious and predatory priest might suggest that such visceral imagery enjoyed a subterranean existence in popular culture until it was able to reassert itself in the discourse of mainstream society. In reality, the historical heritage has been an ambiguous weapon for contemporary claims-makers seeking to "market" the clergy-abuse problem. Generations of jokes and rumors have helped create a willingness to believe the worst of a celibate clergy, so that the reporting of a few authentic cases of pedophilia quickly leads to acceptance of the most extreme charges about systemic corruption. However, the same religious mythology initially made mainstream media more reluctant to give credence to such allegations, for fear of repeating canards that seemed more suitable for vulgar jokes. But the existence of the tradition is beyond question, and works like *A Gospel of Shame* show how far it has shaped contemporary assumptions about the roots and causes of the perceived crisis.

3

The Discovery of Clergy Sex Abuse

An Age of Innocence?

In the past decade the image of the sexually exploitative priest has revived with re-markable vigor. Throughout the century there have been isolated incidents when a Catholic priest was believed to be "visiting the ladies," and such behavior might lead to local scandals, but these rarely attracted wider concern. In only a few instances did cases involving children and minors lead to actual prosecutions, and even then these received little media attention unless the circumstances were highly unusual. In 1977, for example, the Detroit press made much of allegations that a priest had mo-lested a twelve-year-old boy, but this was because of speculation that the incident might be linked to a notorious series of unsolved child murders in Oakland County.[1] This was a rare instance in which the media presented stories, however briefly, about "rampant indiscretions within the priesthood."[2]

The Oakland County case was a glaring exception to a general picture of order and tranquility, which in retrospect we know to have been misleading. There were certainly cases in the 1960s and 1970s when Catholic clergy were found to be sexu-ally involved with children or adult parishioners. However, the media generally cooperated with the church in avoiding scandal. Clerical offenders were dealt with quietly, usually being transferred from their parishes without obvious publicity, and were required to submit to periods of seclusion and therapy that were neither long nor arduous.

Without either media or legal records of any substance, it is impossible to write a history of sex abuse by the clergy, Catholic or otherwise, which makes it difficult to provide a context for the recent upsurge of reports. Two views of recent develop-ments are possible. One suggests that abuse was a relatively constant phenomenon, perhaps going back centuries, but that only in the 1980s did any significant number of cases come to light.[3] An alternative interpretation would see a genuine increase of abusive behavior from the 1960s onward, perhaps an "epidemic" due to a relaxation in the sexual discipline required of priests and to an increasing anomie caused by changing expectations of Catholic clergy. The second view is favored by ecclesiastical conservatives, who believe that the abuse crisis arose from post–Vatican II liberal innovations. However, this position is contradicted by the observed experience of the abuse cases that have earned notoriety in recent years. Many of the most scandalous incidents occurred in the early or mid-1960s, and the perpetrators were priests or religious trained under the traditional preconciliar system. Sexual misconduct by priests long predated the liberal 1960s, but the scale of the problem would not become apparent for many years.

The 1980s

In the early 1980s public attitudes towards child sex abuse were being redefined, and the courts were increasingly willing to hear lawsuits alleging malpractice and negligence by professional groups and organizations. A new environment first became apparent in the civil courts, in sporadic cases in which priests were sued for sexual liaisons either with teenage boys or adult women, and superior clergy were accused of institutional negligence for permitting such conduct. A handful of little-publicized cases established the soon-to-be familiar pattern of a priest eventually subjected to formal arrest and criminal proceedings after years in which his behavior had been known within the church. This was the situation in a 1985 incident in Idaho, in which a priest named Carmelo Baltazar received a prison sentence for lewd behavior with a minor.[4]

From the church's point of view, the most potentially dangerous case in these years involved a ten-year-old New Jersey boy named Christopher Schultz who was abused by Franciscan friar and scoutmaster Edmund Coakeley in circumstances that included sadomasochistic activities. The family received no sympathetic response from church authorities, and Christopher eventually committed suicide in 1979. The Schultzes sued the archdiocese of Newark, the Franciscan order, and the Boy Scouts of America, asking $10.5 million in damages, but their case was dismissed in 1981 on the grounds of charitable immunity; in 1984 the verdict was upheld by the state's highest court.[5] A few years later such a case would probably have received national attention because of the extreme nature of the abuse, the youth of the victim, and the fatal outcome. Moreover, the incident occurred close enough to New York City to attract attention from major newspapers and broadcast media. The relative lack of publicity received by this affair suggests the continuing reluctance to embarrass the church, but the fact that we know about the events at all shows that constraints were relaxing, and a true scandal could not be long delayed.

The Impact of the Gauthe Case, 1984–1989

The major breakthrough in establishing the scale and reality of a "clergy-abuse" problem occurred in the Louisiana diocese of Lafayette in 1984–1985, when Father Gilbert Gauthe was tried on multiple counts of molestation. He was suspected of molesting children of both sexes as early as 1972, and charges involved forcible abuse as well as child pornography. On several occasions, though, church authorities

Table 3.1. Beginning of Clergy-Abuse Scandals, 1983–1986

1983

July	Gilbert Gauthe relieved of priestly duties in Henry, La.
August	Lawyers for families of Gauthe victims request details of diocesan insurance policies

1984

February	Civil lawsuit against superiors of Father Donald Roemer in California, convicted of molestation
June	CBS affiliate in Lafayette, La., reports civil case against Gauthe
July	Father P. Henry Leech of Rhode Island charged with sexual assault of boys
September	Archdiocese of Los Angeles held liable in Roemer case
October	Gauthe indicted

1985

January	Father Carmelo Baltazar sentenced to seven years' imprisonment in Idaho
February	Priest accused of misconduct with several in diocese of Green Bay, Wis.
March	Milwaukee priest resigns license as psychologist following admission of abuse
April	Father William O'Connell of Bristol, R.I. indicted on twenty-two felony counts
	Priest of San Diego diocese pays to settle suit involving improprieties with altar boy
May	Thomas Doyle, Michael Peterson, and Ray Mouton collaborate on report warning of abuse crisis in Catholic church.
June	*National Catholic Reporter* reports Gauthe case and others in progress around the nation. Cases reported in *New York Times* and the *Washington Post*
July	*Time* reports Gauthe case
	Father Alvin Campbell of Morrisonville, Ill. pleads guilty but insane to molesting seven boys
October	Gauthe convicted and sentenced
	Civil suit filed against Father William Authenreith in diocese of Orlando

1986

February	Verdict in civil case resulting from Gauthe affair
April	Canon Law Society meeting at Morristown, N.J., addressed by Thomas Doyle and Ray Mouton, whose remarks on the severity of the abuse crisis are widely quoted in the media
	Priest in Huntingdon Beach, Calif., receives probation for offenses with altar boy
June	Father Peter McCutcheon arrested in suburban Maryland for molesting two boys
	Father William O'Connell sentenced to one year in prison
July	Father Lane Fontenot pleads guilty to molestation related charges in Idaho
August	CBS newsmagazine *West 57th* reports Gauthe case
	Vatican denies Father Charles Curran's right to teach as a Catholic theologian, beginning period of intense intrachurch controversy between liberals and traditionalists (see chapter 6)
September	Vatican removes powers of liberal Archbishop Raymond Hunthausen of Seattle

(Material drawn chiefly from Jason Berry, *Lead Us Not into Temptation* (New York: Doubleday, 1992); Elinor Burkett and Frank Bruni, *A Gospel of Shame* (New York: Viking, 1993); and several stories in the *National Catholic Reporter*, June 7, 1985.)

who learned of his misdeeds responded merely by transferring him to new parishes, where the cycle would begin afresh. External intervention was made more difficult by the religious loyalty of the region, in a diocese where almost two-thirds of the population was nominally Catholic. Gauthe would allegedly molest more than a hundred boys in four parishes, culminating in his position as priest from 1978 to 1983 in a town in Vermilion Parish, Louisiana. In the summer of 1984 a local television station reported a civil suit begun by parents against the diocese, and some months later criminal charges were pressed. The case achieved national news coverage in June 1985, when a detailed account was published by Jason Berry in the *National Catholic Reporter*, and shortly afterward the affair was reported across the nation. In October, Gauthe was sentenced to twenty years' imprisonment. The diocese had originally hoped to silence public criticism by settling discreetly with the families of victims, but one family, the Gastals, pursued the case to a jury verdict, and in early 1986 they were awarded damages of $1.25 million.

The Gauthe affair did much to establish the stereotypical characteristics expected of the "clergy-abuse" offender. Apart from illustrating the extensive harm that one individual could do in a position of trust, the case suggested that the church as a whole had acquiesced in the wrongdoing, perhaps even aggravated it, by refusing to take decisive and punitive action at an early stage. The affair set the precedent that failure to intervene should result in serious financial penalties and compensatory damages for the families. A western Louisiana jury acted according to the legendary sympathies of civil courts in that part of the state in actions setting "little people" against large corporations, and by the end of the decade the affair had cost the Catholic church some $20 million in damages, victim therapy, and legal fees.[6]

The Gauthe case shaped reporting of a series of scandals that broke between 1984 and 1986, in which Catholic priests or religious had sexual contacts with minors, sometimes children who were in their charge in the capacity of pupils or altar boys. Nationwide there were at least forty instances in those years in which Catholic priests would be charged with multiple acts of molestation and outright rape.[7] Courts now showed themselves more willing to intervene in the thitherto confidential disciplinary proceedings of the Catholic church. Prosecutors also became increasingly prepared to press criminal charges in such cases, and in 1985 and 1986 notorious criminal trials ensued in some strongly Catholic communities. In Bristol, Rhode Island, Father William O'Connell was charged with multiple molestation and taking pornographic pictures, and two other priests in the Providence diocese faced similar charges at about that time.[8] Other cases involved Father Donald Roemer in Thousand Oaks, California;[9] Alvin Campbell in Morrisonville, Illinois;[10] and Dennis Dellamalva in the Pennsylvania diocese of Greensburg.[11] "By January 1, 1987, 135 priests or brothers had been reported to the nunciature for molesting youths, in most cases boys."[12]

Another potent legacy of the Gauthe affair was the realization that church authorities already possessed quite detailed knowledge of proven or suspected molesters, though such awareness was never shared with parishes that might be affected. In the Gauthe proceedings, lawyers representing the victims' families succeeded in forcing the Lafayette diocese to open its secret archive concerning complaints alleging abuse or sexual malpractice by priests, and this exposed several individuals who would later face criminal charges. In this one small diocese, there was a clique of priests who were almost overtly sexually involved with children and teenagers, in addition to others known to be actively homosexual, and such flouting of church laws continued over years or decades with minimal official intervention.

Seeking access to such records elsewhere was a powerful tactic. If a suit succeeded, then names were released, and the abuse issue would be strongly publicized;

if it was rejected, then ecclesiastical authorities could be portrayed as concealing their dark secrets. Similar tactics were attempted in other states. In 1988 a newspaper investigation of three priests in the diocese of Pittsburgh expanded to include several additional abuse cases in the neighboring Pennsylvania diocese of Altoona-Johnstown. The *Pittsburgh Press* sued to gain access to sealed records, and the affair resulted in a major scandal and lawsuit.[13]

Facing Facts?

The burgeoning number of scandals evoked deep concern among some Catholic observers, and in 1985 a confidential report entitled "The Problem of Sexual Molestation by Roman Catholic Clergy: Meeting the Problem in a Comprehensive and Responsible Manner" was submitted to the Catholic hierarchy.[14] The authors included Gauthe's attorney, F. Ray Mouton, and two clerics, Thomas P. Doyle and Michael Peterson. Doyle, who became an influential commentator on the incipient abuse issue, was a canon lawyer, one of four American priests at the apostolic nunciature, the Vatican's diplomatic mission in Washington, D.C. Peterson was the founder of an influential therapy program for priests at the Saint Luke's Institute in Suitland, Maryland. Their document considered the impact of the Gauthe case, and noted the impending multimillion-dollar actions to which it was leading.[15] Because some thirty other cases were now in progress, it was reasonable to extrapolate that the financial costs of probable lawsuits might exceed $1 billion within the next ten years.

The group warned of the need to take urgent action in the face of scandals, to react swiftly to complaints, and also to avoid charges of secretive proceedings or cover-ups. The report explored some of the legal nightmares that might soon be encountered, including the criminal charges that could be incurred from failure to report allegations of child abuse to the secular authorities. Furthermore, destroying evidence might be construed as contempt of court or obstruction of justice. The church could no longer rely on the friendship and sympathy of Catholic politicians, judges, and professionals within the criminal justice system; exposure and conviction would be far more likely than in the past.[16] At a meeting of the Canon Law Society in 1986, Doyle spoke publicly about the grave prognosis that he and his colleagues had presented, declaring that it was "the most serious crisis that we in the church have faced in centuries," a phrase that would be much quoted in the following years.[17]

There now occurred a series of conferences on the clergy-abuse issue respectively intended for bishops, priests, and members of religious orders.[18] The National Conference of Catholic Bishops (NCCB) held the first of several confidential discussions on the topic but did not hold the open debate that Doyle and the others had sought.[19] In the fall of 1985 each diocesan bishop received a copy of the Peterson-Doyle-Mouton report as part of a larger discussion of treatment issues. For several years thereafter the bishops would come under repeated attack for their lack of response to the abuse problem, but they contented themselves with issuing defensive statements reiterating the church's commitment to combating child abuse wherever it occurred.[20] Their semiannual meetings (held in June and November) regularly gave the media an opportunity to repeat the charges of inaction or complicity.

The bishops' refusal to take allegations more seriously may have reflected a failure
to see any alternative that could be pursued without risking the very legal troubles
they hoped to avoid. Coming as they did at a time of bitter controversy between
liberal and conservative factions within Catholicism, the attacks intensified the hierarchy's perception of an organized attempt to defame the church, and probably made
the bishops less willing to undertake a wide-ranging investigation. In addition, the
1985 report had specifically recommended a national intervention team to assist dioceses responding to abuse complaints, an interference with local autonomy that was
politically thorny.

It is also tempting to apply here the speech-communications concept of "groupthink," the collective process by which decision makers filter out pressures or
information that might deter them from risky or disastrous strategies. [21] As originally
formulated, the theory proposes a number of characteristics for the group in question, including an illusion of invulnerability; belief in the inherent morality of the
group; collective rationalization; negative stereotyping of outsiders; the illusion of
unanimity; and pressures on participants to conform to group attitudes. If not at
the national level, this seems to offer a perfect model of the forces at work in certain
dioceses facing mounting criticisms of their attitudes toward abuse.

Those years did not produce any one case that attracted national media attention,
though a number of local affairs continued to simmer. Also, in 1987 and 1988 interest in clerical scandals shifted temporarily to the financial and sexual misdeeds of the
Protestant "televangelists," a trend noted with some relief by Catholic papers. [22] As
Our Sunday Visitor commented, "The issue is sin, not celibacy. If it were not so, such
married preachers as Jim Bakker, Jimmy Swaggart and South Africa's Rev Allan
Boesak would not now be in disgrace." [23] The most celebrated instance of mass child
molestation by a cleric in those years involved the Pentecostal preacher Tony Leyva
(see chapter 1). There was still little sense of impending crisis in the Catholic church,
although the Gauthe case continued to be quoted in the child-abuse literature. [24] This
change of emphasis may have encouraged Catholic authorities to believe that the
1985 report had been pessimistic in its predictions of disaster. Such hopes, however,
were dashed by a series of damaging scandals from 1989 onward.

The New Wave of Cases, 1989–1992

In terms of media coverage, by far the most significant incidents involved the cases of
Franciscan Bruce Ritter and former parish priest James Porter, but other widely reported stories involved New Orleans priest Dino Cinel and several unrelated clusters
of cases involving priests and religious in the archdioceses of Chicago and New York
and the Canadian province of Newfoundland. The impact and influence of the various
stories were all the greater because of the repeated opportunities provided for media
discussion and analysis, from the first rumors of scandal through subsequent investigations and trials. Most incidents involved several individual courtroom appearances
and perhaps separate criminal hearings as well as civil litigation, which could be pro-
tracted. In one instance in the Pennsylvania diocese of Altoona-Johnstown, it was an
action originally filed in 1987 that culminated in an embarrassing trial and judgment
in 1994.

The long duration of the cases is suggested by the affair of Minnesota priest Thomas Adamson, who was alleged to have been molesting boys since 1961. Authorities had been made aware of this in 1964, when he discussed the problem with his bishop.[25] Even so, he had since frequently been reassigned to new parishes, his parochial responsibilities alternating with periods of psychiatric treatment for his sexual tendencies. Not until 1987 was he finally removed from ministry, after his activities had on several occasions come to the verge of public exposure.[26] Civil charges were filed in 1984, and in 1990 a Minnesota jury awarded several million dollars in punitive damages to one of his victims.

In some instances, discussion and comment were kept alive for several years after a trial by books, magazine articles, and television documentaries, as well as fictionalized depictions of the stories. The Gauthe story was the subject of television dramatizations in 1990 and 1994, and a major book in 1992.[27] There was thus a lengthy period when all these incidents were more or less simultaneously enjoying great prominence in the media. Although the cases were very different in their details and in degree of malfeasance or neglect charged against church authorities, the concatenation of major cases contributed to perceptions of a national crisis.

The Newfoundland cases were the first of the new wave of scandals. They initially received little coverage in the United States, where Canadian news is underreported, but the affair was extremely damaging to the Canadian Catholic church, and by 1990 the U.S. media were drawing extensive parallels to domestic stories. The cases originally involved criminal prosecutions for repeated molestation committed by two parish priests. In the spring of 1989 attention shifted to the long history of both physical and sexual abuse committed by members of the Christian Brothers order against teenage boys in the Mount Cashel boys home in St. John's.[28] Though seven priests were charged at first, two dozen clergy were said to be implicated in the various complaints, which tainted what had been one of the most prestigious Catholic institutions in the region. Most of the accusations had been known by police and social services as far back as 1975, but the situation had been covered up for the intervening years.[29] During the original clandestine inquiry, some Brothers implicated in molestation had been permitted to leave the province to undertake new assignments. There were no sexual allegations against the province's archbishop, but he resigned in 1990 under attack for church policies during the earlier investigations and cover-up.[30]

Once the story resurfaced in 1989, it stayed in the headlines for several years, with a public inquiry, an internal investigation by the Catholic church, and a series of criminal trials. Public anger at the scandal appears to have reached a height in the fall of 1989, but reports of the trials during 1991 sustained public debate about the ecclesiastical reaction to abuse cases. Hearings at the public inquiry were broadcast daily on television, and analogies to the U.S. Watergate scandal were freely drawn. In 1992 the Canadian television company CBC broadcast a television movie based on the case, *The Boys of St. Vincent*, but a court injunction prevented the showing of the film in much of Canada, giving rise to intense controversy about the right to free speech.[31] The legal dispute enhanced public interest still further, and attracted even greater publicity to the film when it was finally shown over the whole of Canada in

1993 and in the United States in 1994.[32] Though the Newfoundland cases remained the most notorious, there was a series of other scandals in other Canadian provinces in the early 1990s, including other Christian Brothers' schools in Ontario.[33] In 1992 the Canadian bishops' conference concurred that such cases had been made possible by a "general conspiracy of silence" afflicting the church on abuse.[34]

There were analogies between the Newfoundland cases and the several U.S. scandals that came to notice within a few months of each other at the end of 1989. In that November the meeting of Catholic bishops gathered in Baltimore was disturbed by protests about the hierarchy's failures to investigate abuse by priests and subsequent cover-ups.[35] This demonstration followed a pattern that had become popular in dissident Catholic circles as the media had come to regard NCCB meetings as potentially newsworthy because of the likelihood of disputes over topics such as women's rights and homosexuality. Any pressure group therefore stood a good chance of gaining national attention. Activists present at this meeting included Jeanne Miller, who would become a prominent organizer of victim-advocacy and support groups, as well as some militant conservatives who linked the pedophile problem to alleged homosexual infiltration into the clergy. The centerpiece of the 1989 protest was David Figueroa of Hawaii, who charged that he had been molested by a series of parish priests over many years in the 1970s and 1980s, and that one of the culprits was Joseph Ferrario, who had since become bishop of Honolulu. Figueroa began a series of lawsuits that kept the issue in the news through for several years, and in 1991 Bishop Ferrario became the first serving member of the U.S. hierarchy to face civil charges for a sexual offense.

The month following the Baltimore meeting, the *New York Post* charged that Franciscan father Bruce Ritter had been sexually involved with a young man. Ritter became celebrated during the 1980s as the founder of Covenant House, a successful and rapidly growing charity that aimed to rescue street children.[36] He was a visible public figure, well known from his extensive fund-raising mailings, and had been publicly lauded by President Reagan as a model of what could be achieved by the private sector in battling social ills. Covenant House was cited by President George Bush as one of the "thousand points of light" that the administration was cultivating. Reports of sexual misconduct initially attracted skepticism, but over the next two months they were not only confirmed but greatly expanded by similar reports dating back many years. Other charges involved financial impropriety. Early accusations involving a homosexual relationship with a young adult man were broadened to include allegations of relationships with boys and young teenagers, and Ritter was forced to resign his Covenant House position in February 1990.

As in the Newfoundland story, there were suggestions that warning signs had been ignored over two decades. Ritter's lifestyle had long been suspected by journalists and colleagues, and there had been reports and complaints from his sexual partners, though there was no pattern of bureaucratic neglect comparable to that at Mount Cashel or the later cases. In this sense, the Ritter affair was not particularly damaging to ecclesiastical authorities, but the discrediting of so prominent a figure seemed to confirm public suspicions about hypocrisy within the clergy. Ritter himself was celebrated for his puritanical denunciations of pornography and casual sex, and he had even attacked the frank sexual discussions of Dr. Ruth Westheimer while he served on the antipornography commission established by U.S. Attorney-General Edwin Meese.[37] The story also acquired disproportionate visibility from having occurred within close view of most of the major media.

Other American cases proliferated from mid-1991 onward, and concern tended to be regional in nature. The discovery of one or more celebrated instances in a particular diocese led to intense debate and criticism of church authorities. Bishops came under pressure to show themselves to be both frank and vigilant in confronting the abuse problem, and to intervene in situations that might once have been concealed. Realizing the legal dangers, dioceses undertook a process of "housecleaning," examining files for outstanding charges against currently serving clergy and either suspending them or initiating disciplinary proceedings. Growing public sensitivities about molestation further increased the likelihood of both investigation and reporting.

In consequence, one major case would lead to a cluster of others, and the local media portrayed the situation as a generalized problem. National reporting of these local and regional incidents fostered the sense that the issue was ubiquitous, especially when scandals occurred in or near a major metropolitan center such as New York, Boston, or Chicago. The sudden upsurge of cases became an "epidemic," implying that the incidence of the behavior itself was undergoing a dramatic increase rather than simply reflecting increased recognition. Also sinister was the suggestion that a suddenly detected group of unrelated cases in a given city or area might represent a "network" of pedophile clergy, implying a degree of organization or conspiracy. By 1993 Bishop Louis Gelineau of Providence, Rhode Island, was denying charges that his diocese was "engaged in some massive endorsement and coverup of clerical sex abuse rings." Charges of networks or organized activity became all the more likely when litigants and attorneys recognized the enormous advantages that arose from the use of conspiracy or RICO lawsuits in order to recover damages.[38]

Crisis in Chicago, 1991–1994

The archdiocese of Chicago experienced perhaps the most vigorous debate over clergy abuse, in what Andrew Greeley has described as "the pedophile crisis," which reached the point of "explosion" during 1991–1992.[39] In the 1960s and 1970s there had on average been two or three cases each year in which priests were accused of sexual misconduct with minors. The rate rose dramatically to seventeen complaints between 1986 and 1988, and to nineteen in the two years 1990–1991.[40] Between October 1991 and March 1992 charges of inappropriate sexual activity led to the indictment of one priest, Robert E. Mayer, and the removal of six others from their parishes, a purge that is sometimes described as "the October Massacre."

Mayer's case reproduced most of the now familiar themes. He had been the subject of a lawsuit as early as 1982, when he was accused of making sexual advances to a boy whose mother, Jeanne Miller, would later become a prominent activist in the campaign to expose clerical misconduct.[41] As part of the legal settlement, Mayer had been instructed to avoid the proximity of people under twenty-one years of age. However, this rule proved unenforceable, and he had been appointed to a series of other parishes until he arrived at Saint Odilo's parish in Berwyn, where new charges arose in October 1991.[42] The fact that allegations had been known so long provided

Table 3.2. Summary Chronology of the Clergy-Abuse Scandals from mid-1991 through 1995

1991

August VOCAL founded

David Figueroa files civil lawsuit against Bishop Ferrario

October Father Robert Mayer removed from parish in archdiocese of Chicago

Cardinal Bernardin appoints panel to investigate handling of abuse
charges against priests

Father Thomas Chleboski sentenced to eight years for molesting boys in
Washington, D.C., in addition to a twenty-two year sentence in Virginia

November Archdiocese of Chicago removes four priests from parishes

1992

February Father Richard Lavigne indicted in Massachusetts on abuse charges

Father Bruce Ball tried in Wisconsin for offenses involving boy

May Allegations against James Porter broadcast on Boston television station

June Chicago archdiocese publishes report of cardinal's commission on charges against priests
in previous three decades

Canadian bishops' conference issues final report on recent abuse scandals, and
offers guidelines on handling of future abuse cases

August Father Myles White arrested in Illinois for sexual assault

September Cardinal Bernardin announces new archdiocesan policy for responding to abuse charges;
legal controversy between archdiocese and Cook County state's attorney over
identifying priests accused of abuse

Father Ronald Provost indicted on abuse-related charges in Worcester, Mass.

October National conference of VOCAL held in Chicago area

Father Daniel Calabrese found guilty in state of New York

December Sixty-eight of Father Porter's victims announce settlement with diocese of Fall River;
Porter convicted of molestation charges in Minnesota

News media publicize allegations of abuse at Saint Lawrence's Seminary in
Mount Calvary, Wis., run by Capuchin friars

Father David Holley accused of molestation

1993

February Lawsuit against Father Daniel Calabrese

March Four priests removed in diocese of Belleville, Ill.

Archbishop Roberto Sanchez resigns following sexual allegations.

Father James Silva accused of molestation in Rhode Island

April Several clergy involved in homosexual scandal at Sacred Heart School of
Theology in Wisconsin

May Father Edward Pipala removed from his parish in state of New York following
abuse charges

June Report issued by Capuchin order confirms abuse charges at Saint Lawrence's Seminary.

RICO suit filed against priests in New Jersey and Rhode Island

NCCB founds *ad hoc* committee to examine clergy abuse

Pope John Paul II issues statement on abuse scandals in church in the United States

August Suicide of Father Thomas Smith in Maryland following abuse charges

October James Porter pleads guilty to charges in Massachusetts

Camden diocese settles lawsuit against two priests

November Cardinal Bernardin accused of sexual abuse;

Servants of the Paraclete treatment center agrees on financial settlement with
victims of Father Porter

Official inquiry issues report on molestation by friars at Saint Anthony's Seminary in
Santa Barbara, Calif.

December James Porter sentenced in Massachusetts

Archdiocese of Santa Fe announces imminent threat of bankruptcy

Table 3.2. (continued)

1994	
February	Abuse charges against Cardinal Bernardin withdrawn
April	Father Edward Pipala sentenced to prison in New York state
	Civil judgment in case of Father Francis Luddy in diocese of Altoona-Johnstown
May	Several priests accused of abuse in San Francisco archdiocese
October	Class-action lawsuit charges extensive criminal conspiracy by clergy of the dioceses of Camden and Providence

1995	
February	Several priests removed for abuse-related charges in archdiocese of Washington, D.C.

the major grievance for parishioners. The cases received unprecedented attention because they were covered extensively in the *Chicago Sun-Times* columns of Father Andrew Greeley.

In the aftermath of the cases, Chicago Cardinal Joseph Bernardin made a frank admission that the church had been in error on these issues, and specifically apologized to the parishioners of the churches affected directly by the scandals.[43] He demonstrated church concern by appointing an investigative commission with jurisdiction to reexamine any allegations of abuse by priests who had served in the archdiocese in the previous four decades.[44] This wide mandate was intended to ensure that no priest currently in office faced past charges of abusive conduct. In June 1992 the commission reported outstanding charges of sexual misconduct against fifty-nine priests, and determined that allegations against at least thirty-nine of these were probably valid.[45] Several of the men had not been reported to public authorities, and eight continued to serve as priests.[46] This led to a legal and constitutional controversy between the archdiocese and the Cook County state's attorney's office, which demanded that the church hand over all materials involving allegations of abuse of minors by priests.[47] The church refused to do so on grounds of the privileged nature of the communications, and the fact that the allegations were unproven. Courts also held that subpoenas could be resisted on several grounds, including attorney-client privilege as well as mental health and pastoral privilege.[48]

The Chicago cases brought about a grassroots movement to support and assist the victims of abuse by priests, and to demand that the church reform its response to such cases. Jeanne Miller now founded VOCAL (Victims of Clergy Abuse Linkup; later simply The Linkup), and Barbara Blaine founded SNAP, (Survivors Network of those Abused by Priests). The Chicago incidents achieved enormous media coverage, and victims or their families were frequent participants in the many television talk shows and documentary programs that discussed the abuse issue between 1990 and 1994. VOCAL leaders repeatedly challenged the church's secretive handling of the abuse cases, especially in the feud with the state's attorney.[49] Miller served as a source for journalists and others seeking stories in this area, all the more valuable because of the extensive information she had collected on cases nationwide.[50]

Cardinal Bernardin met these controversies with skill and diplomacy, and issued a sweeping new policy statement on abuse cases that appeared to respond to most of the demands of the church's numerous critics (see below). It was ironic therefore that the cardinal himself became the target of allegations of misconduct. In 1993 a former seminarian named Stephen Cook testified that he had been sexually victimized by two priests in the mid-1970s, one of whom was Joseph Bernardin.[51] The cardinal strenuously protested the charges, and he won sympathy from the Catholic community, including sources normally suspicious of the hierarchy, such as Andrew Greeley and the liberal Catholic press. In November, Bernardin's appearance at the meeting of the NCCB was greeted by a standing ovation. Cook withdrew his charges the following February, stating that he now realized the recovered memories to be dubious. Although Bernardin was vindicated, the fact that charges had been made against so popular and visible a figure suggested that virtually any cleric might be implicated. In 1993 his colleague Cardinal John O'Connor remarked, "It's getting increasingly difficult for some priests and some bishops to hold their heads up. Everyone is under suspicion."[52]

The Cases Proliferate

O'Connor warned in May that "a grenade could explode at any time, and another and another."[53] Scandals indeed continued to emerge, often in local clusters reminiscent of the Chicago pattern, and the influence of the Chicago media may be detected in the sensitivity of certain midwestern dioceses to abuse charges. The Illinois diocese of Joliet removed four priests for misconduct with children in a twelve-month period in 1992–1993.[54] In the same state, the small diocese of Belleville experienced a remarkable scandal in 1993–1994 when no fewer than 10 of its 190 priests were removed or suspended following molestation charges, which in some cases dated back to the 1960s.[55] But the phenomenon had become national in scope. In the archdiocese of New York, by mid-1993 molestation had been charged against one priest, Daniel Calabrese in Poughkeepsie, and two others said to be involved with teenage boys.[56] In Orange County, New York, Father Edward Pipala was convicted on multiple counts of sexual misconduct with the members of boys clubs in parishes with which he had been associated during the 1980s. In 1994 the New Jersey diocese of Camden settled legal actions involving no fewer than nine priests, though even more sweeping lawsuits followed shortly; several cases were reported in the archdiocese of San Francisco.[57]

In Massachusetts the diocese of Worcester experienced several scandals between 1990 and 1992.[58] Five concerned priests accused of sexual activities with small boys, either engaging in direct molestation or in taking explicit photographs, and another had raped or molested a number of prepubescent girls. The seventh had sexually exploited a nun who had approached him for counseling. The crimes of one of the priests, David Holley, were considered so serious that he was eventually sentenced to 275 years in prison. In addition, a local treatment and therapy center for sexually troubled priests, the House of Affirmation, was closed in 1989 after the priest who operated it was implicated in a molestation suit.

Other American cases were reminiscent of the Newfoundland affair because they involved the mass abuse of pupils at seminaries or boarding schools. Between 1964 and 1987, dozens of teenage boys were molested by friars at Saint Anthony's Seminary in Santa Barbara, California.[59] "Perpetrators had to use their authority as priests to isolate, intimidate, confuse and manipulate these young boys in order to satisfy their own needs and insure silence."[60] In Wisconsin many former students of a rural boys boarding school alleged that they had been subject to sexual approaches or assaults by Capuchin friars, the incidents having occurred between 1968 and 1992.[61]

"Priest of Porn"

As the cases developed, commentators remarked on a number of features that aggravated still further the pattern of clerical misconduct. For instance, "group" cases were so harmful to the church's reputation because they implied that abuse or pedophilia had acquired an institutional or subcultural character among clergy. Interviews and testimony indicated a quite remarkable flouting of appropriate standards of behavior. Some of the accused priests appeared utterly to lack remorse for their actions or to understand that they were in any sense wrong, and a few suggested that vows of celibacy were violated only by heterosexual contact. This degree of cynicism or cognitive dissonance reflected poorly on the authorities who had tolerated or ignored these offenders for so long. Also damaging were instances in which the nature of the abuse went far beyond what could be defended as fairly innocuous touching, and involved such aggravating factors as child pornography or sadomasochism.

In March 1991 a New Orleans television station broadcast an exposé about a local priest, Dino Cinel, of the parish of Saint Rita's.[62] The affair dated back to late 1988 when large numbers of pornographic videos had been found in his rectory, and because most of them concerned pedophile themes, their mere possession constituted a criminal offense. Cinel had also produced pornographic videos and photographs depicting sexual encounters between himself and several teenage boys, and the scandal was intensified because these had occurred in the parish rectory. However, three months passed before church authorities handed them over to a law enforcement agency. Even then no action had been taken because the the local district attorney was reluctant to embarrass what he termed "Holy Mother the Church." Shortly afterward, Cinel had been quietly transferred from his parochial responsibilities to a well-paying academic job in the City University of New York system. In December 1989 another former Catholic priest named John Bauer was arrested for his role in manufacturing child pornography videos.[63]

There were several other arrests of priests in those years: Thomas Chleboski in Arlington, Virginia, was accused of abusing a thirteen-year-old boy;[64] Father Richard Lavigne in Shelburne Falls, Massachusetts;[65] Father Earl Bierman in Newport, Kentucky. In Maryland, Father Thomas Smith committed suicide after charges emerged that he had fondled a boy in his parish. After his death, the diocesan authorities admitted that he had confessed to molesting other boys during the 1960s.[66] One Georgia case at this time was especially damaging because it aroused ancient suspicions of the cosmopolitan and un-American nature of the Catholic church. In 1989 and 1990 a priest named Anton Mowat was under investigation for molestation when he left the country to be sheltered by the church in his home country of England. This was denounced by the local press as a sinister manifestation of the use of international links to evade justice.[67]

In August 1990 the *Los Angeles Times* reported that more than a thousand cases involving abuse by clergy (Catholic and other) were currently before the courts. By 1992 attorney Jeffrey Anderson could assert that every one of the nation's 188 Catholic dioceses had at least one abuse case in progress.[68] The great majority of actions involved civil litigation, but there were also criminal cases, which by 1994 had resulted in the incarceration of some sixty Catholic priests.[69] Using a 1992 poll of more than a thousand Catholics throughout North America, Stephen Rossetti confirmed that reports and rumors of clergy abuse had risen sharply: no less than 10 percent of respondents said they lived in a parish where a priest had been accused of child sexual abuse; a further 55 percent knew of an instance in their diocese. The 10 percent figure suggests a level of suspicion far higher than might be assumed from any official data on prosecutions or civil litigation, and probably reflects an upsurge of unsubstantiated local rumors.[70]

The media presented "clergy abuse" as a systemic scandal rotting the whole fabric of the American Catholic church, and as so often occurs in social problems, the boundaries of the issue were stretched to include related behaviors that did not fit the original definition. There were two incidents in these years in which senior clergy were involved in well-publicized sexual misconduct, neither of which involved children or pedophilia. Respectively, these concerned Atlanta archbishop Eugene Marino and Archbishop Roberto Sanchez of Santa Fe, New Mexico, both of whom were accused of having had sexual relationships with adult women. However, both incidents were commonly cited in news reporting of "clergy abuse" as illustrative of a general crisis of sexual discipline within the Catholic church. Moreover, news reporting of the Sanchez story in 1993 made extensive reference to the troubles of the Catholic church in New Mexico, where several priests were currently facing charges involving the abuse of minors. This unrelated scandal thus offered a platform for extensive retailing of the child-abuse allegations.[71]

The Porter Case, 1992–1993

The various cases established a familiar stereotypical pattern of a scandal involving a "pedophile priest": a series of accusations over many years to which the church responded by transferring the culprit, possibly after an ineffective spell of therapy, with the inevitable consequence that the cycle would soon begin again in a new parish. These themes were all present in perhaps the most notorious case of the period: the multiple abuse committed by Father James R. Porter in several parishes in the Massachusetts diocese of Fall River, between 1960 and 1967, specifically in the communities of North Attleboro, Fall River and New Bedford. It has been plausibly estimated that the number of children of both sexes molested in those years might have totaled two or three hundred, and he was removed from priestly duties at least eight times in a six-year period on grounds of his sexual activities.[72] Porter left Massachusetts to enter a treatment facility in New Mexico, and was subsequently reassigned to a parish in Bemidji, Minnesota, before leaving the priesthood altogether in 1974. However, he continued to be active in the sexual exploitation of minors, and was convicted of the abuse of a baby-sitter in his Minnesota home.

In 1989 the earlier abuse was recalled by one of his Massachusetts victims, Frank Fitzpatrick, who made contact with other former victims through personal acquaintance and by means of newspaper advertisements. In May 1992 the case was reported on the Boston television station WBZ-TV, which played recorded telephone conversations between Porter and Fitzpatrick, in which the former priest frankly admitted molesting "anywhere, you know, from fifty to a hundred [children], I guess." This exposé naturally encouraged further reporting. With more than one hundred complainants coming forward, the group was able to pressure authorities to prosecute the case, and the Bristol County district attorney announced that he would investigate what might be the largest case of its kind in American history.

In July the ABC network newsmagazine *Primetime Live* reported the Porter affair in two separate items, in which aggressive investigative techniques were employed to force Porter to confront the accusations. The program also played the startling recorded phone conversations. By the closing months of 1992 the Porter case had brought clergy abuse into the headlines and onto op-ed pages of most major newspapers, and also contributed significantly to ensuring that the problem was construed as a specifically Catholic dilemma. Porter himself was separately tried for his misdeeds in Minnesota and Massachusetts during 1993, and his final sentencing in New Bedford in December 1993 became an international media event, with extensive reporting of the sufferings recounted by more than twenty of his victims.[73]

Porter was eventually sentenced to eighteen to twenty years' imprisonment. The case provided a forum for extensive condemnation of church policies by his "educated and articulate" victims and their families. Porter's attorney argued that much of the blame for the crimes rested with the institution: "You've got a church that knew as early as 1963 that there had been 30 to 40 reports of what this man had done, and they kept him supervising altar boys for four more years in this state."[74] The case also put visible faces on what had thitherto been a general impression of wrongdoing in the American Catholic church: "A problem that had existed in disconnected images—a rape in New Jersey one year, a molestation in New Mexico the next—coalesced into a coherent picture when the legions of victims of Father James Porter hit the airwaves."[75]

The Cycle

The sudden upsurge of complaints and prosecutions from about 1989 onward requires explanation, especially in contrast with the relative rarity of such incidents twenty years previously. The post-Gauthe scandals had a snowball effect, in that intense reporting and news coverage encouraged past victims, real or imaginary, to recognize the nature of their past experiences, and then to come forward and register their complaints. One California case provides an illustration of this process. In the case of the Santa Barbara seminary, reports of abuse did not emerge until 1989, when one friar was convicted of criminal charges, and this began an investigation that led to allegations against ten other friars.[76] It was also in 1989, as publicity mounted, that David McCann announced his abuse by Christian Brothers in Alfred, Ontario, as far back as 1960. This began a scandal that led to charges against more than thirty current and former Brothers, and a $40 million lawsuit.[77] In the Saint

Lawrence school in Wisconsin, one man who had been molested as a boy in the early 1970s maintained his silence until 1992, when he published a reminiscence of these events in a Milwaukee newspaper. He was subsequently contacted by other former pupils who reported similar experiences, and the ensuing inquiries resulted in at least six Capuchin friars being implicated in the abuse of dozens of pupils over a twenty-year period.[78]

Changing sensibilities about child maltreatment are suggested by the growing inclusion of female religious as alleged perpetrators of sexual or physical abuse. Formal complaints about such behavior were virtually never publicized before the 1990s, but in 1994 a series of groundbreaking cases charged abuse by nuns. One nun sued her religious order for $3.7 million on the grounds of alleged molestation by her mother superior in the 1960s.[79] An Ontario woman sued the order of Carmelite nuns for $13 million for physical and emotional abuse reportedly suffered in a convent-run orphanage three decades previously.[80] Jeanne Miller remarked, probably correctly, that such charges were "the new wave. You'll be hearing a lot more about it."[81] Such a comment is in a sense a self-fulfilling prophecy as cases influence the expectations of both media and courts, and in turn encourage both reporting and litigation. For the media, such a new angle is likely to be exploited as a welcome embellishment to a story in danger of becoming predictable or stale. From a legal point of view, such charges vastly expand the range of potential actions to include virtually any church-run orphanage or institution, and the trend makes potential litigants of thousands of former inmates of such homes.

Not only were complaints now more likely, it was probable that they would lead to official action. The Catholic church traditionally enjoyed great political power, and in some of the dioceses where scandals occurred the church claimed as believers a substantial share of the local population: 62 percent for Gauthe's diocese of Lafayette; 51 percent in Porter's home territory of Fall River; 45 percent in the diocese of Worcester.[82] Nor do these figures necessarily give an adequate sense of the extent of ecclesiastical power. The Chicago archdiocese declares that about 42 percent of the metropolitan population is Catholic, but Catholics have long enjoyed far greater prominence in Chicago politics and law enforcement than this statistic would imply. In such a setting, police and prosecutors of the 1960s and 1970s were usually content to allow the church to deal with its own malefactors in such a way as to avoid scandal.

After 1985, however, criminal justice agencies realized that traditional qualms about embarrassing church authorities were increasingly questionable, and restraint that once seemed politically wise would now be legally dangerous. Victims and attorneys recognized and exploited the new social environment. Dennis Gaboury describes how early revelations about Father Porter were followed by a torrent of media inquiries, which allowed the complainants to choose which of a wide range of options could best publicize their case. In response, they "formed a committee to match the perfect victim with the perfect interviewer and tailor our coverage to pressure the DA to prosecute." Callers to radio phone-in shows complained that the DA's slowness in proceeding resulted from his "courting the Catholic vote." Following the *Primetime Live* reports, "the new District Attorney . . . became more respectful" and vigorously pursued the case.[83]

The transformation in attitudes is illustrated by the conflict that arose in Chicago in the fall of 1992 when Jack O'Malley, the Cook County state's attorney, demanded the secret records of the Chicago archdiocese. He himself had attracted criticism in earlier years for his allegedly lax attitude toward the wrongdoing of priests, and was currently under attack by a rival candidate in the upcoming November election.[84] In response, his office not only demonstrated remarkable zeal in challenging the archdiocese but also began an investigation against a priest on the basis of events said to have occurred a decade previously. A Chicago journalist explained O'Malley's actions: "He needs a conviction to show that he isn't soft on clergy."[85] There was also an upsurge of civil lawsuits, suggesting that plaintiffs and lawyers saw this as an opportune time both to obtain redress of grievances and to seek financial gain. By late 1992 the church was indeed facing the flood of complaints that Doyle and others had warned of several years earlier.

Restoring Trust

The church was under intense pressure to introduce reforms to prevent or reduce future instances of clergy molestation and to demonstate that it would no longer tolerate the apparent inaction of recent years.[86] Reforms began piecemeal, with the progressive archdiocese of Seattle taking the lead in instituting a policy requiring all clergy to complete training on sexual ethics and sexual abuse, and some smaller communities such as Salt Lake City and Davenport, Iowa, formulated quite elaborate documents as early as 1990.[87] Diocesan policies on complaints varied, but there were several general areas of concern: the speed of proceedings, their secretive nature, and the fact that clergy were being judged by clergy, without external checks or supervision. Also significant was the perceived need to emphasize the needs of the victim at least as much as the rights of the accused priest. A particular grievance was the long-drawn-out internal processes that allowed a priest to remain in contact with children while complaints were heard.

In September 1992 the Chicago archdiocese instituted the most comprehensive changes, including a pledge to remove forthwith any clergy accused of child abuse in order to prevent any potential harm to future victims.[88] A toll-free number was available to encourage the reporting of allegations, and a wholly new review procedure was created to defuse charges that complaints were being dealt with by clandestine internal tribunals. Under the reforms instituted by Bernardin, cases would be examined by a nine-member review board that included three lay professionals (a psychiatrist, a psychologist or social worker, and an attorney), three priests, and three lay representatives (a parent, a member of a parish council, and an abuse victim or the parent of such a victim). The board would thus have a lay majority, and none of the lay people should be church employees. The Victim Assistance Ministry would offer therapy and guidance to those abused by priests, and any substantive allegations would automatically be reported to a state agency.

Where charges were substantiated, priests would in effect pay for the offense for the rest of their lives. There would be years of therapy and counseling, and even after this: "We recommend for each priest that has successfully completed the four year aftercare program: restricted ministry, a mandate restricting access to children, supervised residence, participation in a support group, assignment of a monitor or supervisor for life, and if indicated, ongoing therapy."[89]

The Chicago policy was widely imitated, especially the use of a lay-dominated review board.[90] The American church now sought national policies in response to the continuing scandals, and in June 1992 the president of the NCCB told the assembled bishops, "Far more aggressive steps are needed to protect the innocent, treat the perpetrator and safeguard our children."[91] In November the bishops undertook to create a standard policy based on five principles: prompt response to accusations; swift suspension of an offender where charges were supported by evidence; full cooperation with civil authorities; support for victims and their families; and forthright public explanations of the church's conduct.[92] Pressure for change was reinforced by the presence of a delegation representing victims of abusive priests, including some molested by Father Porter, and groups like SNAP regularly used NCCB meetings to organize demonstrations and press conferences.

In early 1993 the NCCB convened a panel to formulate policy responses to what they described as "a sustained crisis in the church."[93] This group, chaired by Father Canice Connors, comprised thirty-one therapists, officials, and victim advocates, including Jeanne Miller.[94] Following the policies developed in both Chicago and Canada, the panel suggested that if a priest was proven to have molested children, he should be placed under permanent supervision and should have no future contact with children. The following June NCCB created a special *ad hoc* committee of eight bishops to organize a comprehensive plan for treating victims and preventing future misconduct, and this resulted in a standardized policy manual entitled *Restoring Trust*.[95] Church authorities also took steps to improve screening of seminary applicants.[96] The urgency of resolving the crisis was reinforced by the pope, who issued a statement on the scandals in the American church and warned of "the sin of giving scandal to the innocent."[97]

Not Just Catholics

In the aftermath of the Porter case and Chicago's "pedophile crisis," it was inconceivable that the Catholic church should have failed to devise and announce some sweeping policy against sexual misconduct, and church authorities would certainly have been subject to severe criticism if they had failed to undertake major reforms. However, the debates and announcements about disciplinary reforms served to focus public attention sharply on the Catholic aspects of the cases. If even the pope was urging reform, surely the Catholic church was in deep crisis, and must have most to be concerned about. Inaction thus implied neglect; action admitted guilt.

But as has been suggested, this perception of "clergy abuse" would be misleading because clergy of most major denominations were to some extent tainted by such cases from the late 1980s. The most-quoted survey of sexual problems among Protestant clergy states that some 10 percent are involved in sexual misconduct of some kind, and "about two or three percent" are pedophiles, a rate equal or higher than that suggested for Catholic priests.[98] These figures should be viewed skeptically; the methodology on which they are based is not clear, and they seem to rely disproportionately on individuals already in therapy. However, it is striking to find such a relatively high number suggested for both celibate and noncelibate clergy.

There is no central organization that tabulates reports of abusive clergy or ministers, but some data are available from companies providing liability insurance for religious institutions. The Church Mutual Insurance Company reported that by 1993 "it currently has open claims against four hundred non-Catholic clergy and has closed three hundred others since 1984. About half of them concern child sex abuse."[99] By 1993 Survivors International had located more than five hundred reports of clergy molestation; Catholic clergy were involved in a majority, but there were allegations against Episcopal, Methodist, Lutheran, Presbyterian, and Greek Orthodox clergy.[100] In addition, accurate comparison is difficult because of the relative ease of litigation against Catholic dioceses. If we search news reports in a given year, we may find ten cases of abuse involving Catholic priests for every one concerning a Baptist or Methodist minister. However, the Catholic stories will include both current prosecutions and civil litigation on matters dating back many years; the other accounts usually refer to strictly contemporary criminal cases.

Protestant denominations recorded frequent abuse scandals in these years. Andrew Greeley remarks on the basis of anecdotal evidence that Lutheran bishops were as likely to spend just as large a portion of their time dealing with the consequences of abuse scandals as were their Catholic counterparts, and in 1991 a Lutheran bishop in Wisconsin was forced to resign as a result of sexual impropriety. The leading Methodist and Presbyterian denominations in the United States regularly investigated and denounced "clergy abuse" in these years, albeit in the form of harassment or adultery involving adult women, and as in the Catholic church the abuse issue became a potent and divisive weapon in ecclesiastical politics.

The Assemblies of God denomination suffered the Bakker and Swaggart scandals in the late 1980s, and in 1994 paid $1.75 million following multiple charges of child molestation filed against a California minister, described as "a very sophisticated pedophile."[101] As in many Catholic cases, this incident involved repeated abuse over many years, against boys and young men ranging in age from seven to twenty-two.[102] During 1992 alone, molestation charges were brought against Baptist ministers in rural Michigan,[103] in New Orleans, and in Chattanooga, Tennessee. In the last case, multiple allegations of rape and molestation were directed against three brothers from one family, all of whom served as ministers in their respective churches.[104] In 1994 there were molestation cases in Baptist churches in Georgia and in Houston, Texas.

The pervasive nature of the clergy-abuse debate is suggested by the experience of the Episcopal church. This remains one of the most prominent of the traditional mainline denominations, with about 2.4 million members in the early 1990s, about 4 percent of the size of the Roman Catholic body. Episcopalians encountered a lengthy series of misconduct cases, many involving minors; insurance claims for church liability in sexual matters rose from an annual average of five or so in the late 1980s to thirty-nine in 1992.[105] Allowing for differences in denominational size, Episcopalians were not faring significantly better than Catholics, and some incidents affected prominent church leaders. The most damaging involved Wallace Frey, a well-known and popular minister in the diocese of central New York, who resigned in November 1992 after charges of improper conduct with several teenage boys. Frey was currently serving as vice-president of the national House of Deputies, one of the most powerful administrative positions in the church's national structure.[106] In 1993 Bishop Stephen Plummer of the Navajoland diocese was implicated in a relationship with a teenage boy.[107] A Baltimore case involving the abuse of six teenage boys resulted in damage payments to the value of $800,000.[108] In 1994 a new wave of concern followed the assertion by the son of an Episcopal bishop that he had been abused over many years by a priest of the same denomination. The accuser, Jeffrey Haines, became a prominent spokesman for reforming the disciplinary procedures of the Episcopal church in abuse cases.[109] The sister Anglican church of Canada has similarly felt the need to issue a general apology for sexual misconduct by clergy over the years.[110]

As with Tony Leyva, such cases were not widely reported because they did not fit within what had come to be the well-defined frame of the recognized problem, no matter how close the resemblances to the archetypical Catholic incidents. The media both reflected and reinforced public expectations, and reporting now examined the Catholic church to find what had been determined to be a Catholic problem. In so doing, both print and visual media offered remarkably condemnatory interpretations of church actions, and found themselves in alliance with the specific reform agendas of dissident Catholic groups. Consciously or otherwise, the secular media were claiming a role in the making of internal church policies that would have been unthinkable without the impetus supplied by the abuse scandals.

4

The Media and the Crisis

When the mass media reported on the wave of abuse cases, the coverage naturally attempted to offer a context for these incidents, to determine the shape and dimensions of the new problem. The interpretations that now emerged were severely critical not merely of individual priests and clergy but of the Catholic church in general, with charges of systemic corruption and illegality, cynical exploitation of the laity, and extensive sexual perversion. Moreover, the solutions offered to the "abuse crisis" involved a reform of precisely those Catholic characteristics that had so long offended mainstream Protestant sentiment, including mandatory celibacy for priests and religious, the exalted concept of the priestly role, and the seminary system. This approach was all the more influential because there was no effective attempt at rebuttal, no serious effort to indicate distortions or exaggerations in the criticism.

Although the coverage may appear to reflect popular anti-Catholic and anticlerical sentiment, in reality it owed far more to the political interests of the activists and groups who used the media to project their particular interpretation of the putative crisis. The nature of clergy-abuse reporting was determined not so much by any general bias as by the changing commercial, social, and legal environment in which the media operated during the 1980s, together with the selection of the experts who were called upon to interpret the abuse issue.

Reporting the Problem

By the early 1990s reports of sexual misbehavior by priests had become so numerous as to be almost a commonplace of news coverage. Clergy abuse has been regularly covered in articles in magazines and periodicals of all political and cultural shades, and in reports on television news documentaries and talk shows. To take an admittedly crude index of newsworthiness, we can search under the terms *clergy* and *abuse* in the computerized database *Newspaper Abstracts*, which covers major metropolitan papers in the United States. Prior to the late 1980s, the use of these two words almost invariably produced stories about *clergy* being active in the fight against drug *abuse* or child *abuse*, but this picture changed with a tremendous up-surge of stories about clergy themselves being active as abusers. For the three years from 1989 through 1991, 130 such items appeared, or about 40 each year. In 1992 the number of stories rose dramatically to about 240, with 200-plus more during 1993. In the secular media, clergy abuse has probably been the most discussed item of religious news since the upheavals in the Catholic church during the 1960s, and already parallel debates are occurring in the many other nations where the American media play an influential role.

The topic of clergy abuse was also widespread in local media coverage. A few major stories were reported nationally, but others were heavily covered either in the immediate area in which the incident occurred or in the newspapers and television programs of nearby cities. The Cinel case, for example, was often referred to in the *New Orleans Times-Picayune* between 1991 and 1993, and the Porter affair was a recurring theme in the *Boston Globe* long before it was picked up as a national event. Other lesser incidents provided an opportunity for local press and television to explore the familiar themes, all of which served to reinforce the immediacy of the problem.[1]

Between 1991 and 1993 lengthy analyses of clergy abuse appeared in periodicals as diverse as *The Nation,*[2] *National Review,*[3] *Playboy,*[4] *People Weekly,*[5] and *MS,*[6] Detailed case studies were available for all the major cases, including book-length accounts of the Ritter affair and the Newfoundland scandals. The Porter case was described at length in *Rolling Stone,*[7] and *Vanity Fair* analyzed the Dino Cinel story.[8] Other magazines described less celebrated stories, using one particular incident as a vehicle for portraying the scandals of a given city or diocese, as when the *New Yorker* described the problems of the diocese of Worcester.[9] Newsmagazines like *Time* and *Newsweek* regularly referred to the theme,[10] and the intense public interest in the Newfoundland cases led to frequent reporting and analysis in their Canadian counterpart, *MacLean's.*[11] In addition, hundreds of articles have appeared in virtu-ally every religious and denominational periodical during the past decade, includ-ing *Ntional Catholic Reporter* (see below), *Christianity Today, Christian Century,*[12] *America,*[13] *US Catholic,*[14] *Commonweal,*[15] and *Episcopal Life.*[16] In the religious press, more articles appeared on this theme during the single year 1992 than in the previ-ous ten years combined.

The Use of Language

Though the various accounts differed in detail, there were a number of points of agreement, and the media consensus offered a damning view of the Catholic clergy. The sheer volume of reporting suggested that this was a story that demanded public attention and official action. "Crisis" interpretations were reinforced by the hyper-bole that we regularly encounter, especially the memorably brief phrases that attempt to place the issue in a historical context. Andrew Greeley was frequently quoted for the view that the abuse issue represented the greatest crisis facing the Catholic church since the French Revolution, if not the Reformation itself. Thomas Doyle said that pedophilia is "the most serious problem that we in the church have faced in centuries."[17] The problem was a scandal comparable to the worst excesses of secular politics, to disasters such as Watergate.[18] Peter Steinfels wrote that abuse reports "have taken on the dimensions of a biblical plague."[19] Most media analyses cited at least one of these phrases.

The nature of media approaches to the problem can be illustrated from the key words and phrases employed to characterize the issue, terms that repeatedly appeared in the titles of articles and news stories. Any journalist will attempt to use eye-catching phrases that give the prospective reader some indication of the content of a particular story, but the titles are also important in suggesting the message or significance that the audience is intended to derive. In the case of clergy abuse, it is natural to use terminology that a lay audience will immediately recognize as religious or ecclesiastical in nature, but these words inevitably provide an ideological direction to the reporting. The common terms emphasize not merely the wrongdoing of individuals who happen to be priests or ministers, but the institutional context that gives rise to their behavior.

One of the commonest phrases refers to the "sins of the fathers," a Biblical reference that calls to mind the offenses of Catholic priests, who are known as "father." Between 1991 and 1993 the title was used for articles in *Time*, *Newsweek*, *Playboy*, *US Catholic*, *McCall's*, and *The Nation*, as well as countless newspaper items.[20] However, the emphasis on the "fathers" also supports one particular analysis of the problem, which associates abuse with the all-male nature of the priesthood and the patriarchal nature of the institutional church. "Unholy orders" similarly associates the priesthood with wrongdoing or hypocritical behavior, as do "Is Nothing Sacred?", "Breaking the Faith," "Priests Who Prey,"[21] and "Heavenly Silence, Hellish Acts."[22] "Just Following Orders" evokes shades of Nazi Germany and those who undertook vicious or illegal acts in unquestioning obedience of superiors; it was the title of an article by a priest that appeared in the *National Catholic Reporter*.[23]

The title of Jason Berry's *Lead Us Not into Temptation* implies that the abuse is promoted by the "tempting" situation in which the institutional clergy find themselves, a theme emphasized in the book itself. Also much used are terms emphasizing the clandestine nature of the abuse and linking it to the veiled nature of the church in titles such as "The Sacred Secret" and "Clergy Sexual Abuse: Dirty Secrets Come to Light." Although the "secret" might be that held by an individual sex offender, the ecclesiastical context suggests rather that it is the church itself that has prevented the exposure of this behavior. "Unholy Alliances" implies the conspiratorial character of the offenses, again associating the "holy" (clergy or the church) with collective misbehavior and criminality. The harm done by abuse is portrayed in religious phrases that stress the extreme psychic and spiritual damage caused: typical titles include "Soul-Stealing" and "Slayer of the Soul."

Every chapter in *A Gospel of Shame* bears such a religious title, and the book is in the form of a near-religious epic, beginning with the discovery of the Porter case ("While God Wasn't Watching") through subsequent "Revelations."[24] Catholic misdeeds are stigmatized through damning religious terms ("False Idols," "Casting Out

Lepers," and "Cardinal Sins"). Abusive acts are depicted in language that highlights the innocence and suffering of the child victims: "The Crucifixion of Innocence" and, inevitably, "Suffer the Children." "The Silencing of the Lambs" juxtaposes the holy innocence of the victims with the evil, monstrous connotations arising from the popular book and film, which deal with the "ultimate evil" of serial murder. Those who combat such institutional corruption participate in a "crusade."[25] Taken together, the portrait of the Catholic church is of course extremely negative.

In the course of such stories, writers and journalists use analogies to characterize the church structure, and these terms suggest not only the scale and complexity of the church but also its sinister quality. "Mafia" and organized crime analogies are common, as when a journalist describes the code of secrecy said to exist within the clergy: "clerical *omertá* was a given."[26] In a television program broadcast by A&E's *Investigative Reports* in January 1993, Andrew Greeley explicitly compared the church's closed structure to that of the Mafia, with the difference that the Mafia did enforce internal sanctions against deviants: "Even the Outfit . . . has sanctions. The priesthood doesn't." Comparing the church to the Mafia implies size and malevolence, but also (probably unwittingly) evokes alien and conspiratorial qualities of the sort long alleged against Catholicism.

Equally common are metaphors that place opposition to church misdeeds in the tradition of populist activism against overmighty institutions. These ideas have a long and influential heritage in the rhetoric of American politics, but they gained special force following the muckraking exposés of corporate and political misdeeds during the 1970s and 1980s. Attorney Jeffrey Anderson has spoken of his efforts in defending "little guys getting stomped on by the big guys, the behemoths."[27] For Anderson, the church is a "behemoth," and he likens his legal actions against it to attempting to sue General Motors. [28] The corporate crime image recurs when Thomas Doyle becomes "the first whistle blower" by writing the 1985 report.[29] For Greeley, "Pedophilia is the S&L disaster of the Catholic Church."[30] Eugene Kennedy offers an array of similar images and analogies, including "Watergate": bishops and their aides "play roles that in other scripts feature the heads of Union Carbide after thousands died when one of its plants spread a veil of death over Bhopal; the owners of the Exxon Valdez after the Alaskan oil spill; and executives of automobile companies after their vehicles exploded in fireballs."[31] The Catholic church is thus analogous to the Mafia; to the Nixon White House; to a gigantic irresponsible corporation—an "unholy alliance" or "priests who prey," who commit "the sins of the fathers."

The distinctively Catholic nature of the abuse problem is enhanced by the visual imagery employed in television reporting. It is usual to illustrate a theme with related visual footage, and Catholic or "high" ecclesiastical imagery proclaims a religious context much more rapidly than, say, depictions of "low" evangelical services. Church-related footage therefore tends to involve stained glass windows, religious statues, a mass or religious procession, together with plainsong or liturgical music. Though the intent is presumably harmless, the juxtaposition of this imagery with accounts of pedophilia tends to stigmatize traditional "high" Catholic practice, and this visual association supports the stereotypes of lascivious, cynical priests.

The Cartoon Vision

The censorious tone of media reporting of the Catholic church is illustrated by some of the newspaper cartoons that appeared at the height of public outrage. During 1989, for example, a priest in Phoenix, Arizona, named George Bredemann received what was felt to be an unreasonably lenient sentence for child molestation. On a day shortly afterward, two cartoons appeared respectively in the morning and afternoon daily papers in Phoenix. The *Phoenix Gazette* portrayed local bishop Thomas O'Brien using a large crucifix on a chain to assault a figure of Justice, while assuring a monstrous figure labeled "Child Molester," "Don't worry, Father Bredemann, we won't let the lady molest you." In the afternoon, a cartoon of "The Good Samaritan" depicted the same bishop being carried on his episcopal throne, dismissing huddled molestation victims with the words "Oh, stop that whining. We've got to check with our lawyers first." In 1992 the *Arizona Republic* (also Phoenix) portrayed a priest waving at a pair of small children; a thought bubble over his head shows that he is envisioning the two children naked. A sign reads "Suffer the little children." The item attracted controversy and there were numerous letters of protest, but the themes would recur.

The following year a cartoon published originally in the *Hartford Courant* depicted a bishop standing on a carpet, under which can be seen the smirking faces of several men labeled "pedophile priests," while he announces naively, "Perhaps we shall have to change our way of dealing with the problem." Cartoonist Pat Oliphant portrayed an injured child saying, "Somebody call a priest! On second thought, somebody just dial 911," while another character advises, "Leave that priest alone— you don't know *where* he's been." In 1994 Oliphant combined two current abuse panics when he depicted singer Michael Jackson, then facing a much-publicized civil action for sexual misconduct with a teenage boy, alongside a pedophile priest, the point being that both shared the same sexual predilection. Utilizing a priest in this context suggests the degree to which Catholic clergy had been thoroughly and successfully stereotyped as molesters.[32]

Fall from Grace

In fiction, the dark view of the church's role was popularized in Andrew Greeley's best-selling 1993 novel *Fall from Grace,* which describes a situation strikingly similar to the Chicago crisis of 1991–1992, although the author states that it had been substantially completed before these events. The story revolves around a fictional "pedophile priest" named Father Greene, whose seminary nickname had been "Lucifer," and who is indeed portrayed in the most evil terms. ("Lucifer" is also a title applied by Jason Berry to Father Gauthe.)[33] Greene is a sadomasochist and a multiple child molester, specializing in the anal rape of ten- to twelve-year-old boys. The image is enhanced by a conspiratorial element: Greene is "the head of a network of active gay priests in the archdiocese with nationwide links."[34] Even worse, he serves as the renegade priest allegedly required by Satanic cults to perform blasphemous and homicidal rituals such as the "Black Mass," and his rectory is to be the scene of a bloody ceremony that the FBI characterizes as "another Manson case."[35]

In response to such unmitigated evil, the church hierarchy of the Chicago archdiocese responds with a mixture of naive ignorance and cynical self-interest:

> The archdiocese's routine response to such incidents is to cover up, stonewall, intimidate. No police force has ever brought formal charges against a priest within the archdiocese. The media seldom report the charges. With financial deep pockets, the archdiocese is able to overwhelm the parents of the victims (referred to as "enemies" by Ignatius Loyola Keefe, counsel for the Archdiocese), especially by having countersuits for libel filed in the name of the accused priest. The clerical grapevine spreads the rumor that men like "Lucifer" are "cleared" by the police and even that they win suits against the parents of the victims, who are described as drug addicts and alcoholics.[36]

Priests were indeed evaluated and examined by a board of consultants before being returned to ministry, but these experts are "hired guns"[37]—"they share the institutional church's concern to protect priests, to avoid litigation, and to put accused priests back in parishes whenever you can." Meanwhile, civil authorities consistently failed to find proof of charges: "in the territory of the archdiocese of Chicago, Cook and Lake Counties, against a priest, never."[38] In such a setting it is only to be expected that there is a "pedophilia epidemic in the archdiocese."[39]

A Historical Context

The hostile picture of the Catholic church that now emerged was so striking because of the sharp contrast with media depictions of the previous half century. Coverage of clergy abuse reflected an immense shift in media standards toward religious matters, both in news reporting and in fictional presentations. Before the 1970s, the American cinema seldom portrayed a priest in anything other than a heroic or saintly guise, and the best-known images included such near-hagiography as *The Keys of the Kingdom*, *Going My Way*, *Boys Town*, *The Bells of St. Mary's*, and *Angels with Dirty Faces*, all made between 1938 and 1944.[40] A wave of films idolizing priests culminated in 1947 with John Ford's *The Fugitive*, a version of the novel *The Power and the Glory*, in which the mere appearance of the priest hero is usually accompanied by streams of light and angelic music. *I Confess* (1953) featured a priest suspected of murder, but only because of his laudable refusal to breach the secrecy of the confessional.

This obsequious attitude reflected concern about offending such powerful interests, and films with even a tangential religious content had to go to great lengths to avoid commercially disastrous condemnation by church authorities and Catholic groups. By the late 1940s, the Legion of Decency was censoring some 450 films each year, demanding changes in films with a less-than-rosy view of the clergy of any denomination.[41] The National Office for Decent Literature performed a comparable vigilante role for print media. There were also formal legal sanctions. Not until 1952 did the U.S. Supreme Court (in *Burstyn v. Wilson*) strike down a New York State law against showing "sacrilegious" films, the work in question being Rossellini's serious but skeptical study *The Miracle*. This case marked a real turning point in reducing ecclesiastical power over the visual media.

In fiction, it would have been very difficult between about 1930 and 1960 to portray any cleric involved in a situation involving sexual impropriety, and literally impossible for a motion picture to address such a theme in the context of a Catholic priest or nun. (*The Fugitive* even departed from the original book by omitting the alcoholism of the priest.) Nor were church authorities modest about their powers to regulate media treatments of ecclesiastical issues. In 1939 the newspaper of the Philadelphia archdiocese noted that "there were in the course of the year sporadic slurs upon the Catholic church in publications in various parts of the country. In at least one instance the offending publication was a secular college paper. The Government found it necessary to ban certain issues of these publications from the mails."[42]

A change in standards in succeeding decades is suggested by a series of fictional works focusing on such sexual liaisons. The 1977 best-seller *The Thorn Birds* became an immensely popular miniseries, despite (or because of) condemnation by Catholic authorities; controversy was all the greater because the show was first broadcast during the Easter season. Clerical sexuality is the theme of the films *Monsignor* (1982) and *Agnes of God* (1985). The years 1976 and 1977 demonstrated the transition in media attitudes. Apart from *The Thorn Birds*, the dilemmas of homosexual Catholic priests were explored in Iris Murdoch's novel *Henry and Cato* and Patricia Nell Warren's *Fancy Dancer* (both 1976), and clerical sex scandals were depicted in John Gregory Dunne's *True Confessions* (1977). Images of Catholic institutions as corrupt and cynical also appeared in the 1977 film *Nasty Habits*, a Watergate-inspired tale set in a convent.

Another best-selling novel depicting corruption and hypocrisy at the highest levels of the American Catholic church was Andrew Greeley's *The Cardinal Sins* (1981). This was the first of several Greeley books on Catholic misdeeds, and by the end of the decade, some twenty million copies of his novels were in print. Publicity for *The Cardinal Sins* drew attention not only to the scandalous nature of the material but to the changed social environment that it reflected; the blurb to the paperback edition boasted that "thirty years ago, a priest would have been excommunicated for writing such a book. Three hundred years ago, he would have been burned at the stake." Other books used ecclesiastical condemnation as a virtue for advertising purposes. In 1991 a feminist work denouncing "the centuries-old oppression of women by the Catholic church" was prominently identified in the blurb as "the book condemned by New York's Cardinal O'Connor,"[43] and this proved a strong selling point.

There was also a vogue for fictional and "true-crime" stories depicting financial and political conspiracies in the Vatican and the highest circles of the Catholic church.[44] These were inspired by the actual scandals that had occurred in the Vatican bank during the 1970s, which some believed to have contributed to the supposedly sinister death of Pope John Paul I in 1978 and the assassination attempt on his successor in 1981. In 1982, Richard Hammer's *Vatican Connection* portrayed a Mafia-connected fraud conspiracy allegedly directed by a cardinal for the profit of the Vatican coffers; the blurb remarked on the "men in red hats and long robes abusing the power of their religious authority." The incidents involving the Vatican achieved notoriety in the United States through speculative "reconstructions" like David Yallop's *In God's Name* (1984) and in various fictional works. In 1990, Francis Ford Coppola's film *Godfather III* drew on the Vatican scandals, and in the

process made rich use of ecclesiastical settings and Catholic imagery in its portrayals of murder and violence, to an extent scarcely seen since the revenge tragedies of
the seventeenth century. The following year another film satirizing Vatican corruption was controversial chiefly for its tasteless title, *The Pope Must Die*, which under
pressure was altered to *The Pope Must Diet*.

The media were no longer reluctant to embarrass or attack the church, and earlier
sensibilities were criticized in tales of official bureaucracies allying with ecclesiastical officials to cover up scandals. This was the theme of William Caunitz's *One
Police Plaza* [45] and John Gregory Dunne's *True Confessions* (published 1977; filmed
1981), both of which recount incidents in which police collude to conceal the sexually compromising situations in which priests have died. In *True Confessions*, set in
the 1940s, the discovery of a priest who died in a brothel leads to fears that the
media will use headlines like "Manhunt Turns Up Monsignor in Cathouse." [46] Police
move the body to a less embarrassing location, earning the gratitude of the diocesan
authorities, who are well aware of the range of potential scandals and sexual peccadilloes among their clergy. [47] In *One Police Plaza*, the priest dies in the company of a
male transvestite. Clerical criminality and even homicide are the mainstay of a
popular series of detective novels by William X. Kienzle, in books like *Marked
for Murder* (1988) and *Eminence* (1989). Whitley Strieber's 1992 thriller *Unholy
Fire* depicted a priest who becomes a serial killer in response to his own childhood
sexual victimization by another Catholic cleric.

In all the works mentioned, only the Caunitz novel involved a priest in a homosexual liaison, but all explored themes that would once have been viewed as unacceptably offensive to public taste. In the theater, Paul Rudnick's play *Jeffrey*
featured a priest so blatantly homosexual that he described his calling as somewhere
"between a chorus boy and a florist." [48] The extent of the legal and social change
since the 1950s is also suggested by the release of controversial films on the life of
Jesus, including *Monty Python's Life of Brian* (1979) and *The Last Temptation of
Christ* (1988).

The new era was epitomized by two fictional works released in 1995, both of
which would have been regarded as unacceptably daring only a few years earlier.
The film *Priest* frankly explored both homosexual and heterosexual behavior in a
group of Catholic clergy, and this controversial treatment was not only released by a
subsidiary of the Disney studios but was even scheduled to debut on Good Friday,
suggesting a thorough contempt for Catholic sensibilities. Also about this time,
Thomas M. Disch's novel *The Priest* portrayed a cleric as a promiscuous homosexual and child molester, who gives hypocritical public statements on the necessity
to enforce strict sexual morality. Throughout, the book offered a series of highly
negative images of the Catholic church and its clergy of the sort that would once
have appeared only in the most violent anticlerical squibs.

"Conspiracy of Silence"?

Standards of news reporting had also changed fundamentally. At midcentury the
mass media had exercised considerable restraint in investigating or reporting news
stories involving scandals in the mainstream churches. The remarks of a journalist

on one suppressed scandal in Massachusetts in the mid-1970s could be applied to virtually any community with a strong Catholic presence: "If any priest had any sexual problems or was involved in a compromising incident—even if it involved an arrest—the diocese could prevail upon the local papers not to write about it and upon the district attorney's office not to prosecute. To reveal a priest's shortcomings was akin to blasphemy in the eyes of diocesan officials, and they were ever vigilant against such disclosures."[49] As late as 1981 a conservative cleric reminisced that "it was not long ago that the press would file the story of a bishop arrested for drunken driving."[50]

In 1938 George Seldes wrote that the Catholic church was "one of the most important forces in American life, and the only one about which secrecy is generally maintained, no newspaper being brave enough to discuss it, although all fear it and believe that the problem should be dragged into the open and made publicly known." For the media, the consequences of noncompliance could be painful, and Seldes asserted that "to criticize the Catholic church is to invite a boycott, the withdrawal of advertising, loss in circulation and in revenue." In one 1940s case a teenage girl died attempting to escape from a home for delinquents in Washington D.C., and subsequent coverage in one city newspaper painted a hostile picture of the nuns operating the institution, charging what would today be termed physical abuse. Catholic organizations organized an advertising boycott and a campaign among the readership, so that "in two weeks the paper lost forty percent of its circulation."[51] In 1944 even a brief report of a priest found driving drunk with a woman companion attracted costly reprisals against the San Francisco *News*. In response to inquiries, the archdiocesan office responded, probably accurately, that "No one in San Francisco has ever used a story like that"—and the crime referred to was drunk driving, a trivial offense by the standards of the 1940s.[52] At the same time anti-Jewish rioting by Boston Catholics was "concealed behind a thorough news blackout," and was reported in no paper in the city or state.[53] As Paul Blanshard wrote in 1949, "As a result of this policy of siege and boycott, very few publishers in the United States are courageous enough or wealthy enough to deal frankly with Catholic social policy or stories of priestly crime."[54]

By definition, it is difficult to cite specific examples where a newspaper failed to cover a story of sexual abuse by a Catholic cleric, but the Mount Cashel case offers an illustration. The local press in St. John's, Newfoundland, had encountered well-authenticated stories of abuse at the Christian Brothers home at least since the mid-1970s but decided against publication for a variety of reasons, including police objections to interfering with an investigation. A news editor stated that the story was spiked "because he felt it could do more harm than good."[55] Of course, this occurred in the stricter legal environment of Canada, but it may illustrate the attitudes of counterparts in the American media. Media would report only actual criminal charges, and usually not with great prominence. It is possible to find occasional prosecutions reported in local papers throughout the 1970s, but the accounts were virtually never picked up by more nationally oriented publications such as the *New York Times*.

It is inherently unlikely that during the midcentury, stories of priests involved in sexual misconduct would be featured in the mass media or that journalists would actively seek out and investigate such reports because the press collaborated with the church in avoiding public scandal. To some extent, this restraint also survived the precipitous decline in church political power from the 1960s onward. This is suggested by the case of Cardinal Cody of Chicago, who throughout the 1970s had been the subject of rumors concerning his irregular financial dealings, including the transferral of large sums of money to a woman described as his cousin.[56] The prominence of the individual and the nature of the potential scandal would have made this a natural subject for investigative journalism or muckraking, especially in the post-Watergate period. Moreover, the Chicago archdiocese headed by Cody was the largest and richest in the American Catholic church, and its fate was of interest to a large Catholic constituency in the media audience. Despite its newsworthiness, it was not until 1981 that the story surfaced publicly, in Greeley's *The Cardinal Sins* and in the Chicago press.[57]

Changing Media Values

In retrospect, the period between about 1977 and 1981 marked a bold departure for the American press in coverage of Catholic matters. Apart from the Cody scandal, this was also the time that sporadic accounts of child molestation began to appear in newspapers, albeit "unconstructed." In 1980 a syndicated journalistic investigation of fraud and criminality by a group of Pauline Fathers in Pennsylvania won a Pulitzer prize for Gannett News Service, in part because of its groundbreaking willingness to take on clerical malefactors.[58] However, media qualms about this subject did not vanish overnight, and the Bruce Ritter case demonstrates the paralyzing influence of older concerns.

At least since the early 1970s, there had been rumors about sexual contacts between Father Ritter and a number of boys and young men, and by the mid-1980s these were known to several journalists and newspapers, including the *National Catholic Reporter.*[59] However, the charges did not appear in print until the *New York Post* published them in 1989, and even then other New York city papers mounted an active defense of Ritter's character.[60] This was not a typical case, in that Ritter was a powerful and well-connected figure whose charitable activities had earned immense public respect and visibility and his accusers could easily be portrayed as marginal figures, hustlers, and boy prostitutes. The *New York Times* initially "treated the story as a sordid affair beneath its readership."[61] Ritter's survival with such a cloud of witnesses against him shows how difficult it would have been for an isolated account of clergy misbehavior to have been exposed in earlier decades.

This restraint extended to priests far less celebrated than Ritter, and in 1984 Jason Berry's reporting of the Gauthe case in the *Times of Acadiana* led to a costly advertising boycott. Berry remarks how reluctant most mainstream media were to follow up the Gauthe affair, though the remoteness of the rural Louisiana setting may have contributed to the lack of interest.[62] Burkett and Bruni[63] suggest that the media remained very chary about exposing abuse cases until the end of the decade and note instances when newspapers that printed such stories received hate mail that deterred editors and publishers. They argue that the media and civil authorities formed a "unspoken covenant" to protect the interests of the Catholic church.[64] Although this is in line with the two authors' hostile and conspiratorial view of the Catholic church, it is true that a number of major abuse cases received remarkably little coverage in local news media, often after the stories had been picked up further afield. Even while the *Boston Globe* and *New York Times* were reporting the Porter story, the local *Providence Journal* had little to say on the case. Nor did the *Philadelphia Inquirer* report on the long-running suit against a priest in that city and the archdiocese that he served, even while the paper was commenting freely on cases elsewhere in the nation.[65]

On the other hand, presenting media restraint as a simple response to "Catholic power" is misleading because, before the 1970s, similar attitudes prevailed toward the sexual and financial irregularities of all kinds of public figures, including politicians, sports stars, and film personalities. It is for instance inconceivable that the contemporary media would grant a modern president the latitude given to John F. Kennedy over his personal life and medical history. Among institutions, the Catholics received treatment not too different from that accorded both to other denominations and to nonreligious organizations that the media viewed as benevolent and respectable. Throughout the 1970s, the media consistently underplayed recurrent sex scandals affecting the Boy Scouts, failing to mention the scouting affiliations of accused offenders or stating that a convicted offender was a rare "bad apple" rather than the symptom of a widespread problem.[66] Boyle's study of abuse in the scouting movement depicts police and prosecutors struggling to conceal cases from the press, and shows that newspapers were less than active in pursuing connections.[67] This "conspiracy of silence" occurred because editors, publishers, and police chiefs were themselves involved with the movement and were reluctant to see its ideals tarnished. The Big Brothers/Big Sisters benefited similarly.

A definite change in the tone of coverage can be discerned during the 1980s, and this affected the Boy Scouts and the Protestant churches no less than the Roman Catholics. National scandal finally caught up with scouting during 1993, at precisely the time of the Porter case.[68] The discovery of clergy abuse occurred at a time when media values were in rapid transition, in part because of the influence of international media magnates such as Rupert Murdoch and the newspapers and television stations that they had acquired. There was a shift toward sensationalist coverage in many news sources, toward "tabloid" television news shows, prurient talk shows, and "true crime" documentaries that blurred the lines between fact and fiction. Local news shows were affected quite as dramatically as network programming, with a wave of lurid multipart series purporting to investigate and expose some novel social menace.

At both national and local levels, sensationalism ran highest during the three "sweeps" months of February, May, and November, the time when stations scrambled to win the ratings that determined their advertising rates for the coming years. In the Boston area, the May timing of the original Porter revelations guaranteed the most colorful and intrusive investigation of clergy abuse. Throughout the year, media now competed with one another to win sensational stories, a practice that virtually required other papers or television stations to share the new attitudes lest they lose readers. In 1981 the exposure of the Cody scandal was accelerated by journalistic rivalry between the *Chicago Sun-Times* and the Gannett service over which would get into print first.[69]

Once the taboos limiting attacks on the established churches were lifted, the media found that reprisals were not as severe as they might once have been, and that exposés did not in themselves conspicuously offend public taste. In fact, they even appealed to constituencies who actively favored the exposure of abuses. As standards of religious reporting shifted, it became increasingly fashionable to explore the sexual dilemmas of the clergy and to portray the churches as rife with exploitative sexuality. This was as true of fictional works such as TV movies as of purportedly objective news sources and documentaries, and the media became prepared to seek out clerical scandals with an aggressiveness that would have been unimaginable a few years earlier.

Constructing Crisis

In May 1985 Thomas Doyle and his colleagues warned of the rash of abuse cases developing around the country, and commented, "A minimum of six print publications . . . have reporters in place trying to tie the isolated, regional episodes into a national story, presumably one of scandalous proportions."[70] Within weeks the predicted "national story" emerged in the pages of the *National Catholic Reporter*, which would long remain the harshest critic of the Catholic hierarchy in these matters. One issue of *NCR* deserves emphasis for its crucial importance in shaping later commentary, and was indeed the first source to depict a problem that was both systemic and nationwide. Not only did it draw together the various cases into a single account, but it published the actual names and details of the individual scandals. The source was significant because publication in a Catholic paper defused the potential objections that would have arisen if the story had run in a mainstream paper. As an *NCR* correspondent noted, "Had such an article appeared in the secular press, I am sure the shouts of protest would have been raised from all corners of the Catholic church." [71]

In its issue of June 7, 1985, *NCR* devoted the greater part of eight full pages to a report headlined "PRIEST CHILD ABUSE CASES VICTIMIZING FAMILIES; BISHOPS LACK POLICY RESPONSE."[72] Most of the coverage was devoted to Jason Berry's detailed analysis of the Gauthe case, the exposé tone of which is epitomized by the headings "PEDOPHILE PRIEST: STUDY IN INEPT CHURCH RESPONSE"; "MANY KNEW OF FATHER'S PROBLEM, BUT NO-ONE STOPPED HIM"; "LOUISIANA FAMILIES DECEIVED BY JEKYLL AND HYDE PRIEST WHILE CHANCERY SHUFFLED HIM AROUND." Other stories summarized leading cases around the nation: of Donald Roemer in California; of Thomas Laughlin in Portland; of Carmelo Baltazar in Idaho; of Edmund Coakeley in New Jersey; of William O'Connell in Rhode Island; and of others in Wisconsin, Pennsylvania, and California. In each case, the report described a pattern of uncaring and hostile diocesan authorities, of bruising litigation, and of a church that defended its priests while treating parishioners as liars or enemies. The cumulative impression was powerful and unsavory—presumably the effect desired, for the issue had been timed to have an impact on the forthcoming NCCB meeting due later that month.

This one paper contained virtually all the elements that would dominate reporting of the clergy-abuse problem over the next decade. It was presented as a national problem, indeed a "crisis," and it was a mainly *Catholic* problem. This emphasis was inevitable, given that NCR was a Catholic paper addressing issues of interest to its presumed readership and because the journalists concerned had concentrated their investigative efforts upon this aspect of the problem. It was a story of "pedophile priests," a term frequently used therein, and in fact the phrase occured in the titles of the two major reports. Typical remarks included those of a parent who said, "I don't think a pedophile should be able to hide behind a Roman collar." Throughout, pedophilia is presented as being synonymous with a sexual attraction to minors of any age, and this inaccurate usage occurs in even the interviews with psychologists and therapists. The paper's editorial was entitled "Pedophilia problem needs tackling," and the following year, NCR reported on the bishops' reaction to the issue of "clerical pedophilia."

The June 7 issue was controversial, with many readers denouncing it as sensationalistic muckraking, "luridly overdone," "incredibly irresponsible." But it also galvanized others who had observed or experienced such abuse.[73] Victim advocate Barbara Blaine was only one of those who would recall this specific issue as crucial to her decision to confront and publicize her sexual experiences that had begun in 1969: it "sparked a painful yet healing and revolutionary process for me."[74]

NCR had not only defined the abuse problem it had established itself and its journalistic sources as authoritative experts on the question. Indeed, the 1985 NCR stories set in place a generic pattern that was closely followed by virtually all later reports, and that became so predictable that it was noteworthy when one element was missing. Names and places might vary, but overwhelmingly the stories told of repeated rumors of molestation, increasingly troubled parents, and diocesan authorities who ignored warning signs. A disclosure would reveal that this priest or other local colleagues had been known for years to be potential molesters, and the history of "reshuffling" would be made public. Commentary would be provided by a predictable cast of victim advocates and experts on the Catholic church, who would cite a range of similar or comparable incidents. Pundits would usually agree on the depth and severity of the structural crisis facing the church, declaring that the problem was the most serious encountered by that body in centuries.

Most reporting in the mainstream press over the next few years closely followed this model. In subsequent months, the NCR interpretation was essentially that favored in reports on the Gauthe cases in prestigious papers such as the *New York Times*,[75] and the *Washington Post*, as well as *Time*,[76] and on television newsmagazine programs such as *West 57th Street*.[77] At first, media reports of "clergy abuse" drew freely on examples from many denominations and religious groups besides the Catholics and also cited cases in which clerics were sexually involved with adults, but gradually the Catholic and "pedophile" focus pioneered by NCR came to dominate.

This view was reinforced by investigative articles syndicated in Knight-Ridder newspapers during 1987 that described a series of scandals in various parts of the country and also gave national publicity to the 1985 report by Doyle and his colleagues. The stories demonstrated a pattern of misdeeds by Catholic authorities in covering up abuse cases: "In 25 dioceses across the country, church officials have failed to notify authorities, have transferred priests accused of molesting to other parishes, have ignored parental complaints and have disregarded the potential damage to child victims."[78] Clergy abuse was a "time bomb waiting to detonate."[79] In 1988 Eugene Kennedy correctly observed the media trend: to "interpret it as a cover-up story."[80] Most leading newspapers were in agreement that the individual cases coming to light were the tip of a very large iceberg, and the problem was described in major analytical reports.[81] The *Boston Globe* headlined, "Clergy Sexual Abuse: Dirty Secret Comes to Light";[82] the *Los Angeles Times* suggested "Sex Abuse Cases Rock the Clergy."[83]

Experts

The shifting emphasis of reporting toward the "pedophile-priest" model reflected the views of the experts and authorities regularly consulted by journalists. Initially, at the time of the Gauthe case, there was a striking lack of available authorities; no individual or pressure group had yet emerged to make claims about the scale or nature of the issue. Of course, there were therapists with considerable expertise in this area, but they were associated with church-related facilities like the House of the Paraclete or Saint Luke's Institute, and the media regarded such institutions as tainted by their failure to intervene with sufficient force to prevent the return of abusive priests to parish settings. However, this lack of usable authorities was soon filled by a core of people who would come to be respected as knowledgeable commentators from whom the media would seek interpretation of cases. This small group of writers and professionals presented the various incidents as part of one common problem that could be approached and understood.

Two individuals in particular, Jason Berry and Andrew Greeley, could predictably be counted on to appear in most television or newspaper reporting of clergy abuse, and their opinions thus gained great weight. The use of the two requires little explanation. Berry had covered the Gauthe case extensively for the local paper in Louisiana as well as for *NCR*, and by the mid-1980s had become well acquainted with virtually every similar case in progress across the nation, undertaking the research that led to his influential 1992 book *Lead Us Not into Temptation*. In 1986 he received from Thomas Fox of *NCR* the report by Doyle and others that would become one of the most quoted documents in the whole controversy.[84] As Sipe remarks, he was simply the best informed layman on the specific cases and charges.[85]

Greeley, in contrast, claimed no special expertise in the abuse problem but was deeply concerned about the problems and conflicts of the Catholic church both worldwide and specifically in Chicago. In his 1986 autobiography he recited a disturbing litany of recent scandals "in an era when a fifth of the priests in the country leave to get married, when cardinals die in whorehouses, when bishops are arrested for solicitation, when priests are convicted of pederasty, when the Vatican Bank wastes billions, when 80 percent of the laity reject the Church's teaching on birth control and premarital sex, when there are financial scandals all over the American church. . . ."[86] He warned that "It is not unlikely . . . that sexuality, indeed perverse sexuality, will be to the Bernardin archdiocese of Chicago what financial corruption was to the Cody archdiocese."[87] As a best-selling novelist and an overt critic of church policies, he was a natural favorite of the media in search of commentary about Catholic issues long before the molestation cases emerged, and it was predictable that he would retain this role as the crisis progressed.

In their different ways Berry and Greeley were knowledgeable observers, but both were likely to emphasize particular interpretations of the issue. Both were Catholics from strongly Catholic backgrounds, and for both men, the abuse cases with which they were familiar inevitably tended to be incidents involving Catholic priests and religious. From an early stage in the recognition of a problem, both also saw the role of church authorities as disreputable, improper, and devious, and as epitomizing tendencies that also led to difficulties in other aspects of church life. Berry and Greeley differed considerably on specific issues—for example, the extent to which celibacy contributed to the pedophile problem—but both saw many problems in the current structure of the American church and sought reforms broadly along the lines of the liberal Catholic agenda (see chapter 6). Both men were therefore likely to contextualize the abuse cases in such a way as to point out the need for certain institutional changes. The broad sympathy between the two is also suggested by the laudatory introduction that Greeley provided for *Lead Us Not into Temptation*.

Other authorities quoted regularly in such reporting all tended to accept the same basic interpretation of the problem and the reformist agenda. This was the view espoused by the priest Thomas Doyle, and by liberal Catholics such as Eugene Kennedy, who had written on the crisis for *NCR*.[88] Liberal Catholic voices were commonly heard in the *New York Times*, which presented thorough and well-informed coverage of clergy abuse throughout these years. The paper's chief religion correspondent is Peter Steinfels, who formerly edited the Jesuit *America* (Margaret O'Brien Steinfels edits *Commonweal*). Steinfels's articles helped project the local controversies of areas like Chicago as part of a national crisis, while stressing yet again the Catholic dimensions of the problem.

Other experts similarly spoke from positions likely to be hostile to the church hierarchy: pastor Marie Fortune applied a feminist perspective to clergy-abuse issues; attorney Jeffrey Anderson had undertaken much of the civil litigation against the Catholic church over abuse cases. Finally, individuals victimized by clergy were believed to possess a natural authority on the basis of their direct experience, and by the end of the decade it was obligatory for a report on clergy abuse to include a statement from a leader of the victims' support organizations, most frequently Jeanne Miller or Barbara Blaine.[89] Collectively, these were the authorities whose analyses shaped the interpretation of the intensified wave of concern following 1989, who defined and gained "ownership" of the emerging abuse problem.

The relative homogeneity of the "expert community" is apparent from any of the detailed analyses of the problem. In 1991, for example, *Vanity Fair*'s report on Dino Cinel included official comment from the president of the Saint Luke Institute and Mark Chopko, general counsel to the U.S. Catholic Conference, but by far the most-used sources were Jason Berry, Richard Sipe, and Jeffrey Anderson.[90] In a typical story in the *New York Times* some months later, the sources included Anderson, Berry, Chopko, and victim Cristine Clark.[91]

Television

The same group of experts were repeatedly cited and interviewed in television coverage, producing a solid consensus of interpretation. Television reporting began sporadically in middecade with reports on individual cases in magazine programs such as CBS's *West 57th* and ABC's *20/20*, and from 1989 onward, the subject became a staple of talk shows including *Geraldo, Sally Jessy Raphael,* and *Donahue.* In 1989 the Oprah Winfrey show included interviews with Jeanne Miller and Shane Earle, one of the Newfoundland victims whose story was the basis of the film *The Boys of St. Vincent's.*[92] In 1990 Geraldo Rivera featured several leading activists, including Jason Berry, Jeffrey Anderson, David Figueroa, and one of the victims in the Ritter case.[93] In 1992 Jeanne Miller was again the centerpiece of an Oprah Winfrey special. Other victims who appeared frequently on these programs included Dennis Gaboury (who had been molested by Father Porter) and Cristine Clark.[94] Canice Connors remarked, "When we are encircled by talk shows that dwell so frequently on sexual abuse by priests, we begin to wonder if there is anything else that Geraldo or Oprah think about."[95]

During the peak of media concern in 1992 and 1993, the clergy-abuse problem was the subject of many reports on news programs, some of which followed the exposé format pioneered by CBS's *60 Minutes.* These stories described the investigation of a problem or scandal, usually through the heroic efforts of one or more principled individuals. Highly placed perpetrators are interviewed by one of the journalistic team, who are presented as the guardians of the public interest. In July 1992 ABC's *Primetime Live* used this inquisitorial mode of presentation to bring to public attention the case of Father James Porter. In two reports, the heroic role was occupied by Frank Fitzpatrick, the former abuse victim who pursued Porter to his Minnesota home.[96]

The program used the *60 Minutes* technique of having the reporter literally pursue the accused individual in the streets, placing him in the position of apparently hiding from the public eye and implying forcefully that he has much to hide. In this case the priest's crimes were portrayed in the starkest terms: metaphorically at least, "Porter committed murder." The emotional impact of the report was accentuated by images of weeping victims and their parents, and blame was firmly located on the ecclesiastical authorities. Fitzpatrick's "It was like the whole church turned its back on me" found echo in the program's "The church was shutting every door in his face." Porter's frequent reshuffling to fresh parishes was "exactly the pattern of the Catholic church over the years," and the avoidance of scandal was the main goal of a church "that seemed to show little pity for the children." In contextualizing the case, the program asserted that 6 percent of priests were abusers or pedophiles, and implied that Porter was a typical representative of this vast group: "That's three thousand priests."

60 Minutes itself used the "pursuit" device with no less powerful a cleric than Archbishop Roberto Sanchez, in the context of the scandal linking him to several young women.[97] This report in itself was a remarkable departure from earlier broadcast standards: the bishop was interrupted while leading a pilgrimage, an interference with a religious ceremony that would have been inconceivable even a decade previously. In other cases journalistic standards had so thoroughly rejected traditional restraints as to move perilously close to provocation or entrapment. In 1993 the St Louis CBS affiliate KMOV paid the expenses of a male prostitute who arranged a sexual assignation with a priest, placing a hidden camera in the hotel room.[98] This case actually brought the station under criminal investigation.

The Catholic aspects of the abuse problem were analyzed in two major documentary programs broadcast during 1993. In both an *Investigative Reports* special broadcast on the Arts and Entertainment Network[99] and a *CNN Presents* special,[100] the preponderance of speakers were from groups inimical to the clergy and the hierarchy. All suggested that the prevalence of abusive behavior was extremely high, and that the church had for years systematically engaged in cover-ups. Repeated use of the Porter or Gauthe cases as examples implied that such extreme instances were typical of clerical behavior and official responses.

The CNN program "Fall from Grace" used as its point of departure the charges against Cardinal Bernardin, "a prince of the church, a man eligible to become Pope," but also presented an unflattering account of the broader crisis. Although it would obviously be inconceivable to offer "a balanced view" of the issue by having someone defend pederasty, the program effectively presented no speaker who argued that the church had ever responded correctly or honestly to the problem, and even the quite extensive local reforms introduced by some dioceses were described as "a sham." The authorities quoted most extensively included Jason Berry, Jeanne Miller, and of course Andrew Greeley, from whose novel the program derived its title. The main official spokesman for the church was Cardinal Bernardin, who responded to confrontational questions. Individual segments offered a series of harrowing vignettes, such as the Chicago family who found themselves countersued when they attempted to take legal action against a priest. Footage of a VOCAL meeting permitted the airing of other grievances. The program repeatedly suggested that the problem resulted from the church hierarchy's secretive attitudes, and that even the pedophile priests were themselves victims of the excesses of their institutional superiors. The concluding line declared, "It is not just the priests who are falling from grace, it is also the church."

The *Investigative Reports* program "Sins of the Fathers" also dealt with "the sexual abuse of children by Catholic priests," and only one brief clip discussed misconduct by other clergy. The range of experts included the familiar faces of Jeanne Miller, Andrew Greeley, Jason Berry, Richard Sipe, and Eugene Kennedy, and again the Porter, Gauthe, and Cinel cases played central roles. Much of the program involved harrowing case studies told from the point of view of individual survivors and their families, all bitterly critical of the church's structural flaws. Several speeches were presented from the 1992 VOCAL conference, with frequent use of reaction shots showing weeping participants. Dennis Gaboury indicted the whole church as accomplices in his victimization, and declared that "the Church is the real sodomist."[101] In the *Investigative Reports* program Gaboury suggested that the lack of sanctions against priestly misconduct meant that the bishops "might as well be standing behind him and cheering him on" while the priest abused a child. The toleration of extensive clerical homosexuality was one symptom of church hypocrisy, and Berry estimated that up to a half of Catholic priests might be homosexual in orientation. Seminaries were depicted as the home of a flourishing homoerotic subculture. In a memorable

phrase, an FBI expert on child molesters stated, "One of the most dangerous individuals on the face of this earth is a psychopath for God."

Both programs editorialized heavily, usually through the mechanism of presenting remarks in the context of reporting objectively what "victims say" or "critics
say," though there is no doubt that this is the message viewers were intended to accept. CNN typically remarked, "The church's greatest sin, *some say,* is in how it has
dealt with the crisis" (my emphasis). More comprehensively, *Investigative Reports*
followed a series of heinous charges with the comment "Victims say the deeper
issue is an abuse of power, that Church leaders have consistently covered up for the
perpetrators, stonewalled the victims, and in many cases quietly shuffled the abusers
from one diocese to another, leaving parishioners in the dark. Critics also say the
church has been hiding behind its lawyers, and neglecting its moral duty to offer
care and sympathy."

These media portrayals all appeared on nationally syndicated programs, but the
same messages were reinforced by local reports of the sort that commonly followed
a "priest scandal" on the lines of the Porter cases in Massachusetts and Minnesota,
or the Gauthe affair in Louisiana. One example of such local reporting appeared in
Pennsylvania after the conclusion of a locally notorious lawsuit in which a man successfully sued the diocese of Altoona-Johnstown for the consequences of abuse
committed by his parish priest, Francis E. Luddy. The plaintiff alleged that he had
been regularly abused between the ages of ten and sixteen, and that this abuse had
contributed to the erratic behavior that finally led him to commit a series of criminal
offenses. As in many other cases, it was charged that Luddy had also molested a
number of other boys (at least thirteen), and that his diocesan superiors had failed to
intervene, though they had been aware of this misconduct for many years. Moreover, papers revealed during the action showed that several other priests had faced
allegations of abuse in the diocese in the previous two decades.[102]

The series entitled "Sins of the Father" appeared on the local CBS affiliate during
1994,[103] and was heralded by newspaper advertising depicted a praying child with
the caption "Crisis of faith: Do we have a prayer?" The story featured the customary
arguments about the church's secretive and unresponsive character and concentrated
on the supposed contents of its "secret archives," access to which had been a contentious issue throughout. Because diocesan representatives refused to appear, commentary was divided between spokesmen active in the cause of the plaintiff, such as
his lawyer and psychiatrist, and experts who included a former priest and Andrew
Greeley. The final segment essentially challenged the church for its decision to fight
the case and its use of the aggressive defense tactics employed elsewhere. Use of
film from other programs including *60 Minutes* served to contextualize the local dispute as part of a national crisis over clergy abuse.

Even when not explicitly reporting on sexual abuse, other clergy-oriented news reporting of those years reinforced related ideas of clerical hypocrisy and duplicity,
child neglect, and institutional cover-ups. The ABC network took the lead in this matter, as it had earlier done over the issue of ritual child abuse. In March 1993 ABC's
20/20 suggested that the Catholic church was suffering a widespread crisis in its
enforcement of clerical celibacy, and that many priests simply ignored church regulations.[104] In 1994 the same network's magazine program *Primetime Live* aired a

hostile account of abuses in the church's implementation of its policy on marriage annulment, suggesting that a cynical and secretive church bureaucracy harshly treated women and children. Another widely covered story in 1993 concerned the American woman who had clandestinely married an Irish bishop, and borne him a son. Once again, the story implied themes of clerical hypocrisy and covert sexuality.[105]

In May 1993 *Primetime Live* recounted the experiences of children who had been placed in clergy-run orphanages in the province of Quebec during the midcentury. The program alleged that children had been systematically neglected and falsely diagnosed as mentally retarded, and that some orphans had died in mysterious circumstances.[106] As with the sexual abuse cases, crucial testimony was provided by "survivors" of their orphanage experiences, who subsequently returned to confront the clergy and nuns who had mistreated them. Knowingly or otherwise, the report was reviving some of the oldest and most notorious anticlerical canards about violence and covert exploitation within Catholic institutions.

Recreating the Cases

The victims' perspective was also central to the fictional portrayals of clergy abuse in these years. In 1990 the Gauthe case was fictionalized in a made-for-cable movie, *Judgment,* which addressed the church's refusal to give priority to the needs and interests of the child victims.[107] The story was told from the point of view of the Gastals, the parents of a molested altar boy, and their lawyer "Claude Fortier," based upon the real-life J. Minos Simon. Viewers were shown a heroic family and their lawyer engaged in a populist struggle against a monolithic, secretive Catholic hierarchy, which had the power to influence the decisions of secular authorities. As in real-life cases, the diocese knows all too well that some of its clergy are persistent abusers, and yet they are endlessly moved between parishes. The images are not entirely black and white, in that the bishop himself has good motives, but in practice these are overcome by the demands of the lawyers and insurers, who virtually threaten the financial existence of the diocese unless their exact guidelines are followed. All too easily, the church bows to the whims of the world.

Judgment established the "heroic" themes that would dominate media coverage during the following years, above all the centrality of the victims of abuse and their families, and their struggle to achieve justice against a faceless and powerful institution determined to preserve its own image at any cost. In the Canadian *Boys of St. Vincent,* similarly, the effort to expose church misdeeds is complicated by the Catholic hierarchy's close alliance with police and government to protect the orphanage, "one of the most hallowed institutions of this city." In one memorable scene, the local establishment is viewed en masse as the cardinal and a provincial cabinet minister socialize with the police chief under the smiling view of the sadistic pedophile Brother Lavin. In a classically Dickensian juxtaposition, the sumptuous fare at this gathering is contrasted with the lot of the orphans they exploit. Though the children have isolated advocates in the police and social services, the church's local power network thwarts all efforts at achieving justice. Complaints to social services "go upstairs and that's the last we ever hear of them. . . . Have you ever tried to go over the Catholic church in Newfoundland?" In sum, "the high holy church and a bunch of criminal politicians don't give a damn." The film's title is a sardonic reflection of the idealized portrait of the honest and saintly priesthood canonized by the *Bells of St. Mary's*.

Both films took shrewd account of the likely composition of their audiences, emphasizing throughout a female perspective the all-male priestly environment. *Judgment* portrayed the victims' mothers as the guardians of right and conscience against the heartless bureaucracy, and this element may account for the film's long afterlife in frequent reruns on the women-oriented Lifetime cable network. Much of *Boys of St. Vincent's* was recounted from the viewpoint of the two women who were respectively married to the chief pedophile character Lavin (after he had left his religious order) and his victim. At the eventual public inquiry, official malfeasance is revealed through the pointed questions of a woman counsel.

Ironically, it is the fictional portrayal of an *innocent* priest that provides the best epitome of contemporary media attitudes. In a 1994 episode of the television series *NYPD Blue,* a priest is found murdered and partly clothed in a park frequented by male prostitutes.[108] One teenage boy complains that the priest "wouldn't keep his hands off me," and the natural interpretation is that this is yet another example of "a teenager warding off the advances of a sexually predatory priest." However, the charges prove false, and the priest's behavior was in fact above reproach. In the 1990s the surprise ending is provided by the discovery that a priest is *not* homosexually promiscuous.

Defending the Church?

Catholic authorities themselves contributed by default to promoting the bleak image of the clergy. After so many years of favorable media coverage, the Catholic church found itself poorly prepared for the onslaught of denunciation over abuse, and could mount little effective opposition even in the face of the more egregiously hostile news pieces that invoked so many anticlerical stereotypes. As clergy-abuse allegations mounted during 1992 and 1993, Catholic leaders had little success in preparing any effective answer. Insofar as they made statements about the problem, the statements were largely of a negative character, asserting weakly that the issue was not perhaps as bad as it appeared. We can scarcely describe a "debate" over clergy abuse because the public consensus generally accepted certain assumptions about the failings of the Catholic clergy and hierarchy, and the church attempted to show itself willing to seek solutions.

Some dioceses simply refused to respond to journalistic questions, asserting accurately (as in the Luddy affair) that a particular case was in litigation. In practice, this was a disastrous course because it allowed a news program to present a host of allegations, followed by "Church authorities declined our request for an interview." The television station thus fulfilled its legal requirement to provide balance, and church authorities unwittingly cooperated with critics by making it appear that they had no cogent answer to charges. Not until late 1993 did the bishops begin to mend this situation by making the articulate and photogenic Bishop John Kinney their de facto spokesman on abuse charges.

But even when it was decided to contest charges publicly, it was far from obvious what arguments would be most successful. Each of the several possible lines of defense presented serious difficulties in practice, and some would cause more harm than good. For example, it was occasionally argued that the bulk of the offenses involved older boys and teenagers, who might be expected to have a greater degree of responsibility, and who could even be said to have provoked the offense or led the priest on. Such a tolerant approach toward sexual failings contrasted starkly with the absolute standards of moral behavior announced and demanded in public statements. This suggested a dual standard for clergy and laity, all the more so when homosexual behavior was at issue. In addition, the suggestion that a minor provoked sexual contact with an adult was virtually impossible in view of the uncompromising social attitudes toward child abuse that prevailed during the 1980s, amounting to a policy of "zero tolerance." Even to speak of extenuating circumstances was to portray the church as bound to unreconstructed notions of sexual patriarchy, and the neglect of children's interests.

Initially, church leaders argued that media reporting reflected anti-Catholic bias, "Catholic-bashing." This was an effective rhetorical strategy in that it mobilized a common Catholic perception that the church was under attack from the secular world.[109] Fortuitously, the 1989 charges against Bruce Ritter coincided with a controversial demonstration by homosexual activists in Saint Patrick's cathedral, lending at least temporary substance to declarations that molestation charges were part of a broad anti-Catholic conspiracy.[110] When scandals did occur, it was natural to draw on the deep-rooted ideological conviction that disaster and disgrace could be a form of redemptive suffering that would ultimately lead to the vindication of justice.

When several priests were accused of molestation in the Illinois diocese of Belleville, one parishioner noted that the accusation "does seem to fit the season. The priests are being crucified and this is Lent."[111] The Newfoundland cases were similarly described as a "real crucifixion" as the local church passed through its "purgatory."[112] When Archbishop Sanchez was implicated in a sex scandal, a sermon emphasized, "We are living in this moment the Good Friday of the church in New Mexico with the confidence that the resurrection is at hand."[113] The suggestion that the church was being subjected to unjust persecution was apparent in the response of Boston's Bernard Cardinal Law to early reports of the Porter case, when he declared that the stories were exaggerated and "by all means we call down God's power on the media, particularly the *Globe*."[114]

On the other hand, suggestions of anti-Catholic bias were weakened by the visibility of Catholic activists (and clergy) in the assault, and debates within the church had seriously reduced the likelihood of an automatically loyalist response. In only one instance did a cleric accused of sexual irregularities successfully retain the loyalty of the local community by asserting that charges arose from prejudice, and this was when African-American priest George Stallings accused his Catholic superiors of persecuting him on the grounds of his race.[115] Meanwhile, there was no serious question of the guilt of the priests accused in most of the notorious cases. Most charges were substantiated in civil or criminal courts and were accompanied by

Table 4.1. Media Coverage of the Clergy Abuse Scandals, 1991–1993

1991

February	*Christian Century* [1]
August	*Time* [2]
December	*Vanity Fair* [3]

1992

April	*Ms.* [4]
May	*America* [5]
July	*People Weekly* [6]
	ABC's *Primetime Live* broadcasts two segments on case of Father Porter.
Fall	*Human Rights* [7]
November	*Nation* [8]; *Commonweal* [9]; *Redbook* [10]
December	*US Catholic* [11]; *Playboy* [12]
	Legal dispute in Canada over transmission of film *The Boys of St. Vincent's*

1993

January	Arts and Entertainment Network broadcasts special *Investigative Reports* on clergy abuse scandals
March	*America* [13]; *Commonweal* [14]
	60 Minutes segment on Sanchez case
	ABC's *20/20* broadcasts segment on neglect of celibacy rules by Catholic priests
April	*National Review* [15]; *Christian Century* [16]
May	*Primetime Live* segment on maltreatment of orphans in Quebec institutions during the 1950s
June	*New Yorker* [17]
July	*Playboy* [18]; *Newsweek* [19]; *Church and State*
August	*Newsweek* [20]
September	*US Catholic* [21]; *America* [22]; *McCall's* [23]
October-November	*Episcopal Life* [24]
November	*Rolling Stone* [25]; *America* [26]
	Major CNN *Reports* documentary on clergy abuse
December	*Commonweal* [27]

1994

January	*Primetime Live* shows critical segment on Catholic church and marriage annulments
April	*Commonweal* [28]
May	*Time* [29]; *Christian Century* [30]
	60 Minutes segment on aggressive legal countermeasures by Catholic diocese
June	Trial of Massachusetts priest Paul Manning covered on *Court Television* cable channel
October	*Dateline* NBC segment on Paul Manning case suggests police misconduct in eliciting abuse allegations [31]

---

[1] Pamela Cooper-White, "Soul-Stealing: Power Relations in Pastoral Sexual Abuse," *Christian Century*, February 20, 1991, pp. 196–99.

[2] Richard N. Ostling, "Sins of the Fathers," *Time*, August 19, 1991, pp. 51.

[3] Leslie Bennetts, "Unholy Alliances," *Vanity Fair*, December 1991, pp. 224–78.

[4] Angela Bonavoglia, "The Sacred Secret," *Ms.*, March–April 1992, pp. 40–46.

[5] Canice Connors, "Priests and Pedophilia: A Silence that Needs Breaking?" America, May 9, 1992, pp. 400–401.

[6] "Up Front," *People Weekly*, July 27, 1992, pp. 5+

[7] Vicki Quade, "Unholy Wars," *Human Rights*, fall 1992, pp. 18–21.

[8] Thomas M. Disch, "The Sins of the Fathers," *The Nation*, November 2, 1992, pp. 514–16.

[9] "Priests and Sex," *Commonweal*, November 20, 1992, pp. 3–4.

[10] Christine Clark, "Broken Vows," *Redbook*, November 1992, pp. 51–56.

[11] Robert E. Burns, "Should All Priests Pay for the Sins of the Fathers?" *US Catholic*, December 1992 pp. 2.

Table 4.1. (continued)

[12] James R. Petersen, "When The Church Sins,"Playboy, December 1992, pp. 54–55.

[13] Andrew Greeley, "How Serious is the Problem of Sexual Abuse by Clergy?" *America*, March 20/27, 1993, 6–10

[14] Peter Steinfels, "Needed: A Firm Purpose of Amendment," *Commonweal*, March 12, 1993, pp. 16–18

[15] William F. Buckley, "The Church's Newest Cross," *National Review*, April 26, 1993, pp. 63.

[16] Donald E. Clark, "Sexual Abuse in the Church: The Law Steps In," *Christian Century*, April 14, 1993, pp. 396–98.

[17] Wilkes, "Unholy Acts," *New Yorker*, June 7, 1993, pp. 62–79.

[18] Charles M. Sennott, "Sins of the Fathers," *Playboy*, July 1993, pp. 74–76.

[19] Kenneth L. Woodward, "The Sins of the Fathers," *Newsweek*, July 12, 1993, p. 57.

[20] Aric Press et al, "Priests and Abuse"; *Newsweek*, August 16, 1993, pp. 42–44; Kenneth L. Woodward, "Sex and the Church," *Newsweek*, August 16, 1993, pp. 38–41.

[21] Jim Castelli, "Abuse of Faith"; *US Catholic*, September 1993, pp. 6–15; Canice Connors and Tim Unsworth, "Abuse of Faith: How to Understand the Crime of Priestly Pedophilia," *US Catholic*, September 1993, pp. 6–15.

[22] John R. Quinn, "It Is The Best of Times . . . To Be a Priest," *America*, September 18, 1993, pp. 16–17.

[23] David Hechler, "Sins of the Father," *McCall's*, September 1993, pp. 113–19.

[24] Julie A. Wortman, "Pain May Overwhelm Exploited Victims," *Episcopal Life*, October 1991, p. 4; Julie A. Wortman, "Full Disclosure of Abuse Helps Parishes Heal," *Episcopal Life*, November 1991, p. 8.

[25] Dennis Gaboury and Elinor Burkett, "The Secret of St Mary's," *Rolling Stone*, November 11, 1993, pp. 48–54.

[26] Jason Berry, "Listening to the Survivors: Voices of the People of God," *America*, November 13, 1993, pp. 4–9.

[27] Sidney Callahan, "Memory Can Play Tricks," *Commonweal*, December 17 1993 pp. 6–7.

[28] John J Dreese, "The Other Victims of Priest Pedophilia," *Commonweal*, April 22, 1994, pp. 11–14

[29] Howard Chua-Eoan, "After the Fall," *Time* May 9, 1994, pp. 56–58;

[30] James M Wall, "There Ought to be a Law," *Christian Century*, May 4, 1994, pp. 459–60.

[31] Michael Grunwald, "Boy Says He Falsely Accused Priest," *Boston Globe*, October 19, 1994, p. 1.

frank admissions from the culprits themselves, so it was impossible either to defend their conduct or to assert their innocence. Doubts about Father Ritter's guilt soon faded, and Cardinal Law's comment was widely quoted as a perfect example of the "denial" and self-delusion exhibited by the church in dealing with flagrant offenders. Burkett and Bruni denounced the defenses offered by the Catholic hierarchy with terms such as "hysteria," "vicious," "chilling," "venom."[116]

Once it was acknowledged that at least some of the cases were genuine, the best that could be done was to assert that the conduct of a Father Porter was wildly untypical of the behavior of the vast majority of clergy, and that extending blame to other priests in general reflected anti-Catholic stereotypes and controversies. *US Catholic* stressed that the cases affected only a tiny minority of priests, "But let one of these be found guilty of child molesting and bells ring and lights flash in newsrooms across the country."[117] This approach was employed by some Catholic papers, which denounced the sensationalistic concentration on clerical misdeeds and compared the reporting to what might be expected in a tabloid such as the *National Enquirer*. *Commonweal* remarked that "prurient interest . . . exposing the sexual hypocrisy or worse of Catholic priests is an old story and an old controversy,"[118] and similar arguments were used in conservative publications such as *First Things* and

Chronicles.[119] However, these views had little impact in the mainstream media, where they were presented, if at all, as an ineffectual attempt to evade responsibility for past crimes and misdeeds.

The highly critical stories of the early 1990s indicate the extent and rapidity of the change in media attitudes toward the Catholic church as a consequence of the clergy-abuse cases. This shift in reporting was important because it increased the likelihood that individual abuse cases would become widely known, which in turn raised public awareness of the prevalence of the offense and fostered future reporting. There are many anecdotal accounts of how individuals who had been victimized were induced to report the activity after reading a news report or hearing a discussion on a television talk show. Increased reporting helped generate the investigation and prosecution of new cases, which further contributed to the cyclical effect. In addition, the growing emphasis on the Catholic aspects of the issue after 1989 specifically encouraged the exposure of cases in this denomination rather than others, and ensured that the problem was viewed as one of "pedophile priests."

5

Pedophilia and Child Abuse

In recent studies of social problems, the media have come under attack for the dissemination of false or misleading information; an element of "media hype" is widely acknowledged. This is especially true in the presentation of exaggerated statistics.[1] In the issue of missing and abducted children, for example, press reporting of the early and mid-1980s offered wildly inflated figures that promoted a sense of national crisis.[2] Media treatment of clergy abuse certainly has been subject to criticism, but there have been strikingly few complaints about the general accuracy of the problem as it has been depicted. Except in some early coverage, we do not find assertions that charges are false in particular cases, or denials that abuse is widespread, and the church's record of misconduct and neglect is broadly accepted.

In reality, there are three major areas where the construction of the problem was flawed, and where it would have been possible to mount quite a plausible defense of the church's behavior. Respectively, these involve the definition of the offenses charged, the numbers of perpetrators, and the historical context in which most of the gravest allegations were set. All these issues were approached quite selectively in order to render the behavior of the church and its clergy in the most sinister colors. This process of selection is important in illustrating the agendas and policy goals of the groups seeking to define and describe the abuse problem because all benefited to a greater or lesser extent from producing the darkest possible construction of the problem.

Defining the Problem

With so many abuse cases surfacing in the news, it was natural to speculate on exactly how many clergy were involved in the abuse of children, and from the mid-1980s onward media reports usually stated that about 5 or 6 percent of Catholic priests were molesters. This would imply a total of between twenty-five hundred and three thousand at any given time, a figure described by Jeffrey Anderson as "a phenomenally dangerous number."[3] In the cnn film "Fall from Grace," we are told that between two thousand and four thousand Catholic priests are "child sex abusers." The figure derived ultimately from the work of Richard Sipe[4] and Thomas Doyle, and it received national publicity during news programs such as a 1988 segment on abc's *20/20*.[5] Thereafter, the number was rehearsed during virtually every news report and talk show segment on the topic, both because it was memorable and because it implied a vast social menace. If indeed Gilbert Gauthe or James Porter was taken as the typical abusive priest, then several thousand clergy might be engaged in acts of multiple rape and sodomy, and possibly child pornography. However, much remains uncertain about the real scale of the problem, notably about the question of definition. What exactly are we counting?

The problem is usually described as one of "molestation" or "pedophilia." For Thomas Doyle, the "single most serious problem" faced by the church in centuries was "the sexual molesting of little boys by priests."[6] Andrew Greeley published an op-ed piece in the *New York Times* on the "priestly silence on pedophilia," in which he returned time and again to the evocative word: "the head in the sand reaction of most priests to the pedophile problem," "priestly reactions to a pedophile charge," and so on.[7] Canada, meanwhile, "has been rocked by its epidemic of priest pedophilia."[8]

The terms suggest involvement with children ranging in age from toddlers to pubescent youngsters, and *pedophile* implies coercion, exploitation, and even violence, so that to show any tolerance or sympathy for the condition is socially unacceptable. At the very least, the words imply a breach of trust by a crucial authority figure ("father"), and in many cases the acts involved were committed against children in institutional care, who had no alternative but to submit to the sexual desires of an adult. Using *pedophile* adds rhetorical momentum to the critique of the institutional failings of neglect and secrecy that permitted this situation to arise. A placard carried by a member of snap at a bishops' conference during 1992 declared "Child rape is a cardinal sin." Apart from indicating that the sexual activity is both forcible and directed at small children, the phrase implicates high church authorities (cardinals) in tolerating and defending perpetrators.

The Porter case indeed involved some of the worst instances of molestation and child rape, and similar acts were involved in other notorious cases. However, by no means all the scandals involved "molestation," and many did not include victims we can accurately characterize as "children." When considered in detail, the cases often suggest sexual liaisons between priests and boys or young men in their late teens or early twenties. This behavior may be reprehensible in terms of violating ecclesiastical and moral codes of sexual conduct, and breaching vows of celibacy, and the power relationship between priest and young parishioner renders it difficult to speak of the behavior as fully consensual. However, it is not properly *pedophilia*, which according to the standard psychiatric manual *DSM-III-R*, specifically refers to "sexual activity with a prepubescent child."[9] When a thirty-year-old priest has a sexual relationship with a sixteen-year-old male, the act may be described in many ways, but "pedophilia" is as inaccurate as "child abuse" or "molestation."

Contemporary English lacks a common word for the behaviors included in the great majority of "clergy-abuse" cases, in which the "abused" is often fifteen or sixteen years old. The best and most comprehensive term is probably *pederasty*, the erotic love of a youth (Greek, *pais*), which is etymologically very close to *pedophilia* but covers relationships with any young person, usually male, up to the age of full adult maturity.[10] The difficulty is that in general usage, *pederast* has fallen into disfavor as a derogatory epithet applied inaccurately to homosexuals; as late as the 1970s, the *Oxford English Dictionary* gave *pederast* and *sodomist* as synonyms. Moreover, *pederasty* fails to include sexual activities with young girls. These difficulties explain the recent preference for the medically precise *pedophile*, but the result is that sexual activities with teenage boys have fallen into a linguistic limbo. To describe this activity as homosexuality fails to take account of the age difference between partners, and thus the inability of one partner to provide legal consent. We are therefore left with the obscure word *ephebophilia*: the sexual preference for boys, *epi hebe*, upon puberty. Not surprisingly, few writers seeking a popular audience use such a word, which until recently was not even defined in major dictionaries. They therefore fall back on the better-known but inaccurate *pedophilia*, with all its connotations.

The difference between ephebophilia and pedophilia may seem purely semantic, but it has many implications in terms of the potential for treatment and therapy. In the prevailing psychiatric opinion of the 1970s and early 1980s, it would have been quite appropriate to return to a parish setting a man who had been successfully treated for ephebophilia but not for pedophilia, and it was precisely this issue of the employment of past offenders that led to such scandal following the Gauthe case (see below). It was dangerous for church authorities to permit a known pedophile such as James Porter to be in unsupervised contact with children, but such a decision would have been defensible with an ephebophile or homosexual.

The distinction is crucial, if rarely made or understood. In the words of Nova Scotia bishop Colin Campbell, following the Mount Cashel scandal, "We are not dealing with classic pedophilia. I do not want to argue that homosexual activity between a priest and an adolescent is therefore moral. Rather it does not have the horrific character of pedophilia."[11] The case that ruined Bruce Ritter involved a man of twenty-five who generally passed for nineteen. Other incidents were said to affect somewhat younger boys, but even if all the allegations against him were true, he would not count as a pedophile. Suggesting that the church concealed or tolerated pedophiles is much more destructive than the charge that it granted a certain degree of tolerance to priests involved in consensual relationships with older boys or young men. In Catholic church law, the age of heterosexual consent is sixteen rather than the eighteen common to most American jurisdictions.

Catholic authorities were surprisingly oblivious to the rhetorical significance of the terms used. It was both inaccurate and politically unwise for the U.S. Catholic Conference to have issued a statement on clerical "pedophilia," which was portrayed as synonymous with sexual abuse or misconduct with minors.[12] As the church struggled to deal with the problem in the early 1990s, diocesan policies on "child abuse" usually made no distinction between other underage sexual activity and pedophilia, and customarily defined "child abuse" as misconduct with anyone under the age of eighteen.[13] In the Los Angeles archdiocese, "any sexual misconduct on the part of a priest involving a minor constitutes sexual abuse."[14]

The problem of definition is complicated by the nature or degree of sexual contact, whatever the age of the young person involved. The Porter case involved the most extreme types of misconduct, including oral and anal intercourse, but again it is difficult to generalize. Many of the cases involved far slighter degrees of contact or interference, such as fondling or kissing. The acts may have been immoral and disturbing, but they stood at the opposite end of the spectrum from the behavior of one of the well-known predatory pedophiles. Although acts of forcible rape have been known, violence does not occur in the overwhelming number of instances.

These distinctions make it difficult to know exactly what is meant by the assertion that "five or six percent" of Catholic clergy are involved in abuse. Crucially, Sipe's much misquoted estimate was that 2 percent of priests were pedophiles and 4 percent ephebophiles, but he was referring to sexual *tendencies* and not actual behavior: "six percent of America's 52,000 priests are at some point in their adult lives sexually preoccupied with minors."[15] Although that in itself says nothing about misconduct, other sources expand the "five or six percent" to cover all priests physically involved with anyone under eighteen, or even twenty-one. Jason Berry writes that the figure refers only to pedophiles, and takes no account of ephebophiles. In addition, the "clergy-abuse" literature sometimes subsumes into this category acts of consensual intercourse between clergy members and adults, either men or women. With the definition of the problem so vague, it is not surprising that the estimates of the frequency of clergy abuse vary so widely.

How Many Priests?

With these difficulties in mind, it is possible to suggest a general range for the frequency of priestly misconduct, whereby the problem appears considerably less serious than it is sometimes said to be. Generally, commentators suggest that a given number of priests are implicated in abuse, and extrapolate from this to estimate the proportion of the current number of Catholic priests (about fifty thousand) who are "pedophiles." However, many of those accused, like Porter, had long ceased to be priests at the time that the accusations surfaced, and a more accurate gauge of misbehavior would take into account the total number of men who had served in the priesthood since, say, 1960. Although this would not affect the total number of cases proved or alleged, it would indicate that abusive priests represented a smaller proportion of the whole than sometimes appears.

Jason Berry writes that between 1982 and 1992, "approximately four hundred priests were reported to church or civil authorities for molesting youths."[16] However, many of these were accused for incidents dating back to the 1960s and 1970s, and this number should be placed alongside the total number of individuals who served as priests in those years, well over a hundred thousand men in the United States alone. Presumably, Berry is being precise in referring to "priests" as opposed to religious, but other sources quote it differently, and the cnn program "Fall from Grace" stated that five hundred "priests and Catholic brothers" had been implicated by late 1993. If religious were included, the total population of current and former clergy would approach 150,000 in the United States alone. Furthermore, Berry's statistic seems to refer to North America as a whole rather than just the United States. The Canadian Catholic church is about one-fifth the size of its U.S. counterpart, and if Canadian offenders are indeed included, the total for present and former clergy should be increased by about 20 percent, to perhaps 180,000.

Berry accurately states that this was the number "reported," and there were cases where priests were accused on flimsy or malicious grounds. But even if we assume that all those reported to authorities were in fact guilty of the acts charged, this suggests an offense rate of less than 0.2 percent. Of course, the number formally reported omits a substantial "dark figure" of unrecognized abusers, but Berry's figure is suggestive, and it is confirmed by other data. Between 1983 and 1987, two hundred priests or religious were reported to the Apostolic Nunciature for abuse-related charges.[17] By 1993 Saint Luke's Institute had treated two hundred priests for abuse-related problems, and a similar number had been treated by the New Mexico house of the Servants of the Paraclete.[18] The figure is in the hundreds, nowhere near "five or six percent."

In assessing numbers, one of the most valuable sources is the Chicago study carried out by a commission appointed by Cardinal Bernardin. The personnel files of all men who had been priests in the archdiocese between 1951 and 1991, or 2,252 individuals, were examined. Between 1963 and 1991, 57 of these priests and 2 visiting clerics had been the subject of allegations of sexual abuse.[19] The commission reviewed all charges, not by the standard of criminal cases, which insists on proof beyond a reasonable doubt, but on the less stringent civil criterion of the preponderance of evidence. Further, evidence was used that would not have been acceptable in a court of law, including hearsay testimony. Where there was doubt about a case, the commission decided to err on the side of the accuser rather than the priest involved. By these quite generous standards, the charges in 18 cases were judged not to involve sexual misconduct: 4 cases were based on "groundless" testimony; in 14 others "there was inappropriate and immature behavior which did not rise to the level of child sexual abuse or molestation," behavior such as "tickling and questionable language."[20] Removing these 18 cases left valid charges against 39 priests in the archdiocese, and the 2 externs.

This study offers a likely range for the incidence of sexual misconduct sufficiently serious or obvious to lead to complaints: 2.6 percent of archdiocesan clergy were the subject of complaints, and charges were thought to be justified for 1.7 percent of priests. Because the cardinal's commission was under intense public pressure to examine the records thoroughly and frankly, we can probably be confident about the validity of its figures. Extrapolation to the national situation is much riskier, but there is no immediately apparent reason that clergy in this diocese should have been significantly more or less prone to misconduct, or that parishioners should have reported abuse at a rate much higher or lower than the national average.

The Chicago findings offer the first and, to date, the only systematic review of so large a cohort of clergy over so long a period to become publicly available. (Comparable studies were also undertaken elsewhere, notably by the Boston archdiocese.) The figures gain importance from their use by Andrew Greeley to demonstrate the scale of the "pedophile danger." In 1992 Greeley reacted to charges that the abuse

danger had been exaggerated by declaring that the Chicago statistics proved that
nationwide "an estimate of one out of ten priests as sexual abusers might be too high
and an estimate of one out of twenty might be too low." The statement, however, is
based on what appears to be miscalculation: he asserts that the thirty-nine proven
abusers represented about 5 percent of the men who had served as priests in Chicago
during that period, a proportion that is much larger than the actuality. Abuse was
confirmed in the cases of about one-sixtieth (about 1.7 percent) of the corps of Chicago priests rather than the suggested 5 to 10 percent, evidence of how even a writer
of such competence and integrity can fall into error.[21]

Greeley's mistake is compounded by his estimate that an abuser might have between two hundred and three hundred victims. Using what he calls "a conservative
estimate," he suggests that nationwide twenty-five hundred priests might have molested fifty children each, to give a "not unreasonable estimate of the victim
population" well in excess of one hundred thousand victims over a twenty-five-year
period: "each one a human being who has suffered a terrible personal tragedy at the
hands of a slayer of the soul." Victim-advocate groups have suggested that Greeley's
figures are an underestimate, but in reality the misapprehension appears to lie in the
opposite direction. For example, the number of victims assigned per hypothetical
abuser is far too high. There are indeed professional works that propose figures in
the hundreds, but all are based on interviews with incarcerated offenders who represent the extreme upper range of deviant behavior, the most severe and predatory
pedophiles. *National Catholic Reporter* has gone further: "the average pedophile
priest abuses 285 victims."[22] In reality, Greeley's figures exaggerate the number of
both abusers and victims; the same data have been used by other observers to estimate a total of 15,000 victims over forty years—a difference in magnitude of more
than 1,000 percent.[23] However, his estimate continues to be cited as authentic in
media outlets as widely read as *Time* and the *New York Times*.[24]

Very few abusers are pedophiles. One of the most experienced persons in the treatment of disturbed clergy is Father Canice Connors, the director of the Saint Luke's
Institute, and he suggests that true pedophiles are quite rare. Connors contends that
about 3 percent of American Catholic clergy might have tendencies toward the abuse
of minors, but that pedophiles make up only 10 percent of this group, or 0.3 percent
of the whole body of the clergy.[25] If this is correct, then it is quite justifiable to argue
that "*it is rare to find a true pedophile in the priesthood or religious life*," however
much this contradicts the recent popular literature.[26] Of the fifty-seven accused priests
examined in the Chicago survey, forty-nine cases involved teenagers: thirty-nine
boys and ten girls, and the commonest complaint involved boys of fifteen or sixteen.
"*The overwhelming number of cases, in other words, involved homosexual ephebophilia, in other words priests sexually attracted to young teenaged boys. . . . There
was only one founded case of pedophilia, involving a priest-uncle with two six-year-
old nieces.*"[27] Without this one sad individual, the "pedophile crisis" in Chicago
would have conspicuously lacked pedophiles.

The Chicago data indicate that less than 2 percent of all serving American priests
are or have been involved with minors, about a thousand "pederasts" in all nationwide, with the great majority of this group being homosexual ephebophiles. True
pedophiles would be counted at most in the hundreds, and "predators" like Gauthe

or Porter constitute a small handful of priests accused of abuse, a few dozen at any given time in the whole of North America. To assert this is in no way to play down the damage that can be done by such individuals or to deflect the culpability of any superior who might have tolerated their activities, but it does provide an essential context for appreciating the dimensions of the "abuse problem." The number of "pedophile priests" has been magnified by a factor of twenty or more.

Child Abuse: A Historical Context

Questions of number and definition illustrate how popular constructions of the clergy-abuse issue made it appear larger and more pernicious than the evidence would justify. Also significant here is the historical context of the scandals, many of which occurred before or during what must be seen as a radical transformation in social attitudes during the early 1980s—the surge of concern about child sexual abuse. A number of the clergy-abuse incidents that came to light after 1989 involved activities that had occurred long before, a quarter of a century in the case of James Porter's career in Massachusetts and the scandals at Mount Cashel, and the events and the later reactions were separated by a gulf far more significant than a period of years. Church authorities in the 1990s thus found themselves judged in retrospect for actions carried out in an utterly different social context, and it is important to reconstruct the attitudes that prevailed before these near-revolutionary changes.

Under various names, incest, pederasty and child molestation have been recognized behaviors in most societies, though different communities vary greatly in how they view the gravity of such actions, as well as the age at which a person is presumed to be responsible for his or her sexual actions. It is far from obvious that a given sexual act between individuals of widely differing ages constitutes immoral or criminal behavior, still less that it causes grave harm to either participant. This is also an area where the traditional double standard remains powerfully apparent, in that Western culture attaches little stigma to a relationship between an underaged boy and an adult woman. Even when the activity involves "true" molestation, by an adult male, the intensity of social concern tends to be cyclical rather than constant. Contemporary theories about the nature and prevalence of sexual exploitation have been established only since the late 1970s, and they marked a dramatic reversal of the notions prevailing between about 1955 and 1975. In turn, these views were very different from the ideas of the previous quarter century. The history of public attitudes toward sex offenses can with some oversimplification be summarized as shifting from near-panic in the 1930s to complacency in the 1960s, and back to panic in the 1980s. Many of the clergy abuse *incidents* occurred in the age of complacency, but the resulting *scandals* occurred in the later era.

The Age of Complacency

During the 1930s and 1940s sex offenders were viewed as a major public danger, and even the most trivial sexual deviations were contextualized together with the most serious assaultive offenses, including serial rape and homicide. The issue of predatory sex offenders was accentuated by a series of widely publicized cases, and there was intense "anxiety about sexual crimes, particularly those having violent overtones or involving children."[28] Most American states passed draconian and ill-defined "sex-psychopath" laws to stem the alleged tide of sexual violence.[29] As in more recent years, child molestation was usually discussed in the context of rape, and concern about the two offenses rose and fell together.

During the 1960s an intense public campaign against sex-crime laws drew on the rhetoric of civil liberty and procedural justice, and this was seen as part of the more general due-process revolution initiated by the U.S. Supreme Court. Between 1966 and 1973 a series of cases in federal and state courts asserted the need for due-process safeguards to be implemented in the investigation and detention of sex offenders, even if these processes were notionally civil in character. Opposition to sexual-psychopath laws was one part of the movement against the civil commitment and forcible treatment of mental patients, and the leading cases included evidence of what would later be classified as child sexual abuse. In the 1968 case *Millard v. Harris*, U.S. Judge David Bazelon stated that the confinement of a compulsive exhibitionist was scarcely justified on the grounds of "harm" because the behavior affected only "unusually sensitive adult women and small children."[30] Courts regularly decided against the constitutionality of sexual-psychopath laws, asserting that the danger posed by sex offenders was too slight to justify the incursions on legality and individual rights.

Both court decisions and academic works suggested that the sexual-offender laws reflected the prudery of an earlier generation, which had similarly stigmatized consensual activities such as homosexuality, fornication, and the enjoyment of pornography. Although the various behaviors were not all on a moral par, none merited the invocation of legal sanction in an increasingly tolerant society. Overturning penal laws against nonviolent molesters, exhibitionists, and other "sex deviants" should therefore be seen in the context of the concurrent liberalization of "puritan" morality laws in these other areas, especially concerning homosexuality. All were part of the recognition of what Kittrie has termed "the right to be different."[31]

In the scholarly and professional literature between about 1955 and 1975, the real "problem" about sex offenses was not the activity itself but the public hysteria surrounding it and the ill-considered legislation to which it contributed. Liberal therapists and academics led a reaction against what they perceived as hysteria, and aimed to quiet public concern by debunking excessive claims about rape, incest, and sexual violence. Criminological pioneer Edwin Sutherland published in 1950 a study that showed the extreme rarity of forcible rape and sexual violence. In 1955 another prestigious criminologist, Paul Tappan, denounced what he regarded as "some myths about the sex offender."[32] These false ideas included the beliefs "that tens of thousands of homicidal sex fiends stalk the land. . . . That the victims of sex attack are 'ruined for life.' . . . That sex offenders are usually recidivists. . . . That sex psychopathy or sex deviation is a clinical entity."

Similar views are reflected in all the most-used textbooks and manuals of the period. A typical criminological text noted in 1959:

> The most serious [of sex crimes] are associated with rape, particularly forcible rape, or with assaults on young girls or elderly women. But contrary to public opinion, there are

few outright cases of this type. Most of the rape cases deal with statutory rape. . . . So far as forcible rape is concerned, it has been much overrated. In many cases the female has offered little resistance, and in others she has "framed" the male. In other cases the female has reported the man only after he has jilted or abandoned her.[33]

Concern about sex-crime laws was enhanced by charges of structural racism. From 1930 to 1967 blacks made up 90 percent of those legally executed for the offense of rape, these in addition to numerous instances of lynching. The belief that blame was attributed on slight evidence was reinforced by memories of the Scottsboro Boys scandal of the 1930s.

Incest or child molestation was regarded as so rare as not to require mention in most general works on crime and deviance, and when it was discussed (however briefly) it was in the context of a sympathetic response to acute family dysfunction. There was a general acceptance of the "collusion" of daughters in sexual relationships with fathers.[34] Statistical evidence for the offense was controversial. In 1948 the Kinsey Report suggested a high prevalence of adult-child sexual contact, affecting some 25 percent of girls, but this document was gravely flawed methodologically. The definitive study of incest published during the 1950s estimated that the behavior affected perhaps one American child in a million, and this was the orthodox view for the next two decades.[35]

Formulating Child Abuse

Between about 1950 and 1977, mainstream professional opinion did not regard child sexual molestation as a serious danger or indeed as a significant social problem. Modern concepts of child abuse grew out of the recognition from about 1962 of "baby battering" and other forms of violence inflicted on children in their homes, usually by members of their families. Though the idea was controversial, it came to be accepted in professional circles that the battering and physical abuse of children were common phenomena, affecting families of all social strata, and that this sort of behavior could pose a lethal danger to the young. By the mid-1970s, these perceptions had been disseminated in the mass media, and political and bureaucratic responses took the form of increased funding for research and prevention. In 1974 Congress passed the Child Abuse Prevention and Treatment Act, which mandated the reporting and investigation of abuse allegations, and similar measures were soon passed by all states with little opposition.

Discussions about child *physical* abuse repeatedly emphasized the same themes: an enormous problem that could threaten any child in any type of home; "tip-of-the-iceberg" statistics; a refusal to acknowledge that such appalling acts could occur; and a general lack of groups or agencies with the will or power to intervene. From the mid-1970s onward, these same ideas were increasingly applied to the phenomenon of sexual acts committed against children, to what became known as "child sexual abuse," and increasingly appropriated the generic term of *child abuse*.

Concern over child sexual abuse was in part an outgrowth of feminist campaigns against rape, which asserted that the overwhelming majority of sexual assaults remained unreported and unpunished.[36] Susan Brownmiller's classic 1975 study of rape, *Against Our Will,* included a pioneering section on the frequency of incest, "father rape," as part of "the absolute dictatorship of father rule."[37] Developing research and feminist activism focused attention on younger victims, and theorists such as Diana Russell extended their interests from the rape of adult women to the abuse of minors.[38] The new sensibility reflected shifting emphases within the therapeutic professions and brought into being an institutional foundation for the study of child maltreatment: in specialized clinics and in some university departments dealing with social work and social problems. Though we cannot exactly speak of a freestanding child-abuse profession, something approaching this developed out of existing traditions in social work, therapy, and counseling. There now emerged a network of academic and professional experts in the field of child abuse, with accompanying societies, conferences, and journals.

The child-protection issue was further publicized by politicians of various ideological shades who saw enormous potential in the emotive theme. Concern over sexual abuse became a leading issue in the media and in political debate between 1978 and 1984, and it led to a profound reassessment of social priorities. Between 1976 and 1986, the number of reports of child abuse and neglect in the United States rose from 669,000 to more than 2,000,000, with a further increase to 2,700,000 by 1991.[39] Increased sensitivity to child abuse tremendously enhanced the likelihood that incidents would be reported.[40] Predictably, commentators suggested that the increase reflected a genuine rise in the behavior itself, an "epidemic" of child abuse. The head of the Children's Defense Fund wrote in 1994, "About three million [children] a year are reported to be neglected, or physically or sexually abused—*triple the number in 1980.*"[41]

A letter to the *New York Times* in 1993 described the radical change in attitudes toward child abuse:

> A decade or so ago, the state of the art on incest was limited to the work of a half-dozen professionals . . . . who bravely researched and treated and pondered the forbidden ancient taboo. Enlightened treatment for victims was limited to a few women therapists. The courts, presided over by male judges, coddled perpetrators. The police, disbelieving and demeaning, further damaged victims.[42]

This exaggerates the suddenness of the change, and there were far more than half a dozen professionals by 1980, but developments were rapid. The first signs of reviving concern appeared in 1977, with congressional hearings on the "sexual exploitation of children" through abuse, prostitution, and pornography. This interest was reflected in the wave of books that appeared over the next two years.[43] Within a few years studies were available from influential and much-quoted scholars such as Ann W. Burgess,[44] David Finkelhor,[45] Judith Herman,[46] Roland Summit,[47] and C. Henry Kempe.[48] It was about 1980 that a causal link was asserted to exist between childhood sexual abuse and multiple-personality disorder in later life, a linkage that emphasized still more sharply the devastating effects of childhood trauma;[49] 1980 also brought the first published account of ritual child abuse.[50]

These were also the years of scandals and news stories that appeared to confirm a general danger to children: the child murders case in Atlanta; the murder of Adam

Walsh; the abduction of Etan Patz; a panic over missing and abducted children; and a new upsurge of urban legends and rumor panics concerning kidnapping and Halloween sadism.[51] Congress held hearings on child pornography; on pedophilia; on missing, murdered, and exploited children; and on changing the courtroom environment in abuse cases.[52] These occasions gave a platform to a proliferating body of child-welfare advocates, politicians like Paula Hawkins and Paul Simon, activists like John Walsh and Kenneth Wooden.[53] State legislatures responded with a flood of measures to protect missing or abused children, to register sex offenders, and to investigate day-care centers: across the nation, 265 such bills were begun in the first three months of 1985, more than double the total for the whole of 1984.[54]

New views of the abuse danger are suggested by the emphasis on child pornography, proven or rumored, in accounts of molestation cases. That molesters were photographing or filming their victims suggested the deliberate, repeated, and premeditated quality of their actions, which might be undertaken as part of a network, a "pedophile ring." Obtaining commercial gain from such a venture showed that molesters were dehumanizing abused children, treating them as commodities to be bought and sold. From the late 1970s onward, child pornography was depicted as such an unqualified social threat that its mere possession was harshly penalized, a stigma hitherto reserved for the most dangerous addictive drugs.

Scale and Effects

The child-welfare advocates of this era asserted that sexual exploitation was at least as widespread a problem as physical abuse. Between 1982 and 1984, Diana E. H. Russell published her influential research, suggesting that nearly 40 percent of girls had been sexually abused before the age of eighteen.[55] Therapist E. Sue Blume argues that "it is not unlikely that *more than half of all women* are survivors of childhood sexual trauma."[56] Media accounts eventually settled on a consensus figure that abuse affected between 20 and 30 percent of children.

Initially, the family was now seen as the usual setting for this abuse, with the father and other male relatives or authority figures as the commonest offenders.[57] Feminist writing extended the term *incest* to other sexual acts involving such adults with a relationship of authority or trust with the child involved: "a parish priest, a next-door neighbor, a police officer, pediatrician, an FBI agent or a Scout leader."[58] In this broad context, "even to call incest an epidemic is to understate the case."[59] Therapists treated the victims from "the front lines of the unbridled epidemic of sexual assault."[60] The quantitative claims now proposed gained credibility from the precedents of earlier campaigns against physical abuse. Once it would have been angrily denied that tens of thousands of children were targets of violence within their homes, but now that fact was broadly accepted. According to believers in the sex-abuse danger, similar issues of "denial" might initially impede acceptance of the supposed hazards from this direction, but here too the problem would be confirmed.

Opinions about the potential harm wrought by sexual abuse changed quite as dramatically as estimates of the frequency of the offense. Medical opinion had thitherto been divided over the degree of real or lasting trauma, and there was real skepticism about the effects of a sole incident of fondling or exhibitionism.[61] Paul Tappan had rejected the view "that the victims of sex attack are 'ruined for life' " as one of the pernicious myths diverting social policy. He argued, in contrast, that little lasting harm *need* be caused by the experience of "rape, carnal abuse, defloration, incest, homosexuality or indecent exposure":

> In some instances the individual does carry psychic scars after such an experience. Characteristically the damage is done far more, however, by the well intentioned associates of the victim or by public authorities than by the aggressor. This is not to condone the offense, but merely to emphasize that its implicit danger has been grossly exaggerated, and that the possible traumatizing of the individual is almost always a product of cultural and individual responses to the experience rather than because of the intrinsic value of that experience itself. . . . [T]he young individual in our own society who has not been exposed to an excess of parental and community hysteria about sex can absorb the experience of a socially disapproved sexual assault without untoward consequences.[62]

This tradition dominated the professional literature for many years, and even a text coauthored by C. Henry Kempe argued in 1978 that "a single molestation by a stranger, particularly of a nonviolent kind, appears to do little harm to normal children living with secure and reassuring parents."[63] Another authoritative text stated: "Early sexual contacts do not appear to have harmful effects on many children *unless the family, legal authorities or society reacts negatively.*"[64]

By the late 1980s such comment would appear callous because the new orthodoxy was asserting the devastating and lifelong consequences of even brief or isolated sexual impropriety committed against minors. Inevitably, such an intellectual environment severely narrowed the acceptable range of discussion on issues of children's sexuality and their right to grant even limited consent. It was argued that the common pattern of molestation went far beyond mere exposure or fondling, and might well involve anal or genital rape, but even the lesser types of contact were ruinous. The change of attitude is suggested by the frequent application of the term "*survivor*" to victims of rape, incest, or sexual abuse, with the implication that they had passed through an ordeal comparable to that of a natural disaster or homicidal attack, and that the experience would in a sense define much of the rest of their lives.[65] Rhetorically, the term disarms potential criticism of the victim and demands public sympathy, while indicating that one individual is a "survivor" implies that others have not been so fortunate as to escape with their lives. The word was used in association with "incest," even where the perpetrator was not a blood relative, reinforcing the breach of faith and trust that an "incest survivor" would need to repair.

The belief in the lasting damage caused by abuse contributed to raising public and political awareness of the issue and to the sense of urgency in finding remedies. Therapists argued that repeated child abusers were likely themselves to have been abused as children, and abused women were likely to become the wives of abusers, and to connive in their crimes against a new generation of children. If not sexual exploiters, abuse victims were believed to be at high risk to become juvenile delinquents or adult violent criminals.

Reframing the Sex Offender

New concepts of child abuse transformed attitudes toward offenders, and hence the nature of interventions required to reduce the problem. Once again, there was a reversal of the attitudes prevailing in the two decades prior to 1975. In those years there was contention between those who advocated purely therapeutic solutions, and the libertarians concerned with the excessive use of enforced therapy under the sexual-psychopath laws, but neither side showed any sympathy for penal solutions to a relatively trivial and nonthreatening symptom of sexual inadequacy.[66] Nor were sex offenders necessarily the persistent monsters of popular mythology. Paul Tappan had argued that "sex offenders have one of the lowest rates as repeaters of all types of crime," and only homicide offenders were less likely to repeat their crimes. As late as the mid-1970s, the standard psychiatric textbooks either scarcely mentioned pedophiles or trivialized the condition, emphasizing that the behavior was "a one-time activity."[67]

This view was precisely contrary to modern assumptions, which treat an incident of abuse as symptomatic of a dangerous compulsive disorder unlikely to respond to limited or short-term measures. If not exactly irredeemable, child abusers are strongly resistant to either cure or deterrence. In the aftermath of one recent clergy scandal, the president of the National Coalition Against Sexual Assault remarked, "I don't know of one treatment plan other than death where they can promise that recidivism will not occur."[68] A lawyer representing some of Father Porter's victims asserted simply that "pedophilia is not a curable condition."[69] Molesters are extremely active and persistent in their deviant careers, having sexual contact with very large numbers of children over many years. "To report one abuser is perhaps to save scores of future victims."[70]

An analogy may be drawn to drunkenness, which had traditionally been viewed as a deterrable moral failing but which in the twentieth century had been recognized as a likely manifestation of the disease of alcoholism. Similarly, sexual acts with children were seen less as isolated occurrences that could be deterred or discouraged and more as symptoms of a serious personality disorder or compulsive psychological condition identified by a clinical term like *pedophilia* or *ephebophilia*.[71] The alcoholism analogy would be drawn frequently, for example, in the complaint by one of Father Porter's victims: "You don't put an alcoholic back behind the bar. You don't put a pedophile back in a parish."[72] Andrew Greeley argues that "alcoholics are dangerous only to themselves, their families, and the people they smash with their cars, but each pedophile is a threat to the future lives of hundreds of children."[73]

The belief that child sexual abuse is widespread, persistent, and very harmful has obvious policy consequences. If the offense was a disease rather than a moral lapse, then therapeutic responses might be appropriate, but such programs for offenders were deeply unpopular in the 1980s. Because repeated incarceration seemed to have little deterrent effect on persistent pedophiles, and even prolonged programs of treatment or therapy were of only limited value, many jurisdictions increasingly turned to harsh penal solutions involving lengthy periods of incapacitatory detention: a revival of the sexual-psychopath laws, in substance if not in name. Criminal justice

and social service agencies were urged to be much more proactive in dealing with
this type of offense and to regard the protection of children as an absolute priority
that overrules the supposed sanctity of the family unit. These ideas would be implemented in law and official policies over the next few years, with wide-ranging
implications both for the legal system and for professional bodies that came into
contact with children.

Framing Clergy Sex Offenders

The discovery of clergy abuse as a national problem during 1985 therefore occurred
during the peak of concern about child molestation, when the most extravagant
claims were being made about offenders and the consequences of their actions. Since
the mid-1970s the image of the sex offender had changed from that of a pathetic
social and sexual inadequate to the much more threatening portrait of a violent
predator potentially associated with abduction, child pornography, and even serial
homicide. During 1984 and 1985 extreme allegations about the pedophile menace
were given immense publicity by the McMartin preschool case in California, in
which a number of teachers were accused of abusing hundreds of infants in ritualistic
settings, apparently for the purpose of manufacturing child pornography. (Almost
certainly, the charges were entirely spurious.) The affair was sweepingly reported in
its own right, and it also gave the media a centerpiece or "tag" for the swelling torrent
of news stories and features that intensified popular awareness of new formulations
of the sexual-abuse problem.[74]

The McMartin case contributed to shaping perceptions of clergy abuse by
showing that severe molestation could occur in any setting where children were separated from their parents. Not surprisingly, families became highly sensitized to any
hint of institutional abuse, with the result that a host of preschools and kindergartens
experienced investigations and scandals over the next few years. Many of these occurred in churches and religious institutions, and even if clergy were not directly
accused, there was likely to be a legacy of suspicion against any adults connected
with the enterprise. The scandals enhanced the probability of abuse suspicions
against any adult who worked closely with small children, and encouraged investi-
gators to seek evidence of accomplices in organized molestation. The McMartin
case confirmed the worst possible fears about the scale and harmfulness of sexual
abuse and pedophilia, providing a rich mythology on which claims-makers could
draw to demonstrate the severity of the threat to children.

When *NCR* reported on the problem of "priest pedophiles," the concept inevitably
acquired many of these threatening connotations. The paper claimed that pedophiles
formed enormous conspiratorial networks with their own newsletters and toll-free
numbers; they engaged freely in "murder, kidnapping and child molestation"; and
every year hundreds of unidentified bodies of their child victims come to light.
"Each year, 1.5 million children are reported missing . . . many are kidnapped by
strangers."[75] Declaring that the clergy problem was one of "pedophilia" instantly
elevated the question from the area of morality into the realm of criminal violence
and demanded an appropriate response. It also *ipso facto* condemned all existing
church practices and policies in dealing with sex offenders.

Treating Clergy Abusers

In retrospect, the behavior of the Catholic church in dealing with James Porter and other errant priests of that generation seems at best remarkably naive. In the film *Judgment*, the pedophile priest is ordered to take refuge in the House of Affirmation, and is promised that "it works miracles on the spirit." This accurately reflects the attitudes prevailing prior to the mid-1980s. There is an anecdotal account of a young priest detected molesting children: "at the time, no one quite knew what to do about it. The young priest, however, subsequently announced that he himself had taken care of the situation. He had gone to confession and the problem was over."[76] This casual response is sometimes summarized by the phrase "Pray and it will go away." A harsher view suggests that official failure to recognize the danger of such behavior was cynical to a degree that is at present incomprehensible. If, however, we place the response of the church in the context of the prevailing expert attitudes of the 1960s and early 1970s, they become more understandable.

There was then very little scholarship available on what would later become known as pedophilia, and what scholarship there was emphasized concepts that would not be acceptable to a later generation of professionals and scholars. In line with mainstream psychiatric and criminological opinion, religious leaders acted on the assumption that adult sexual activity with children was quite a rare phenomenon. When it did occur, the church initially responded to the behavior as a form of sin that required penance, but it gradually came to accept therapeutic models, on the model already accepted for alcoholism.[77] "Before the 1980s, church people usually viewed sexual offenses against minors as isolated moral lapses calling for prayer, a motivational talk, and greater willpower."[78] To quote Cardinal O'Connor, it was assumed that the priest "had learned his lesson by being caught, reported and embarrassed."[79] As the hierarchy declared in 1989, "However such cases may have been handled in past decades—when psychology was less sophisticated and when child abuse may have been viewed simply as a moral failing for which one should be repentant rather than a psychological addiction for which treatment was mandatory—today things are different."[80]

Sexual activity with minors was believed to reflect the inadequacy or confusion of the perpetrator, and merited therapy rather than punishment under the outdated legal system that harked back to more punitive times and retained "puritan" prejudices against homosexual conduct of any kind. And although the activity was illegal, this was true only in the technical sense that permitted the survival of the commonly unenforced statutes which many states possessed against adultery, sodomy, and most forms of unorthodox sexual behavior. It was improbable that the behavior would cause any long-term harm to the child concerned, provided the case was not "made an issue of" by police or courts. Further (in this view) the child might well have colluded with the offender or else was inventing the report out of malice or fantasy. In short, the Catholic authorities acted exactly according to prevailing liberal opinion, although they demonstrated excessive generosity or credulity in permitting an individual to reoffend repeatedly before taking decisive action. Liberal ideas were at their most influential between about 1964 and 1974, exactly the years that church authorities were making their decisions about James Porter.

Church attitudes were also conditioned by demographic changes within the priesthood, which suffered an alarming decline in numbers from 1968 onward. Particularly in western and southern dioceses, the shortage of clergy became acute, and by the 1980s there was a growing number of "priestless" parishes, in which many clerical functions were exercised by laypeople or women religious. In consequence, clergy and seminarians were a scarce commodity whose careers should not be lightly jeopardized. For that reason, dioceses granted a wider latitude in accepting ordinands of suspected homosexual disposition, and were reluctant to take severe action against priests with a sexual predilection for minors. Clerical authorities were predisposed to place their hopes in the efficacy of treatment and therapy rather than punitive measures.

Local shortages of priests also made it relatively easy to dispose of clergy who had encountered problems in one jurisdiction; they could usually find a ready welcome in another region or even overseas. This could be justified as offering a "new start" for a troubled individual who had recognized the error of his ways, but frequent transfers made it less likely that any one diocese or authority would track the record of an abusive priest, whose national or international career of molestation might thus continue unchecked for years. Such repeated international transfers characterized the career of the Irish Norbertine priest Brendan Smyth, who over a forty-year period was accused of abuse in numerous parishes in Ireland, Great Britain, and the United States.[81]

Ecclesiastical attitudes toward clerical sex offenders are well represented by the values of the various clinics and institutes that offered treatment and therapy to troubled priests, places such as the Saint Luke's Institute in Suitland, Maryland, and Villa Louis Martin, the house of the Servants of the Paraclete in Jemez Springs, New Mexico.[82] All based their treatment on an essentially optimistic outlook about the curability of sexual disorders, although recognizing that matters would be more difficult for true pedophiles, obsessed with prepubescent children, than for men involved with older boys or teenagers. If abusers might be cured or reformed, then they could safely be restored to ministerial settings, whether or not in regular parish life.

Moreover, the Catholic institutions retained these views some years after they had been attacked by other therapists and professionals. Father Canice Connors of the Saint Luke's Institute was the most visible spokesman for the older view, which he continued to advocate through the most severe controversies of the early 1990s. In 1992 he wrote in very unfashionable terms of "priest abuse," arguing, "We are not involved with the dynamics of rape but with the far subtler dynamics of persuasion by a friend. As we speak to and about the victims we must be aware that the child sometimes retains a loving memory of the offender."[83] He even repeated the much-maligned idea that formal intervention might be detrimental to the victim: "Sometimes well-meaning but dramatic reactions cause additional trauma for the young person."[84]

Nor was Connors unique. In 1990 a group of clergy and therapists published a collection of essays on clergy abuse under the title *Slayer of the Soul*. Although granting the extreme harm that might be caused by abuse, they came to conclusions that were much more optimistic than would be accepted even two or three years later. Two of the group (Rossetti and Lothstein) argued strongly that sexual contact with young people need not incapacitate a priest from pursuing his vocation, even in a parish setting; "more than a few" clergy had already been "successfully returned to ministry."[85] However, they drew a key distinction between pedophiles and ephebophiles; the condition of the latter was much more amenable to treatment. Frank Valcour, medical director of the Saint Luke Institute, stated, "Pedophilia and ephebophilia are quite treatable and successful treatment programs have flourished in church affiliated institutions."[86] In support of this opinion, he reported a study undertaken by the institute in 1989 that examined fifty-five priests who were child molesters and who had completed its program. "Most were in active follow-up programs and among this group there were no known relapses and no new allegations of improper behavior occurring after treatment. Of the 55, 32 were in some form of active ministry."[87] Such policies would come under attack, but as late as 1988 a court sentenced a priest convicted of molesting three youths to probation, with a requirement that at least a year be spent at the Paraclete house.[88]

This therapeutic view of the sex offender was associated with an ambiguous depiction of the other party in the sexual activity, who was occasionally seen less as a pure victim than an active participant, all the more so when the case involved a boy in his mid or late teens. It was one of the more sensitive and liberal members of the Catholic hierarchy, Archbishop Rembert Weakland, who remarked of a 1988 case, "Sometimes not all adolescent victims are so 'innocent', some can be sexually very active and aggressive and often quite street wise." We should thus avoid the impression that "any adolescent who becomes sexually involved with an older person does so without any degree of personal responsibility."[89] In the Newfoundland cases, Nova Scotia bishop Colin Campbell noted, "If the victims were adolescents, why did they go back to the same situation once there had been one pass or suggestion? Were they co-operating in the matter or were they true victims?"[90] Such remarks could be used to offer a partial defense in instances of "clergy abuse," as in a New York State case in which a priest had had sexual contact with a sixteen-year-old after plying him with vodka.[91] The defendant archdiocese was rebuked for contending that the boy had at least partially consented to the offense, a view that would have been quite orthodox and mainstream during the 1960s or 1970s but that now seemed to place the stigma on an innocent "survivor" rather than a predatory offender.

The Catholic authorities thus suffered for maintaining an essentially liberal and therapeutic approach years after that approach had been overtaken by events that wrought a revolutionary change in the public consciousness. By 1985 those who believed in the magnitude of a sex-abuse problem had succeeded beyond all expectation in establishing as plausible quite far-reaching notions about the scale and seriousness of the issue, and the incurably predatory nature of sex offenders. It was at precisely this point that media attention turned to the first major cases involving priests as abusers. The Gauthe trial in particular occurred at a crucial point in the evolution and publicizing of ideas about the problem, ideas that constituted a significant new paradigm for social science and policy.

Once the new views were accepted, it was intrinsically likely that the churches would encounter significant criticism over child abuse, and that once a few cases earned public notice, intense investigation would follow. The deepest suspicion was likely to attach to a predominantly male institution dealing with children on a daily basis, where the adults possessed strong claims to authority by virtue of their office. This was all the more true when that institution had strong traditions of enforcing discipline internally and a powerful reluctance to invoke the formal authority of either the criminal justice system or welfare agencies. If the child-abuse theorists were correct, this would be an ideal criminogenic environment: individuals would be presented with both frequent temptations and almost unlimited opportunities to commit illegal acts, with little chance of either detection or punishment. As a few cases came to light, it would swiftly be argued that these represented a huge dark figure, and that reform was urgently needed. The discovery of the phenomenon of clergy abuse was thus all but certain to lead to perceptions of a major structural problem, which is precisely what occurred over the next few years. And once investigations began, it would rapidly be found that the churches, and especially the Catholic church, had been repeatedly guilty of applying the standards that had prevailed before the revolution in social sensibilities.

The common construction of "pedophile priests" thus distorted reality in a number of important areas, exaggerating the scale and seriousness of the problem, and placing an anachronistic interpretation upon the conduct of the Catholic church. To some extent, this reflected the normal tendency of the media to present any question in a simple and readily understood form, and simultaneously to highlight the drama of the story by exaggerating the heroic or villainous characteristics of participants. However, the particular formulation of the problem also served the social, political, and ideological interests of a diverse range of groups. By far the most active and successful were those within the Catholic church itself, for whom the abuse problem offered an invaluable weapon in campaigns for comprehensive structural reform.

6

Conflict in the Churches

The "abuse crisis" was not inevitable. The individual cases could have been interpreted in a manner more sympathetic to the institutional churches, and the media need not have accepted the extremely high estimates of clerical misconduct advanced by certain authorities. The atmosphere of belief and acceptance had to some extent been created by the general concern over child abuse during the previous decade, but specific concerns about the churches were enhanced by the vigorous debates then in progress within the religious bodies themselves, and especially the Catholic church.

In the furor over abuse by Catholic clergy, several major themes emerged recurrently: the authoritarian nature of the church and its hierarchy; the special privileges accorded to priests; the apparent neglect of the interests of children and women; and an ambiguous and hypocritical attitude toward sexuality. As Jeffrey Anderson argued, "The real scandal is not that there's exploitation by clergy. It's the mendacity, the duplicity, the complicity, the ignorance and the indifference of the hierarchy."[1] All these issues and allegations had been under intense discussion within Catholic circles for two decades before the Gauthe case, from which they now acquired an urgent focus. At precisely the time that the abuse cases came to light, the Catholic church was embroiled in a series of bitter struggles about such matters as the balance of lay and clerical power in the church, the power of the hierarchy and the special role of the clergy, and gender concerns.

The neat fit between these earlier debates and the new problem can be explained in various ways. Perhaps the earlier critics of the hierarchy had been prophetic in their analysis of the ills afflicting the church and in foretelling imminent disaster. An alternative view suggests that the dissidents were successful in using clergy abuse as a vehicle for projecting their long-established grievances, so that the construction of the problem reflected the internal politics of the Catholic church. In either case, the abuse problem must be situated in the context of the ongoing "Catholic civil war"

that since the 1960s had divided conservatives and radicals, traditionalists and reformers, ecclesialists and modernizers.

It would be convenient if activism over the issue of clergy abuse could be neatly
associated with one particular cause or faction, for example if we could argue that liberals and feminists publicized molestation cases in order to embarrass the hierarchy
with which they were at odds on so many issues. Undoubtedly, something like this
did occur, but the situation was complicated by the parallel activism of conservatives,
who drew attention to the same cases for motives precisely opposite to those of the
liberals. The abuse crisis attracted so much attention precisely because it was so valuable, rhetorically and symbolically, to so many political causes within the church.

The Origins of Conflict

The midcentury church succeeded in projecting an image of cohesive unity under the
leadership of the National Catholic Welfare Conference, precursor of the later U.S.
Catholic Conference: "an efficient and aggressive organization that is the envy of
many other American religious groups."[2] Those suspicious of Catholic ambitions
viewed the hierarchy as an Orwellian juggernaut:

> The bureaus of the N.C.W.C. are full of busy young priests, lobbyists, pamphleteers,
> journalists and lawyers who coordinate the Catholic population of the country as one
> great pressure group when any "Catholic issue" arises. The Press Department sends out
> about 60,000 words a week in the form of news releases and feature articles to 437
> Catholic papers in this country and beyond. . . . [I]n American Catholicism the bishops
> speak for Catholic power.[3]

This monolithic image belied a long tradition of internal dissent within the American
church; conflicts about the relative power of clergy and laity had occurred regularly
over the previous century.[4] However, disputes became more public following the
Second Vatican Council (1962–1965), when internal critics attacked such fundamental aspects of the church's structure as its hierarchical structure, its male priesthood, and its claim to a special divine revelation. Since the 1970s a complex array of
organized factions and pressure groups have existed, each with its distinctive publications and media outlets.

During the 1960s the rapid pace of reforms raised expectations about an increased
role and status for the laity, and a reconceptualization of the role of clergy that might
permit an end to mandatory celibacy. There now began a period of radical liturgical
innovation, which had as its main theme the reduction of the special role accorded to
the priest and an enhanced idea of the congregation as the community of God. It was
hoped that the church would play a social and political role more in accord with the
changing attitudes of its lay faithful, demonstrating greater liberalism regarding
sexual issues such as contraception and more concern with racial and social justice.
A current of "liberation theology" emphasized the duty of Christians to struggle
against all forms of social and political oppression.[5]

Liberal hopes were dashed by the pope's reaffirmation of the church's opposition
to artificial means of contraception in the 1968 encyclical *Humanae Vitae*, which led
to public protests on an unprecedented scale by clergy and religious.[6] The specific

question of contraception was perhaps less significant than the related issues of the basis of church authority.[7] The Vatican was accused of enforcing as absolute doctrine the sexual mores of particular times and cultures, to the neglect of the changing moral sensibilities of large sections of the educated laity. The extensive neglect of this prohibition by Catholic families over the next two decades suggests declining respect for the absolute moral authority of the church. In addition, traditional clerical structures were placed under grave stress by the growing uncertainty about the role of clergy in a contemporary society.[8]

Clerical celibacy was among the most contentious problems, for the extreme degree of symbolic separation it demanded between the priest and his community and for its implied misogyny and denigration of sexuality. The discipline raised practical problems for the recruitment and retention of adequate numbers of priests, and the celibacy issue contributed to the exodus of clergy from the late 1960s onward.[9] From 1968 through 1973 resignations of priests were so numerous that three-quarters of all ordinations were required just to fill these gaps, not counting losses from death or retirement.[10] Between 1965 and 1994 the number of priests in the United States fell from almost 59,000 to 53,000, and this at a time of considerable growth in the Catholic population due to immigration.[11] The ratio of priests to the lay population fell from 1:600 in 1945 to 1:850 in 1975; the projected ratio for the year 2005 is 1:2,200.[12] In 1990, about 10 percent of Catholic parishes in the United States lacked a resident priest: by 2005 the figure may be 30 percent.

The situation in the seminaries was particularly grave in that a decline here has disastrous long-term consequences. Between 1966 and 1993 the number of students fell by 85 percent; "in the pre-Vatican II era, young Catholic males were about ten times as likely to study for the priesthood as they are now."[13] Women were especially affected by the changes of those years, and the number of women religious in the United States fell from 180,000 in 1966 to 94,000 in 1994. Between 1966 and 1976 alone, some 50,000 nuns left their religious orders, and many who remained became increasingly radicalized.

Gender, Sexuality, and Authority

During the 1970s and 1980s conservative and radical factions within the American church battled over familiar issues such as liberation theology and sexual ethics, and Catholic clergy and theologians demanded the right to support moral and political positions contrary to official teaching.[14] Liberals mobilized in events like the Women's Ordination Conference (1975) and the national Call to Action (1976), which produced a sweeping reformist agenda. In 1977 controversy surrounded the publication of a liberal text, *Human Sexuality*, which critically explored church teachings on such matters as premarital sex and masturbation. Consultants on this book included prominent liberals such as Charles Curran, Gregory Baum, and Richard A. McCormick, all of whom were likewise active in a 1977 symposium held to discuss "Vatican III," a hypothetical future General Council. Other reformers present included Eugene Kennedy and Andrew Greeley.[15] Though they complained about attempts to silence them, the American dissenters enjoyed far greater latitude to criticize official positions than in any recent period of Catholic history, and there was a rarely precedented degree of licence to engage in liturgical and credal diversity. Liberal and radical opinions were freely expressed in Catholic papers such as *America*, *Commonweal*, and especially *National Catholic Reporter*.

The already acrimonious debates were intensified by disagreements over the role of women in the church. Catholic feminism became a vigorous force in the 1970s, and the thwarting of demands for the ordination of women contributed to the development of a range of groups and organizations that virtually constituted a parallel church. Catholic divisions were especially sharp during the mid-1980s. While the feminist movement was growing apace with the new "Women-Church" movement, the political Left had been galvanized by opposition to the Reagan administration. Liberation theology found an immediate focus in opposing U.S. government policies in the largely Catholic nations of Central America. The Catholic Left was broadly sympathetic to the Sandinista regime in Nicaragua, and was vehemently hostile to the repressive rightist governments of El Salvador and Guatemala. The movement had acquired martyrs in the four American nuns and churchwomen murdered by the Salvadorean military during 1980. Within the church, radicals and liberals criticized the hierarchy for its failure to confront the administration over these issues, as well as other touchstones like nuclear disarmament and social policies, while it actively supported right-wing positions on moral issues.[16]

Abortion was important in this context. Throughout the century the official position of the Catholic church had militantly denounced both abortion and "artificial" means of contraception. During the 1970s and 1980s the Catholic church had emerged as by far the most vocal foe of legalized abortion, and the question enjoyed enormous prominence in Catholic political and social rhetoric. It also facilitated the forging of alliances with right-wing evangelical Protestant organizations such as the Moral Majority. The NCCB's Committee for Pro-Life Activities has for a decade been "the broadest, best organized and most powerful group" in the anti-abortion cause.[17] Within the church, pro-life militancy alienated the hierarchy still further from the feminists, who saw abortion as a matter of women's rights and interests. The political Left attacked the reassertion of individual moral issues at the expense of political and social causes.

Conflicts within the church reached a climax in 1986–1987, "the year that shook Catholic America."[18] In 1984 the Catholic hierarchy denounced Democratic vice-presidential candidate Geraldine Ferraro for her support of abortion rights, and liberal Catholics characterized this as an impermissible interference in secular politics. When a number of nuns and other religious signed a petition organized by Catholics for a Free Choice, church authorities took steps to discipline the nuns (the "Vatican 24") and the Vatican began a general investigation of American religious orders.[19] Hostilities flared again in 1986 over the question of granting platforms to pro-abortion politicians in premises associated with the church, and there were attempts to silence or discipline leading liberals who had criticized church regulations on sexual or political matters. Theologian Charles Curran lost his license to teach at the Catholic University of America; Seattle Archbishop Raymond Hunthausen suffered a sharp reduction of his archdiocesan powers; Jesuit John McNeill was condemned for urging a liberalization of church attitudes toward homosexuality (he was a cofounder of the pressure group Dignity). Meanwhile, there were attempts to force the Dominican order to silence Matthew Fox and his mystical "Creation Spirituality" movement. American Catholic periodicals followed closely the parallel efforts to discipline radical theologians in Europe or Latin America, and the proceedings of the "new inquisition" against Leonardo Boff, Hans Küng, and Edward Schillebeeckx each became a *cause célèbre.*[20]

Liberals alleged that these acts were part of a concerted "Roman Restoration" in the United States, a deliberate scheme to re-establish Vatican orthodoxy and strict hierarchical control over the church. There were related suspicions about interference from conservative political leaders. "The Vatican's repeated denials that [Hunthausen's] peace activities had anything to do with his troubles with the Vatican failed to convince many Catholics, who believed the Reagan White House had been instrumental in working revenge against a thorn in its side. He stood up for the rights of homosexuals, blacks, Hispanics and women."[21] In March 1986 the *New York Times* published another petition from more than a thousand Catholics, asserting their right to dissent from official church teaching.

The demands of the Catholic opposition were epitomized in a petition published on Ash Wednesday 1990, and signed by more than forty-five hundred individuals; this "Pastoral Letter" called for the ordination of women, an end to mandatory celibacy, revision of church teachings on sexual morality, adoption of gender-neutral language in the liturgy, and an end to official restraints on academic theologians. Similar issues were discussed within the church hierarchy. In 1992 the prelates gathered at the NCCB were deeply divided over a proposed pastoral letter on the role and concerns of women, a document that had been under discussion for nine years.[22] The document sought to be conciliatory in offering a heartfelt denunciation of sexism, but it also condemned abortion and contraception and rejected future discussion of the ordination of women. Ultimately, the document proved so contentious that no agreement could be reached on a final form.

The Catholic hierarchy faced an organized "opposition" in the form of several left-liberal groups, all founded since the late 1960s: Dignity (1969) represented gay Catholics, both clerical and lay; Corpus (1974) was an organization of men who had left the priesthood in order to marry (the name was an acronym derived from Corps of Reserved Priests United for Service); and Pax Christi (1945) was an antimilitarist network that included a number of bishops in its ranks. Also influential was the Women's Ordination Conference (1975), and there were ad-hoc liberal groups like Catholics for a Free Choice, Catholics Speak Out, and the Association for the Rights of Catholics in the Church.

Dissent was often manifested at the semiannual deliberations of the NCCB where, as *NCR* headlined, "No Meeting [Is] Complete Without Protesters."[23] In vivid contrast to the NCWC meetings of the 1940s or 1950s, contemporary bishops can expect to hear a range of irate voices. In 1992, for instance, feminists concentrated their ire against the pastoral letter, and the bishops were again confronted by a delegation from Dignity.[24] The following year, the NCCB meeting provided a forum for protests by groups of clergy-abuse survivors (SNAP, VOCAL, Protect the Child) as well as Pax Christi, Catholics for a Free Choice, and Catholics Speak Out.

Homosexuality

Homosexuality was another area in which official Catholic policies and doctrines were under attack. Traditionalists found natural allies with the evangelical Right, for both opposed legislation providing civil rights protections for homosexuals, and liberals called for greater toleration. Some radical theologians, such as Charles Curran and John McNeill, urged a theological reassessment of the Catholic condemnation of homosexuality, but in the stringent atmosphere of the mid-1980s this contributed to their official condemnation. Battles over homosexuality were exacerbated by the perception that many priests were themselves homosexual, at least by inclination and often in practice. As the priest shortage became acute during the 1970s, the church was apparently willing to accept homosexual clergy on the understanding that they remained strictly celibate on the model expected of their heterosexual counterparts.[25]

Probably there always have been active homosexuals within the clergy of the Catholic church and other ecclesiastical bodies, and men and women of homosexual inclination are disproportionately likely to be attracted to the single-sex environment of a celibate clergy or religious order. In modern times changing political conditions have made it possible for homosexual clerics to express their preferences publicly, or at least to discuss them in the context of a support group like the Catholic organization Dignity or the Episcopal Integrity, and informal networks are numerous.[26] In 1976 it was NCR (yet again) that broke new ground by publishing an interview with an anonymous but avowedly gay priest.[27] Since that watershed, a number of autobiographical books have described the authentic experience of homosexual clergy, both male and female.[28]

In contrast to the scandalous semipornographic productions of the nineteenth century, a 1970s novel such as Patricia Nell Warren's *The Fancy Dancer* could freely explore the conflicts of a Catholic priest discovering his homosexuality in encounters with a young former convict. In sympathetically portraying the real-life work of Dignity, the book examined the lively gay subculture among Catholic priests, manifested in the strongly sexual symbolism of a Eucharist organized by the group. And although not favoring overt manifestations, the local bishop acknowledges, "I would be less than honest . . . if I didn't admit that your affliction is a common one in the priesthood. Maybe commoner than temptations to the fair sex. . . . And by no means is it limited to the rank and file."[29] The theme of the priest's discovering his homosexual nature occurs in another novel written in the same year, Iris Murdoch's *Henry and Cato*.[30]

Based on an extensive survey of Catholic clergy over a twenty-five year period, Richard Sipe argues that "approximately 20 percent of all clergy have some homosexual orientation. Approximately 10 percent of clergy . . . involve themselves in homosexual activity."[31] He further states that the number of priests reporting homosexual tendencies or serious questions about sexual identity doubled between 1978 and 1985, from about 20 to 40 percent.[32] The growth of gay clergy was widely rumored, and occasionally discussed in the media. In 1982 the National Federation of Priests' Councils noted, "Of more recent and urgent concern is the increasing number of priests who have a homosexual orientation."[33]

A gay rights movement already at odds with the Catholic church was further galvanized by the AIDS epidemic of the 1980s, and once again the church was seen as a stronghold of reaction for its refusal to support any health policy involving condom use. Complaints also came from the Catholic charitable agencies and groups that dealt with populations most directly at risk from AIDS in consequence of either drug abuse or high-risk sexual practices. AIDS was of course a threat to homosexual priests, and in 1987 the disease claimed its most visible clerical victim to date, with the death of Michael Peterson of the Saint Luke Institute. As controversy grew, the Vatican in 1986 issued a document that not only reaffirmed traditional teaching that homosexual conduct was morally wrong but went on to assert that this form of sexual orientation was "a tendency ordered towards an intrinsic moral evil and thus the inclination itself must be seen as an objective disorder." Pressure groups like Dignity were condemned in language that was unambiguous, even though the group was not explicitly named, and over the next year the bishops excluded Dignity chapters from church premises.[34]

By 1989 gay rights groups such as ACT-UP (AIDS Coalition to Unleash Power) and Queer Nation adopted increasingly militant tactics against the Catholic church, holding demonstrations that interrupted church services and including salacious parodies of clerical figures in gay rights parades and protests.[35] Among the most contentious incidents were the ACT-UP protest in Saint Patrick's Cathedral in New York City during December 1989 and the 1991 dispute over ACT-UP's violently polemical film *Stop the Church*, which was presented on the Los Angeles public broadcasting station after being canceled on most PBS affiliates. In 1990 an ordination service held by Boston's Cardinal Bernard Law was interrupted by chants of "two-four-six-eight, How do you know your priests are straight?"[36] Protesters staged parodies of the Sermon on the Mount and the Eucharist, distributing condoms in the latter. One potent source of grievance in many cities was the Saint Patrick's Day parade, a cherished part of Irish-American cultural life. During the early 1990s there were prolonged legal battles over the right of gay groups to march officially in the parades in cities such as New York and Boston. Conflicts became so embittered that organizers threatened to cancel events rather than permit gay participation in what were notionally Catholic celebrations. When the pope visited the United States in 1993, protesters in Denver, Colorado, described him as "the biggest homophobe in the world" and accused the Catholic church of "sins of sexism, homophobia and abuse of power."[37]

Traditionalists

The Catholic church in the 1980s therefore faced both internal and external dissension, and these conflicts contributed to the process of making and establishing claims about clergy sex abuse. However, the topic belonged to no one strand or faction. On the topic of clerical homosexuality, for instance, the alleged prevalence of gay priests was valuable to liberal or gay rights activists, who could denounce the church's hypocrisy and argue that sexual repression directly led to the molestation of children. On the other hand, the issue also benefited the conservative and traditionalist critics of the hierarchy, groups that believed that the post–Vatican II reforms had gone too far. Many conservatives were prepared to denounce clergy who demonstrated even the slightest sympathy for feminism or liberation theology. Like the liberals, they too had their organized pressure groups, such as Catholics United for the Faith, and their own press, in papers such as *The Wanderer* and the *Lay Witness*.[38] For traditionalists, clergy abuse was a natural outcome of liberal and Vatican II excesses, specifically the sinister invasion of the clergy by homosexuals, for in this view there was no effective distinction between homosexuals and pedophiles. Child-abuse campaigns offered an effective platform from which to denounce the toleration of homosexuality in the church and in society at large.

When the pioneering protest by abuse victims and activists was organized at the NCCB meetings in Baltimore in 1989, a staunch conservative element among the campaigners was exemplified by Pat Morley, Tom Phillips, and especially Michael Schwartz, who was the main spokesman.[39] Schwartz was a vigorous critic of episcopal laxity in the face of the abuse problem, and he formed the pressure group Catholics for a More Open Church specifically to address the issue. He was active in the Catholic League for Religious and Civil Rights and wrote a number of conservative books, pamphlets, and audiotape presentations such as "Abortion: The Nazi Connection" and "The Supreme Court versus the American Family." He also co-authored with Enrique Rueda a book on homosexuality and AIDS, which portrayed a multitentacled homosexual movement seeking to impose its deviant values on mainstream society.[40] Homosexual influence in the churches was of acute concern, and the authors charge that even the trend toward gender-neutral language was part of a scheme to induce gender confusion.[41] They warn, "Churches, once they have been infiltrated by the homosexual movement, constitute one of its most important allies." Any religious body "is of great interest to, indeed is a target of, the homosexual movement."[42]

Schwartz's cooperation with Rueda points to the enduring concern with homosexual issues on the Catholic Right. Rueda was most celebrated for his 1982 book *The Homosexual Network*, an encyclopedic exposé of gay infiltration into the churches and other areas of society, and it was largely through his efforts that the phrase "homosexual network" entered the lexicon of social conservatives.[43] Predictably, the book already stressed pederasty as one of the many nefarious aspects of the issue.[44] Rueda's investigation was undertaken at the request of archconservative ideologue Paul Weyrich, founder of the right-wing Free Congress Foundation, which throughout the 1980s did much to develop and propagate such influential ideas as the "Culture War," and the aggressive defense of traditional values. Schwartz directed a division of the Free Congress Foundation, and both Schwartz and Rueda were prominent in a foundation offshoot named Catholic Center for Free Enterprise, Strong Defense and Traditional Values. Throughout the decade, the Catholic Center denounced the liberal views of the Catholic hierarchy on such matters as Central America and nuclear disarmament. The center led the assault on Archbishop Hunthausen, among other things for his sympathy for homosexual rights, and it was blamed by liberals for the Vatican campaign against radical theologians. Long before the abuse cases came to light, the center's stated goal was to generate "significant negative publicity for the bishops" to make them "squeal and scream in anguish."[45]

The cast of antiabuse activists in 1989 bore some resemblance to the coalition that had destabilized Hunthausen, including as it did the Catholic Center and the "Weyrich-*Wanderer* network."[46] Once again liberal prelates were being targeted, and pedophile charges permitted the revival of older grievances on sexual issues. In the mid-1980s, for example, Archbishop Weakland of Milwaukee was under attack from conservatives for liberal policies on matters such as AIDS education and for his permitting a priest to serve as chaplain to a Dignity chapter. Rueda had bracketed him with Hunthausen for their "soft position on homosexuality."[47] By 1988 the campaign to enforce traditional moral standards in Milwaukee came to focus on sexual misconduct between local parish priests and teenage boys, with conservative activist Tom Phillips as a leading Weakland opponent.[48] Schwartz invited Phillips to participate in the Baltimore protest.

Pat Morley, similarly, had campaigned against Honolulu bishop David Ferrario for his enthusiastic support of Vatican II reforms, and she supported the efforts of David Figueroa to expose the bishop's alleged history of sexual abuse.[49] The discrediting of Ferrario was the culmination of a long campaign by "archconservatives" to expose what they viewed as homosexual and liberal hegemony in the diocese, the "homosexual network" of Hawaiian priests, and the supposed "homosexual persecution" of conservatives.[50] The political environment of these activists seems far removed from the liberalism of writers like Jason Berry, who nevertheless writes sympathetically of their endeavors. At one point, he recalls how the Hawaiian conservatives had "exposed Ferrario as a Modernist," a surprisingly partisan way of referring to their traditionalist stance.[51]

This advocacy from the ecclesiastical Right was more than an idiosyncratic decision by a handful of unusual individuals. The campaign against clergy "pedophilia" was associated with strenuous opposition to real or imagined homosexual infiltration into the priesthood, and especially to the liberalism of bishops such as Hunthausen, Weakland, Ferrario, and Bernardin.[52] *The Wanderer* has explicitly blamed the Left for the pedophilia crisis, and suggested that the problem would be solved by a purge of leftists and "communists."[53] Bernard Lynch, a priest who attracted visibility in the New York archdiocese for his militant advocacy of gay rights and AIDS issues, linked his 1989 prosecution on molestation charges to the activity of "right wing groups of Catholics, highly articulate and more dangerous than I ever realized."[54]

The linkage between homosexuality and pedophilia is frequently drawn, to the extent that the victimization of young girls is all but excluded from the usual construction of the problem. Conservative Catholic author Malachi Martin portrays a "self-protective network of gay church officials which covers up for other homosexuals *and* child sex offenders in the priesthood."[55] In the Gauthe case, the attorney for the victims' families explicitly connected the pedophile issue with alleged homosexual infiltration. He argued that the diocese of Lafayette offered a "safe haven" for homosexuals because "someone in authority knowingly condones homosexual behavior." Both types of activity were ultimately "rooted in celibacy."[56]

Similar associations appear in the works of writers who are viewed as liberal on many points. Berry asks if Jesus would approve of an "ecclesiastical culture [that] harbors child molesters, tolerates homosexual activity."[57] In 1989, in the same week as the Baltimore protest, Andrew Greeley published a controversial article in *NCR*, denouncing official toleration both of clerical sexual misconduct with young people and of networks of gay clergy. He wrote, "Blatantly active homosexual priests are appointed, transferred and promoted. Lavender rectories and seminaries are tolerated. National networks of active homosexual priests (many of them church administrators) are tolerated."[58] He alleges that homosexual priests are effectively granted official licence to hold assignations and meet regularly for sexually oriented parties, behavior that would not for a second be tolerated for heterosexual clergy. Greeley argues, admittedly on anecdotal evidence, that "perhaps a quarter of the priests under 35 are gay, and perhaps half of that group are sexually active,"; the United States is developing a "substantially homosexual clergy, many of whom are blatantly part of the gay subculture."

Greeley is generally careful to distinguish between homosexuality and pedophilia and had attracted Rueda's ire for this very point, but he does imply that lax standards on homosexual contacts contribute to toleration of clergy sex abuse.[59] In a significant juxtaposition, he urged in 1990 that the archdiocese of Chicago "clean out the pedophiles, break up the active gay cliques, tighten up the seminary, and restore the good name of the priesthood."[60] "The two phenomena" of homosexuality and pedophilia "shade into one another." In the novel *Fall from Grace*, the bishop who is so reluctant to believe or investigate tales of clergy abuse had himself been involved in a sexual relationship with a man who proves to be a member of a pedophile ring. The appalling pedophile Father Greene is also the leader of a tolerated group of sexually active gay priests.

Conservative approaches to clergy abuse are reflected in discussions of the harm caused by the behavior, and whether molestation or childhood sexual activity could indeed condition the victim's future sexual orientation. An older stereotype suggested that boys molested by men themselves became homosexual, so the condition was almost contagious, and this pedophile association was much used by opponents of homosexuality. In gay rights campaigns from the 1970s onward, moral traditionalists and religious groups sometimes employed the slogan "Homosexuals aren't born—they recruit." Gay rights advocates naturally rejected this association, generally arguing that sexual preference is determined before birth. If true, this would favor the expansion of civil rights protections for homosexuals on the grounds that their sexual identity is involuntary and immutable. However, the clergy-abuse cases reassert the older view of the effects of pedophilia, chiefly to emphasize the darkest possible view of the behavior for ideological or legal ends.

One lawyer representing alleged victims of abuse by priests in New Mexico asked rhetorically, "How do you compensate a young man who was *programmed to lead a gay life style*, who lost his faith, who faces a lifetime of depression and will require a lifetime of therapy? There's no amount of money that will fully compensate him."[61] Stephen Cook similarly alleged that abuse by Cardinal Bernardin and other clergy had caused his subsequent homosexual lifestyle, and thus indirectly led to his contracting AIDS. Jeffrey Anderson remarked that each of the child victims of Father Adamson "suffered a terrible arrest of personality development and sexual identities. Some are now homosexuals, some don't know what they are."[62] There is a significant contradiction here between the assertions of some clergy-abuse claimsmakers and the liberals with whom they often share common ground.

Clergy Abuse as a Liberal Issue

It would be simplistic to present Catholic activism in regard to sexual abuse as entirely the product of the Left/liberal wing of the church, but it was these latter dissenters who did most to shape and define the issue during the 1980s. The liberal critique of the American Catholic church would be central to the understanding of later debates over clergy abuse, a linkage that will be apparent if we consider the failings alleged against the church during the feuds of those years.

For the liberal reformers, the church's organization was resolutely founded upon patriarchal values, and it confounded those socially based male interests with absolute or supernatural Christian beliefs. This was exemplified in the church's failure to admit women to clerical responsibilities, even those as seemingly harmless as altar girl (a concession on this issue was granted only in 1994). In the secular realm, this patriarchal conservatism took the form of the determined opposition to women's reproductive rights and alternative forms of sexual expression. On sexuality generally, the church was dangerously out of touch with social or psychological reality, and its celibacy policies reflected a mystical and unrealistic attitude, "unworldly" in the pejorative sense of the word. Priests were victims of an unfair and unnatural burden, which they could resolve only by suffering psychic scars or by secretly exploring their own sexuality in ways that made nonsense of their vows of chastity. There were estimates that as many as half of all priests might be ignoring the church's regulations by illicitly engaging in sexual relationships with women.[63] Charges of mass hypocrisy and clandestine sexuality were widespread before any serious public attention was paid to "priest pedophilia."

Central to the liberal critique was the definition of "the church." It is common to speak of "the church" as synonymous with the institutional body and specifically the bishops and clergy, so that one conventionally refers to a man's taking clerical orders as "going into the church." The Second Vatican Council reemphasized the identity of the church as the community of Christian believers, so that the laity were as much or more "the church" than were the clergy. In the 1980s those who disagreed with official Catholic teachings referred to this doctrine, and drew a distinction between "the church" (the body of the faithful) and the "institutional church," what Eugene Kennedy describes as "the official church, never to be confused with the people of God."

Opposition was directed not against the church as such but against its authorities, cardinals and bishops, who were described in terms like "the hierarchy." When the institutional church was reflecting the policies of the papacy and the Roman Curia, this would be emphasized by drawing a distinction between "the American church" and "the Vatican." In this populist and patriotic view, "the hierarchy" and "the Vatican" are portrayed as unsympathetic to the autonomous and democratic traditions of American religion, manifested by the official church's regressive attitudes on matters of gender. Echoing nativist traditions, some exponents of this view portray the hierarchy as the servants of foreign and un-American masters in the Vatican.

The debates of the 1980s publicized charges that the church, or at least "the hierarchy," was a hermetically sealed elite in which policies were formed and discipline enforced with little or no consultation of the laity and lower clergy. The church was a law unto itself, enforcing almost unlimited power over its own clergy and faithful while rejecting attempts to bring it into line with the standards and values of contemporary life. Secretive, byzantine, bureaucratic, patriarchal: these hostile images of the church gained credence from frequent retellings in the media. This approach was most clear in the pages of the *National Catholic Reporter*, "the stalwart evangelist of the Catholic Left," and the foremost enemy of the "Roman Restoration."[64] Radical and liberal Catholic groups stood to gain much from an exposure of clergy abuse; even if there had never been a single confirmed case of abuse by a Catholic priest, most of the same rhetorical elements would still have been employed in intrachurch debate, though without the urgency provided by the putative threat to children.

The Media and the Catholic Reformers

In the mid-1980s, NCR took the lead in exposing and publicizing the abuse cases. Jason Berry found NCR to be one of the few national media outlets that would report on the Gauthe case,[65] and the paper published reports and opinion by all the most visible commentators. At the height of media controversy during 1992 and 1993, the paper retained its position as the most trenchant critic of church policies.[66] It argued that the hierarchy was covering up "the see-no-problem, hear-no-problem, speak-no-problem problem."[67] It offered extended and unfailingly sympathetic coverage of the efforts of VOCAL and Jeanne Miller, and used the organization's 1992 conference as an opportunity to report the views of several leading protesters and dissidents, including Thomas Doyle, Richard Sipe, Andrew Greeley, and Jason Berry.[68] Thomas Fox and Jason Berry cowrote an article with the title "AS NATION DISCUSSES PEDO-PHILIA, EVEN POPE ADMITS IT'S A PROBLEM," implying that the natural tendency of the pope and the Vatican was to deny or conceal such difficult issues.[69] This was the message of other 1993 headlines such as, "MOVING BEYOND DENIAL, SEX ABUSE EXAMINATION BEGINS." Readers could be in no doubt that, as Fox wrote, the abuse affair was "viewed by many as the greatest crisis the Catholic church has faced."[70]

The Catholic character of NCR permitted the paper to pioneer structural interpretations of the abuse problem that would have been intolerably controversial had they appeared in a non-Catholic setting. It is inconceivable that *Time* or the *New York Times* would produce a major study of sex scandals in the Catholic church under the banner headline "BISHOPS AS ACCOMPLICES: SEX, CELIBACY AND THE COLLAPSE OF THE CLERICAL STATE," which was the heading used by NCR for a review of recent incidents.[71] "Rome," the "hierarchy," the "official church" were all denounced in a way that would brand a secular publication as overtly anti-Catholic. For one writer, the central message of the pedophile crisis was that "Rome can make disastrous moral errors. The autocratic character of Roman Catholicism is hostile to pastoral well-being . . . the gospel of Christ is tainted by its vesture of totalitarianism."[72] Eugene Kennedy commented on the failure of "official Catholicism" to examine or investigate abuse and other problems arising from celibacy, perhaps because its root cases have "become so much a part of the weave of overall ecclesiastical culture that they cannot be teased out without tearing the cloth itself."[73]

Criticism of church authorities was by no means universal, and NCR found kind words for those who made sincere efforts at reform. The paper praised Bernardin's reforms in Chicago and defended him against the Cook charges,[74] while holding up Canadian reforms as a model for the U.S. church.[75] However, the paper reflected the opinions of those radical reformers who believed that the abuse problem was so serious as to force a church schism, in Catholic terms an extraordinarily serious threat. Greeting the 1992 VOCAL conference, Sipe declared that those assembled were present together at "Wittenberg," recalling the site of Luther's protest against the "celibate/sexual system" of the Catholic church, which was in need of "profound reformation."[76] After recollecting recent feuds over issues such as women's ordination, celibacy, homosexuality, and academic freedom, Thomas Fox continued, "Yet another division has been added to the list pushing lay Catholics into further conflict with their clerical teaching authorities. This issue also deals with sex and authority." "If abuse of indulgences was the last straw when Augustinian friar Martin Luther split with the Catholic church, then clergy sexual abuse might well be that proverbial last straw should a split occur in our lifetimes."[77]

Liberal Catholic papers like *NCR* do not reach a large audience, but their point of view has won support because of the ways in which the mass media find Catholic experts on the abuse issue. The broadcast media have long demonstrated sympathy to feminist and liberal stances on religious issues, as suggested by the overwhelmingly unsympathetic coverage of the church's reluctance to ordain women priests and the generally hostile reporting of the church's position on abortion.[78] On women priests, news programs generally depict maintainers of the status quo as hidebound reactionaries, while devoting most of a given report to the concerns and ambitions of the reformers. Throughout the 1980s the customary experts sought on such conflicts had been prominent Catholic reformists. No partisan intent necessarily lay behind this choice; the media were demonstrating their customary penchant for visible and articulate commentators, and popular authors such as Andrew Greeley and Eugene Kennedy ably filled this role. The result, however, was to ensure a distinctly reformist and antihierarchy emphasis in news coverage. More conservative church spokesmen rarely appeared in the mainstream press, and thus the authorities employed to present "the Catholic view" of the question generally denounced the hierarchy and its procedures. Once the abuse issue did arise, it was predictable that the media would seek comments from the familiar group of reformists, who would place the emerging problem in the context of grievances like celibacy. Relying on the reformist core meant that views that had once been limited to the pages of *NCR* were now disseminated through the mainstream media.

The Rhetoric of Reform

In rhetorical terms, clergy abuse was invaluable for church critics, provided that the focus could be shifted from the individual misdeeds of a few clerics to the structural hypocrisy of the church hierarchy. The consequences might be presented in terms of sharp contrasts and contradictions: the church affected to speak for traditional values and sexual restraint, but its clergy were heavily involved in sexual excess and exploitation; while the Church denounced homosexuality between consenting adults, its clergy committed homosexual acts against vulnerable children; and the church's "pro-life" stance asserted the absolute value of human life and the defense of small children, but the institution made strenuous efforts to protect clergy who assaulted and raped the young. The church "is paying millions of dollars to do penance for the sexual amusements of supposedly celibate priests while it seeks to minimize, if not eliminate altogether, the sexual pleasures of married lay people."[79] Jason Berry explicitly compares the treatment of the heterodox theologian, who is stigmatized and silenced, and that of the pedophile priest, who is tolerated and re-shuffled: "Such inertia stands in jagged contrast to the persecution of Charles Curran and Archbishop Hunthausen."[80] Curran himself remarked that the 1993 book *A Gospel of Shame* reached to "the heart of the matter—the credibility of the Catholic church today."

Ray Mouton observed that "the Roman Catholic church cannot credibly exert moral authority externally in any area where the public perceives it as incapable of maintaining moral authority internally."[81] To quote Jason Berry, "When the bishops say that life in the womb is sacred and at the same time for years have been playing musical chairs with pedophiles, something doesn't wash, there is an inconsistency here, there is a tremendous problem of credibility."[82] The same themes appear in the letters that appeared in Catholic papers following the exposure of the various sex scandals. For example, "Do you think Archbishop Sanchez used birth control or that the pedophiles used safe sex? Hypocrisy and double standards live on in the Catholic church, except this borders on criminality."[83] "The Catholic church is confronted with its failure to eradicate pedophilia within the ranks of the clergy. Millions wonder why an organization that presumes to call the world to moral and religious excellence can be so corrupt."[84] This rhetoric of hypocrisy and contradiction threatened to subvert the most successful aspects of the Catholic position on social issues.

The political value of the clergy-abuse problem can be illustrated by comparing today's debates over church reform with those of twenty years ago. In the 1970s there were vigorous movements within the church calling for the ordination of women and abolition of compulsory clerical celibacy, at the same time that liberal activists were attacking the church for its stand on moral issues such as abortion and homosexuality. Catholic reformers used the rhetoric of religious and moral justice, of compliance with divine law, and of conformity to contemporary secular standards of fairness and social equality. All were powerful arguments, but none had the im-mediate force of the contemporary debate, in which it is declared that the reforms are imperative to protect children, to prevent ruined lives, and to forestall the new cycles of abuse believed to stem from such exploitation. Similarly, secular argu-ments based on liberal ideals and enlightenment are nothing like as potentially powerful as the rhetoric of hypocrisy, which in effect rejects the whole moral foun-dation of the Catholic church, its hierarchy, and any of its representatives.

Reform as Remedy: Celibacy and the Seminaries

The potential of the abuse issue for church reformers can be best appreciated in the context of the remedies proposed for the problem. These included essentially all the major changes that had been advocated by liberal Catholic reformers for decades, though now with the added force supplied by the pedophile theme. Reformers argued that each would in its way contribute to the protection of the young. In the protest meetings of parishioners and other citizen groups following exposure of the Mount Cashel affair in Newfoundland, a typical statement was that "the only way to purge the Church was to allow priests to marry and to open the seminary doors to women. Other radical means were proposed, including the abolition of confession so that fallen priests wouldn't have an easy means of homing in on their victims."[85]

The Catholic church had always regarded celibacy as a matter of discipline rather than faith, and therefore an area in which change was theoretically possible, in contrast to the ordination of women. In the 1980s liberals and reformists usually advocated this reform, and their cause gained much impetus from the abuse cases. Notre Dame theologian Richard McBrien suggests that any reform measures in the abuse area would be palliatives unless they extended to the core problem in "the seminary pipeline. And at the root of the seminary problem is celibacy."[86] Eugene Kennedy argues the point in *NCR* under the heading "Seminary System Rates Quick Christian Burial." Attorney Jeffrey Anderson explicitly links the problem to the church's "failure to deal openly and honestly with issues around sexuality and sexism. And that manifests itself in a lot of their religious practices, such as the tenet of celibacy."[87] One weighty voice in this debate was that of Ray Gunzel, a priest of the Servants of the Paraclete, who had worked extensively with sexually troubled priests. He opposed returning men to ministry without considering "deeper issues of church structure . . . a system that establishes celibate men in positions of power and authority, separating them from the community of the faithful."[88]

Richard Sipe's book *A Secret World* (1990) was widely cited to demonstrate the supposed neglect of celibacy regulations by many priests.[89] Sipe places the abuse issue in the context of the celibacy debate,[90] arguing,

> The celibate/sexual system that surrounds clerical culture fosters and often rewards psychosexual immaturity. . . . Child abuse by clergy, the tip of the iceberg, does not stand on its own . . . we are certain that the hierarchical and power structures beneath the surface are part of a secret world that supports abuse. . . . [W]hen the whole story of sexual abuse by presumed celibate clergy is told, it will lead to the highest corridors of Vatican City.[91]

From 1989 onward, clerical celibacy became a lively issue in the secular media no less than the religious press. The issue was discussed in publications as diverse as *Time*,[92] *Newsweek*,[93] *Jet*,[94] and *USA Today*,[95] as well as religious periodicals such as *Commonweal*,[96] *America*,[97] *Christian Century*,[98] and *US Catholic*.[99] On television, analyses of the abuse problem invariably concentrated on the theme of celibacy. The A&E program "Sins of the Fathers" favorably quoted church critics who seek "drastic" remedies "shutting down the seminaries or making celibacy an option for priests instead of a demand," while "many" saw a partial solution in ordaining women.[100] CNN's "Fall from Grace" similarly identified celibacy as a primary evil: the celibate priesthood offered "an attractive hiding place for men struggling with deviant sexual urges," "a safe hiding place for men struggling with sexual conflict."

Media coverage attempted to demonstrate freedom from bias, but the underlying assumptions were difficult to conceal. Following the scandal at the Capuchin school in Wisconsin, the lawyer for the victims stated that the problem arose from mandatory celibacy, for creating "a priestly world where 'women and children are the enemy.'" In reporting this remark, *Time* magazine continued, "Whether or not that is fair, the accumulating scandals signal the need for reform."[101]

Interpreting Clergy Abuse

The political and ecclesiastical implications of clergy abuse are apparent in the two major books that have so far appeared on the scandal: Berry's *Lead Us Not into Temptation* and Burkett and Bruni's *A Gospel of Shame*. Both perceive the individual cases as manifestations of a structural crisis, the roots of which they find in fundamental aspects of Catholic belief and practice as currently constituted, and both use the scandals to advocate sweeping changes in the church. Both present a picture of structural failings as thorough and damning as those depicted by the most vigorous anticlericals through the centuries.

Lead Us Not into Temptation was a widely reviewed and quoted best-seller that offered an effective manifesto for most of the major themes of contemporary liberal Catholicism. It succeeded in reaching both a popular and a professional audience because of its combination of writing styles and genres, beginning with a detailed "true-crime" reconstruction of the Gauthe case. Berry then suggests that cases like this are commonplace, and that in most the behavior of Catholic authorities has been cynical and disreputable. Although the church claims to be the children of "Mother Church," it is in fact a "dysfunctional family,"[102] based on "a warped elitism: priests and bishops above, shunning lay people below." "Harboring child molesters is akin to the dynamics of an incestuous family."[103] He has remarked elsewhere of the abuse cases that "every one of these stories is about the abuse of ecclesiastical power and about the ecclesiastical power structure trying to conceal the internal corruptions that have long been tolerated."[104]

Berry writes, "I had come to see pedophilia as part of a deeper ailment within a culture premised on celibacy,"[105] and a major portion of his book consists of a lengthy tract, "The Political Dynamics of Celibacy." He exposes the failings of clerical celibacy and its alleged by-products of homosexuality, pedophilia, misogyny, and hypocrisy. Following Sipe, he argues that celibacy was not part of the original teaching of Christianity, and cites numerous instances from the early and medieval church where clergy were known to be uncelibate. He describes the misogyny associated with this view and notes instances where celebrated saints and theologians demonstrate an apparent loathing of sexuality and the human body.

Berry argues consistently that celibacy is the major cause of many evils in the church, and blames celibacy for the overt "gay clericalism" flourishing in certain dioceses and the way in which homosexual subcultures have become rooted in the seminaries.[106] He contends that many of the notorious abuse cases of the 1980s had their origins in this milieu. "What did they expect in a church that shunted women to the ministerial margins and rewarded unmarried men?" Effective responses were to be found only in the end of mandatory celibacy and the introduction of a married priesthood. He shares the common liberal belief that these problems can be traced to the excessive power of the central church and the papal authorities. Berry refers to the morality that condemns all sexual activity outside marriage as the "Vatican mindset,"[107] and denounces "the corruption of clerical life in a nation of

60 million Catholics, which sends more money to the Vatican than any other nation on earth."[108]

Berry writes as a Catholic dissident. Burkett and Bruni agree with many of his positions, about the structural problems of the church and the particular problems caused by celibacy, but they also venture much further into what can only be described as a radically anticlerical position that parallels the anti-Catholic literature of previous centuries. They denounce the corruption of a church that "creates a class system—bishop above priest, priest above common man, man above woman, adult above child—that bestows privilege and respect in accordance with a person's role rather than merit, garb rather than deed."[109] Sexual abuse is an inevitable outcome of the church's present structure: "the kind of men attracted to its priesthood, the pressures placed on them, the status granted them and the hierarchy in which they were tucked away."[110] "Abuse thrives in hierarchical, authoritarian institutions—particularly sexually repressive ones. When experts describe such institutions, they seem to be characterizing the Catholic church."[111]

The book concludes with an explicitly religious message, calling for an advance beyond Catholicism to what the authors perceive as the primitive religious community advocated by Jesus Christ.[112] The final sentence presents the familiar contrast between the "official" and "real" churches in describing Cardinal Bernardin's refusal to attend the 1992 VOCAL conference; they quote Jeanne Miller: "It's not as if the Church didn't come to us tonight. The cardinal didn't come to the Church."[113] This radical rejection of "official" Catholicism appears quite regularly in the victims' rights movement and is not peculiar to *Gospel of Shame*. Burkett and Bruni suggest that victims have moved on from Catholicism to "finding in themselves a more mature faith—less dependent on deference than on conscience."[114] In the CNN film "Fall from Grace," similarly, VOCAL members assert, "We are the church," and the reporter notes, "Others say they no longer trust Catholicism but they have a stronger, more mature belief in God, and a deeper understanding of their role." Catholicism, it seems, is for the deferential, immature, and shallow.

Impact of the Scandals

The growing media consensus on the structural problems of the Catholic church has naturally inspired some angry reactions. Andrew Greeley describes the attention paid to celibacy in this matter as a manifestation of "bigotry," "intolerable anti-Catholic bigotry": "It is intellectually dishonest Catholic-bashing to blame celibacy for the problems of the church or the priesthood."[115] However, the campaign appears to have originated in Catholic circles, and to have had a significant impact on Catholics' perceptions of their own church.

Using a 1992 poll of American Catholics, Stephen Rossetti found a serious lack of confidence in priests and their relationships with children. Among lay respondents who did not know of an abuse case in their diocese, only half agreed with the statement "I believe that the church will safeguard the children entrusted to its care." The proportion in affected dioceses was 33 percent, and in parishes where scandals had occurred, it fell to 25 percent.[116] A similar gradation is found in numbers supporting priestly celibacy: from 32 percent in unaffected dioceses to 18 percent in parishes with known scandals.[117] Rossetti argues that "Catholics trust their priests less, and are less inclined to want their sons to be altar boys or priests. . . . Pedophilia is the lightning rod for disaffected Catholics who find their church unresponsive or their priests inadequate. . . . When people read of abuse by a priest, it is seen as the abuse not [by] a single priest but [by] the entire church."[118]

The consequences were especially dramatic in demands for the reform of church discipline and practice. Already in May 1992, before the worst publicity about the Porter case, a Gallup poll found that the number of American Catholics favoring women priests had grown to 67 percent, up from 40 percent in 1979 and 47 percent in 1985.[119] The same poll found that more than 70 percent supported married priests, up from 58 percent in 1983, and large majorities (in excess of 80 percent) favored the toleration of artificial contraception and of the use of condoms to prevent AIDS. In 1993 a *Newsweek* survey of American Catholics suggested that 71 percent of respondents favored the ordination of married men, and 62 percent supported the ordination of women.[120]

The consequences were still more dramatic in Canada. In 1989 the Canadian hierarchy began to encounter intense popular pressure to permit married priests, and surveys indicated that abuse scandals have been the chief factor in motivating support for reforms.[121] In a large 1993 survey, 37 percent of Canadian Catholics reported that their faith had been shaken by recent abuse scandals, and 64 percent agreed that the celibacy requirement was a major cause of sexual abuse by priests.[122] Liberal positions were now supported by substantial majorities: 84 percent for clerical marriage, 78 percent for women's ordination. Catholic sexual teachings had also lost favor, and the number approving of contraceptive use exceeded 90 percent.

In assessing the role of Catholic factions in constructing the abuse issue, it is useful to compare the actual situation of the past decade with what might hypothetically have occurred if a series of similar scandals had developed in an earlier period, for example the 1920s. The cases reported then would almost certainly have gained little credence within Catholic circles and would have been dismissed as the result of anti-Catholic bigotry. It is inconceivable that they would have been accepted sufficiently by Catholic groups and factions to be employed as political or ideological weapons. In forming this interpretation, Catholics would have been influenced by their recent historical experiences and the consciousness that persecution and discrimination were a likely reality, a view all the more likely for ethnic groups like the Irish and Poles. The circumstances of the 1980s were so different because of a major shift in the sociological character of the American church, which radically transformed cultural and political expectations. Large sections of educated opinion were actively predisposed to accept sinister interpretations of the hierarchy's behavior, especially in areas affecting sexuality and priestly privilege. Far from automatically rejecting the truthfulness of the charges, it was the Catholic intelligentsia who were most active in stating that the individual cases were only the visible manifestations of a very large hidden problem, a crisis that urgently needed to be exposed and confronted.

7

"Sins of the Fathers": The Feminist Response

A recent book on pedophilia and other sex crimes notes in passing that "*However quintessential its patriarchy*, the Catholic church is not alone in the perpetuation of attitudes that tolerate sexual assault."[1] This casual statement makes two seemingly natural assumptions that in fact reflect a substantial history of ideological development: respectively, that the Catholic church is the epitome of a form of bias or prejudice known as patriarchy, and that this patriarchalism contributes directly to clergy abuse. Both ideas are well represented in recent writing, for instance, in the work of Jason Berry and of Richard Sipe, and the fact that they can be presented without substantiation suggests the degree to which feminist arguments have permeated mainstream discourse in the theme of sexual abuse. "The sexism of the Catholic church"[2] is seen as a given.

Women's groups and feminist activists were instrumental in the discovery of child sexual abuse as a social problem, and it is not surprising that women's issues should have been so central to shaping the clergy-abuse issue. The involvement of clergy showed that molestation was ubiquitous, regardless of the pretensions or ideological claims of different groups, and the finding was useful in social and political controversies with the Catholic church. Moreover, feminist writing customarily expands the domain of the abuse problem to include relationships between clergy and adult women, and in this form ("clergy exploitation") the issue is employed to stigmatize patriarchal authority in other mainstream churches. All churches thus share to some degree in the "abuse crisis" recognized in the Catholic context and need to take comparable remedial measures.

This emphasis on the sins of the fathers supports claims that the patriarchal social system is founded upon the real or symbolic sexual oppression of the powerless, specifically women and children, and that the religious beliefs used to underpin this system are themselves based on abuse and hypocrisy. Within the churches themselves, the scandals provided additional justification for expanding the role of women, and for developing distinctively feminist theological and ritual structures.

Feminism and Sexual Abuse

When the modern women's movement emerged in the years after 1968, the themes of rape and sexual molestation were central to its political rhetoric.[3] These offenses were seen as analogous to lynching and terrorism against racial minorities and were framed as gender-based victimization in which one part of the population engages in behavior systematically intended to subdue and repress another part. This is the view expressed in Brownmiller's classic formulation of rape as a "conscious process of intimidation by which *all* men keep *all* women in a state of fear."[4] Initially, the chief concern was with the offenses such as rape and domestic violence that were committed against adult women, but by the early 1980s attention had expanded to included the molestation of children.

Child sexual abuse was increasingly contextualized with acts such as rape, domestic violence, and "femicide" as part of a vast problem of sexual violence.[5] This social crisis was attributed not to the deviant characteristics of certain individuals, but to masculine characteristics shaped by the structures of a male-dominated society. "Under patriarchy, whole groups of persons—women, children, and persons of color—are terrorized by sexual violence so that their existence is marginal."[6] Feminist literature employs sexual assault as an ideological weapon not so much against men as a category but against the "patriarchal" society they dominate, with the implication that the degree of patriarchy conditions the rate of sexual violence. These ideas have become widely accepted far beyond the circles of feminist activists or academics and have been popularized in the mass media through news articles and television programs, made-for-television movies, and magazine features. Feminist campaigns against sexual violence provide the movement with its most effective tools for social mobilization: protests against the pornographic materials believed to inspire rape; grassroots endeavors to assist the victims of rape and violence; school campaigns to warn children of the dangers of abuse and assault.

This approach to child molestation in general helped determine the feminist response to the more specific problem of clergy abuse. The ubiquity of sexual abuse meant that any institution dealing with children would be likely to encounter the problem, and this probability was all the greater when dealing with a patriarchal and (it was asserted) antifemale body such as the Catholic church. The "believe-the-children" ideology meant that feminists accepted the intrinsic likelihood of allegations against the clergy, while also suggesting the appropriate package of policy responses and safeguards.

Feminism in the Churches

The impact of clergy abuse was all the greater because feminism had made such rapid advances in the American churches, and issues concerning the role and importance of women were by the 1980s extremely controversial within the world of organized religion. The allegation that male clergy were systematically engaged in the exploitation of minors was a powerful weapon in such debates because it proved the need for a reevaluation of religious structures and attitudes that would be fundamental if not revolutionary. This was especially true within the Roman Catholic church but also affected other denominations.

Since the 1960s, changes in American society had resulted in a general weakening of traditional family structures and an increasingly independent role for women. Within the religious communities, some churches had accommodated women's demands for greater visibility and power, the "fomenting feminism" so crucial in "reshaping normative religious styles."[7] However, the Catholic church remained obdurate to calls for changes in attitudes toward matters such as divorce, abortion, and contraception, as well as to demands for women's ordination and an end to priestly celibacy.[8] In the moral and social issues that were pivotal to American politics during the 1980s, the Catholic church had become a prominent and powerful force on the side of patriarchal conservatism and traditional values.

Feminists reciprocated with protests that were strongly anticlerical and anti-Catholic, especially during open disputes between pro-choice and pro-life demonstrators. One common feminist slogan told the church, "Keep your rosaries out of our ovaries." When U.S. Surgeon General Joycelyn Elders addressed a crowd of pro-choice activists, she denounced pro-lifers, who were conducting a "love affair with the fetus" at the behest of "a celibate, male-dominated church."[9] For radical feminists, Catholicism was "a weary, dated religion where women are incubators and servants."[10] "The church is two hundred years behind the times . . . light-years behind."[11] For abortion-rights advocates such as Lawrence Lader, Catholic activism on abortion was part of a troubling "challenge to American pluralism," which raised serious doubts about the church's commitment to democratic values.[12]

These ideas obtained sympathy in the mainstream news media, which were generally sympathetic to women's demands for greater representation in the churches and in society at large. In 1991, for example, the nomination to the Supreme Court of Catholic-educated conservative Clarence Thomas occasioned a flurry of hostile cartoons depicting the sinister nuns and conniving bishops who would now influence secular policy in matters like abortion. Popular hostility to official Catholic attitudes was also suggested by another newspaper cartoon syndicated in 1994. A senior Catholic cleric is depicted stating, "We strongly condemn increased participation by radical groups in the upcoming UN population conference," while the priest accompanying him adds, "For example, say . . . women!"[13]

Meanwhile, women within the churches were being profoundly influenced by new social ideas. Catholic feminism originated in the late 1960s with the work of academics like Mary Daly.[14] At first, the primary demand was for women to be ordained as priests, and from 1975 onward the main pressure group was the Women's Ordination Conference, WOC. Campaigns of this sort had generally succeeded in mainline American churches by the 1970s, and the Episcopal church approved the reform in 1976. Beginning in the mid-1970s, the mainly Protestant World Council of Churches had regularly issued denunciations of sexism and patriarchal domination in the churches, but the Catholic church proved adamant on the ordination issue. An ongoing dialog between representatives of WOC and the NCCB initiated in 1979 reached deadlock in 1981.

Catholic feminism found a large constituency among present and former nuns, and among the thousands of women involved in institutes of theological education, both seminaries (Catholic and non-Catholic) and secular theological schools. This was a broad movement, including many moderates whose aspirations would largely have been met by incorporating women into the official structure of the church more or less as currently constituted. Feminist approaches influenced liberal reformers in the church and activists such as Rosemary Radford Ruether and Joan Chittister, who found a platform as columnists for the *National Catholic Reporter*.[15] When in 1994 the pope issued a statement categorically declaring that the prohibition on women priests was nonnegotiable and permanent, indeed eternal, NCR printed a cover depicting a woman saying Mass under the caption "Not Now, But One Day."[16]

The influence of the new ideas is indicated by opinion surveys, which suggested that by the late 1970s the ordination of women was favored by almost half of younger Catholics, those aged between eighteen and thirty.[17] On the basis of these surveys, about a third of the women in the cohort could be described as "feminist," with far more liberal attitudes on abortion and other sexual matters than those of their female elders.[18] A decade later, support for liberal causes was even stronger among younger Catholics.[19] Among "baby-boomer" Catholics today, 80 percent of women favor women's ordination.[20]

However, the implacable opposition of church policies to any such change transformed into a dissident act even a group of women's reciting the Mass in its present form, with one woman acting the role of priest. The focus of agitation now shifted from the priesthood to the whole nature of ministry and hierarchy, and the movement inevitably came to incorporate the insights of other radical groups. From liberation theology, Catholic feminists drew their belief that although authentic Christianity demanded a wholesale questioning of oppressive social structures, the church's male hierarchy exemplified the worst of these traditions. Its "absolute" morality merely reflected and reinforced the conventions of particular male-dominated societies over the centuries, and so did much of its theology. To identify God as male was to deify masculinity and male social structures, and Mary Daly has suggested that "if God is male, then the male is God."[21] The course of feminist influence can be traced through the gradual triumph of gender-neutral "inclusive" language in the liturgy and Scripture translation of most mainline denominations during the 1980s. Enemies of priestly celibacy have especially emphasized its misogynistic assumptions, what Sipe calls the "equations of unredeemed patriarchy" employed to justify the sexual prohibition.[22] A Benedictine nun told a conference of Catholic women in 1986 that "the Roman church, presided over by a Supreme Pontiff and a male, celibate, hierarchically ordered clerical class since the fourth century, has deliberately, even if unconsciously, denied itself access to the experience of women's spiritual gifts."[23]

It was in these years that Christian feminism developed its most radical critique and rejected many aspects of traditional Christian orthodoxy, including the uniqueness of the Christian revelation. The Catholic church argued that it held a special role as the guardian of divine truth, and that other religions at best might have a small share in this insight. Catholic feminists enthusiastically explored what they believed to be authentic and empowering rituals from other religious traditions, including Native American belief and "Wiccan" paganism.[24] During the 1980s, feminist thealogy (*sic*) drew heavily on "Goddess" traditions, which were also associated with radical environmentalism.[25] Appropriate ritual practices were strictly nonhierarchical, involving for example the passing of bread and wine by members of a congregation, rather than consecration by one (male) priest.

During the early 1980s the radicalism and self-confidence of the Catholic feminists developed rapidly, and the more extreme groups attracted new interest.[26] Through the work of scholars such as Elizabeth Schüssler-Fiorenza, feminist biblical scholarship attained wide visibility.[27] The movement developed a number of institutional structures, with several interlinked organizations. woc held national conferences in 1975 and 1979, and in 1983 the various groups were brought together by the "Woman-Church Speaks" conference, held in Chicago. The following year, the new movement began regular meetings under the name Women-Church Convergence. In 1986 another organizational focus was provided by the first annual conference, "Women in the Church."

Between 1982 and 1986 the ideas of the movement were disseminated by a series of conferences, retreats, and "consciousness-raising" events held across the country, often under the auspices of Catholic colleges and religious institutions. In 1985 Rosemary Radford Ruether's book *Women Church* proposed a wholesale reorganization of the institutional church on the model of the "base communities" pioneered by Latin American liberation theologians and identified these spontaneous grassroots communities with "covens." By the mid-1980s the "Women-Church" movement was developing so rapidly and was so distancing itself from traditionally Christian concepts that continued affiliation with the churches seemed tenuous.[28]

The conflicts were especially intense for Catholic feminists, but similar issues affected mainstream Protestant denominations. In 1993, for example, some two thousand women attended a Minneapolis conference entitled "Re-Imagining," sponsored by the Presbyterian and Methodist churches.[29] The gathering included a feminist eucharist involving milk and honey, and prayers were offered to "Sophia," the feminine Wisdom of God. Traditional Christian concepts and practices were rejected in startling language, so that one speaker suggested that "I don't think we need a theory of atonement at all. I don't think we need folks hanging on crosses and blood dripping and weird stuff." Catholic feminist Mary Hunt remarked on the centrality of the quest for justice: "Whether it is Christian or not is frankly, darling, something about which I no longer give a pope."[30] Hunt has also denounced much traditional Catholic teaching on sexual matters as constituting "theological pornography" in its own right. At "Re-Imagining," Beverly Harrison denounced the Roman Catholic hierarchy as "the pedophile capital of the world."[31] Like the Catholic liberals, the feminists were similarly warning of the necessity for a break from the official church, a "second reformation," "much more basic and important to the health of humankind than the first."

The Theology of Abuse

Even before the immense public interest in abuse by members of the male clergy, the new feminist activists and theologians were already incorporating concepts of abuse, victimization, and domestic violence as weapons into their assault on religious patriarchy. One important text on this theme was *Sexual Violence: The Unmentionable Sin*, by Marie M. Fortune, which explored the contribution that religious groups could make to the healing of sexual assault, a term that included battering, rape, and child abuse.[32] This work placed the issue of sexual violence firmly on the agenda of religious feminism and stimulated discussion about the churches' role in causing and preventing maltreatment and exploitation.[33] Reports and data about rape, abuse, incest, harassment and battering were collected and publicized by groups that served as women's caucuses in the mainstream churches, such as the Commission on Women and the Churches in the United Presbyterian Church, the United Methodist Office of Women in Crisis. The same theme emerged as major issues in denominational publications such as *The Lutheran* and *Episcopal Life*.[34]

For the feminist theologians, sexual abuse and violence were rooted in the patriarchal structure of the whole society, including the churches, and only by thorough social reconstruction could they be eradicated. The crimes of patriarchy were a glaring manifestation of structural sin, which merited ecclesiastical condemnation quite as vigorous as that previously accorded to such individual failings as fornication or adultery. In the feminist literature, child sexual abuse became a paradigm of social injustice and absolute sin, and the rhetoric that now emerged naturally foreshadowed much of the later attack on the Catholic church over clergy abuse.

Already in 1985, Ruether's proposed liturgies for the Women-Church movement included a "disaffiliation from patriarchy," a kind of exorcism that commands, "Powers of domestic violence, which assault children, women, and the weak and elderly in the home and hold them in bondage to fear and self-hatred, begone!"[35] Other texts included the "rite of healing for wife battering," which drew heavily on Del Martin's influential feminist text *Battered Wives*.[36] The "ritual of healing for an incest victim" "estimated that one in three females are sexually abused as children by their fathers or other male relatives or friends of the family."[37] Freudian errors had interpreted these genuine experiences as childhood fantasies and dreams, so that in consequence, "sexually abused children carry the guilt and shame of these experiences much of their lives, and it is probably one of the biggest factors in female mental illness."[38] Another feminist collection, *Sexual Assault and Abuse,* similarly contained a section of appropriate liturgies, including "Devotions" and "Services of Healing" for the sexually abused.[39]

Sexual exploitation and violence are repeatedly emphasized in these texts as structural flaws: "rapists are the shock troops of patriarchy, while wife batterers are the army of occupation."[40] These remarks could have come from any feminist tract of the decade, but they are here placed in a decisively religious context, with the patriarchal church held responsible for the "holocaust of women," including those thousands killed as witches and heretics.[41] The Catholic church is stigmatized because it "has taken the lead in the crusade against women's control of their own bodies."[42] Another strong advocate of feminist positions is Matthew Fox, who complains of the manifestations of "adultism" that have so blighted our culture, to create "a society that devours its youth." Adultism and male oppression lead to mass child abuse and child pornography, and to "the religious and spiritual abuse of our child-rcn" in the form of the Christian hostility to sexuality and the body. This constitutes "another instance of sexual abuse that feeds the other, more blatant kind of pornography in our culture."[43]

In 1989 an impressive range of leading feminist theologians contributed to a major work, *Christianity, Patriarchy and Abuse.*[44] Essays by Marie Fortune, Rosemary Radford Ruether, Mary Hunt, and others suggest the truly radical implications of recent feminist theology, especially the "theology of abuse," which is employed to justify revolutionary revisions of Christian theology. In this model, God becomes the ultimate abuser, the patriarchal prototype of the molesting father or priest, and the atoning sacrifice of his son is an act of monstrous tyranny. In Christianity, "divine child abuse is paraded as salvific."[45] "As an aspect of Trinitarian thought, Christology is often based on implicit elements of child abuse."[46] One Episcopal feminist challenged the theology of the crucifixion on the grounds that "to me, it is an abusive act of a father toward a child. The theology of sin in the church is all about human worthlessness." Another from the same denomination suggested that people "see our Christology as a prescription for child abuse."[47] "We need to ask whether the image of God in the crucifixion is abusive."[48] The Trinity becomes the celestial archetype of the dysfunctional family.

Both in theory and practice (it is said), patriarchal Christianity justifies child abuse, and abuse in turn contributes to indoctrinating its victims into the values of patriarchal religion. The feminist theologians reject the necessity for humility and penance, contrary to traditional Christian virtues of self-abnegation and redemptive suffering, and urge the virtues of pride and self-empowerment. Even forgiveness is prohibited in many instances because the offense of child abuse is so immeasurably severe, and because forgiving gets in the way of the "healing" of the alleged victim. In this view, guilt and the sense of sin represent the psychic scars of primal rape and abuse suffered by the believer, hence "we do not need to be saved by Jesus' death from some original sin. We need to be liberated from the oppression of racism, classism and sexism, that is, from patriarchy. . . . Peace was not made by the Cross. . . . [S]uffering is never redemptive, and suffering cannot be redeemed."[49]

Feminists and Clergy Abuse

In such an intellectual environment, the leaders of the traditional churches are already implicitly portrayed as exploitative patriarchal figures participating in gender oppression and intimidation. Once evidence became available that some clergy had been participating in literal rather than metaphorical sexual abuse, these charges would be widely cited as confirmation for the validity of feminist positions in religion.[50] Feminist groups thus had a strong predisposition to accept charges of sexual abuse by clergy and to integrate them into a theological and political framework. They also had a disproportionate opportunity to promote their particular interpretation because of the role of Marie Fortune and other feminist writers as visible and knowledgeable experts to whom the media could resort for commentary on the "abuse crisis." In 1994, Joan Chittister was one of the speakers at the national Link-Up conference, where she joined such familiar faces as Thomas Doyle, Richard

Sipe, and Jeanne Miller. She argued that the church's abuse crisis stemmed from its patriarchal nature and asserted that the solution was to be found in making domination "a sin rather than a right."[51]

The publications of the religious feminists do not necessarily reach a wide public, but their assumptions and commonplaces have enjoyed an enormous influence, to the extent that they almost represent a social orthodoxy. By 1992 even a committee of the Canadian Conference of Catholic Bishops could state, "Child sexual abuse flourishes in a society that is based on competition and power, and which is undermined by sexual exploitation and violence against women."[52]

Since 1990 there have been lengthy and repeated discussions of clergy abuse in the secular mass media directed chiefly at a women's audience, in magazines as diverse as *McCall's*[53] and *Ms.*[54] *Vanity Fair* published a lengthy investigative study of the Dino Cinel case,[55] while *Redbook* offered a reminiscence by "survivor" Cristine Clark.[56] All emphasize the familiar feminist themes: the frequency of the offense, its roots in patriarchal values and beliefs, and the structural inability of the church to eradicate the problem without abandoning traditional gender roles. Each story was told through a case study of one particular woman and her struggles to obtain justice. The *Ms.* article was characteristic in its portrayal of a teenager who had allegedly been sexually involved with seven Catholic priests. This individual story was then used as a foundation for an account of an apparently widespread problem, the "sacred secret" of sexual liaisons between clergy and parishioners, that occurred in all denominations.[57] The article cited such cases from Protestant, Jewish, and even Buddhist groups, as well as Catholic, so that "sexual abuse at religious institutions seems to be epidemic."

As in most of the feminist literature, "clergy sex abuse" is here taken to include sexual relationships between clergy and adult women, as well as the molestation of children.[58] In this extended sense, clergy abuse is contextualized alongside other forms of female victimization, including rape, "femicide," and incest, all of which arise from the unjust distribution of power in a patriarchal society.[59] The broader idea of clergy exploitation emerged during the mid-1980s, and incest parallels were freely drawn: ". . . similar to incest . . . what takes place is not so much an expression of human sexuality. It is rather a misuse of power and a breach of trust."[60] Writing in *Christian Century*, Pamela Cooper-White is one of many to emphasize the role of unequal power relations in this type of abuse, and draws an extended parallel between clergy sex abuse and wife-battering.[61]

Clergy exploitation also shared the stereotypical characteristics of sexual harassment, an area in which feminist views had been rapidly popularized in the early 1990s. The watershed event was the televised Senate hearings on the nomination of Clarence Thomas for the U.S. Supreme Court in 1991, when Anita Hill testified about Thomas's misconduct toward her. Also influential was the Tailhook scandal of 1991–1993, in which navy fliers were accused of inappropriate sexual conduct and harassment, an affair that placed harassment in the context of sexual violence and coercion. Following so closely on the Anita Hill affair, Tailhook reaffirmed the feminist interpretation of sexual harassment as pervasive and destructive. Federal courts, meanwhile, expanded the right to sue and gain substantial damages in harassment cases, and the number of actions brought in public and private institutions began to spiral upward.

Marie Fortune contextualizes the child-abuse scandals with both the Hill and Tailhook cases, and compares the relatively effective response of the navy to the inadequate policies of the organized churches of all denominations. She remarks, "How equally astonishing it would be to see another patriarchal institution, the church, respond in similar unequivocal fashion to the endemic problem of sexual abuse by its clergy."[62] Fortune complains about the tendency of both ecclesiastical and civil authorities to disbelieve and disparage victims, suggesting the intense hostility to women in mainstream religious systems. To quote *Ms.* magazine, "Reaching back to their Biblical roots, some Judeo-Christian clerics blame the woman." Other writers draw on the literary analogy of the *Scarlet Letter*.[63]

The expansion of "clergy abuse" to include adult heterosexual relationships ("clergy exploitation") deserves emphasis.[64] Fortune's best-known book, *Is Nothing Sacred?*, concerns a minister who had engaged in sexual relationships with at least six of his adult female parishioners.[65] Although there were allegations of coercion of force, the definition of *abuse* in this instance was based on accusations such as the following: the clergyman "misused the power and authority of his ministerial office to manipulate, coerce or intimidate parishioners. . . . These included giving promises of marriage, use of abusive and profane language regarding church members, threats of retaliation, and misrepresentation."[66] Fortune argues that the minister was given licence by "the patriarchal structure . . . to use his pastoral role and position in the church to engage in the abuse of women for years and then protected him from the consequences. . . .The patriarchy prevented the women from getting justice within the church."[67] He was assisted by "the hesitancy of some men to confront other men's behavior."[68] For the analysis of religious patriarchy, Fortune refers the reader to the works of Ruether, Schüssler-Fiorenza, Daly, Beverly Harrison, and others.

Fortune did much to popularize this interpretation of "clergy abuse," all the more successfully because of the popularity of her work in mainstream Protestant media. When discussing the prevalence of "abuse," she cited the instances of Bruce Ritter and James Porter alongside that of an Episcopal diocese sued for failing to prevent an affair that occurred between one of its priests and a woman parishioner.[69] (See chapter 8 for this case; Fortune appeared as an expert witness for the woman plaintiff.) She then declared that "as many as 38 percent of clergy are sexually involved with their congregants," a figure that whatever its origins clearly does not solely refer to child abuse. Other accounts repeat the figure that 10 percent of clergy are or have been sexually involved with someone other than a spouse.[70] *Ms.* similarly cites high statistics to substantiate the claim that clergy habitually engage in inappropriate sexual activity with parishioners or employees, and the assumption is that those receiving such advances are adult: "On the whole, religious institutions have chosen to protect their offending clergy and themselves rather than the *women victims*."[71]

The rhetorical goal here is to enhance the gravity of a behavior that many would not find reprehensible (adult sexual relationships by clergy) by associating it with the universally condemned act of child molestation. Applying the generic term *clergy abuse* thus links the two behaviors on the debatable grounds that both involve an abuse of trust by figures holding a form of patriarchal authority. In the early 1990s the feminist concept of clergy exploitation was propagated and discussed in the workshops and seminars that were held by most denominations in the aftermath of the abuse scandals. Even in the Catholic archdiocese of Los Angeles, the concept of sexual exploitation was incorporated in the sweeping 1994 policy on abuse by priests: "When adults are involved, sexual abuse occurs when a priest takes advantage sexually of another person, when there are unwanted sexual advances or suggestions, or when the sexual contact takes place in the context of providing pastoral care."[72]

The Uses of Abuse

In the Catholic church the issue of misconduct with minors provided a weapon in the arsenal of reformers anxious to restructure the church away from traditional concepts of hierarchy, male dominance, and clerical elitism. In other denominations, the problem served a similar function, but necessarily cast in broader terms. The exact definition of the question differed somewhat in bodies where the reformers had already made significant progress. By the 1980s most of the traditional mainline Protestant churches had married clergy of both sexes, and the denominations were broadly sympathetic to liberal approaches on social issues. This was certainly true of the major Methodist, Presbyterian, Episcopal, and Lutheran denominations, for whom the crucial areas of conflict had now shifted to even more sensitive questions, such as as the ordination of actively homosexual clergy and the blessing of homosexual marriages.[73]

However, "abuse" and harassment were still cited to justify the need for defending and advancing reform. In the United Methodist church, for example, several churches experienced harassment and misconduct cases in the early 1990s that were generally reported in the media as involving "clergy abuse" or "church abuse," terms that emphasized the grave and predatory nature of the conduct.[74] These incidents provided the basis for extensive debate at regional or national denominational conferences and permitted women's groups and especially women clergy to assert their grievances. The consequence was the codification of ethical and professional policies that strictly defined the limits of appropriate sexual conduct. Apart from providing a possible legal resort for women in the denomination, the mere existence of the codes was a potent symbolic statement of the need for protection and affirmed the feminist belief that male clergy were likely to exploit women. Victory was made easier because it was difficult to mount an effective opposition: few male clergy wished to appear less than zealous in the campaign against "abuse" and hence were reluctant to speak or vote against a motion condemning abusive pastors.

The very term *clergy abuse* experienced a metamorphosis in those Protestant denominations, where concern was expressed about the sexual abuse and harassment of clergy by clergy: specifically of women ministers by male pastors, seminary professors, and congregational leaders.[75] By linking this behavior to the emotive term *abuse*, the new generation of women clergy were asserting their dignity and professional standing, all the more necessary in light of frequent charges that feminist clergy and theologians were advancing heterodox or unbiblical views. The language of abuse and sexual violence was metaphorically extended to cover such polemics as well as the actual behavior. Among Presbyterians, for example, conservative and evangelical factions denounced the "Re-Imaginings 1993" conference as neopaganism or witchcraft; in response, feminists rejected criticisms as "spiritual rape."[76]

The integration of the abuse issue into continuing factional polemics can be illustrated by the experience of the Episcopal church, which had already accepted a considerable redefinition of traditional gender roles.[77] Three women bishops were consecrated between 1989 and 1993, and the presiding bishop was sufficiently open to dialog with homosexual groups to address the convention of Integrity, the Episcopal counterpart of the Catholic Dignity.[78] There were even irregular ordinations of actively homosexual clergy in these years. By Roman Catholic standards, the liberals had already triumphed in the Episcopal church, but internal debate was still fierce, and there were powerful conservative and traditionalist organizations like Episcopalians United and the Episcopal Synod of America.

As in the Catholic church, matters of gender and sexual preference continued to divide the Episcopal factions, and here too, the abuse issue was used by the liberal and feminist wings to attack what was depicted as the pervasive patriarchy of the traditional male-dominated church. There were well-publicized incidents involving clergy in sexual relationships with women, affairs that earned public condemnation as "abusive" because the women had approached them in a pastoral or counseling capacity and could therefore assert that a breach of professional responsibility was involved. Some philandering ministers were termed "serial abusers." This epithet is effective because it rhetorically unites the stereotypical characteristics of both compulsive sexually violent offenders and child molesters, although the behavior concerned involved neither force nor minor victims.[79]

Throughout 1991 and 1992 the abuse issue was frequently discussed in the editorials and correspondence columns of major denominational papers such as *Episcopal Life*, with typical headlines declaring "Exploitation a Major Church Problem." The topic was the basis for a well-attended debate at the church's triennial General Convention, which met in Phoenix, Arizona, in 1991; this gathering was addressed by Marie Fortune, who suggested that all churches "are in crisis over the long hidden issue of sexual abuse."[80] The convention agreed on a statement that "declares sexual abuse, exploitation, coercion and harassment of adults and minors by clergy and church employees are abuses of trust and contrary to Christian character" and established the Committee on Sexual Exploitation to develop a policy and code of conduct on clergy abuse and to report on its work to the next General Convention at Indianapolis in 1994.

As in the Roman Catholic church, the Episcopal response to the "abuse crisis" involved quite draconian measures that in effect accepted the guilt of an accused minister before he had been tried or convicted in either a formal trial or internal disciplinary proceedings. Statutes of limitations were extended and are to be counted from the time that an offense is "discovered" or recollected instead of when it is alleged to have occurred, and standards of proof in such cases were reduced from "beyond a reasonable doubt" to "clear and convincing evidence."[81] Conservative clergy attacked these reforms as unfair and uncanonical; women clergy denounced them as inadequate. As in the Methodist church, the call for emergency legislation implied a crisis that needed urgent action. Clergy abuse, broadly defined, again proved a vital ideological weapon in cementing and expanding feminist gains and in stigmatizing opposition as sinister and "patriarchal."

Conclusion

Feminists stood to gain greatly from the discrediting of institutions that presented the most vigorous opposition to their political causes, but the expanding concept of clergy abuse was valuable in other ways. Feminist claims-makers successfully defined the problem of abuse by clergy in a broad way that would cause the greatest benefit to themselves ideologically and, as they believed, to women as a group. They were here employing a familiar rhetorical technique: seeking to use an issue that is widely known (and accepted as posing a real social danger) to expand the domain of this known issue to include other behaviors that do not obviously appear to be related. In terms of social-problem theory, the feminist expansion of the abuse concept was a model of successful interest-group politics.

Political and ideological conflicts ensured that the abuse cases would be employed to produce the worst possible view of the institutional failings believed to have produced the offenses. However, this rhetorical activity was made easier by social changes that created an environment highly favorable to the making and establishing of claims about the extent and seriousness of the problem. Legal developments in particular contributed to the damage potential of the individual cases and provided a real incentive for the reporting and publicizing of incidents. The legal context must therefore be understood because it created a critical forum in which activists could put forth their demands.

8

The Legal Environment

If a scandal like the Porter affair had erupted many years earlier, say, during the mid-1950s, church authorities would have feared social consequences very different from those imagined by their modern-day counterparts. In the 1950s a hypothetical priest-abuse scandal might well have affected the political position of the culprit's superiors. The affair would have been discussed for its likely impact on anti-Catholic movements and politics, and might have affected the electoral position of Catholic-supported candidates or parties. Earlier still, there might have been fears of riots and social disorder. However, the worst speculations about the case's impact would have differed radically from modern circumstances in that they would not have included a financial or legal impact vaguely comparable to that of the recent cases. When observers of the mid-1980s considered the likelihood of future abuse scandals, it was natural to emphasize the financial dimension because damages from legal actions might well run into billions of dollars. Incidents of this sort can now be very expensive for those adjudged guilty of malpractice or professional misconduct, and successful plaintiffs can receive enormous sums of money. This may seem an obvious point, but litigation of this sort is a relatively new phenomenon in American history, and the legal environment that permits it has developed quite recently, mainly in the past quarter century.

Intensive litigation and high damage awards effectively create a range of interest groups with a powerful interest in discovering and exposing new clerical-abuse cases, and in the most visible public forum. Apart from individual victims of abuse, potential beneficiaries of the new environment include attorneys and the therapists and others likely to serve as expert witnesses. Legal circumstances vastly enhance the likelihood that individual instances of clerical misconduct will be reported, and that each particular abuse lawsuit will in turn encourage the reporting and prosecution of new cases. Conversely, it becomes far less likely that a victim will forgo resorting to formal legal processes following the recognition or recollection of abuse because this decision might mean renouncing a multimillion-dollar legal settlement.

Litigation is actively encouraged by a number of trends in contemporary social ideology, especially the movements asserting the rights of children and victims of sexual violence. In this view, vigorously pursuing a lawsuit is by no means a manifestation of greed or vengeance; it seeks a higher social goal. It gives the opportunity to publicize a grave injustice and perhaps to protect future potential victims, as well as to seek redress for individual wrongs. An urge for retribution might be combined with a belief that litigation promotes healing for the victim or the family concerned. Only where an individual possesses a strong countervailing ideology of absolute loyalty to the institutional church, and thus a wish to avoid embarrassing it, is it likely that he or she would fail to take advantage of such clear opportunities.

The legal system has thus played a vital role in the definition and shaping of the clergy-abuse problem. Moreover, legal ideas and doctrines contributed to focusing the issue on the Roman Catholic church, as opposed to any of the less centralized or bureaucratic organizations whose ministers had been implicated in misconduct.

The Litigation Explosion

The proliferating lawsuits over child abuse should be seen in the context of the "litigation explosion." This trend was first noted in the 1960s, but it can be traced ultimately to the reform of the Federal Rules of Civil Procedure in 1938, which expanded the access of litigants to the federal courts.[1] During the 1980s there were frequent complaints that excessive litigation had become so severe a problem as to cause a "liability crisis," in which hospitals, child-care facilities, and others were unable to obtain insurance. In retrospect, much about this "crisis" appears suspect in that at least some of the difficulties arose from self-interested complaints by the medical profession and others about the size of malpractice awards by juries, and the insurance companies had aggravated the situation by irresponsible marketing.[2] However, it is true that damage awards have become substantially larger since the 1960s because courts expanded the permissible grounds that a jury might take into account in assessing payments to include intangible factors such as fear and emotional distress.[3] Currently, an award in a personal injury suit in Great Britain might have been anywhere from thirty to a hundred times larger if the case had been tried in a comparable American court. Punitive damages have also become more common since the 1960s. The size of awards rose inexorably following a series of heavily publicized product liability cases in the late 1970s and early 1980s, such as the $125 million award in the 1978 Ford Pinto case. These judgments created an expectation about the appropriate level of damages to be expected from future juries.[4]

The United States is genuinely characterized by a much higher level of civil litigation than comparable Western countries, and it has many more lawyers per capita. Reforms of legal procedure since the midcentury have made it easier for American lawyers to begin actions without having to define precisely the grounds of the alleged malpractice or misconduct, in the hope that substantive evidence of wrongdoing might emerge during the process of discovery. American courts also differ from European in the range of evidence that is regarded as admissible in civil suits and in the use of experts paid for by the contending parties themselves.[5]

International differences have grown enormously in recent decades, in part because the American legal profession abandoned earlier ethical restrictions on seeking clients or fomenting lawsuits, and the increasing acceptability of contingency-fee arrangements makes litigation both more likely and more profitable. Professional restrictions on lawyers advertising their services were withdrawn by a series of decisions by courts and bar associations during 1976 and 1977. In 1985 the U.S. Supreme Court declared that lawyers could actively canvass for clients wishing to sue a particular company or institution.[6] Other court decisions of the 1960s and 1970s facilitated the launching of class-action suits. Taken together, these reforms constituted a deregulation of the business of litigation at least as significant as any of the other industrial or commercial reorganizations of these years. Peter Huber describes these events as a "liability revolution" based on the fundamental assumption "that most accidents have preventable outside causes that can be effectively deterred by litigation."[7]

Various areas of the law have successively attracted the interest of attorneys, and a similar pattern can be discerned in each. A few celebrated decisions created precedents that were exploited by lawyers and their clients, and there swiftly emerged a subfield specializing in that particular type of law. Once litigation developed in a given area, it was likely to snowball because the plaintiff stood an excellent chance of gaining at least a partial victory. Throughout the 1980s about 60 percent of personal injury cases decided by juries were won by the plaintiffs, and that does not include the numerous cases in which a compromise settlement was reached prior to verdict. In such instances, "from a cost-benefit analysis, it's cheaper for the deep pockets to settle rather than to try the case and win it."[8]

Initially, suits were chiefly aimed at wealthy institutions such as municipal governments, but the growth of litigation resulted in a general recognition of a need for liability insurance among all sorts of professional groups and agencies rendering services to the public. Ironically, this in turn increased the likelihood that these institutions would themselves become the targets of profitable suits. In the 1960s much of the activity concentrated on personal-injury and malpractice litigation, with product liability as a major interest in the next decade. During the 1980s litigation affected an ever-increasing range of professionals and service providers. For example, suits alleging improper contact between psychiatrists or psychologists and their women patients became so common that in 1985 the insurance industry officially excluded coverage for this form of liability.[9]

Litigating Child Abuse

The growing emphasis on child abuse cases in the 1980s reflected radically new social and legal attitudes toward the credibility of child witnesses, and the accuracy of memories recollected by adults who had been victimized as children. Molestation cases thus became far easier to litigate successfully. In the mid-1980s day-care centers and play schools were hit by a series of liability claims arising from alleged instances of child maltreatment. In addition, courts and legislators largely accepted the expansive charges made in these years about the scale of the behavior and its damaging consequences.

One striking index of the new attitudes was the rapid spread of mandatory re-porting statutes in the 1970s and early 1980s.[10] Many states passed laws requiring individuals or institutions who suspected child abuse to report that behavior to the police or social services. Such laws attributed to child protection an overriding social importance that outweighed notions of professional confidentiality, and some went so far as to deny the privilege traditionally accorded to conversations between a lawyer and a client or remarks made to a priest or minister.[11] Nor was this a mere oversight; several states discussed clergy exemption but specifically decided not to grant it in these cases, despite the potential for severe conflicts between church and state. In theory at least, this even covered remarks heard by a Catholic priest in con-fession, though no jurisdiction has hitherto pressed charges in these circumstances. The threat of abuse was seen as sufficiently serious as to demand the reduction or elimination of traditional clergy exemptions and privileges under law and to create a "pending gauntlet to the free exercise" of religion.[12]

By the mid-1980s little prophetic skill was needed to realize that church insti-tutions were shortly to encounter serious legal difficulties with molestation suits, especially because traditional internal defenses were withering. In earlier years canon law provided excommunication for any Catholic who sought redress against a priest or religious in a secular court, and in the 1920s a notorious ecclesiastical dis-pute in Rhode Island led to a group of sixty laymen's being excommunicated for suing their bishop and diocese in a dispute over parochial schools.[13] Because most victims of abuse by priests came from Catholic families, this was a valuable deterrent for potential litigants as long as excommunication remained a viable weapon, which it had long ceased to be by 1980.

There was also some doubt whether church institutions were vulnerable to litiga-tion of the sort then assailing the schools and kindergartens because at least some were covered by the doctrine of charitable immunity. In Massachusetts, for example, suits against charitable institutions were limited to $20,000, which by the 1980s ap-peared paltry. Obstacles to litigation were highlighted in 1984 and 1985: the liability suit following the death of Christopher Schultz was once more in the news, and feminist attorney Gloria Allred instituted a pioneering suit on behalf of Rita Milla, an adult woman who had had sexual relations with a number of Catholic clergy.[14] Both suits failed, and the court in the Milla case asserted that the archdiocese of Los Angeles could not be held liable for behavior by priests "beyond the course and scope of employment." However, the fact that the cases were brought and reported suggests a changing legal environment, and as early as 1982 NCCB/USCC staff were discussing civil liability dangers with two dioceses facing abuse scandals.[15] Sympto-matic of new attitudes, it was also in 1984 that the Boy Scouts of America was being assailed by abuse lawsuits that were beginning to demand redress from the organi-zation rather than the individual offender.[16]

The legal situation was revolutionized by the Gauthe settlement and the Roemer case.[17] In 1988, Father Peter McCutcheon was held liable for civil damages in con-nection with the molestation of three boys, on grounds of negligence, malpractice by a member of the clergy, and assault.[18] In 1990 the lawsuit against Father Thomas

Adamson was the first to involve damages that were punitive rather than merely compensatory, on grounds that the church's behavior had been reckless as well as negligent. In the late 1980s the courts became less willing to accept that churches were completely protected by the doctrine of charitable immunity, a concept denounced by Jeffrey Anderson as "archaic, antiquated, outrageous . . . the vestiges of that influence that religious organizations have exercised in lawmaking in our culture."[19]

Clergy Abuse in the Courts

Successful lawsuits proliferated from 1985 onward.[20] By the start of 1993 there were two thousand suits nationwide involving Catholic clergy alone, and the number was escalating month by month.[21] During 1991 the archdiocese of Chicago paid $1.8 million for therapy and in damage judgments to victims, and Andrew Greeley has plausibly extrapolated from this fact that the Catholic church in the United States was spending $50 million a year by the 1990s.[22] Berry estimates a financial loss to the Catholic church of $400 million by 1992. This is calculated on the basis of adding damage settlements ($200 million), legal expenses ($165 million), and medical expenses ($41 million).[23] All these figures have since increased substantially, lending credence to estimates that total costs by the end of the decade might exceed $1 billion.

The attractiveness of the church as a target for litigation is not difficult to explain. At the most cynical level of interpretation, the church represents a multibillion-dollar economic enterprise with vast holdings in property and real estate. Its total assets in the United States in 1986 had a possible value of $200 billion.[24] In 1984 the Chicago archdiocese alone reported assets of $2.3 billion in real estate and securities, the New York archdiocese, $1.2 billion—and these figures do not include the property of colleges, hospitals, and religious orders located in those metropolitan areas. Measured another way, the expenditures of the Milwaukee archdiocese during 1993 reached $1.25 billion. Ecclesiastical lawsuits also had the practical advantage that it was easy to establish a chain of responsibility. Many dioceses operate as a "corporation sole," which means that the bishops "take total control of all real estate, stocks and assets in their diocese, and no internal or external check can limit their power. The individual bishop and his aides reign as a one man corporation."[25] This created the opportunity for a cleric like Chicago's Cardinal Cody to rule as a virtual despot. It also raised the danger that litigation would target the diocesan authorities who were liable for actions carried out by priests in the course of their employment, under the familiar legal doctrine of *respondeat superior.* Detailed record keeping provided a paper trail that could not only demonstrate a pattern of official misconduct in one particular case but also might lead to the names of other suspected malefactors.

The sums involved might be substantial. When Stephen Cook accused Cardinal Bernardin and another priest, he demanded $10 million in damages. During 1994 alone, the archdiocese of New York faced suits demanding $500 million for the repeated abuse charged against Father Edward Pipala. The archdiocese also faced a large suit from a man who said he had been abused by Father Daniel Calabrese, and who sought damages of $25 million from the priest and a similar amount from his archdiocesan superiors. Such sums were far from typical, but even the "ordinary" judgments were expensive. The diocese of Camden paid more than $3 million to settle charges against nine of its priests,[26] and the diocese of Altoona-Johnstown paid almost $2 million in a case resulting from abuse by Father Francis Luddy. In the United States the average settlement currently runs at about $1 million a victim. The large sums were justified by litigants on the basis of the extreme psychic trauma alleged to have been caused by abuse, damage too severe ever to be compensated fully. As Dennis Gaboury wrote, "How much does it cost to rape a child in the state of Massachusetts?"[27]

Though most attention has focused on U.S. conditions, very large sums have also featured in the Canadian clergy lawsuits, despite the traditional reluctance of that country's courts to emulate the largesse of their U.S. counterparts. In the case of the Ontario Christian Brothers, plaintiffs have demanded compensation in the tens of millions of dollars.[28] Clergy-abuse suits have been instrumental in dramatically increasing both the expectations of Canadian litigants and the attitudes of the juries to whom they pleaded their cases.

There are already a few well-known American attorneys who specialize in clergy-abuse cases.[29] By far the best known is Jeffrey Anderson of St Paul, Minnesota, who since 1984 has specialized in representing alleged victims of abuse by priests and other clergy, mainly Catholic but also including Episcopalians.[30] By 1991 he was litigating more than eighty cases of clergy abuse around the country, including those of David Figueroa and the victims of Father Thomas Adamson; by 1993, more than two hundred clients in twenty-six states. "Geographically these cases are coast to coast."[31] Some attorneys may be sincerely dedicated to obtaining justice for their clients in the face of perceived church villainy, and Anderson in particular represents some individuals on a *pro-bono* basis, but for others the potentially lucrative rewards of church litigation are an obvious temptation.

Expanding the Liability Net

A charge of clergy abuse has financial implications that go far beyond the particular individual accused, and here again the church encountered the consequence of the "litigation explosion." The courts have accepted an ever-expanding net of liability that includes any group or institution that can in some measure be associated with the misconduct in question. In the case of drunk driving, for example, a series of cases in the 1980s extended the concept of liability to the bars or hosts who served the driver, or who failed to prevent the driver from driving away in an intoxicated condition; and some suits tried to trace the blame back to the distiller of the offending liquor.[32]

For clergy, lawsuits commonly include the priest's diocesan employers and also superiors who might have had cause to suspect his misdeeds but failed to intervene. Following the exposure of James Porter, a lawsuit was begun by a group of Minnesota men who had been abused by him in the 1970s. Codefendants included the two dioceses that at various times had employed Porter, respectively in Massachusetts (Fall River) and Minnesota (Crookston), and the New Mexico treatment center run

by the order Servants of the Paraclete, in which Porter had been treated following his departure from Massachusetts. Subsequent actions further charged abuse
in a New Mexico parish, which thereby implicated the archdiocese of Santa Fe.
One case alone, albeit an extreme manifestation of the problem, thus involved litigation in three states and threatened grave financial consequence for three Catholic
dioceses.

Other cases attempted to stretch still further the possible chain of association and
liability. In 1993 a suit launched in federal court in Camden, New Jersey, charged
that plaintiffs had been abused by two priests during the 1960s (one of the victims
was himself a priest). Also named were the parish churches of the alleged culprits,
as well as "six priests and bishops in supervisory positions who the suit says knew
or should have known the abuse was taking place, the National Conference of
Catholic Bishops, and the United States Catholic Conference." The following year,
a related class-action suit alleged involvement by twenty-seven priests of the dioceses of Camden and Providence, many in positions of ecclesiastical authority, and
declared that a pattern of abuse had been systematically covered up since the found-
ing of the Camden diocese in 1937. Plaintiffs called for the removal of Camden's
bishop and the dissolution of the diocese.[33]

In a singularly dangerous development for the churches, the Camden suits invoked
the federal RICO (Racketeer Influenced and Corrupt Organizations) act, charging that
in effect the collusion between the various parties entitled them to be described as a
racketeering organization. Under RICO, once a particular group has been found guilty
of two of a broad set of criminal offenses within a specified period, it becomes liable
to designation as a "racketeer organization." This opens the door to numerous penalties and disadvantages, including federal seizure of the organization's assets, the
tripling of damages in civil lawsuits, and even the freezing of assets prior to final
judgment, thus crippling the chance of mounting a successful defense. Apart from
federal RICO, most states have comparable statutes.[34]

It might seem grotesquely improbable that a Catholic diocese or institution could
earn the title of "racketeer" (the bishop of Providence termed the idea "ludicrous"),
but on several occasions priest-abuse cases have involved criminal charges that
would technically count as RICO violations.[35] These include pornography and child
pornography, and breaches of the federal "Mann Act," in transporting any person
across state lines for immoral purposes. Traditionally, criminal prosecutors had been
reluctant to press charges against clergy, but by the 1990s they were demonstrating
real ingenuity in their quest for legal remedies. In the 1993 RICO case, prosecutors
charged that a priest had traveled from one state to another for the specific purpose
of molesting boys, creating the interjurisdictional element necessary to invoke federal statutes. The 1994 Pipala case used the Mann Act, accusing the priest of having
taken a boy across state lines for the purposes of molestation. Nor would it require
great legal ingenuity to prosecute a parish or diocese for the RICO offenses of mail
fraud or wire fraud in such a case if it misrepresented the background of a priest in
order to secure him a position. An attempt to shield a suspected priest or conceal
documents could be construed as obstruction of justice. Perhaps the most remarkable legal aspect of the clergy-abuse affair to date is that RICO has been so sparingly
employed, for its potential is vast.

In 1984 the litigation surrounding the Gauthe case had reached the bizarre point where the pope himself was named as a codefendant in civil litigation against the Catholic diocese. At the time this merely seemed an eccentric legal formality, but there were more serious later attempts to stretch the concept of liability to the summit of the church's leadership. In 1994 a Texas lawsuit tried to include the pope as codefendant, on the grounds that he was the head of a business operating within that state (the court held that the pope was exempted on the basis of diplomatic immunity). And although responsibility was harder to prove in Protestant denominations, Catholic institutions were not the only ones to suffer from such an expansive concept of liability. When an Assemblies of God minister was sued for abusing a number of boys, the several codefendants included his church, his national denomination, and its regional district.[36]

The courts were sympathetic to extending the grounds on which superiors might be held liable for negligence, and though by no means did all the cases involve Catholic institutions, the rulings had serious implications for clergy of all denominations. The Supreme Court of Alaska noted that research showed that those abused as children were themselves more likely to become abusers as adults. Therefore, it held, a church might be found negligent for molestation by employees such as day-care workers if it failed to ask them if they themselves had been victims of abuse.[37] The implications for seminary training are obvious.

Equally damaging was the concept of the special duty and responsibility that any professional had toward a client who might be in an emotionally vulnerable or dependent situation, a trend that permitted legal action against clergy whose sexual misconduct was entirely confined to adults. In 1991 Mary Tenantry won more than a million dollars in damages after having a sexual relationship with an Episcopal minister to whom she had turned for counseling and pastoral guidance. Though the affair was a consensual affair between adults, she succeeded in suing his employer, the Episcopal diocese of Colorado. Such actions extended to individuals of any age the idea of the breach of trust and abuse of power that were believed to characterize child molestation, a crucial aspect of the feminist view of clergy exploitation. By 1992 six states had passed legislation that specifically forbade sexual relationships of any kind between clergy, therapists, or counselors and those clients or parishioners to whom they had a pastoral responsibility.

The Effects of Litigation

In many cases of alleged child abuse by clergy, the reported offenses had occurred some years previously and were thus sheltered from prosecution by a statute of limitations. This meant that legal action had to be pursued through civil litigation, which made it easier to establish and publicize misconduct. For example, civil cases are decided on the basis of a preponderance of the evidence rather than the criminal criterion of proof beyond a reasonable doubt. In addition, litigation can be begun on the basis of relatively slight evidence, unlike the substantial evidence normally required to launch a criminal prosecution. However, once a civil case is begun, news reporting often tends to treat it as authentic, if only through the careless use of terms like "accused child molester Father X," which suggests that the priest is "a molester who has been accused."

The accusations against Cardinal Bernardin apparently commenced when Stephen Cook began to "recover" memories with the assistance of an unlicensed hypnotist who had not followed the guidelines required for such testimony to be admissible in court. Nevertheless, this provided the basis on which Bernardin was added to an existing suit against another priest, and the accusations were then repeated in news programs "virtually every half hour throughout the weekend."[38] In the Camden diocese, the 1994 class-action suit was launched in a 275-page document containing numerous allegations against named individuals both living and dead, with some charges derived from anonymous sources and others quite uncorroborated, but this was sufficient for most regional newspapers to report the cases in front-page accounts. Like most professional groups, clergy are not protected by the laws limiting medical malpractice suits, which in many states demand that any action must be substantiated by a medical professional who believes there are plausible grounds for proceeding with an action. In sex-related cases, the plaintiff can even remain anonymous, a privilege not granted to the accused.[39]

Nor do civil suits offer an accused person the protections he or she would receive in a criminal court for actions committed many years before. A statute of limitations has many justifications, including the likelihood that memories will fade and that eye-witnesses will no longer be available or credible after so many years. In the clergy cases, however, there is the added issue that social and legal attitudes toward the offenses have changed so radically that to prosecute now for acts committed twenty or thirty years ago is virtually to create an *ex post facto* law: to punish someone for a behavior that was not criminal at the time it was committed. This was not true of an individual such as Father Porter or Gauthe because their actions would have been liable to severe sanction if discovered at the time, but the case is nothing like as clear for other priests whose behavior had been less extreme. In the 1970s, say, the virtual certainty that "minor" cases of molestation would not lead to legal consequences explains the otherwise puzzling frankness of priests in admitting their faults to superiors, often in writing. Decades later, the documents entered the public domain, with ruinous legal consequences.

New concepts of the appropriate response to abusers were also damaging to the superiors of the priests concerned. Diocesan authorities in the 1960s or 1970s had rarely intervened suddenly or dramatically to an allegation of abuse; it was assumed that priests could be reintegrated into parish ministry after rest and treatment. In the more severe atmosphere of the 1980s, this policy exposed therapeutic institutions to lawsuits charging that they had negligently permitted dangerous pedophiles to be unleashed against the children of a particular parish.

The consequences are suggested by a case against the religious house of the Servants of the Paraclete in New Mexico, which in the 1960s had played host to Father James Porter after the exposure of his sexual misdeeds in Massachusetts.[40] The house is generally described as a center for the treatment of troubled priests, although the institution presents itself only as a retreat for prayer and counseling, and not until 1977 did it officially begin to offer therapeutic programs for the sexually troubled.[41] After his sojourn here, Porter had been placed in a Minnesota parish, where he abused at least twenty-one young people during 1969 and 1970. In 1994 the Servants of the Paraclete were adjudged guilty of negligence in releasing Porter to parochial ministry, and agreed to pay more than $5 million to the Minnesota victims. Nor was this case unique. Another Massachusetts priest was David Holley from the diocese of Worcester, who recognized his sexual problems as early as 1962, and who had repeated confrontations with his diocesan superiors. In 1971 he found himself at the New Mexico treatment center, and there received weekend assignments in local parishes, where the pattern of abuse resumed.

The location of the New Mexico house proved uniquely unfortunate for the local archdiocese because Holley and Porter were only two of many troubled clergy from various parts of the country who spent time at the Paraclete house. Most had been given some parochial responsibilities, and a few had subsequently relocated permanently to parishes in the region, where clergy were scarce. Because some had reoffended in this area, the archdiocese of Santa Fe found itself under overwhelming legal assault from liability cases, with charges that between forty-five and fifty priests had abused more than two hundred people in a thirty-year period. Victims' attorney Bruce Pasternack painted a dark picture of the consequences for New Mexico. The state had become "the ecclesiastical dumping ground of the United States," one end of a "perverts' pipeline" for the most disreputable of clergy.[42]

By 1993 the archdiocese was on the verge of declaring bankruptcy to seek protection from creditors and liability claims on the order of $50 million.[43] The diocese's potential bankruptcy attracted much publicity, but the suit against the Servants of the Paraclete was perhaps more significant because it established a troubling precedent that any institution, religious or otherwise, would be legally liable for harm done by a former patient if the treatment did not succeed.[44] Carried to its logical extreme, this would threaten overwhelming litigation against any and all therapeutic institutions.

Defending the Suits

Civil litigation was dangerous for any institution, but especially so for a body such as the Catholic church, which was greatly dependent on maintaining a positive public image of its integrity. As other institutions had faced legal challenges, a number of aggressive devices had emerged to discredit or discourage litigants, and there is some evidence that these countermeasures were effective with juries, who by the early 1990s were increasingly likely to demonstrate hostility to what were perceived as grasping lawyers and plaintiffs. Between 1989 and 1992 alone, the proportion of personal injury cases decided for plaintiffs declined from 63 to 52 percent.[45] However, the Catholic church encountered a severe ideological and practical dilemma in utilizing these defenses. Although the institutional continuity of the church depended on the maintenance of its property, the ideological framework of Christianity notionally disdained material goods and praised peacemaking and reconciliation. The injunction to love enemies was all the more urgent in the context of fellow members of the church, and most suits in these years were begun by Catholic laity. Using aggressive legal tactics, "playing hardball," drew charges of hypocrisy; failing to use them invited financial destruction.

In media reporting of clergy-abuse suits, the legal defense efforts of Catholic dioceses assumed a central position as manifestations of a cynical contempt for the interests of the laity and a vindictive response to genuine public grief and outrage. The CNN program "Fall from Grace" typically complained that Sunday donations were finding their way to the defense of pedophile priests.[46] Another program described such defense efforts as the church's "hiding behind its lawyers."[47] Such accounts sometimes use the metaphor that the children in the cases are doubly abused, once by the priest and once by his implacable institutional superiors, a powerful image that suggests that vigorous legal defenses almost constitute official complicity in the misconduct.[48]

This theme is found in Greeley's *Fall from Grace*, where loyal Catholic families are depicted being asked demeaning questions as part of "the archdiocese's goal of delay and harassment."[49] These scenes bear many resemblances to the case of the parents suing the diocese over abuse allegedly committed by Chicago priest Robert Lutz.[50] Greeley had earlier commented on this case: "To make the families of the victims of priests the enemy is evil, damnable."[51] He gives the name of "Ignatius Loyola Keefe" to the diocesan attorney, a name that suggests traditional suspicions and stereotypes about crafty and unprincipled Jesuits.

In 1994 (May 15) an extremely critical report on the CBS magazine program *60 Minutes* described the "hardball" legal maneuvers employed by various Catholic dioceses to defend against lawsuits; lawyers had asked alleged victims a series of complex and intimate questions about their sexual histories.[52] The emotional tone of the program was enhanced by interviews with victims and their families, who denounced the church's apparent cynicism in these actions, and commentators included the familiar figures Andrew Greeley, Jeanne Miller, and Barbara Blaine. In one Philadelphia case, the church's lawyers responded to an abuse suit by asserting that the man's parents should have known about the behavior and were therefore liable for contributory negligence. The program depicted the weeping mother reporting her actions on hearing this charge: "And it was like I had electric shocks going through me all through my body and they all entered into my heart at one time. But I knew that it wasn't Our Lord doing that to me. I know it was the authorities, who didn't even care."

Such reporting is somewhat misleading in suggesting that ecclesiastical tactics were in any sense unusual in confronting these potentially crippling suits; expansive counteractions and countersuits have become a fundamental weapon of insurers and their lawyers, and are an essential tool of self-defense in a social and legal environment as litigious as the contemporary United States. They are used to create bargaining positions to whittle down large damage claims, against suits that can begin with demands in the tens or hundreds of millions of dollars. The extraordinary inflation of damage claims virtually demands a vigorous defense. Cardinal O'Connor of New York has written that although harassing countersuits should be avoided, the archdiocese would still make its best efforts to defend against "excessively punitive measures" or suits meant "to teach the church a lesson." "Lawsuits based on an assumption that the church is a bottomless financial well are simply unjust."[53]

Equally controversial was the common practice in civil suits of requiring as part of the settlement that both sides maintain strict secrecy about not only the terms of the settlement but also the events leading to the case. This has led to charges that the Catholic church has sealed the records of pedophile clergy, who can then be placed in unsuspecting parishes. However, the church is by no means unique in demanding confidentiality; this is common practice for corporations and insurers.

The condemnations of church conduct do assume that all plaintiffs are accurately recounting genuine abuse and that no charges are either spurious or based upon false recollection. This was not true in one of the most celebrated of all cases, the Bernardin affair, and the truth of some other allegations remains to be proven. It is disingenuous to suggest that every plaintiff has impeccable credentials. In Chicago, the cardinal's commission found a high proportion of cases in which the original charges were either exaggerated (fourteen cases out of fifty-seven) or wholly spurious (four cases). Almost a third of these instances of alleged "clergy abuse" would thus have merited serious challenge and investigation before the church conceded blame. Many of the remaining cases, the thirty-nine that were judged to be valid, received this affirmation only by the loosest and most expansive standards of proof, criteria that would not necessarily stand up in a court of law.[54] To take one of the best-publicized examples, the Lutz case was widely cited as a scandalous instance of the church defending a heinous offender, and it was presented in this light by Jason Berry and Andrew Greeley, as well as a substantial segment in the CNN program "Fall From Grace." However, both the priest and a codefendant were swiftly acquitted on criminal charges, though a civil suit remains pending.[55]

The dilemmas faced by the church are illustrated by the question of admitting blame. In the various media reports, victims and their families frequently assert that they chiefly sought amends in the form of an apology and assistance in therapy, and that the failure to obtain this had led them to seek financial damages. This is attractive in the context of the religious belief system shared by the victims and the church, but the proposed solution is virtually impossible in a legal setting because an acknowledgment of blame removes the chance of defending against any future lawsuit. In the *60 Minutes* report, a victim said that once he complained, he was viewed "as the enemy. Not once did anyone in the church say, David, I believe you; David, I'm sorry what happened to you. We're going to do something about this." However, such a response could have been legally crippling. As Cardinal Bevilacqua of Philadelphia pointed out in debates about appropriate church responses, even a gesture as apparently simple and humane as an offer to pay for therapy for victims could be construed as an admission of guilt.[56] To quote Dennis Gaboury, "Forcing the first dollar out of the church was forcing an admission of complicity."[57] The radically adversarial nature of the civil legal environment creates intolerable ideological conflicts for a religious entity such as the Catholic church, and there is a rich potential for these contradictions to be exploited by activist groups and mass media.

Consequences

Media reporting reinforced a sinister public interpretation of the Catholic church's response to abuse cases, and in such a public mood, it is likely that jurors will be sympathetic to plaintiffs and will make generous awards accordingly. This mood contributed to making clergy-abuse litigation a tempting field by the early 1990s, and the lawsuits had an impact on the internal policies and values of the churches concerned that went far beyond simple financial cost. Churches in effect have now acquired an external supervisory authority in the form of the insurance companies. Regardless of doctrine or tradition, church organization has to be molded according to the wishes and interests of these companies, who provide the liability coverage without which no group can operate and that pays the damage awards. By a tragic coincidence, the upsurge of clergy-abuse lawsuits in 1985 occurred at precisely the time at which overextended insurance companies were cutting back dramatically on general liability policies and were canceling existing policies even for many clients who appeared to be perfectly sound risks.[58] The specter of abuse suits now made churches and day-care centers prime candidates to lose coverage. By the end of the decade, most religious institutions could no longer obtain liability insurance covering sexual misconduct, which gravely limited their ability to perform virtually any activity in which children participated. (This withdrawal of coverage is much cited, with the suggestion that the Catholic church was uniquely notorious for potential child abuse scandals. In fact, as we have seen, it was only one manifestation of quite a common tendency in mid-decade.)

Where policies remained in effect, the companies sought to avoid payments by arguing that the churches had been partially responsible for any misconduct. When a number of priests who had been treated at the House of the Paraclete were sued for abuse in various New Mexico parishes, the insurer asserted that it was not liable for misconduct that was intentional or foreseeable, and "from the past history of these men, the Archdiocese could have expected injuries to happen."[59] Claims in this case totaled about $50 million. In the Porter case, similarly, Continental Insurance sued the church to avoid having to pay damages, on the grounds that church authorities had failed to take action upon learning of the abusive behavior.[60] In response, dioceses became increasingly scrupulous about the slightest hint of molestation, and the Ohio diocese of Youngstown typically required several thousand full- and part-time employees to sign affidavits certifying that they had never been involved in any form of abuse.[61] The primary goal, of course, was to avoid legal or insurance problems of the sort that had crippled the diocese of Santa Fe.

The companies were demanding that the churches thoroughly reform their treatment and supervision of personnel, and sometimes the directives were clear and explicit. In 1993, for example, the Church Insurance Company, which provided policies for Episcopal parishes, announced a radical revision in its coverage of sexual-misconduct cases. The value of liability coverage was sharply curtailed, and parishes could obtain coverage only if they agreed to a series of measures to limit or prevent abuse, including background checks on all prospective clergy and church employees that would examine past *allegations* of misconduct in addition to proven charges. Clergy who behaved improperly would have to undergo a specified course of treatment and rehabilitation before being reassigned to ministry.[62] Cost control thus justified a thorough restructuring of the disciplinary procedures of at least one major denomination.

Conclusion

In 1994 the *Cincinnati Enquirer* published a cartoon depicting a Catholic priest at a baptism ceremony; he is saying, "You hold the child until my lawyer gets here. . . ." The implication is that he is too afraid of abuse charges to perform any functions involving children except with the safeguard of legal advice.[63] Allowing for humorous license, the image is an accurate reflection of the impact of legal considerations on church policies. For example, legal factors go far toward explaining the quite radical nature of the reforms introduced by many Catholic dioceses in procedures for hearing and assessing complaints against clergy.

Following the lead of the Chicago archdiocese, these changes have usually built a substantial lay element into the mechanism. Historically, churches have been very slow to change internal procedures, even over issues that seem trivial to outsiders, and the Catholic church has been slower than most. Moreover, lay involvement in complaints procedures has been a source of deep contention for many professional groups. In the area of law enforcement, for example, civilian participation in complaints procedures was the main detonator of the vigorous police militancy of the 1970s. One might attribute the responsive Church attitude of recent years to the far-sighted attitudes of leaders such as Cardinal Bernardin, but even if the hierarchy had been less sensitive, changes would have had to occur. Pressures resulting from litigation and the threat to insurability have caused quite rapid reforms in the rules governing clergy behavior, even to the point of adopting procedures that may be questionable under the canon law that traditionally guided discipline.

The classic legal definition of a corporation is a person lacking a soul, and since the early days of muckraking, this phrase has been used to complain that great business corporations lack soul and heart, in the sense of humanity or decency. In the case of a religious corporation such as a church, there is the difficult question of whether a formal property-holding institution can act consistently according to higher or spiritual aspirations, or if practical worldly considerations such as self-defense must always take precedence. Can a church maintain its "soul" in the face of so wide ranging a legal challenge? The assaults of the past decade suggest the enormous pressures on the churches to conform to secular standards of legality and bureaucratic procedure.

9

Defending Therapy

Like lawyers, therapists as a group have a vested interest in the promotion of distinctive views of the clergy-abuse problem. For purposes of litigation, there is a natural commonality of interest between therapists and child-abuse experts on the one hand and the lawyers who are seeking to prove the extent and harm of clergy abuse on the other. The earlier recognition of the child sexual abuse phenomenon had greatly enhanced the authority and visibility of therapists and psychologists as experts claiming a peculiar competence in dealing with this problem. Throughout the 1980s this expertise had been established and expanded as a result of a series of court battles and legal encounters, and it was to be expected that the therapeutic community would be closely involved in the new clergy-abuse problem. The common assumptions and interests of that profession helped to determine the ways in which the problem would be formulated.

Moreover, once accepted as a genuine menace, clergy abuse offered therapists and psychologists support in a number of public controversies in which they had become engaged. In the early 1980s an expanding therapeutic profession had succeeded in gaining public acceptance of certain central ideas about child abuse. Over the next decade, however, pursuing these ideas to their logical conclusion resulted in serious disputes in which therapists were variously accused of incompetence, credulity, or unscrupulous greed, and these charges were publicized in the mass media no less than the professional literature. Criticisms over matters like memory therapy and alleged ritual abuse reached a crescendo during 1992 and 1993, when public skepticism about child molestation was growing steadily. This threatened the gains not just of the therapeutic professions but of the feminists and other activists who had come to set such ideological store by the portrayal of an abuse menace. It is in this larger context of contemporary debates about the value and potential of therapy in dealing with child victims that we must place the "pedophile priests" affair. For a profession accused of inventing abuse or else exaggerating trivial incidents out of all proportion, it was invaluable to find in clergy abuse a type of offense concerning which the earlier orthodoxies remained unchallenged and expert pronouncements retained public respect.

Believing the Children

New attitudes toward child abuse in the late 1970s were largely inherited from the antirape campaigns, which had struggled to overcome legal skepticism about the evidence of adult women. Anglo-American legal orthodoxy had been summarized by the classic statement of Sir Matthew Hale: "Rape is an accusation easily to be made and hard to be proved, and harder to be defended by the party accused, though never so innocent."[1] During the 1970s legal procedures had been extensively revised to reflect the presumption that the woman alleging assault was indeed a survivor, a victim of a brutal crime, rather than merely one party in a contest, whose assertions were inherently neither more nor less likely than those of the offender.

Prior to the 1980s both lawyers and psychologists had been similarly skeptical about the value of children's charges about sexual abuse, a doubt influenced by Freudian beliefs about the power of infantile fantasy, usually directed against parents or other authority figures.[2] Since the early twentieth century the expert consensus on such matters had been that children were "the most dangerous of all witnesses."[3] Children's testimony was pivotal to molestation cases, but the courts were suspicious of their truthfulness. Smaller children were often deemed unfit to testify; older children were liable to cross-examination in circumstances that were widely deemed to be hostile and potentially traumatizing. Prosecutors saw abuse cases as a particularly risky venture, with a high chance of failure due to the disqualification or withdrawal of child witnesses. The stereotype of these years was that excessive tenderness for the rights of accused molesters permitted many to escape punishment and that their victims experienced another form of child abuse through their experiences on the witness stand.[4]

Following the redefinition of the child-abuse problem after 1977, matters changed substantially. Psychologists and therapists now commonly accepted the very high figures offered for the incidence of child molestation and argued that many or most cases involving alleged abuse were genuine. Research on the capacity of children to report truthfully at different developmental stages was believed to show that children virtually never lied when making allegations of sexual abuse and that charges were all the more plausible when stemming from very young children.[5] This was most evident when children lacking knowledge about sexuality offered detailed testimony about the actions of an accused molester. However, the younger the child, the greater the need for expert assistance to elicit his or her evidence.[6] A whole new professional field of therapists specialized in the detection and treatment of sexual abuse, and these individuals were employed as convincing expert witnesses in the courtroom. The phrases "believe the children" and "listening to children" became articles of faith for child advocates, and they conveniently summarize the goals of a decade of legal reform.[7]

In the 1980s reformers tried to eliminate these presumed difficulties. States passed laws removing the obligation of the child witness to confront the individual against whom he or she was testifying. Some permitted children to give testimony from behind screens or through the medium of videotape, and a few sought to reduce the ability of counsel to undertake hostile interrogation or cross-examination. These reforms were controversial, and received a mixed reception from a divided U. S. Supreme Court, but enough of the new laws withstood challenge to alter substantially the legal environment of child-abuse cases.

New attitudes toward child sexual abuse radically changed the position of therapists and psychologists within the courtroom. Expert witnesses had long been employed to assess the credibility of a particular child, but it was now asserted that children's evidence was difficult to elicit or present except through the medium of a therapist. This might occur in discussions or treatment occurring outside the courtroom, where the investigator used tactics like play therapy that were at best novel to the legal environment, and leading questions were regularly employed in such sessions. There were prolonged debates about whether and how such evidence could be presented in the criminal court. Did a child's statements reflect objective reality, and even if so, could testimony be presented by the child with the direct assistance of the therapist?

The reaction against earlier skepticism went so far that it became virtually unacceptable to suggest that such charges might be false, the product of either fantasy or deliberate lying. To reject children's testimony was presented as, at best, a psychological problem of "denial" on the part of the critic and, at worst, the moral equivalent of acquiescence in the act of molestation. It was "blaming the victim." This in effect challenged the legitimacy of employing conventional criteria of probability, plausibility, or evidentiary quality when assessing claims about sexual abuse. The near-orthodoxy asserted that children were most likely to be telling untruths when they denied being victimized, rather than the opposite. Using the analogy of post-traumatic stress disorder, psychologists argued that abused children were inherently likely to deny the occurrence, perhaps to obliterate it from their memories, and only expert therapy could overcome this "child abuse accommodation syndrome."[8] While acknowledging the traumatic effects of stress, such an argument offered a "heads I win, tails you lose" approach: if a child admitted abuse, the abuse had occurred; if the child denied it, then the abuse had been all the more severe. The issue, then, was whether intense questioning to induce a child to admit to sexual exploitation might lead him or her to make a false admission or might even instill false recollections in the alleged victim.

Ritual Child Abuse

The dilemmas involved in this approach are suggested by the ritual child-abuse cases that came to light in 1983 and 1984.[9] The first charges occurred in the McMartin school case, in Manhattan Beach, California, but similar allegations soon appeared in may parts of North America.[10] Most such incidents began with allegations of "ordinary" sexual abuse made by one or more children. However, intense investigations by therapists produced startling allegations against a number of adults, who were said to indulge in bizarre ritualistic practices, such as the killing of animals and humans, and acts of cannibalism, blood drinking, or coprophilia.[11]

Charges of this sort still continue to occur, but it is now widely accepted that many such allegations arise from the particular therapeutic techniques employed to question children.[12] Children were questioned repeatedly, on the assumption that they were concealing the fact of abuse. Eventually, they would concede that something improper had happened, and would then attempt to describe what they felt to be a plausible description of misbehavior, usually with the leading of the interrogator. The extravagant statements involved what the children felt to be the worst concepts imaginable, involving blood, excretory functions, and violent death, and numerous participants were named. Therapists and others interpreted these remarks as indicating genuine activity by a ritualistic or satanic cult.

As the charges became widely believed and disseminated, they formed the expectations of other therapists about the directions that questioning might take in subsequent investigations, and it is not surprising that the same allegations (robes, pentacles, blood drinking) recur so freely in other cases. The ritual-abuse concept derives from the absolute conviction that children do not lie about abuse, no matter how bizarre the charges may initially seem or how extreme the violence and perversion said to be involved. The belief gained importance in public debate from a series of publicized cases in which individuals or groups were tried and occasionally convicted for perpetrating such crimes, and therapists invariably played a crucial role in eliciting or presenting the damning evidence in the courtroom.[13]

Believers in the objective reality of ritual abuse drew analogies to the earlier discoveries of physical abuse in the 1960s and sexual abuse in the following decade, and—as in the earlier cases—it was hoped that public skepticism would be proved false as the number of reports rose. Accounts did indeed increase, so that by 1994 the total of reported instances exceeded twelve thousand across North America, but ritual abuse never acquired a like degree of credibility. This was because of the scale and complexity of the conspiratorial networks rumored to be involved, and the total absence of corroborating evidence.[14] The McMartin affair was one of several cases that collapsed ignominiously, among grave doubts about the professional techniques employed in interviewing child witnesses. The whole "ritualistic" concept was under attack from about 1987, and by 1990 the skeptics were in the ascendant. In the early 1990s both the courts and the media were far less willing to accept the likelihood of mass abuse, especially when testimony had been elicited through therapists. Although sexual abuse was still believed to be a vast social problem, there was also concern about the methods used to combat it.

The Recovered-Memory Debate

The issue of interviewing children soon became linked with the still more difficult question of repressed memory and the problem of whether therapists were able to draw forth early memories that an adult subject had concealed because they were too troubling for the conscious mind to confront.[15] The objective reality of hidden memories remains unresolved, and many writers regard them as perilously likely to be false rather than merely suppressed recollections.[16] Belief in recovered memory derived from a powerful therapeutic trend of the mid-1980s, a view publicized in best-selling self-help books such as *The Courage to Heal*, by Ellen Bass and Laura Davis.[17] From this perspective, failings and anxieties encountered by adult patients could be traced to forgotten early instances of childhood sexual abuse, which the therapist was able to recover through hypnosis or suggestion. Once identified as "incest survivors," patients were in a position to confront their problems and begin a process of healing, usually through self-help groups of comparable survivors, based on the familiar model of Alcoholics Anonymous.

However, the matter was controversial because therapists were so willing to assume that abuse had occurred despite the lack of corroborating evidence, except for ill-defined "symptoms" that others might identify as accidental personality traits. *The Courage to Heal* assured readers that "if you are unable to remember any specific instances . . . but still have a feeling that something abusive happened to you, it probably did. . . . If you think you were abused and your life shows the symptoms, then you were."[18] Skepticism was discouraged: E. Sue Blume wrote, "If you doubt you were abused, minimize the abuse, or think 'Maybe it's my imagination', these are symptoms of post-incest syndrome."[19] In the most extreme cases, for example, involving cult or ritualistic abuse, the psychic trauma might be so severe as to have caused a multiple-personality disorder, with the various personalities emerging under therapy to testify about the infantile exploitation.

The number of therapists or psychologists active in this type of treatment expanded dramatically from the late 1980s onward, and their ideas initially gained credence. There have been a few cases where recovered memories have resulted in individuals being convicted of serious crimes. In a notorious California case decided in 1991, George Franklin was convicted of a 1969 homicide on the basis of testimony from his daughter Eileen, who claimed to have repressed the memory for twenty years.[20] Memories of victimization also provided the basis for civil actions, and in 1990 California became the first state to extend the statute of limitations in abuse cases from the age of nineteen to twenty-six, and also to permit actions to be brought within three years after the time that a person of any age *recalled* an offense: a lead followed by more than twenty states in the next two years.[21] In Minnesota, the statute permitting suits within two years after the recollection of abuse (rather than the event itself) was drafted by Jeffrey Anderson, who had earned celebrity for his litigation against abusive clergy.[22] This sort of reform expanded tremendously the potential for civil litigation, and several hundred suits followed in the next three years, generally involving adult women suing members of their families. The trend raised fears that the quest for hidden memory might offer a temptation for unscrupulous therapists or plaintiffs.

Throughout the 1980s some academics and psychologists had been skeptical about the possibility of recovering supposedly lost memories, suspicious both of the techniques employed in therapy and of the chance that recollections would accurately reflect events that had genuinely occurred.[23] This critique became all the sharper because of the regularity with which patients were reporting phenomena that were extremely improbable, such as ritual abuse, or downright impossible, including abduction or rape by aliens and occupants of UFOs.[24] By 1992 the mass media were becoming increasingly vocal in their attacks on recovered memory and other aspects of the child-abuse movement, and hostility was expressed in major newspapers and magazines. The obvious charge was that the concern over sex abuse had led to the creation of a therapeutic "industry" with a vested interest in the identification of sexual trauma and that innocent individuals were being falsely accused in consequence of dubious therapies, There were also concerns that the recovery and self-help movements were being used to deny personal responsibility, and that child abuse had become a scapegoat for all flaws and failings.[25] One widely quoted article was entitled "Victims All? Recovery, Co-dependency and the Art of Blaming Somebody Else."[26] Skeptics pointed to the rapid rise in the number of identifiable psychiatric disorders, with the suggestion that at least some were spurious: the first standard diagnostic manual, in 1952, listed 106 disorders; in 1975 there were 265; in 1987, 292.[27]

The recovery movement was the target of a wave of attacks in magazine articles and syndicated stories in the early 1990s.[28] In 1993 a *New York Times* article entitled "Beware the Incest Survivor Machine" attracted furious rebuttal from therapists and patients alike.[29] *Time* magazine had already attacked the reliability of recovered memories in 1991,[30] and in 1993 a major investigation, "Lies of the Mind," not only challenged the validity of memory recovery techniques but suggested that particular therapists and clinics were serving as "memory mills," virtually guaranteed to induce such recollections in a patient.[31] A *Newsweek* cover headlined a story on the case of the Souzas, a couple accused of molesting grandchildren on the basis of testimony elicited by therapists; the case was used as the basis for an examination of false allegations in child-abuse cases.[32] Stories in other publications gave favorable attention to representatives of the False Memory Syndrome Foundation, a group of families and individuals who say they have been falsely accused by such means.

Similar themes occurred in television news programs. Prominent among these was *60 Minutes*, which from as early as 1987 had criticized the investigative techniques employed in the McMartin school case. More recently, the show had run exposés of other alleged instances of ritual or mass abuse, and one *cause célèbre* was the story of teacher Kelly Michaels, whose abuse conviction was overturned in 1993.[33] In 1994 a *60 Minutes* report on the abuse allegations made by television star Roseanne Arnold attacked the exponents of recovered memory therapy and favorably quoted professional critics of the movement.[34] PBS's documentary series *Frontline* suggested that faulty methods of interviewing child witnesses lay behind the mass abuse case in the North Carolina community of Edenton.[35]

In 1993 a report on the ABC newsmagazine *Primetime Live* suggested that therapists were creating false memories of ritual abuse in adult patients, a theme also argued later that year in a CNN news special.[36] In mid-1993 the media began sympathetic reporting of the academic work of psychologist Stephen Ceci, who showed how repeated questioning of children over lengthy periods could generate false but plausible-sounding memories that the subjects would report with absolute conviction as objective reality.[37] This provided the basis for a story on ABC's *20/20*, that emphasized the inability of experts to distinguish between accounts of authentic and artificially generated memories.[38] All these stories showed the practical damage done

Table 9.1. Controversy over Therapeutic Responses to Child Abuse, 1991–1995

1991	
October	*Harper's* article attacks "victim culture" allegedly constructed by therapists[1]
November	Syndicated article in Knight-Ridder press alleges that therapists are instilling false memories of abuse[2]
1992	
January–February	Series of articles in Knight-Ridder press on false memory and dangers of improper therapeutic response to abuse charges
March	*60 Minutes* segment on false abuse allegations against the Swan family, including charges of improper conduct against therapists and prosecutors
1993	
January	Carol Tavris article in *New York Times,* on "Beware the Incest-Survivor Machine" *Ms.* article defends concept of ritual abuse[3] ABC's *Primetime Live* shows segment suggesting that therapists are creating false memories of ritual abuse in patients
March	New Jersey Supreme Court overturns conviction of Kelly Michaels, accused of mass child abuse in a day-care center
April	*Newsweek* special on the case of the Souzas, who are also portrayed sympathetically on many talk shows and news programs.
May	CBS's *48 Hours* devotes one-hour program to the Kelly Michaels case, strongly arguing for her innocence *New Yorker* articles attack ritual abuse[4]
May–June	Media reporting of the scientific findings of Stephen Ceci on the generation of false memories in children
June	*Vanity Fair* article defends ritual-abuse idea[5]
July	PBS *Frontline* attacks the convictions of those accused in the mass abuse of children in day care in Edenton, North Carolina
August	CNN special on false memory
October	ABC's *20/20* feature on suggestibility of children in accepting and believing stories
November	Major *Time* feature, "Lies of the Mind" Acquittal of Dale Akiki, accused of multiple molestation in day-care center in San Diego County, California
1994	
April	False memory addressed in two *60 Minutes* segments: one, on the Kelly Michaels case, is highly sympathetic to the falsely accused defendant; the other, on Roseanne Arnold, suggests the harmfulness of false memories of child sexual abuse
May	Damages awarded to Gary Ramona in case against therapists accused of implanting false memories in his daughter's mind
June	Grand jury investigating Dale Akiki case depicts extensive error and mismanagement of prosecutorial process *Redbook* article denounces ritual abuse theory[6]
July	*20/20* report on family falsely accused of sex abuse as a result of memory therapy
December	*Primetime Live* report on Dale Akiki case
1995	
April	PBS *Frontline* shows two-part program entitled "Divided Memories" on the issue of how false memories are invented in the course of therapy

[1] David Rieff, "Victims All: Recovery, Co-dependency and the Art of Blaming Somebody Else," *Harper's*, October 1991, pp.49–56.

[2] Darrell Sifford, "When a Parent is Wrongly Accused of Sexual Abuse," syndicated Knight-Ridder article in *Centre Daily Times* (State College, Pa.), December 26, 1991.

[3] Elizabeth S. Rose, "Surviving the Unbelievable: Cult Ritual Abuse." *Ms.*, January 1993, pp. 40–45.

[4] Lawrence Wright, "Reporter's Notebook: Remembering Satan," *New Yorker*, May 17 and 24, 1993.

[5] Leslie Bennetts, "Nightmares on Main Street," *Vanity Fair*, June 1993, pp. 42–62.

[6] A. S. Ross, "Blame it on the Devil." *Redbook*, June 1994, pp. 86–89+.

by false reports and recollections, in the form of divided families and ruined reputa-
tions, as well as lawsuits.[39]

The media campaign against recovered memory therapy reached a climax with a
1994 *20/20* exposé of a Maryland case in which a girl under treatment for an eating
disorder was induced to accuse her family of sexual abuse, including satanic cult
activities.[40] This "American horror story" was a tale of "outrageous and destructive
lies" and "devastating betrayal," all caused by "so-called recovered memories" and
the therapists and social workers who credited the bizarre fiction. It was a "Salem"
case that confirmed yet again that "the issue of false accusations will be the Big Bang
that will rock therapy in the 1990s."[41]

Denunciations of memory therapy customarily included a disclaimer that no
doubt was being cast on the truthfulness of the majority of abuse complaints, and
indeed that false allegations were so pernicious because they might lead to unjus-
tified skepticism about authentic complaints. However, this debate inevitably caused
significant damage to the model of child sexual victimization that had gained such
near-universal acceptance a decade previously, above all the ideology of "believe
the children." Coming so shortly after the ritual-abuse controversy, the affair harmed
the image of the therapeutic profession, which had benefited substantially from the
child protection movement. In popular culture, the therapist assisting a child patient
to confront or recollect sexual abuse had been portrayed as a heroic crusader against
prejudice and injustice, but in the early 1990s public stereotypes were reverting
to the older image of the gullible quack, vulgarly parodied as "Sigmund Fraud."
Doubts about abuse accusations were enhanced by numerous well-reported instances in which spurious charges were employed as weapons in cases involving
divorce and child custody.

By 1994 recovered memory was the theme of numerous cartoons and comedy
sketches, and episodes of comic strips such as *Doonesbury* and Berke Breathed's
Outland. In the latter, a boy whose allowance has been canceled pressures his father
by announcing a sudden recollection: "The Satanic rituals at age four! You put a
goat's head on me while your poker buddies danced round naked in the living
room!"[42] A cartoon of this sort lays no claims to academic respectability, but it does
more to influence public stereotypes than a thousand scholarly articles.

The reversal of the public mood was symbolized by a growing number of legal
cases in which patients alleged malpractice against psychiatrists who had led them
to believe in earlier experiences of abuse, often ritual or satanic in nature, and these
trials further fueled media complaints against therapy.[43] In a California case decided
in 1994, a man won $500,000 in damages against therapists who were judged to
have falsely convinced his daughter that she was the victim of childhood incest. In a
ritual-abuse case decided the same year, also in California, the acquitted defendant
demanded $110 million in damages against the county that had prosecuted him.
Therapists were being portrayed as a social problem in their own right.

This revival of earlier skepticism was troubling to child-protection advocates.
Feminist psychologist Judith Herman remarked of current trends, "We're back
where we were twenty years ago. This is a mobilization of accused perpetrators and
their defenders to take the spotlight off perpetrators of crimes and put it back on victims and issues of their credibility."[44] Skeptical articles like those in the *New York*

Times were denounced as part of a social reaction, "a backlash against survivors," an attempt "to go back to square one in our understanding of incest."[45] There were even charges that "pedophile advocates" were themselves influencing the false memory charges in order to conceal their own misdeeds.[46]

Recovered Memory and Clergy-Abuse Allegations

The upsurge of allegations of clergy abuse from the late 1980s onward occurred against a political and intellectual background that offered some potential dangers for the therapeutic profession. In these scandals, at least, the vast majority of the charges were confirmed, either through confessions or successful legal proceedings. This substantiated claims of a thitherto unrecognized menace that necessitated expert counseling and therapy to counter its worst effects. It was particularly important that this detection gained such a fillip from *recovered* memories, above all in the Porter case.[47] This scandal began when Frank Fitzpatrick examined the "great mental pain" with which he lived and eventually realized that it reflected "a betrayal of some kind" involving sexual abuse more than twenty-five years earlier, when he had been twelve years old.[48] Some weeks later he recalled the perpetrator as the priest James Porter.

Fitzpatrick succeeded in finding other former parishioners and urging them to confront their collective experiences. Some victims reported recalling the abuse in sudden flashbacks. One man reported having suppressed all memory of the abuse until hearing of the case on his car radio.[49] Fitzpatrick's sister described television coverage as the catalyst that permitted her to recollect the offenses: "I've had flashbacks for a number of years about being sexually abused. But it wasn't until I saw the TV show that I connected it to Father Porter."[50] The victims reported a range of symptoms close to that described in the therapeutic literature: "depression, problems with relationships, alcohol and drug abuse, difficulty keeping jobs, and a loss of faith in religion. Some said they had attempted suicide." Dennis Gaboury writes of the Porter survivors, "When we told each other about the intervening decades of our lives, it turned out to be a litany of sexual confusion and broken marriages, depression, suicide attempts and psychiatric instituionalization. . . . Drug abuse and alcoholism were nearly as common a bond as the terrible childhood guilt we had felt after Porter's predations."[51] One former altar boy asserted that "shame and guilt became the foundation of my being."[52]

Thus far the retrieval of memories followed almost exactly the pattern outlined in such works as *The Courage to Heal*, and these ideas benefited enormously when, ultimately, Porter's victims were vindicated in court. Nor were Porter's victims the only ones who said they had repressed their memories. Jeffrey Haines declared he had lost for fifteen years the recollection of childhood abuse by an Episcopal minister, and only in 1993 did he report the case in circumstances that would cause great controversy within that church (see chapter 3). Burkett and Bruni recount other such cases, including one in which memories of abuse were reported to have lain dormant for more than twenty years before emerging to become the subject of a lawsuit during 1991. "Sometimes victims stay silent because they simply don't remember what happened. Their minds have blocked it out. . . . [R]epressed memory is most common when the abuser is an especially trusted figure, such as a priest."[53] Not surprisingly, Ellen Bass herself has praised *A Gospel of Shame* as "courageous, compelling and necessary."

At conferences and meetings of survivors, accounts of recovered memories became commonplace. A middle-aged woman recalled having a body massage, and when the masseuse touched her thigh, she suddenly realized that she had been a victim of abuse by a priest: "It wasn't just like seeing him do it to me. It was that I became that little girl again screaming 'Don't do it! Don't do it!'"[54] Another woman stated that she had had no recollection of abuse "until she read a story about clerical sexual abuse in a newspaper. She stopped and broke into uncontrollable tears."[55] Such recollections may of course be wholly valid, but other individuals have presented equally plausible sounding recollections of experiences far less intrinsically probable, so the memories need not be accepted without challenge. However, the confirmation of many stories gave heart to therapists and feminist critics, whose parallel work on recovered memory and ritual abuse acquired plausibility from the clergy-molestation stories.

As the attack on false memories gained momentum during 1992 and 1993, the experiences of Fitzpatrick and others like him would repeatedly be cited as solid evidence of the value of therapy. In news articles on recovered memory, the pro side of the debate would customarily be represented by two well-validated examples: the Franklin murder case and an instance of recalled clergy abuse. In the *New York Times*, for instance, a 1992 article, "Childhood Trauma: Memory or Invention?" used the stories of Ellen Franklin and Frank Fitzpatrick to support the authenticity of recollection, and the same pairing appeared in later studies.[56]

Clergy Abuse and Ritual Abuse

The clergy allegations also helped validate ritual abuse, and controversial cases involving satanic charges became more believable by association with the proven reality of "priest pedophilia." The significance of juxtaposing the two types of incident is apparent when compared with the treatment of ritual charges in unsympathetic media outlets. If one describes mass-abuse charges and then compares them with cases known to be false, such as the Salem witch trials, the McMartin school, or the Kelly Michaels affair, there is an obvious message that the newspaper or television program is gravely skeptical of the allegations. On the other hand, if ritual charges are set alongside accounts of Father Porter, there is an implied message that both stories share the same essential qualities. Both involve betrayal by trusted local figures, priests in one context, teachers and child minders in another, and again public incredulity is blamed for permitting the suffering of children.

In the magazine *Vanity Fair*, the same journalist who in 1991 had published a detailed account of the clergy-abuse crisis published in 1993 a similar analysis of a comparable "hidden epidemic," this time of ritual child abuse, the "nightmares on main street."[57] Both pieces emphasized the same themes, of intimate betrayal, of official "denial" overcome by heroic survivors aided by determined journalists and therapists. In Canada likewise, the linkage was quite explicit. In 1991–1992, an alleged mass-abuse scandal in a day-care center in Martensville, Saskatchewan, was said to involve ritualistic and satanic elements, and the scandal achieved national notoriety. The regional *Western Report* demonstrated its skepticism by contextualizing the cases with Salem and McMartin. In contrast, the national newsmagazine *Maclean's* compared the story with other "abuse charges against trusted officials," namely the recent allegations against Christian Brothers institutions in Newfoundland and Ontario.[58]

By far the most visible juxtaposition of ritual charges and clergy abuse occurs in Andrew Greeley's 1993 novel *Fall from Grace* (see chapter 4). Greeley is of course a popular novelist in quest of interesting and exciting themes, but his book also has a crusading aspect in its attempts to publicize the clergy-abuse problem. This real-world quality lends credence to the bizarre claims for ritualistic crime, including human sacrifice and Black Masses.[59] Greeley is by no means unskeptical, and notes the lack of positive material evidence for this "ultimate form of sexual abuse."[60] On the other hand, the characters become far more willing to accept the charges as the novel progresses, and a therapist is depicted using hypnosis to assist a ritual-abuse victim to recover the memories of her sufferings. He comments, "There's no doubt in my mind . . . that the young woman was drugged and ritually abused by her parents and by others."[61] In the novel, at least, the refusal to accept ritual-crime charges echoes the earlier "denial" of molestation by clergy, and the two problems gain acceptance in parallel. The book's climax includes a thwarted satanic ritual that would have been presided over by the homosexual pedophile priest Father Greene, "Lucifer": the ultimate reunion of the twin mythologies of anti-Catholicism and Satanism.

Defending Therapy

Clergy-abuse cases reinforced therapeutic assumptions about the treatment and healing of abuse, not least through the near-universal acceptance of the idea that abuse victims urgently require extensive psychological treatment. That this concept seems so self-evident is in itself strong testimony to the recent influence of the child-abuse ideology and the assumption that molestation caused extensive psychic damage. The appropriate expertise for treatment was believed to lie with professionally trained therapists rather than the religious resources offered by the churches themselves.

In the fictionalized version of the Gauthe case in the film *Judgment*, the motivation offered for the family's remorseless pursuit of a legal remedy is the deep trauma suffered by their young son, whose life has been transformed by molestation into a continuing nightmare of anxiety and terror. However, he is so traumatized that he cannot describe his sufferings in words. He cannot assist in bringing his exploiter to justice, and the lawyer points out how even a determined child witness would be harangued and insulted in the courtroom cross-examination. The son's process of healing begins only when he receives professional treatment from a psychologist who leads him to confront the past through play therapy. As the expert explains, "That's what children do. They don't talk. They act." A key scene offers the memorable image of the boy simulating his experiences by playing with two dolls, one of which wears a clerical collar.

The media confirmed the necessity for professional intervention for clergy-abuse victims. Payment for therapy was usually a basic demand in legal actions, and there was remarkably little argument about the large financial commitment involved. In the real-life Gauthe case, a therapist estimated the cost of treatment at up to $50,000 over several years; extrapolating this figure for the tens of thousands of clergy victims cited by some sources gives some idea of the huge sums at stake in the controversy.[62]

Survivor Movements

Equally in line with therapeutic views was the development of self-help groups to support and counsel victims of clergy abuse. The most celebrated were the chapters of VOCAL/The Linkup and SNAP.[63] VOCAL originated with the work of Jeanne Miller, who had written a pseudonymous account of her conflict with the archdiocese, and this book, *Assault on Innocence,* had been read by other "survivors" and their families.[64] Following the outbreak of the major scandals in Chicago, she formed VOCAL in 1991.[65] By 1993 the Linkup had forty-five hundred members and SNAP had twelve hundred. At least eight such groups were active by 1993, including local networks in Albuquerque and Milwaukee, and this does not count *ad-hoc* groups like the Survivors of Father Porter in Massachusetts. In Ontario, David McCann founded a Kingston-based self-help group for survivors of clergy abuse, and systematically contacted several hundred former residents of Christian Brothers' schools to invite them to discuss their experiences.[66]

VOCAL and SNAP were prominent activists in public debate over the appropriate policy response to the abuse problem, and Miller and Blaine were both frequently interviewed by the media as authentic representatives of the victims' point of view. In 1992, for example, the special commission organized by Cardinal Bernardin interviewed both women, together with two other VOCAL members. In 1993, Miller addressed the normally academic gathering of the Catholic Theological Society of America, where the abuse issue emerged as a central theme of debate.[67] When the Chicago archdiocese established its special review board to judge complaints against clergy, one of the nine members was to be an abuse victim or a member of a victim's family, giving a remarkable institutional status to the "survivors." By the time of its 1994 conference, a "visibly matured" Linkup movement even held its gathering on church premises, at an abbey and the connected university in Collegeville, Minnesota.[68]

Victim groups drew on the familiar rhetoric of the survivor movements that had earlier mobilized victims of rape, abuse, or incest, and they promoted recognition of the new problem by encouraging frank recognition of each member's history of abuse.[69] The familiar recovery rhetoric of this latest survivors' movement is illustrated by one of Father Porter's victims, speaking on a television talk show in 1993:"This is about a faith, but it's about a belief in self. My life's changed twice. The second time it's changed has been during the past eighteen months when I've been recovering and the only way that I've recovered has been believing in myself and having faith in me, in the fact that I'm a good person and I can make decisions." [70]

The fact that the majority of such groups had well-authenticated stories to recount undoubtedly contributed to obtaining public respect and sympathy, which by this point was not necessarily true for purported "survivors" of recollected incest or ritual abuse. One Gauthe victim, Calvin Mire, was the subject of a television movie aimed at children and intended to heighten their awareness of the potential danger from sexual abusers.[71] Skepticism was thus minimized and media coverage of VOCAL was consistently favorable, so here at least the "courage to heal" remained a noble aspiration. Thus validated, the clergy-abuse survivors' groups were successful in keeping the issue in the news by a variety of tactics. They organized protests and press conferences at official church gatherings such as the NCCB meetings, where they claimed a right to speak as the voice of thitherto unrepresented child victims. In October 1992, VOCAL held a widely reported national conference in the Chicago area, using as motto "Breaking the cycle of silence," with all its connotations of recovering and confronting past traumas. Victim groups regularly provided articulate speakers to be interviewed for news programs and documentaries.[72] They were especially visible on talk shows, where audiences offered loud applause for the courage of survivors recounting their experiences. This visibility in turn encouraged admissions and recollections by more reticent victims past and present.

Especially during 1992 and 1993, public responses to clergy abuse seemed to hark back to the attitudes prevailing a decade previously, when there was general acceptance of the need for a child-abuse crusade. Therapists had validated their admittedly daring techniques, victims were lauded for their courage, and those who attempted to deny or challenge the charges met anger and contempt. As in the early 1980s, there was little sympathy for alleged abusers who tried to defend themselves against the charges, and the media denounced "hardball" legal responses as in a sense repeating the original abuse.

Backlash

In the year following the exposure of the Porter case, clergy abuse offered a buttress for the therapeutic approach, but the issue proved to be a mixed blessing. A crucial turning point came with the allegations against Cardinal Bernardin. Though the charges received widespread and sensationalistic coverage, there were from the beginning reasons to doubt them. Stephen Cook, the former seminarian who initially believed he had been abused, stated that the offenses had taken place when he was seventeen years old, which is unusually old for events of this type to be so thoroughly repressed. Skepticism was expressed by newspapers that could normally be expected to criticize church conduct. The *National Catholic Reporter* commented that Cook had been counseled by a priest who had long been critical of the cardinal,[73] and *Commonweal* used the case to remark on the perils of using false memories as legal evidence.[74]

When Cook announced some months later that he had come to doubt the accuracy of the memories recovered under hypnosis, the case was reported as another reason to cast doubt on memory therapy and as a reminder of the dangers that could arise if another complainant were not as scrupulous as this one. In the state of Illinois the affair led directly to legislative attempts to restore the statute of limitations, which had been eased only the previous year.[75] Another less publicized case involved a

Minnesota therapist's being sued by five women "who say she implanted memories of satanic ritual abuse." The same therapist had treated two women who alleged sexual misconduct against Bishop Gerald O'Keefe of Davenport, Iowa, but later withdrew their charges.[76] The two women asserted they had been abused by the bishop as children in the 1960s. Both were said to suffer from multiple personalities, and one of the complainants also asserted that she had been abused by a satanic cult and was in contact with a UFO.

Hostility to therapeutic claims was reflected in cartoons and satire. In 1993, at the time of the original Bernardin charges, a syndicated cartoon from the *Philadelphia Daily News* portrayed a client at the offices of "Dr. Vic Timm," whose price list indicates rates for the recollection of different types of abuse, with "memory of abuse by a priest" at $30,000, the largest sum. A secretary is asking, "How much abuse can you afford to remember?"[77] In the months following the Bernardin case, the widely syndicated cartoon strip *Doonesbury* returned to the theme on a number of occasions. In one series a character undergoing hypnosis is repeatedly being led by the therapist to transform innocent statements into terrifying accounts of homicidal and abusive parents, as well as UFO abductions.[78] Another series depicted a cunning lawyer attempting to emphasize the difficult life led by his client. He asks, "In fact, you were abused, right? By a priest, perhaps?" The client replies, "A priest? Sure, why not?"[79]

In recent decades, concern over child abuse has followed a cyclical pattern, in each stage of which the recognition of a problem is followed by the making of extravagant claims and the passage of far-reaching legislation. After some years the public grows skeptical about the extent of the claims and the nature of the new laws, and a reaction sets in, so that the "crusade" itself becomes the problem. This was the pattern with the sex-offender panic of the 1930s and the 1940s, and the false-memory issue might foreshadow a comparable setback for the child-abuse problem that has achieved such visibility during the past twenty years. For the therapeutic community, the clergy-abuse controversy should be viewed as a rearguard action, an opportunity to reverse dangerous trends. The mixed success that the claims-makers enjoyed bodes ill for their future success in this area.

10

Meanings and Directions

The construction of the clergy-abuse problem can be approached in a number of ways. The issue's origins can be traced to the interplay of various interest groups, who made effective use of opportunities arising from developments in the mass media and the legal environment. However, the whole affair also illustrates deeper structural changes in American society that have had a profound impact upon religious thought, and the effects are likely to continue in future years. Perceptions of a crisis over clergy abuse suggest how far the particular charges violated powerful new sensibilities and value systems. Public outcry reflects a fundamental shift away from traditional attitudes toward religious authority, in the direction of secular standards more in keeping with liberal and feminist beliefs. The specific instance of clergy abuse may thus foreshadow other problems and crises that will be experienced by American churches in the next decade or so. In terms of the Catholic church, the practical and ideological effects are likely to be devastating for traditional structures.

Constructing the Problem

Successive studies of social problems and moral panics have suggested a number of critical preconditions for the generation and acceptance of a given issue, for a problem to "succeed," and clergy abuse exemplifies most of these. Ideally, a successful problem should be sufficiently familiar for the audience to be able to recognize its broad characteristics and potential for serious harm, which is why new issues are sometimes portrayed as subsets of existing topics. "As an acknowledged source for concern, a well established social problem becomes a resource, a foundation upon which other claims may be built."[1] Once "child abuse" has been established as a menace, there is widespread public knowledge and acceptance of the stereotypical characteristics of the offense, and often of an accompanying terminology and body of

153

assumptions (survivors, the statistical dark figure, the cycle of abuse, and so on). It then becomes easier for subsequent claims-makers to build their particular issues upon this narrative framework, so that "ritual abuse," "elder abuse," or "clergy abuse," require less detailed explanation or construction.

Also, the clergy affair illustrates yet again the significance of naming and contextualization in the creation of a problem, of declaring the appropriate limits of the issue's domain. This process determines the quest for solutions to the problem identified, for the policy consequences for "pedophile priests" would be utterly different if the issue were defined instead as merely clergy molestation or the feminist concept of clergy exploitation. The triumph of one particular view reflects the success of activism by the rival Catholic pressure groups, who from 1985 onward pioneered the exposés of the individual cases and were the first to offer a systematic explanation of the issue.

However, the clergy-abuse story also suggests a number of points that are not often emphasized in the abundant literature on problem construction, above all the central significance of the legal dimension. Social problems are described in terms of the claims-making activity of interest groups and the role of the mass media, and these were major factors in the events described here. However, neither the media nor the activists would have had many cases on which to draw, any "raw material" for construction, were it not for the substantial changes in the character of litigation and the legal profession in the decade after 1975. The deleterious effects of the "litigation explosion" and the related liability revolution can be long debated, but no account of problem construction in the contemporary United States should ignore the impact of extended legal liability, whether one wishes to study issues of public health, education, medicine, or social policy. The powerful incentive to seek remedies through the courts reinforces and rewards what has been described as the "victim culture," the tendency of groups and individuals to seek external culprits for disorders or difficulties that afflict them.[2] A threat or promise of large damage payments has become a powerful force motivating the reformulation of social issues.

The example of legal change also points out the necessity of studying social problems in the broadest historical context. Though the first major cases of clergy abuse were not publicized until 1984–1985, we can discern a chain of historical causation that leads back at least into the 1960s. It was the civil rights movement that transformed attitudes toward the role of courts and law, and promoted the view that litigation might be a healthy and socially desirable means of redressing injustice. "Litigating for rights" was appropriate when cases were fought on behalf of classes of hitherto unrepresented victims opposing powerful corporations or institutions, and this concept justified the ethical and legal changes of the 1970s and early 1980s. The radical political ideas of the 1960s also left an inheritance in the feminist movement, which shared with civil rights activism concepts such as structural oppression and group victimization. There is a linear connection from the feminist movement to the surging concern with child sexual abuse that caused so comprehensive a revision of social attitudes during the 1980s. Also, the bitter factionalism of the Catholic church during the mid-1980s was a continuation of disputes that developed during the 1960s, especially during the watershed year of 1968.

Though these different phenomena appear quite unrelated, all were necessary pre-conditions for the generation of the abuse problem. Without the requisite ideology, there would not have been the upsurge of child-abuse prosecutions, nor would anything have appeared amiss about the church's handling of its offending priests. Without the litigation explosion, attorneys would have lacked the ability to begin the investigation and prosecution of church authorities that so swiftly developed a cyclical and self-sustaining character. And had the Catholic church not been so divided, it would have been easier for the hierarchy to win credence for assertions that the charges were simply another chapter in the American pattern of hysterical anti-Catholic agitation. Finally, the critical news coverage of the abuse cases owed much to the revived muckraking traditions that had grown out of the Watergate affair and the antiwar protests, and that caused a general distrust of government and powerful institutions.

Although it is improbable in the extreme that even the most perceptive observer in 1980 could have predicted the extent of the crisis that the Catholic church was about to undergo, there were already symptoms of impending trouble. To take one example from many, it was in 1981 that the conservative Catholic monsignor George Kelly wrote *The Battle for the American Church*, warning of the many signs of real and potential conflict within American Catholicism. He cited the growth of factionalism, the radical change in concepts of the priesthood, and the impact of feminism on women's religious orders. He also noted how the media had lost the respectful restraint traditionally shown toward churches and priests, especially in the Catholic context: "But lately news for news' sake is the compelling moral norm for revelations regardless of the consequences. . . . Magazines like *Newsweek* have a penchant for shocking audiences with stories about irregular priests. . . . [I]n a secularized culture, however, nothing is sacred, especially the sacred. Deflating or dethroning authority figures is fashionable."[3] He was referring to stories that in retrospect seem remarkably mild, about priests engaged in dating and casual heterosexual liaisons, but it took little imagination to see how rival factions might use larger scandals for polemical purposes. Had Kelly also noted the changing legal atmosphere, he would have included all the major components of the impending crisis

If for some reason the Gauthe case had not reached a public forum or had not achieved wide publicity, it is certain that one of the other instances would eventually have had a similar impact. Quite independent of events in Louisiana, there were by 1985 several separate legal actions involving clerical sexual misconduct. Between 1983 and 1985 countless news stories and articles emphasized that abuse could occur in any circumstance, and some observer sooner or later would cite a clergy lawsuit, making the point that "even a priest" was not immune. The McMartin affair made this danger acute. Once the incident was publicized, there were several groups with an interest in collating evidence about errant priests, in order to support an ideological point about the evil effects of "gay clericalism"; about the cynicism of the hierarchy; about the hypocrisy of a male institution that denounces abortion and homosexuality yet tolerates pedophiles. Given the political circumstances of the mid-1980s, it was also probable that Catholic groups and factions would adopt the theme and focus attention on Catholic misdeeds. Once set in train, it was only a

matter of time before the lawsuits and investigations now begun would bear full
fruit in a major scandal involving a true predatory pedophile who could be used,
however unfairly, as a symbol of all clergy sexually involved with minors. It is more
likely than not that reactions to this case would tend to revive anti-Catholic stereotypes and speculation.

The Church and the World

Inevitability is not a concept with which historians feel comfortable, but a clergy-
abuse problem was to say the least extremely likely to occur during the mid-1980s.
There were also structural factors within the Roman Catholic church that greatly enhanced the likelihood of scandals' occurring at about this time, and these incidents
would probably address a range of themes broadly similar to what was actually encountered in the abuse cases. Clergy abuse, in short, was inherently likely to be
transformed into "priest pedophilia."

This study has emphasized the role of specifically Catholic disputes in encouraging the construction of the problem, but divisions must be seen as part of a
longer-term conflict over the distinctive nature of the American Catholic church. In
summary, this body was in the middle of a difficult process of transition from a "sect"
into a "church," and the transformation dangerously enhanced the risk of scandal and
internal dissension. It may seem paradoxical to describe so large and powerful a
movement as Catholicism as lacking true "church" status, but a sociologist of religion would draw a significant distinction between the two terms depending on
the "degree of tension between religious organizations and their sociocultural environments."[4] "To the degree that a religious body sustains beliefs and practices at
variance with the surrounding environment, tension will exist between its members
and outsiders. . . . When a religious body has no beliefs or practices setting it apart
from its environment, no tension will exist." The more accommodating latter bodies
are churches; the former are sects, "religious bodies in a relatively high state of tension with their environments." Other scholars would add different criteria to the
distinction, for example, that sects require a significantly higher degree of commitment from their membership; they impose stricter discipline; and a higher proportion
of members enter the group by voluntary choice rather than by birth and early so-
cialization. Over time sects generally accommodate to the surrounding environment,
and achieve the stability and conventionality that demonstrate their evolution into
churches.

Sects are often regarded as numerically small fringe groups, but in American
history the Roman Catholic church has shared most elements of the definition of a
sect and has consistently maintained a "relatively high state of tension" with the assumptions of the broader culture.[5] Since the 1960s reforms within the church have
demonstrated all the classic symptoms that customarily mark the transformation of
a sect into a church: the erosion of distinctions in ritual, theology, and religious practice; the reduction or elimination of "cultural markers and symbolic boundaries"
such as Friday fasts and the Latin liturgy.[6]

This process of assimilation has occurred in other bodies, and once begun it soon
develops a powerful momentum. As activists or reformers begin to reduce tradi-

tional distinctiveness, they receive rewards and reinforcement from outside sources anxious to promote reform, including the existing churches and the media. Changes are encouraged as components of normalization or modernization: they may be described as "seeing the light," "being brought into the twentieth century," or achieving freedom from superstition. A movement to conventionality may also reduce historic tensions and conflicts with secular legal authorities over matters such as education or family structure. In fact, the pressures to assimilate become so strong that they are difficult to resist except perhaps by a thorough geographical separation. After a few years, a hypothetical sect is largely brought within the mainstream, except for diehard conservatives who might secede to form a new and still stricter exclusive body.

Religious changes begun in the 1960s had an enormous impact on all sections of the American Catholic church, and naturally aroused expectations that progress would be pursued to its logical conclusion, in effect the elimination of obstacles to complete harmonization with the liberal Protestant churches. This would mean the end of distinctive institutions like mandatory celibacy, the all-male priesthood with all its attendant prestige, the extreme emphasis on hierarchy and the autocratic episcopate, and liturgical or disciplinary practices such as confession. Reforms won the wholehearted support of the secular media, for whom they represented a convergence with conventional ideological goals: ideas such as the expansion of democracy and representative institutions, the decline of a privileged priestly caste, and the ending of gender discrimination. What could be less American than "the Catholic church's history of monarchical rule, grounded in celibacy"?[7] There is a nationalist or patriotic agenda here, in that the Romanness and internationalism of the Catholic church represent one of the sharpest areas of conflict with social assumptions. The movement to assimilation is sometimes characterized in partisan and quite loaded terms, as when a writer attacking Catholic political power observed that "the next decade may decide whether the internal conflicts of Catholicism will turn an autocratic church into a people's church, in tune with both ecumenism and constitutional principles."[8] The *Roman* Catholic church in America would thus become, in the fullest sense, the *American* Catholic church.

However, the experience of American Catholicism has differed fundamentally from that of other sectarian communities because although the process of assimilation developed an impressive momentum, it soon encountered insurmountable obstacles. A "natural" or predictable process was thwarted because the American church is only one component of a much larger international structure. Final decisions about the extent of reform lie outside the nation's borders, in a Vatican that must take account of the 90 to 95 percent of Catholics who are not Americans. The papal decision on contraception in 1968 reasserted the gulf between the church and contemporary cultural assumptions and kept alive the basic conflict between American Catholicism and "the world." High expectations raised in the 1960s were precipitously dashed, with severe consequences of disappointment and disillusion.

The defeat of "normalization" was especially bitter for the clergy, whose traditional role had been undermined without a new concept's being properly formulated or understood. Confusion about expectations contributed to the hemorrhage of priests from the late 1960s, and the ensuing clergy shortage contributed significantly to the later abuse scandals. Conflicts over Catholic distinctiveness exacerbated tensions between the leaders and the led. Most of the hierarchy continued to affirm Roman orthodoxy, but the relative assimilation of the laity is suggested by indices such as the sharp decline in the practice of confession from the late 1960s onward and the rising use of contraceptives among married couples to rates little short of the Protestant norm.[9]

Sects and Scandals

The American church of the past decade was vulnerable to scandal and conflict precisely because it lay somewhere between the sociological categories of sect and church. In seeking to abandon its sectarian status, the church also forfeited its protections against public hostility. In a *church*, belief and organizational structure are by definition unlikely to offend prevailing social attitudes and mores, so isolated crimes and scandals will not be denounced as reflective of grave structural flaws. External criticism of *sects* is likely to run much deeper, according on the degree of variance from accepted social norms.[10] Sects perform a convenient integrative function by providing a common enemy, a "dangerous outsider," against which the mainstream can unite and reassert its shared standards and beliefs. Depending on the legal and cultural environment of a given society, the tension between sects and the mainstream community might result in active persecution or it can take the form of ostracism and negative stereotyping.

Hostile constructions of a movement or group are achieved by imaginative or prurient exaggerations of precisely those aspects of belief or practice that distinguish the sect: for example, its sexual unorthodoxy, charismatic leadership, or communal lifestyle. The anti-Catholic polemics of the nineteenth and early twentieth centuries are indistinguishable in their emphases from the anticult literature of the past two decades.[11] Even modern controversies over deprogramming cult members were precisely foreshadowed in the efforts of nineteenth-century families to kidnap and reconvert daughters who had entered convents.

The structure of sectarian organizations makes them vulnerable to scandals. In many groups, the leadership operates with a huge amount of discretionary authority over matters like finance and administration. The possession of power without responsibility offers temptations to corruption or sexual misdeeds, which are all the more serious because the leaders themselves fall short of the lofty or puritanical standards of behavior that ordinary members are expected to meet. As Bruce remarks of new religious movements, NRMs,

> Many religious innovators and NRMs deliberately draw attention to sexuality. NRMs often claim moral and ethical as well as spiritual superiority. They are often ascetic and present either explicit or implicit challenges to the rest of us about our laxity. If we feel indisposed to accept the NRMs' claims to ascetic superiority, we may throw the challenge back with the simple technique of inversion.[12]

There is a potential for recurrent scandals of the most damning nature, based on obvious charges of hypocrisy. However, sects have internal mechanisms that tend to reduce both the likelihood and the severity of public scandals. Members prize the internal and informal resolution of disputes rather than resort to the procedures of a sinful outside world, so that disagreements or even crimes are less likely to come to light. Even if formal complaints or prosecutions do occur, members discount them as the inevitable product of popular prejudice. Vituperation from outsiders may even have a positive ideological effect on the group, reinforcing the members' sense of alienation and separateness from the social mainstream. The blame for scandal may thus fall on the person who denounced the crime rather than on the actual perpetrator. In these circumstances, the sect may heighten its resolution to remain a "peculiar people" or may even increase the degree of peculiarity. In the language of cognitive dissonance theory, "the more an individual suffers for something, the more positively he/she will evaluate it."

In the 1980s the American Catholic church was still sufficiently different to excite criticism, but its members no longer responded by "circling the wagons," as they had so predictably in the past. As has been argued in chapter 6, the scandals actually offered a rich opportunity for reformers to pursue their goals. The derailed process of assimilation had produced a substantial corps of dissenters within the American church whose grievances emphasized the continuing areas of distinctiveness that caused the greatest offense or puzzlement to the religious mainstream. Their critique was undertaken by means of a rhetoric drawn from the dominant secular culture, with ideas of individual rights, formal legality, and gender equality, all within a national and patriotic framework that opposed Roman domination. Instead of a charismatic priesthood subject only to church law, reformers demanded the disciplinary standards of a modern secular profession (see, for example, Andrew Greeley's complaint: "The priesthood may be the only profession in this country that makes no attempt to police itself against unprofessional behavior").[13] The clergy-abuse cases stigmatized exactly those aspects of Catholicism that had long been denounced and derided by outsiders, notably the "sectarian" tendency to resolve internal offenses quietly and informally. Despairing of achieving their goals within the organization, dissenters promoted reform (more daringly, "a reformation") by resorting to the mechanisms available within the secular society, especially the courts and the mass media. The influence of these ideas is indicated by the willingness of laity and even clergy to sue the church; a less "sectarian" response would be difficult to imagine.

The paradoxical expectations of the church hierarchy (the "official" church) explain the rhetorical response to the abuse cases. For example, dissidents demand that the church hierarchy observe formal legal/bureaucratic standards and norms in dealing with abuse cases, in effect that it act as a "normal" organization acts and claim no special privileges. On the other hand, when church authorities respond to charges with the conventional legal defenses appropriate to a comparable secular body, they are condemned for this failure to act consistently with their announced goals and aspirations. When church authorities are sufficiently accommodating to conventional standards as to admit or tolerate actively homosexual clergy, they open themselves to attack from both liberal and conservative factions for their failure to enforce announced policies. American Catholicism has forfeited the advantages of being a sect without gaining the "normal" status and respect appropriate to a church.

Values, Authority, and Religious Change

For the Catholic church, the clergy-abuse issue provided a focus for underlying conflicts between the attitudes and assumptions of the wider culture and those of the ecclesiastical organization. However, the Catholic experience was by no means unique; the crisis exemplifies long-term cultural changes that have affected many aspects of American religion, regardless of denomination. The affair says much about values, in the sense of those things that are most prized in a given society and the extent to which these values are now in flux. As the values and the attitudes of the surrounding culture change, so all churches find themselves under pressure to conform to their environment, a process marked by external criticism and internal controversy. In the past decade debates over sexual abuse and exploitation have regularly provided a forum for the exploration and resolution of underlying conflicts over values and authority.

The experience of the 1960s can again be cited to account for the sharp decline in all traditional models of authority, secular or religious, that challenged the position of the churches in general and the Catholic church in particular. Potential conflicts were for some years masked by the wholehearted commitment of the churches to political struggles on behalf of liberal concepts of rights, justice, and equality, especially in racial matters. However, the growing significance of issues of gender and sexual preference during the 1980s accentuated tensions between the traditional churches and the liberalism that prevailed in the mainstream society. In consequence, to use the seismic analogy suggested by Robert Wuthnow, the crucial fault lines in American religion now run *within* denominations rather than between different traditions and communities.

The centrality of women's issues and concerns has been apparent in the life of most major churches during the past two decades. For most religious organizations, the central ideological conflicts concern the related core issues of authority, tradition, and gender relations. In the 1970s the crucial goal was the advancement of women within existing institutional and credal structures, but in recent years concern has shifted to more fundamental questions of theology and authority. In the feminist view, the whole system of religious belief and organization is evaluated on the basis of its relevance and contribution to women's social and intellectual experience, and ideally will be preserved or discarded on this basis. Recent debates on "Goddess worship" represent an extreme manifestation of a thorough reassessment of the bases of authority within the Christian churches.[14]

Through most of the history of Christianity, models of authority have been found either in tradition or Scripture, mediated through an institutional church or clerical structure. In the feminist mold, such traditional warrants of authority are likely to be insufficient and also to be a significant part of the problems facing society. The churches are seen as bureaucratic institutions shaped by the social and economic interests of elite groups over successive centuries, and usually pursuing policies likely to align them with the government or groups holding social power. This is reflected in the common emphasis of religious bodies on issues of individual sin (rather than social or structural evil) and the support of family and patriarchal authority.

The increased social status and assertiveness of women has made suspect any institution that explicitly asserts masculine and patriarchal authority, and (in the Catholic church) refuses to countenance even notional equality within its professional leadership. In terms of the ideologies generally accepted since the 1960s, such traditionally based policies are easily stigmatized as severe violations of social values, using words like *discrimination, bias, sexism, misogyny,* and *prejudice.* These disparaging terms are enhanced or escalated by association with pernicious historical references, concepts such as medievalism, the Inquisition, or other manifestations of religious persecution. Although patriarchal power can be lambasted in abstract terms, feminist arguments gain rhetorical force from the problem of clergy abuse and exploitation. This exemplifies both the harmful consequences of the conservative ideology and its enduring hypocrisy in sexual matters.

The critique of patriarchal authority has also addressed the interests and rights of children, whom feminists regard as a traditionally neglected and exploited social group, and the influence of these ideas is indicated by the triumph of the child-abuse ideology between about 1978 and 1984. This had a transforming effect on many aspects of American culture: in law, the media, education, and religion. At least rhetorically, contemporary American culture has come to place a high premium on certain concepts of childhood, and these values must be protected even at the cost of sacrificing what were once considered centrally important religious beliefs, such as the sanctity of the priesthood, the secrecy of the confessional, and so on. The ease with which legislatures omitted clergy privilege from laws mandating the reporting of abuse is a striking manifestation of a new cultural environment. The rhetorical affirmation of children's interests has provided a versatile trump card that can be used to overwhelm older values such as the sacrosanctity of family discipline. During the Branch Davidian siege in Waco, Texas, in 1993, a decision to intervene militarily was justified on the basis of an alleged discovery that children within the compound were being abused.

Issues of authority are inextricably bound up with the question of credibility, which is the heart of the matter in virtually all child-abuse allegations. In a conflict between two competing versions of a given situation, whom should one be predisposed to believe: the individual and family or the large institution; the layperson or the cleric; the child or the adult; the therapist or the cleric? In every instance the recent abuse cases demonstrate an overwhelming public tendency to lean toward the credibility of the lay individual against the cleric or church, the child rather than the adult, the woman not the man; throughout, the prestige of religious sanctions or justifications has been overwhelmed by the influence of secular ideologies.

Changing values are reflected in the degree of discretion that can, according to social consensus, be safely granted to particular groups or institutions. In the past decade agencies affecting to defend children's interests have seen a vast enhancement of their resources and legal powers. This makes it far easier to remove children from homes and families believed to practice abuse, and without the legal formalities and procedure hitherto required. Conversely, church-run children's institutions were assailed for alleged involvement in physical abuse and neglect in addition to the better-publicized sexual exploitation. Whereas once the religious institutions would have been thought worthy of enforcing internal standards of behavior and morality, the current trend is to seek external controls from the civil and criminal law, and to impose the value systems of nonreligious groups.

The clergy-abuse scandals demonstrated a near-collapse of public confidence in the integrity of church institutions. In Chicago, for example, it was a political necessity that the investigative review board established by Cardinal Bernardin have a substantial lay majority. A relative decline of clerical status is reflected in the increased willingness of the mass media to investigate ecclesiastical misdeeds, especially involving women or children. In this sense, we can thoroughly agree with the remarks quoted earlier from Monsignor Kelly about changing social criteria for the groups and individuals who merit respect and reverence: "Deflating or dethroning [male, traditional] authority figures is fashionable."

Therapeutic Values

A crisis of belief in traditional authority was accompanied by questions about the standards by which behavior and morality could be judged. In this sense, the clergy-abuse issue was a further engagement in the ongoing conflict between the different value systems represented by organized religion on the one hand and the orthodoxies of the therapeutic and behavioral-science professions on the other, and the impact that each had in the mainstream culture. Secular and religious responses to the abuse cases both indicate a dramatic decline in the influence and social acceptability of traditional religious ideologies. At every stage the debate shows how far contemporary religious consciousness has been transformed by the insights of psychology, despite the apparent contradiction with traditional Christian doctrinal assumptions such as the belief in the power of sin and the necessity of repentance.

The changing concept of wrongdoing might be illustrated by imagining a priest known to have embezzled a substantial sum of money from a particular parish, but whose church superiors decide not to report the misdeed to civil authorities. Following a period of some years of retreat and self-discipline, the same individual is given a fresh start in a new parish. If known, such a decision would probably receive sympathy or even praise as a humane and generous measure, and one moreover that was closely in tune with the announced ideological goals of the church of encouraging forgiveness and redemption. It would also be justified by numerous scriptural passages commanding Christians both to forgive wrongs, "seventy times seven" if necessary, and wherever possible to avoid involving the civil authorities in internal church matters.[15] In fact, it is rather the decision to *exclude* the lapsed priest from future service that would be denounced as an act of hypocrisy and cruelty, given the religious and ideological framework of the organization.

The question then arises how such a hypothetical case differs from the notorious decision of a given diocese to return to ministry a man implicated in the sexual molestation of minors. An obvious answer is that this behavior differs from theft in that it is now commonly believed to reflect a compulsive or addictive personality disorder, which cannot be cured or deterred by even the most determined act of will on the part of the offender. The near-universal acceptance of this compulsive model suggests the continuing expansion of medical and deterministic interpretations of wrongdoing and the consequent reduction or revision of the concept of individual sinfulness, especially in matters of sexuality. Sin necessarily implies free will; psychological and therapeutic models are deterministic in their analysis of how character and behavior are formed by family, upbringing, and social development.

A fundamental change of value is also apparent from the response deemed proper to a particular act of wrongdoing. Historically, Christian ethical values emphasized the free responsibility of the individual both to make moral choices and to suffer the consequences of those decisions. In most churches the assumption was that a wrong act merited punishment and perhaps required penance but did not necessarily brand the culprit for life as having the stereotypical characteristics of an offender. A man who performed a sexual act with a boy had committed an act of sodomy or pederasty but did not thereby become a pederast who was inevitably likely to reoffend, any more than a man who visited a prostitute acquire the indelible label of "lecher." Nor was an individual who became drunk necessarily an irredeemable drunkard; he or she could reform and repent. Basic to the Christian value system is a belief in the worth and potential of repentance as a decision of the individual. In the therapeutic assumption, however, an increasing number of offenses are pathologized, regarded as the outcome of circumstances determined by factors beyond the individual. As such, they require diagnosis or classification with a medical term such as *alcoholic*, *pedophile*, or *ephebophile*, followed by appropriate treatment procedures.

During the 1970s and 1980s psychological values and assumptions had permeated the religious world no less than the secular culture, often through the vehicle of self-help and recovery movements.[16] In Protestant churches, small groups proliferated so rapidly from the early 1980s onward that their total membership surpassed that of Sunday schools, and with ever-eroding boundaries between "religious" Bible-study groups and more general self-help units.[17] Among the expanding range of twelve-step recovery movements are "Fundamentalists Anonymous" and groups offering recovery from "religious abuse." This condition is manifested by symptoms such as guilt, obsessive praying, hostility to sexuality, a preference for faith over inquiry, fasting, and attitudes of conflict toward the values of science and conventional education.[18]

Therapeutic ideas found many points of contact and similarity with contemporary political movements, especially the feminist and radical ideas currently transforming religious consciousness. For example, suffering and injustice are not necessarily inherent to a divine or providential plan for the world but commonly result from human or social agency and can be changed, reformed, or abolished. Passive acceptance of the sufferings either of oneself or of others is by no means a virtue, and neither is any attempt merely to ameliorate the worst of these conditions through acts of benevolence. The theory demands active political involvement to achieve structural change in social arrangements. Bad conditions and human suffering are not necessarily or even probably the fault of oneself, and the blame lies rather in the hands of others. Guilt, penance, and the sense of individual sin are not only unnecessary but actively counterproductive in the promotion of essential social change.

In the feminist context the locus of political change shifts to the personal arena and the realm of the family and domestic arrangements, and here too the sense of individual sin is questioned or refashioned. The response to personal problems and dysfunctions involves virtues such as empowerment, pride, assertiveness, and self-reliance, qualities that collectively made up a large part of what older Christian theology had customarily regarded as the fruits of sin. New ideas are reflected in the sweeping assault on the "abusive" implications of orthodox theology, Christology, and theodicy (see chapter 7).

The rejection of sin and the sense of guilt in the society at large was also influential in the courts. In 1987 a California court found a Protestant church liable following the suicide of a young man, accepting his parents' contention that the church had exacerbated his "pre-existing feelings of guilt, anxiety and depression." Legal writer Peter Huber aptly comments, "Perhaps it had. But the mission of many religions is to challenge heart and conscience, so as to promote a sense of contrition leading to absolution." [19]

An intellectual chasm separates the operating assumptions of the Catholic church and other traditional religious bodies from those of mainstream therapy and psychology. The medicalization of wrongdoing radically circumscribes the areas in which clergy can appropriately exercise their professional jurisdiction, and this loss of acknowledged expertise to therapists and medical authorities both symbolizes and accelerates a substantial decline in professional status for priests and ministers. However, not only were the clergy-abuse scandals generally interpreted according to therapeutic views and policies but the churches themselves adopted at least the rhetoric of the therapists. The standard operating assumptions of secular therapy dominated the main church-run treatment center, Saint Luke's Institute, and the center's director included in an essay the "twelve steps of Sexaholics Anonymous." [20]

When an abuse crisis was acknowledged by the early 1990s, the Catholic church did not react with the devices that might have seemed appropriate decades earlier: religious responses such as local or national days of prayer and repentance. The vast majority of public statements by the Catholic hierarchy accepted the basic belief about the compulsive and essentially irredeemable nature of adult sexual activity with children and admitted the quite radical belief that priests so involved should never again be restored to parish ministry. They also accepted that child victims urgently required therapy, treatment that should be provided by secular psychologists and counselors, itself a rejection of the means of healing offered by the church. Official Catholic documents accepted with little challenge the expansive claims made by therapists and child-abuse advocates about the vast extent of sexual abuse and its devastating and lifelong consequences, all ideas that are in reality open to serious challenge.

To take a minor but representative example of accommodation with therapeutic orthodoxy, when the cardinal's commission made its recommendations for reducing the future incidence of sexual misconduct by clergy of the Chicago archdiocese, it placed high emphasis on seminary training and the choice of proper individuals to be admitted and ordained. However, this reform was to be achieved not by a reassertion of any criteria drawn from any Catholic tradition but by the most advanced current methods of social and behavioral science. Seminaries were directed to maintain and refine their use of such psychological screening techniques as the MPD (Ministerial Potential Discerner), and where appropriate, sexual dysfunctions were to be diagnosed through the MMPI survey technique (the Minnesota Multiphasic Personality Inventory). [21]

Again, the Catholic church is far from unique in this regard, and many churches responded to the perceived crisis with an explosion of seminars, workshops, retreats, and "consciousness-raising" events, all of which promulgated the insights of therapists and counselors dealing with sexual abuse and harassment. In the Seattle archdiocese, for example, Archbishop Raymond Hunthausen responded to recent abuse allegations by requiring all priests and staffers to attend a workshop by Marie Fortune. Other denominations organized events with titles such as "Women, Abuse and the Bible."[22] Resorting to therapeutic authorities implies respect for if not full acceptance of their underlying value system no less than their methodologies, and the response to the abuse issue increases still further the influence of these assumptions within the churches. It is difficult to imagine that trend will not have doctrinal consequences in the decades to come, in areas as significant as Christology and the Trinity.

The Rhetoric of Religious Problems

The religious setting of the clergy-abuse issue sets it apart from other social problems involving themes such as drunk driving, illegal immigration, and drug abuse. Of course, religious problems cannot exist wholly independent of general secular fears and concerns, for (with a few extreme sectarian exceptions) both activists and potential audiences are inevitably influenced by the media and the social environment. However, the religious environment does presuppose a number of peculiar characteristics.

Social problems are often identified when a group or individual makes claims with the ultimate goal of changing laws or social policy. The legal separation of church and state means that claims-makers in a religious environment are usually seeking to affect the policies not of a government but of a particular church or sectarian tradition. Activists must operate within the church's distinctive rhetorical and cultural traditions and its own political mechanisms, and they are unable to use such familiar publicity devices as hearings before congressional committees. In fact, religious problems can arise or be exacerbated by an improper crossover between church and state, as with the allegation that the Catholic church drew on its allies in law enforcement to cover up abuse scandals. Within the religious organizations themselves, change comes through means very different from those that might be expected from a democratic or commercial concern: there is no electorate in the usual sense, and there are no shareholders to influence. As conservative Catholics are fond of repeating, the church is not a democracy, and perhaps never will be. Pressure groups must therefore appeal to a dual audience, using conventional rhetoric and demands suitable for a general secular public but also framing problems in a way that will influence the internal structures of the church or religious organization.

As it came to be constructed, the clergy-abuse problem carried a simple but powerful message about the urgent necessity for ecclesiastical reform. The effectiveness of this message is suggestive for the contemporary state of argument in religious matters, for the best means of making and establishing claims, and for the most reliable warrants to justify change. In all these areas there has been some convergence with secular concerns. The contrast with recent events might be illustrated by imagining the nature of religious debate in a previous century, in which the needs

or interests of a particular group were in serious conflict with the policies of a dominant church. Usually, the dissident approach would be primarily historical. This
might take several forms, including an assertion that the dissident group was basing
itself on a superior or more authentic tradition, or a declaration that the group relied
on Scriptures other than those emphasized by the church. All these strategies have
been employed in recent engagements between the Catholic church and its feminist
or liberationist foes, who have retrieved the Christian tradition of political protest
and argue that women played a substantial if largely forgotten role in the early
church. Assertions of gay rights can similarly employ the historical argument that
modern hostility to homosexuality was not present in the early or medieval church.[23]

What separates contemporary polemics from its predecessors is the absolute necessity to link historical or theological assertion with arguments that are pragmatic
and utilitarian. In contrast to earlier centuries, it would be unsound today to base an
argument solely on traditional religious criteria ("The Bible says . . . "; "The Church
has always believed . . . "), or indeed on traditional authority of any kind, whether
scriptural or traditional. To state, however controversially, that the medieval church
blessed same-sex "marriages" might be dismissed as talk of a historical curiosity. To
argue that a particular doctrine is wrong because it causes actions that are recognized as immediately harmful is far more effective, and it is imperative that the
harm be comprehensible in secular terms. Even the opponents of "Goddess worship" who use Scripture to denounce religious syncretism link their attacks to
warnings of practical evils such as satanic cults and ritual abuse.

In view of contemporary social ideologies and commonplaces, issues gain power
if they can be linked either to defending and promoting the status of women or to
any threat that can be postulated against children. This is by no means a new rhetorical development; it was ably pioneered in the early twentieth century by the
temperance movement. Pornography is depicted as evil and worthy of prohibition
not because it violates the biblical seventh commandment but because it leads to
child pornography and to sexual violence against women. Consuming illegal drugs
appears superficially to represent consensual victimless crime, but the offense leads
to the innocent suffering of "crack babies," "ice babies," and the rest. A celibate
clergy is wrong not because it is antiscriptural but because it creates a situation in
which priests molest boys in the sacristy. Homosexuality is not wrong because the
Bible (arguably) says so but because it is associated with pedophilia, and as long as
sexual preference remains a contentious issue, pedophile charges are likely to be the
weapon of choice in opposing homosexual aspirations in the churches or in society
at large. The rhetoric of contemporary social problems thus illustrates the essential
importance of placing the interests of women and children in the forefront of any
feasible issue in order to take advantage of new sensibilities. In the case of clergy
abuse, such a shift of emphasis has already permitted the undermining of what once
appeared impregnable ideological positions.

"The Greatest Crisis"?

The abuse crisis has had grave consequences for the Catholic church in North
America, an impact that is perhaps disguised by the inflated claims made by some

commentators. Activists calling attention to an issue make claims that appear extravagant, exaggerating the scale of the phenomenon or its impact on the community. It is not difficult to find examples of this rhetorical escalation in the area of priest pedophilia, described in phrases such as "perhaps the most serious crisis Catholicism has faced since the Reformation"[24] and "the greatest crisis the Catholic church has faced."[25] This is a familiar form of hyperbole, and it is not unprecedented. The theological liberalism of the 1890s was similarly said to have precipitated "The Great Crisis in American Catholic History," though this is today remembered by few nonspecialists.[26]

From a global perspective, the "greatest-crisis" language is fatuous. The contemporary abuse issue directly affects perhaps a few hundred priests on one continent, and it fades into insignificance beside such political conflicts as the spread of Islam and Protestantism in the early modern period, the rise of communism and fascism in the early twentieth century, and such intellectual crises as the Enlightenment and the growing hegemony of science and rationalism in the nineteenth century. Is this really a greater crisis for the whole church than, say, the year 1940, when Europe faced the imminent prospect of partition between Hitler and Stalin? To take a contemporary example, many would argue that the gravest single danger facing world Catholicism today comes from the massive inroads of evangelical Protestantism in Latin America, the home of perhaps a third of all Catholics.

The present problem might usefully be compared with the situation of the European church in the last quarter of the eighteenth century, when most major Catholic nations had dragooned into obedience the church structures on their own territories and secularized much church property. Major religious orders were dissolved at the behest of secular governments, and the prevailing intellectual tone of the era was profoundly hostile to any aspect of traditional or revealed religion such as Trinitarian belief. The revolutionary government in France was systematically executing hundreds of bishops, priests, and religious, and the same regime abducted and imprisoned two successive popes. When Rome fell to the French in 1798, it would have taken great optimism to believe that the Catholic church would survive into the nineteenth century. Only the most extreme hyperbole could suggest that the North American scandals of 1992 were somehow more threatening or damaging than the genuine crises of 1940, the 1790s, the 1520s, or of many other years when the Catholic church faced appalling perils.

Though falling short of these other menaces past and present, the abuse problem has already had complex effects on North American Catholicism, and there may be serious long-term consequences. Catholic observers frequently note how easily outsiders are misled by the divisive and even vicious tone of controversies within the church; in reality these have little impact on "real" Catholic life, which revolves around the enduring verities of the parish and the Sacraments. In the abuse issue, however, lies a serious threat to exactly these core phenomena that have survived unscathed the decades of skirmishing over matters like contraception and women's ordination.

It is barely a decade since the Gauthe trial revived the image of the pedophile priest, but in that short time the torrent of publicity has substantially changed popular attitudes toward the Roman Catholic church and its priesthood. One harrowing change is the revival of stereotypes that most observers believed long extinct. *A Gospel of Shame* accurately notes that the abuse issue has caused an outpouring of humor and folktales concerning priests and illustrates this by recounting a vulgar joke about a man who stands in for a priest at the confessional.[27] Hearing a confession from an admitted molester, the man struggles to find an appropriate penance, and then asks the altar boy what Father George gives for sex with a twelve-year-old boy. The boy replies, "Usually, I get a dollar bill and a candy bar." Citing this story well illustrates public attitudes, but the authors are incorrect in suggesting that it was a novel outcome of recent events, "a joke making the rounds among many Catholics in 1992." This tale is certainly decades old and, in different guises, may long predate this century. Although opposition might properly be termed anticlerical or antihierarchy rather than anti-Catholic, the pedophile issue has legitimized patterns of rhetoric and prejudice that would have been quite familiar in the era of the Know-Nothings.

There is a classic sociological account of how people come to determine the shape of reality, the "real" being defined as those things that exist independent of our volition, the inevitable things we take for granted. Berger and Luckman write that "the reality of everyday life maintains itself by being embodied in routines, which is the essence of institutionalization. Beyond this, however, the reality of everyday life is ongoingly reaffirmed in the individual's interaction with others. Just as reality is originally internalized by a social process, so it is maintained in consciousness by social processes."[28] In the past decade a sinister and unsavory vision of the Catholic church has come close to being a routine part of perceived reality in this culture, with the required institutional quality provided by recurrent reinforcement through newspaper headlines and television news stories, rumors, and jokes. Collectively, these symbolic actions draw upon and define social reality. Whether a news program introduces a story with visuals of a church or a mass, or a cartoon depicts a bishop, or a comedian begins a story about a priest, there is the same expectation that the likely and predictable outcome will involve scandal, improper sexuality, and exploitation, or at least misogyny. When the same message is repeatedly offered by all forms of media and confirmed by conversation with friends or associates, then it has been legitimized as social fact, for Catholics as well as non-Catholics.

The savage anti-Catholicism of the nineteenth and early twentieth centuries did not prevent the church from maintaining high popular prestige or indeed from recruiting large numbers of prospective priests. At that point, however, the dark picture of the church was only one competing reality, which was not shared by Catholics themselves. The environment of the 1990s is different in many ways, and the number of priestly vocations stood at a historic low even before the present crisis. That the situation will grow worse in the short term appears inevitable. Priestly prestige has been severely damaged, and even in traditionally loyal Catholic communities there is evidence of intense family opposition to boys' entering seminary or even becoming altar boys. The apparent need to restrict personal contacts between clergy and children sends a symbolic message that this is a dangerous or tainted profession, even where no specific allegation has been made. In the Los Angeles archdiocese, for example, stringent policies now forbid priests from engaging in such apparently innocent activities as "hugging, tickling and wrestling that involve physical contact with minors."[29] The cases "have made it difficult for anyone who wears a clerical collar to so much as smile at a child, let alone stroll past playgrounds."[30] Anyone considering the priesthood must be aware of the greatly intensified risk that a career will be damaged, perhaps irreparably, by a scandal resulting from either false charges or misconstrued horseplay.

The betrayal of children is all the more devastating for Catholics because of the emphasis that the church in the past half century had placed on children's interests and activities. In many parishes it is precisely the child-centered activities that attract the highest degree of lay commitment: the church school and the children's choir, in sports, scouting, and recreational events. These stand at the heart of parish life and traditionally supplied the cohesion and sense of community that overrode any factional or theological grievances. If priests are to be severely constrained in their dealings with children, they lose much of their *raison d'être*, which is simultaneously undermined by the concession of their distinctive areas of expertise to therapists and medical professionals. Whereas celibacy once served as a token of charismatic power and status, it has today become for many a stigma warning of frustration and sexual impropriety. To use an economic analogy, the Catholic priesthood always offered both high costs and high rewards. Although it traditionally made intense demands on an individual, it offered commensurate rewards in terms of prestige and a lifelong career. The past decade has simultaneously slashed the potential rewards and escalated the costs to a level that many will find prohibitive.

Vocations will assuredly decline, though this trend will not have its full effects until early in the next century, when an already predicted shortage of priests could become significantly worse than yet imagined.[31] By that point, if not sooner, there will probably be a dramatic rise in lay pressure for measures to increase the number of priests, certainly including an end to mandatory celibacy; the restoration of priests who left their positions in order to begin families; and probably the ordination of women. If the American church were autonomous, there is little doubt that these measures would be implemented, but because it is not, no prediction can be made about the eventual outcome. The choices appear limited: either a radically transformed and more "American" church or an increasingly stressed and conflict-ridden community with a sharply declining number of individuals authorized to perform essential rituals. In either case the result would be completely different from the most sweeping change envisioned only a decade ago. This grim scenario is not the consequence of the pedophilia controversy alone, which should be seen, rather, as a catalyst accelerating existing trends. As in other denominations, however, the problem of clergy abuse has developed a momentum that is unlikely to slow before the end of the decade.

Understanding Clergy Abuse: Activism and Audience

In the 1970s sociologists developed the concept of the "moral panic" in order to analyze social problems and fears.[32] A panic is a sudden manifestation of exaggerated public fear and concern over an apparently novel threat:

> When the official reaction to a person, groups of persons or series of events is *out of all proportion* to the actual threat offered, when "experts" . . . *perceive* the threat in all but

identical terms . . . when the media representations universally stress "sudden and dramatic" increases (in numbers involved or events) and "novelty", above and beyond that which a sober, realistic appraisal could sustain, then we believe it is appropriate to speak of the beginnings of a *moral panic*.[33]

The panic reaction occurs not because of any rational assessment of the scale of the particular menace but as a result of ill-defined fears that eventually find a dramatic and oversimplified focus in one incident or stereotype, which then provides a visible symbol for discussion and debate.[34] Panics are important because they reflect deep underlying social tensions over matters as diverse as ethnicity, social change, and a crisis in values and social attitudes.

It is tempting to see a moral panic in the "sudden and dramatic" concern over the "novelty" of priest pedophilia, though the theory cannot be applied precisely and the concept has been subject to criticism. The very term *panic* is heavily value-laden and suggests that virtually any fears analyzed are *ipso facto* irrational and wildly overblown. To an even greater degree than "constructed," to speak of "panic" implies dismissive skepticism. Although many statements and estimates about clergy sex abuse are distorted or exaggerated, the verifiable core of the phenomenon is still sufficient to justify a degree of public concern. Pederast priests and ministers do exist and can cause harm, though the elements of an appropriate policy response are not self-evident.

Where the moral panic concept is useful is in its emphasis on the audience for a putative problem as much as on the claims-makers, and on the agendas that that audience brings to a particular issue or text. In this view, social reaction is the determining force in transforming individual crimes or abusive acts into general problems, which are interpreted according to preexisting public concerns and fears rather than by any intrinsic quality of the acts themselves. As in other historical periods in which there has been intense hostility to the church and its clergy, it is not necessary to suppose that the frequency or gravity of clerical misdeeds has increased significantly in recent years. What has changed is the moral perception of the public and, crucially, of the Catholic laity themselves, who now provide a hungrily receptive audience for claims of priestly atrocities. As the media and the various interest groups present new stories to feed the emerging market, so the attitudes and expectations of the audience become ever more skeptical of clerical virtue and authority.[35]

The resulting cycle has no natural or inevitable resolution, but such anticlerical insurgency has historically portended periods of sweeping and often painful internal reform for the church, marked by growing intrusions from the secular state and its legal apparatus. Though not yet anything approaching a "greatest crisis," the historical precedents are not comforting. The original Protestant Reformation owed less to any theological discovery and more to a tectonic shift in notions of the rights and status of the laity. As so often in the past, contemporary anticlericalism is the symbolic assertion of this new lay mood of self-confidence and self-awareness.

Given the changing nature of public perceptions and expectations in recent years, it is quite possible to imagine an influential "clergy-abuse problem" arising from real phenomena far less numerous and damaging than those that actually have occurred. If the abuse crisis had not existed, then some other problem involving priestly deviance and sexuality would probably have developed, drawing on the same range of issues, and that problem would have had quite as substantial an impact on the churches. The clergy-abuse issue has attained the force it has because it epitomized the diverse interests and fears of a broad array of social constituencies at a time of dizzying transition in their expectations about matters as basic as gender relations and family structure.

Notes

Abbreviations

APA American Protective Association

NCCB National Conference of Catholic Bishops

NCR National Catholic Reporter

SNAP Survivors Network of those Abused by Priests

USCC United States Catholic Conference

VOCAL Victims of Clergy Abuse Linkup (later "The Linkup")

WOC Women's Ordination Conference

Chapter 1: The Construction of Problems and Panics

1. R. C. Fuller and R. D. Myers, "The Natural History of a Social Problem," *American Sociological Review* 6 (1941).

2. Philip Jenkins, *Using Murder: The Social Construction of Serial Homicide* (Hawthorne, N.Y.: Aldine de Gruyter, 1994); Philip Jenkins, *Intimate Enemies: Moral Panics in Contemporary Great Britain* (Hawthorne, N.Y.: Aldine de Gruyter, 1992); Joel Best, *Threatened Children* (Chicago: University of Chicago Press, 1990); Malcolm Spector and John Kitsuse, *Constructing Social Problems* (Hawthorne, N. Y.: Aldine de Gruyter, 1987).

3. Erich Goode and Nachman Ben-Yehuda, *Moral Panics* (Oxford: Blackwells, 1994); Joel Best, ed., *Images of Issues* (Hawthorne, N.Y.: Aldine de Gruyter, 1989); Stan Cohen and Jock Young, eds., *The Manufacture of News: Social Problems, Deviance and the Mass Media* (London: Constable, 1973); Stan Cohen, *Folk Devils and Moral Panics: The Creation of the Mods and Rockers* (Oxford: Blackwells, 1972).

4. Jenkins, *Intimate Enemies*; Jenkins, *Using Murder*.

5. Best, *Threatened Children.*

6. See chapter 9, below.

7. Stuart Hall et al., *Policing the Crisis* (London: Routledge, 1978), p. 54.

8. David Ray Papke, *Framing the Criminal* (Hamden, Conn.: Archon, 1987), p. xvii; Erving Goffman, *Frame Analysis: An Essay on the Organization of Experience* (New York: Harper & Row, 1974).

9. Best, *Threatened Children.*

10. Hall et al., *Policing the Crisis,* pp. 223–26.

11. Jason Berry, *Lead Us Not into Temptation* (New York: Doubleday, 1992).

12. Elinor Burkett and Frank Bruni, *A Gospel of Shame* (New York: Viking, 1993).

13. A. W. Richard Sipe, "Celibacy and Imagery: Horror Story in the Making," *National Catholic Reporter,* July 2, 1993, p. 5; A. W. Richard Sipe, "To Enable Healing," *National Catholic Reporter,* September 17, 1993, pp. 6–7. A. W. Richard Sipe, *Sex, Priests and Power: Anatomy of a Crisis,* (New York: Brunner/Mazel, 1995). Also see below, chapter 5.

14. Berry, *Lead Us Not into Temptation.*

15. Ronald Smothers, "Preacher's Journey: Long Trail of Abuse," *New York Times,* November 15, 1988, p. A1.

16. Thomas Schilling and Charles Mount, "Suit Charges Moral Misconduct by Arlington Heights Priest," *Chicago Tribune,* December 24, 1982, p. B1; compare Jeanne Miller, *Assault on Innocence* (Albuquerque, N.M.: B&K Publishers, 1988; originally published under the pseudonym Hilary Stiles).

17. Mark Curriden, "Third Brother in Family of Ministers Facing Charges of Child Molestation," *Atlanta Journal and Constitution,* March 28, 1992, p. A3.

18. Said Deep, "Cleric Held on Sex Abuse Charges," *Detroit News,* November 18, 1992, p. G6; Said Deep, "Pastor Faces New Charges of Raping Four Year Old," *Detroit News,* November 19, 1992, p. B4. The driver was subsequently acquitted.

19. Aric Press et al., "Priests and Abuse," *Newsweek,* August 16, 1993, pp. 42–44. The only text that attempts a broad ecumenical overview of clergy malfeasance is Anson Shupe, *In The Name of All That's Holy* (Westport, Conn.: Praeger, 1995).

Chapter 2: The Anti-Catholic Tradition

1. Elinor Burkett and Frank Bruni, *A Gospel of Shame* (New York: Viking, 1993), p. 28.

2. Ibid., p. 178.

3. Ibid., p. 28.

4. The continuing survival of nativist stereotypes is well described in Andrew Greeley, *An Ugly Little Secret* (Kansas City, Mo.: Sheed, Andrews & McMeel, 1977), though this work understates the force of the sexual rhetoric in this area. Michael Schwartz, *The Persistent Prejudice* (Huntington, Ind.: Our Sunday Visitor, 1984).

5. Jose Mariano Sanchez, *Anticlericalism: A Brief History* (Notre Dame: University of Notre Dame Press, 1972).

6. John Miller, *Popery and Politics in England, 1660–1688* (Cambridge: Cambridge University Press, 1973).

7. Denis G. Paz, *Popular Anti-Catholicism in Mid-Victorian England* (Stanford: Stanford University Press, 1992); Philip Jenkins, "G. K. Chesterton and the Anti-Catholic Tradition," *Chesterton Review* 18(3) (1992): p. 345–69.

8. From a large literature, see, for example, E. W. McFarland, *Protestants First! Orangeism in Nineteenth Century Scotland* (Edinburgh: Edinburgh University Press, 1991); Cecil J. Houston and William J. Smyth *The Sash Canada Wore* (Toronto: University of Toronto Press,

1980); Steve Bruce, *No Pope of Rome: Anti-Catholicism in Modern Scotland* (Edinburgh: Mainstream, 1985).

9. Quoted in Steven Marcus, *The Other Victorians* (London: Corgi, 1969), pp. 62–63.

10. Sydney E Ahlstrom, *A Religious History of the American People* (New Haven: Yale University Press, 1972); Jenny Franchot, *Roads to Rome: The Antebellum Protestant Encounter with Catholicism* (Berkeley: University of California Press, 1994), pp. 87–98.

11. Franchot, *Roads to Rome*, pp. 99–111; Bryan Le Beau, "Saving the West from the Pope," *American Studies* 32(1) (1991): 101–14.

12. David H. Bennett, *The Party of Fear* (New York: Vintage, 1990), pp. 171–82; Schwartz, *The Persistent Prejudice*; Donald L. Kinzer, *An Episode in Anti-Catholicism: The American Protective Association* (Seattle: University of Washington Press, 1964); John Higham, *Strangers in the Land: Patterns of American Nativism, 1860–1925* (New Brunswick, N.J.: Rutgers University Press, 1955).

13. Marcus Bach, *They Have Found a Faith* (Indianapolis: Bobbs-Merrill, 1946), p. 14. For the Klan, see Richard K. Tucker, *The Dragon and the Cross: The Rise and Fall of the Ku Klux Klan in Middle America* (Hamden, Conn.: Archon, 1991); Leonard J. Moore, *Citizen Klansmen: The Ku Klux Klan in Indiana, 1921–1928* (Chapel Hill: University of North Carolina Press, 1991); William D. Jenkins, *Steel Valley Klan* (Kent, Ohio: Kent State University Press, 1990); Philip Jenkins, "The Ku Klux Klan in Pennsylvania, 1920–1940," *Western Pennsylvania Historical Magazine* 69(2) (1986): 121–37.

14. Edmund A. Moore, *A Catholic Runs for President* (New York: Ronald Press, 1956). Higham's remark is quoted from the *Catholic League Newsletter* 16(10) (October 1989): 6.

15. Quoted in Geoffrey R. Elton, *The Tudor Constitution* (Cambridge: Cambridge University Press, 1960), p. 323.

16. There is a rich anthology of such charges in the essays collected in Peter A. Dykema and Heiko A. Oberman, eds., *Anticlericalism in Late Medieval and Early Modern Europe* (Leiden: E. J. Brill, 1993). See, for example, pp. 29–30, 276–77; see especially Albrecht Classen, "Anticlericalism in Late Medieval German Verse" pp. 91–114.

17. Dykema and Oberman *Anticlericalism in Late Medieval and Early Modern Europe*, pp. 250–52.

18. Mark Twain, *Letters from the Earth*, ed. Bernard DeVoto (New York: Perennial Library, 1974), p. 53; Franchot, *Roads to Rome*, pp. 120–26.

19. Bennett, *The Party of Fear*, p. 175.

20. Nancy Roberts, "Are There Really Tunnels Linking Rectories and Convents?" *US Catholic*, January 1, 1990. Craig E. Harline, *The Burdens of Sister Margaret* (New York: Doubleday, 1994), explores fantasies of rape and harassment among nuns themselves.

21. Walter L. Arnstein, *Protestant versus Catholic in Mid-Victorian England: Mr. Newdegate and the Nuns* (Columbia: Mo.: University of Missouri Press, 1982); Ray Allen Billington, *The Protestant Crusade, 1800–1860: A Study of the Origins of American Nativism* (Gloucester, Mass.: Peter Smith, 1963; originally published 1938), pp. 67, 360–66.

22. David Brion Davis, "Some Themes of Counter-Subversion: An Analysis of Anti-Masonic, Anti-Catholic, Anti-Mormon Literature," in *From Homicide to Slavery* (New York: Oxford University Press, 1986), pp. 137–54; H. Montgomery Hyde, *A History of Pornography* (London: Four Square, 1966).

23. Marcus, *The Other Victorians*, pp. 62–63; Henry Spencer Ashbee, *Index of Forbidden Books* (London: Sphere, 1969).

24. The Marquis de Sade, *The Complete Justine, Philosophy in the Bedroom, and Other Writings* (New York: Grove, 1966), p. 741.

25. Iain McCalman, "Unrespectable Radicalism: Infidels and Pornography in Early Nineteenth Century London," *Past and Present* 104 (1984): 86–91.

26. Billington, *The Protestant Crusade,* pp. 67, 80; Franchot, *Roads to Rome*, pp. 105–6.

27. Ashbee, *Index of Forbidden Books*.

28. Billington, *The Protestant Crusade.* pp. 361–62.

29. Compare Ronald Pearsall, *The Worm in the Bud* (London: Pelican, 1971), pp. 418–19.

30. Franchot, *Roads to Rome,* pp. 135–61; Billington, *The Protestant Crusade*.

31. *Awful Disclosures of Maria Monk* (Philadelphia: T. B. Peterson, n.d. [ca.1840]; first published 1836).

32. Compare James A. Lewis, "Mind-Forged Manacles," *Mid-America* 72 (3) (1990).

33. Charles Chiniquy, *Fifty Years in the Church of Rome* (Montreal: Drysdale, 1886).

34. Bennett, *The Party of Fear*, pp. 175–76.

35. David F. Greenberg, *The Construction of Homosexuality* (Chicago: University of Chicago Press, 1988), p. 289.

36. Quoted in Jason Berry, *Lead Us Not into Temptation* (New York: Doubleday, 1992), p. 270.

37. Kent Gerard and Gert Hekma, eds., *In Pursuit of Sodomy: Male Homosexuality in Renaissance and Enlightenment Europe* (New York: Harrington Park Press, 1989), pp. 79–81, 95–96, 410–14, 447.

38. James M. Saslow, "Homosexuality in the Renaissance," in Martin Bauml Duberman, Martha Vicinus, and George Chauncey, eds., *Hidden from History: Reclaiming the Gay and Lesbian Past* (New York: New American Library, 1989), p. 93.

39. Originally published 1894: reprinted in Brian Reade, ed., *Sexual Heretics: Male Homosexuality in English Literature from 1850 to 1900* (London: Routledge & Kegan Paul, 1970).

40. Reade, *Sexual Heretics*; compare George Chauncey, "Christian Brotherhood or Sexual Perversion?" in Duberman, Vicinus, and Chauncey, *Hidden from History,* pp. 294–317.

41. McCalman, "Unrespectable Radicalism," 86–91; Iain McCalman, *Radical Underworld* (Cambridge: Cambridge University Press, 1988).

42. *Rugby Songs* (London: Sphere 1967), pp. 161, 166.

43. Norman Cohn, *The Pursuit of the Millennium* (London: Secker & Warburg, 1957), pp. 86.

44. Clorinda Matteo de Turner, *Aves sin nido* (New York: Las Americas, 1968).

45. Mongo Beti, *The Poor Christ of Bomba*, African Writers Series (London: Heinemann 1971; originally published 1956).

46. Billington, *The Protestant Crusade* pp. 361–62; Franchot, *Roads to Rome*, p. 125.

47. Quoted in Richard Hofstadter, *The Paranoid Style in American Politics* (Chicago: University of Chicago Press, 1979), p. 34.

48. Burkett and Bruni, *A Gospel of Shame*, 28.

49. Richard Grunberger, *A Social History of the Third Reich* (London: Penguin, 1974), pp. 557–58.

50. Nathaniel Micklem, *National Socialism and the Roman Catholic Church* (New York: Oxford University Press, 1939), pp.156–61.

51. "Nazi Charges of Immorality Are Poorly Founded," *Catholic Register* (Altoona-Johnstown, Pa.), November 7, 1937, p.1; "Immorality Trials Extended to Austria," *Catholic Standard and Times* (Philadelphia), July 8, 1938, p. 1 .

52. Micklem *National Socialism and the Roman Catholic Church*, pp. 156–61

53. Grunberger, *A Social History of the Third Reich*, pp. 557–58.

54. Micklem *National Socialism and the Roman Catholic Church* , p. 159.

55. Ibid., pp. 159–60.

56. Samuel Walker, *In Defense of American Liberties* (New York: Oxford University Press, 1990); compare Emmett McLoughlin, *People's Padre: An Autobiography* (Boston: Beacon Press, 1954).

57. Throughout these years, the *Converted Catholic Magazine* continued to provide a forum for extravagant charges of papist wrongdoing and conspiracy.

58. Bennett, *The Party of Fear,* pp. 319–22. There was a brief upsurge in the publication of anti-Catholic tracts and conspiracy books. See especially Emmett McLoughlin, *American Culture and Catholic Schools* (New York: Lyle Stuart, 1960); Emmett McLoughlin, *Crime and Immorality in the Catholic Church* (New York: Lyle Stuart, 1962); Emmett McLoughlin, *An Inquiry into the Assassination of President Lincoln* (New York: Lyle Stuart, 1963).

59. James F. Richardson, Joel Best, and David Bromley, eds., *The Satanism Scare* (Hawthorne, N.Y.: Aldine de Gruyter 1991).

60. Philip Jenkins, *Using Murder: The Social Construction of Serial Homicide* (Hawthorne, N.Y.: Aldine de Gruyter, 1994); Philip Jenkins, *Intimate Enemies: Moral Panics in Contemporary Great Britain* (Hawthorne, N.Y.: Aldine de Gruyter, 1992).

61. Jenkins, *Intimate Enemies.*

62. "Cult Abuse of Children: Witch Hunt or Reality?" special issue of *Journal of Psychohistory,* spring 1994.

63. See chapter 9 below, for ritual and satanic abuse.

64. Lorraine Boettner *Roman Catholicism,* (1st British ed. (London: Banner of Truth Trust, 1966), p. 399.

65. Karl Keating, *Catholicism and Fundamentalism* (San Francisco: Ignatius, 1988).

66. Paul Boyer, *When Time Shall Be No More* (Cambridge: Harvard University Press, Belknap Press, 1992), pp. 274–75.

67. *What's Behind the New World Order* (Jemison, Ala.: Inspiration Books East, 1991).

68. Michael Hirsley, "Anti-Catholic Blitz Again Spurs Group to Action," *Chicago Tribune,* June 1, 1990, p. C7.

69. *Alberto* (Chick Comics, 1979), p. 12; compare McLoughlin, *An Inquiry into the Assassination of President Lincoln.*

70. Gerald Sussman, "The Goyspel [*sic*] According to Bernie," in *National Lampoon's Tenth Anniversary Anthology* (1979), 1:155–60.

Chapter 3: The Discovery of Clergy Sex Abuse

1. Tommy McIntyre, *Wolf in Sheep's Clothing* (Detroit: Wayne State University, 1988), pp. 163–64, 222–29.

2. Ibid., p. 224.

3. Mark E. Chopko, "Restoring Trust and Faith," *Human Rights,* fall, 1992, pp. 22–24.

4. Jason Berry, *Lead Us Not into Temptation* (New York: Doubleday, 1992), pp. 30–31.

5. Patrick Boyle, *Scout's Honor: Sexual Abuse in America's Most Trusted Institution* (Rocklin, Calif.: Prima, 1994), pp. 97–112; 200–202.

6. Compare Walter K. Olson, *The Litigation Explosion* (New York: Dutton 1991).

7. Jonathan Friendly, "Catholic Church Discussing Priests Who Abuse Children," *New York Times,* May 4, 1986, p. A26.

8. See table 3.1; Elinor Burkett and Frank Bruni, *A Gospel of Shame* (New York: Viking, 1993), pp. 159–60.

9. Berry, *Lead Us Not into Temptation,* 73.

10. *Chicago Tribune,* July 30, 1985.

11. Berry, *Lead Us Not into Temptation,* p. 232.

12. Ibid., p. 233.

13. Jim Cuddy, "Boys Story: How Trust of Priest Turned Into Sexual Abuse," *Pittsburgh Press,* October 23, 1988, p. A1; Lawrence Walsh, "Press Challenges Two Sealed Lawsuits," *Pittsburgh Press,* October 23, 1988, p. A1; "Pittsburgh Press Seeks Abuse Case Records," *Editor and Publisher,* November 19, 1988.

14. "Brief History: Handling Child Sex Abuse Claims," *Origins* (Catholic News Service) 23 (38) (1994): 666–70; Burkett and Bruni, *A Gospel of Shame*; Berry, *Lead Us Not into Temptation*; Leslie Bennetts, "Unholy Alliances," *Vanity Fair,* December 1991, pp. 224–78 ; Michael Harris, *Unholy Orders: Tragedy at Mount Cashel* (Toronto: Penguin, 1991), p. 257.

15. Berry, *Lead Us Not into Temptation,* pp. 98–101.

16. Burkett and Bruni, *A Gospel of Shame,* pp. 162–65.

17. Friendly, "Catholic Church Discussing Priests Who Abuse Children."

18. Peter Steinfels, "Inquiry in Chicago Breaks Silence on Sex Abuse by Catholic Priests" *New York Times,* February 24, 1992, p. A1; Peter Steinfels, "New Panel in Chicago to Study Sexual Abuse of Children by Priests," *New York Times,* June 16, 1992, p. A17; Peter Steinfels, "Bishops Vow Firm Action on Sexual Abuse by Priests," *New York Times,* November 20, 1992, p. A18; Berry, *Lead Us Not into Temptation,* pp. 110–12.

19. "Brief History: Handling Child Sex Abuse Claims" (Origins).

20. Ibid.; "USCC Pedophilia Statement," *Origins* (Catholic News Service) 17 (36) (1988): 624; "Catholic Bishops Defend Response to Child Abuse," *Education Week,* February 17, 1988, p. 2.

21. Irving Janis, *Groupthink,* 2nd ed. (Boston: Houghton Mifflin, 1982).

22. Charles E. Shepard, *Forgiven: The Rise and Fall of Jim Bakker and the PTL Ministry* (New York: Atlantic Monthly Press, 1989); Larry Martz and Ginny Carroll *Ministry of Greed* (New York: Weidenfeld & Nicholson, 1988).

23. "Scandals," *Our Sunday Visitor,* August 19, 1990, p.18.

24. See, for example, John Crewdson, *By Silence Betrayed: Sexual Abuse of Children in America (*Boston: Little, Brown, 1988), pp. 115–16.

25. Burkett and Bruni, *A Gospel of Shame,* pp. 153–56.

26. Berry, *Lead Us Not into Temptation,* pp. 281–86; Bennetts, "Unholy Alliances."

27. Berry, *Lead Us Not into Temptation.*

28. Glen Allen, "A Church in Crisis," *Maclean's,* November 27, 1989, p. 66; Glen Allen, "Breaking the Faith," *Maclean's,* July 30, 1990, pp. 16–17.

29. Harris, *Unholy Orders.*

30. Allen, "Breaking the Faith"; Gary Kinsman, "The Mount Cashel Orphanage Inquiry," in Chris McCormick, ed., *Constructing Danger: The Mis / Representation of Crime in the News* (Halifax, Nova Scotia: Fernwood), 1995.

31. Ruby Rich, "Far from Mainstream Films," *New York Times,* May 29, 1994. pp. 2:9.

32. The film also had a great impact when shown in Great Britain and the Irish Republic during late 1994: Fintan O'Toole, "Tracing Father Brendan's Forty Years of Child Abuse," *Irish Times,* October 8, 1994.

33. Judy Steed, *Our Little Secret: Confronting Child Sexual Abuse in Canada* (Toronto: Random House, 1994); Art Babych, "Price of Canada Scandals Hits $23 Million," *National Catholic Reporter,* July 2, 1993, p. 6.

34. "Every Parent's Nightmare," *Maclean's,* June 22, 1992, pp. 24–25; "Fifty Recommendations: The Church and Child Sexual Abuse" *Origins* (Catholic News Service) 22 (7) (1992); *From Pain to Hope: Report from the CCCB Ad Hoc Committee on Child Sexual Abuse* (Ottawa: Canadian Conference on Catholic Bishops, 1992).

35. Michael Hirsley, "Accusations Distract Bishops from Agenda," *Chicago Tribune,* November 7, 1989, p. 1:2.

36. Bruce Ritter, *Sometimes God Has a Kid's Face* (New York: Covenant House, 1988); Charles M. Sennott, *Broken Covenant* (New York: Simon & Schuster, 1992).

37. Ritter, *Sometimes God Has a Kid's Face,* pp. 97–101.

38. "Letter After Charges Involving Local Priest," *Origins* (Catholic News Service) 23 (7) (1993): 112. In 1995 the Catholic parishes of suburban Maryland became the scene of an expanding scandal that led to charges of an "ecclesiastical meltdown" in the archdiocese of Washington, D.C.: see Arthur Jones, "Washington Priests Admit Abusing Altar Boy," *National Catholic Reporter,* February 17, 1995, p. 7; Arthur Jones, "Sexual Abuse by Priests: The Unrelenting Crisis," *National Catholic Reporter,* March 3, 1995, p. 6: Arthur Jones, "As Scandal Keeps Growing, Who is Accountable?" *National Catholic Reporter,* March 3, 1995, pp. 6–7. For RICO and the legal dimension of abuse accusations, see chapter 8, below.

39. Andrew Greeley *Fall from Grace* (New York: G. P. Putnams, 1993).

40. Julia Quinn Dempsey, John R. Gorman, John P. Madden, and Alphonse P. Spilly, *The Cardinal's Commission on Clerical Sexual Misconduct with Minors: Report to Joseph Cardinal Bernardin, Archbishop of Chicago* (Chicago: The Commission, 1992), p. 21. Cited hereafter as *Cardinal's Commission.*

41. Berry, *Lead Us Not into Temptation,* p. 325.

42. Michael Hirsley, "Panel to Examine Priests in Sex Cases," *Chicago Tribune,* October 26, 1991, p. 1:5; Michael Hirsley, "Removal of Priests Angers Parishioners," *Chicago Tribune,* November 21, 1991, p. 3C:1; Michael Hirsley, "Removal of Priests Leaves Parishes Torn," *Chicago Tribune,* November 24, 1991, p. 2C1; Tim Unsworth, "Church, State, Wrangle Over Pedophilia Cases," *National Catholic Reporter,* September 25, 1992, p. 14.

43. "Bernardin Apologizes," *Christian Century,* November 13, 1991, p. 1056.

44. Steinfels, "Inquiry in Chicago Breaks Silence on Sex Abuse by Catholic Priests."

45. See chapter 5, below.

46. *Cardinal's Commission*; Steinfels, "New Panel in Chicago to Study Sexual Abuse of Children by Priests"; Peter Steinfels, "Church Panel to Investigate Sexual Abuse Charges" *New York Times,* September 22, 1992; Michael Hirsley, "Archdiocese Seeks Answer to Sex Abuse Clergy," *Chicago Tribune,* March 16, 1992; Michael Hirsley, "Victims' Group Criticizes Church Sex Policy," *Chicago Tribune,* June 17, 1992.

47. Cheryl Lavin, "O'Malley Charges Church Hampering Abuse Probes," *Chicago Tribune,* September 2, 1992, p. 1:1; Terry Wilson, "O'Malley-Archdiocese Rift Widens Over Allegations of Sex Abuse," *Chicago Tribune* September 4, 1992.

48. Randall Samborn, "Church Fights State over Sex Abuse Files," *National Law Journal,* September 28, 1992, p. 10; Joe Loconte, "Pastoral Privilege Questioned," *Christianity Today,* January 11, 1993, p. 42.

49. Hirsley,"Victims' Group Criticizes Church Sex Policy."

50. Berry, *Lead Us Not into Temptation,* p. 345.

51. Maureen Graham, "Archbishop of Chicago Is Accused of Sex Abuse," *Philadelphia Inquirer,* November 13, 1993.

52. Jim Castelli, "Abuse of Faith," *US Catholic,* September 1993, p. 8.

53. Quoted in Peter Steinfels, "O'Connor Orders Priests to Meetings on Sexual Conduct," *New York Times,* May 26, 1993, p. B1; Richard N. Ostling, "The Secrets of St. Lawrence," *Time,* June 7, 1993, p. 44.

54. Burkett and Bruni, *A Gospel of Shame,* p. 37.

55. "Man Sues, Charges Abuse and Priest Sex Parties," *National Catholic Reporter,* April 21, 1995, p. 5; "Belleville Priest Accused in $15 Million Suit," *National Catholic Reporter,* March 10, 1995, p. 7; Robert McClory, "SNAP Says Belleville Treats Abuse Victims Best," *National Catholic Reporter,* January 13, 1995, p. 4; Don Corrigan, "Clergy Sexual Misconduct Stories Hidden for Decades, Say Survivors," *St. Louis Journalism Review* 23 (June 1994: 6+);

Robert Kelly, "Belleville Diocese Monitors Sex Abuse Cases," *St. Louis Post-Dispatch,* January 31, 1994, p. 1A; "Four Priests Linked to Sex Misdeeds," *New York Times,* April 2, 1993.

56. Steinfels, "O'Connor Orders Priests to Meetings on Sexual Conduct"; Douglas Martin, "Feeling Slighted by Church Officials, New York Youth Sues over Abuse by His Priest," *New York Times,* February 24, 1993, p. B4; Patricia Lefevere, "$50 Million Suit Filed Against N.Y. Archdiocese," *National Catholic Reporter,* March 5, 1993, p. 5.

57. Maureen Graham and Larry Lewis, "Sex Abuse Suit Claims Cover-Up by Bishops," *Philadelphia Inquirer,* November 1, 1994, p. A1; Don Lattin, "Archbishop Discusses Pedophilia," *San Francisco Chronicle,* May 11, 1994, p. A15; Don Lattin, "Three Priests Sued— Molestation of Boys Alleged," *San Francisco Chronicle,* May 24, 1994, p. A1; "Sex, The Church and the Cops" (editorial), *San Francisco Chronicle,* August 21, 1994.

58. Paul Wilkes, "Unholy Acts," *New Yorker,* June 7, 1993, pp. 67, 74; Paul Wilkes, "Priests Who Prey," *New York Times,* September 26, 1992, p. A21.

59. Thomas H. Stahel, "A Pastoral Response to Abuse: Interview with Joseph P. Chinnici OFM," *America,* January 15–22, 1994, pp. 2–4.

60. Seth Mydans, "Eleven Friars Molested Seminary Students, Church Inquiry Says," *New York Times,* December 1, 1993, p. A1; Seth Mydans, "Report on Friars' Abuse Eases a Victim's Burden," *New York Times,* December 2, 1993, p. A18.

61. Ostling,"The Secrets of St. Lawrence."

62. "In Box," *Chronicle of Higher Education,* April 14, 1995, p. A16; Berry, *Lead Us Not into Temptation,* pp. 291–98; Bennetts, "Unholy Alliances."

63. John H. Lee, "Priest of Porn Is Arrested," *Los Angeles Times,* December 14, 1989.

64. Bennetts, "Unholy Alliances"; Mary Burns, "Unsacred Trust," *Washington Post,* February 19, 1995, p. C1.

65. James L. Franklin, "Sexual Misconduct Seen as Serious Problem in Religion," *Boston Globe,* October 23, 1991, p. 24.

66. "Church Says Priest Who Died Was Accused of Child Abuse," *New York Times,* August 31, 1993.

67. Anne Cowles, "Church Officials Admit Helping Mowat Stay Free," *Atlanta Constitution,* June 6 1990, p. D1.

68. Thomas C. Fox, "Clergy Sex Abuse Survivors Break Silence," *National Catholic Reporter,* October 30, 1992, pp. 3–4.

69. Dawn Gibeau, "Link-Up Gains Momentum on Road to Healing," *National Catholic Reporter,* August 26, 1994, p. 3.

70. Burkett and Bruni, *A Gospel of Shame,* pp. 215–16.

71. Peter Steinfels, "Archbishop Concedes He Had Relationships with Three Women," *New York Times,* March 10, 1993, p. A12; Peter Steinfels, "Archbishop Is Resigning After Accusations of Sex," *New York Times,* March 20, 1993, p. A6.

72. Dennis Gaboury and Elinor Burkett, "The Secret of St. Mary's," *Rolling Stone* November 11, 1993, pp. 48–54+; Fox Butterfield, "Silent Decades Ended, Dozens Accuse a Priest," *New York Times,* June 9, 1992, p. A18; Fox Butterfield, "Priest Accused of Sexual Abuse Is Extradited," *New York Times,* September 23, 1992, p. A25; Fox Butterfield, "Report Says Ex-Priest Admitted Sex Abuse to Pope," *New York Times,* October 25, 1992, p. 1:20; Fox Butterfield, "Diocese Reaches Settlement With 68 Who Accuse Priest of Sexual Abuse," *New York Times,* December 4, 1992; Peter Steinfels, "Data in Priest Abuse Case Show Pattern of Treatment," *New York Times,* October 22, 1992, p. A12.

73. Burkett and Bruni, *A Gospel of Shame,* passim.

74. Quoted in "Former Catholic Priest Sentenced to 18 to 20 Years for Sex Crimes," *New York Times,* December 7, 1993, p. A22.

75. Burkett and Bruni, *A Gospel of Shame,* p. 33.

76. Mydans, "Eleven Friars Molested Seminary Students, Church Inquiry Says"; Mydans, "Report on Friars' Abuse Eases a Victim's Burden."

77. Art Babych, "Former Students Sue Order for $40 Million," *National Catholic Reporter,* September 16, 1994, p. 6; "Every Parent's Nightmare," *Maclean's,* June 22, 1992, pp. 24–25; Harris, *Unholy Orders,* pp. 368–69.

78. Ostling,"The Secrets of St. Lawrence."

79. *National Catholic Reporter,* July 29, 1994, p. 18.

80. "Addenda," *National Catholic Reporter,* October 7, 1994, p. 5; compare "Clergy Sex Abuse at Orphanage Alleged," *Denver Post,* August 12, 1994, p. B3.

81. Gibeau, "Link-Up Gains Momentum on Road to Healing."

82. *Official Catholic Directory,* 1994.

83. Burkett and Bruni, *A Gospel of Shame,* p. 51.

84. Robert McClory, "Bernardin Issues Rigorous Pedophile Policy," *National Catholic Reporter,* October 2, 1992, p. 3; Steinfels, "New Panel in Chicago to Study Sexual Abuse of Children by Priests."

85. Unsworth, "Church, State, Wrangle Over Pedophilia Cases."

86. Norbert Rigali, "Church Responses to Pedophilia," *Theological Studies* 55(1) (1994); Peter Steinfels, "Ancient Rock in Crosscurrents of Today," *New York Times,* May 29, 1994, p. A1; John D. Vogelsang, "From Denial to Hope" *Journal of Religion and Health* 32(3) (1993).

87. "Child Abuse Policy: Diocese of Salt Lake City," *Origins* (Catholic News Service) 20 (3) (1990): 42–44; "Sexual Abuse Policy: Diocese of Davenport," *Origins* (Catholic News Service) 20 (6) (1990): 93–94.; "When a Cleric Is Accused of Sexually Exploiting a Minor: Sioux City Diocesan Policy," *Origins* (Catholic News Service) 22 (10) (1992): 178–79.

88. "Chicago Policy Regarding Clerical Sexual Misconduct with Minors," *Origins* (Catholic News Service) 22 (16) (1992): 273–83; Steinfels, "New Panel in Chicago to Study Sexual Abuse of Children by Priests."

89. *Cardinal's Commission,* p. 46.

90. For the reforms in the New York archdiocese, see Peter Steinfels, "O'Connor Orders Priests to Meetings on Sexual Conduct," *New York Times,* May 26, 1993, p. B1; Peter Steinfels, "Policy Is Issued on Investigating Abuse by Priests," *New York Times,* July 2, 1993, p. A1; for Boston, see "Pastoral Policy: Allegations of Clergy Sexual Misconduct with Minors—Boston Archdiocese," *Origins* (Catholic News Service) 22 (34) (1993): 580–83; for Los Angeles, "Policy on Sexual Abuse by Priests: Los Angeles Archdiocese," *Origins* (Catholic News Service) 24 (5) (1994): 70–74.

91. "Painful Pastoral Question: Sexual Abuse of Minors," *Origins* (Catholic News Service) 22 (10) (1992): 177–78.

92. Peter Steinfels, "Bishops Vow Firm Action on Sexual Abuse by Priests," *New York Times,* November 20, 1992, p. A18.

93. "Bishops Struggle over Sex Abuse by Parish Priests," *New York Times,* June 18, 1993, p. A1.

94. Robin Edwards, "Bishops Advised on Sexual Abuse," *National Catholic Reporter,* March 5, 1993, p. 5; see chapter 5, below, for Connors.

95. "Washington Meeting," *Catholic New York,* November 17, 1994; Peter Steinfels, "Beliefs: On Sexual Abuse by Catholic Clergy," *New York Times,* October 8, 1994, p. A30; "NCCB Establishes Committee on Sexual Abuse," *Origins* (Catholic News Service) 23 (7) (1993): 104–11.

96. Mary Crystal Cage, "Seminaries Review Screening of Applicants in Wake of Sex Scandals Involving Priests," *Chronicle of Higher Education,* July 28, 1993, pp. 6–7.

97. Thomas C. Fox and Jason Berry, "As Nation Discusses Pedophilia, Even Pope Admits It's a Problem," *National Catholic Reporter,* July 2, 1993, pp. 2–3; Peter Steinfels, "Pope

Vows to Help U.S. Bishops Oust Priests Who Molest Children," *New York Times,* June 22, 1993, p. A1.

98. Lloyd Rediger, *Ministry and Sexuality* (Minneapolis: Fortress Press, 1990), p. 55; compare chapter 5, below.

99. CNN, "Fall from Grace," 1993; see chapter 4, below.

100. Aric Press et al., "Priests and Abuse," *Newsweek,* August 16, 1993, pp. 42–44; Berry, *Lead Us Not into Temptation,* pp. 278–79. Shupe, in *In The Name of All That's Holy,* also discusses comparable scandals in New Religious Movements.

101. John W. Kennedy, "$1.75 million Paid to Abuse Victims," *Christianity Today,* June 20, 1994, p. 56.

102. For another recent case in this denomination, see Jane Kwiatkowski, "Preacher Accused of Sexual Abuse," *Buffalo News,* July 30, 1994, p. C1.

103. Said Deep, "Cleric Held on Sex Abuse Charges," *Detroit News,* November 18, 1992; Said Deep, "Pastor Faces New Charges of Raping Four Year Old," *Detroit News,* November 19, 1992. Compare Ann Sweeney, "Preacher Gets Probation for Molesting Young Girl," *Detroit News,* August 25, 1994.

104. Mark Curriden, "Third Brother in Family of Ministers Facing Charges of Child Molestation," *Atlanta Journal and Constitution,* March 28, 1992.

105. David Skidmore, "Parishes Face Limits to Insuring for Sex Abuse," *Episcopal Life,* April 1993, pp. 1, 7.

106. Dennis Hevesi, "Episcopal Priest Resigns Among Sex-Abuse Charges," *New York Times,* October 7, 1992; *Episcopal Life,* November 1992, p. 1.

107. *Episcopal Life,* November 1993.

108. Skidmore, "Parishes Face Limits to Insuring for Sex Abuse."

109. Nan Cobbey, "Bishop's Son Accuses Priest of Sexual Abuse," *Episcopal Life,* October 1994, p. 5; Nan Cobbey, "Clergy Discipline Canons Fairer to Victim, Accuser," *Episcopal Life,* October 1994, p. 14. The Episcopal church was also beset by a number of scandals involving heterosexual misconduct, including the case of Bishop David E. Johnson of Massachusetts, whose numerous extra-marital affairs came to public attention following his suicide in 1995: Gustav Niebuhr, "Episcopal Church Reveals Sexual Misconduct by Bishop," *New York Times,* January 27, 1995, p. A13; "Episcopalians: Money, Sex and Power Distract Bishops," *Christianity Today,* April 3, 1995, 95.

110. Reginald W. Bibby, *Unknown Gods* (Toronto: Stoddart 1993), p. 72.

Chapter 4: The Media and the Crisis

1. Richard Cunningham, "Sex, the Church and the Press," *Quill,* May 1991, p. 12.

2. Thomas M. Disch, "The Sins of the Fathers," *The Nation,* November 2, 1992, pp. 514–16.

3. William F. Buckley, "The Church's Newest Cross," *National Review,* April 26, 1993.

4. Charles M. Sennott, "Sins of the Fathers," *Playboy,* July 1993, pp. 74–76; James R. Petersen, "When the Church Sins," *Playboy,* December 1992, pp. 54–55; Robert Scheer, "Such Unholy Business," *Playboy,* June 1990, pp. 55, 169+.

5. "Up Front," *People Weekly,* July 27, 1992.

6. Angela Bonavoglia, "The Sacred Secret," *Ms.* March–April 1992, pp. 40–46.

7. Dennis Gaboury and Elinor Burkett, "The Secret of St. Mary's," *Rolling Stone,* November 11, 1993, pp. 48–54+.

8. Leslie Bennetts, "Unholy Alliances," *Vanity Fair,* December 1991, pp. 224–78.

9. Paul Wilkes, "Unholy Acts," *New Yorker,* June 7, 1993, pp. 62–79.

10. See, for example, Aric Press et al., "Priests and Abuse," *Newsweek,* August 16, 1993, pp. 42–44; Kenneth L. Woodward, "Sex and the Church," *Newsweek,* August 16, 1993, pp. 38–41; Kenneth L. Woodward, "The Sins of the Fathers," *Newsweek,* July 12, 1993, p. 57; Richard N. Ostling,"The Secrets of St. Lawrence," *Time,* June 7, 1993, p. 44; Richard N. Ostling, "Sins of the Fathers," *Time,* August 19, 1991, p. 51.

11. For example, see Glen Allen, "Breaking the Faith," *Maclean's,* July 30, 1990, pp. 16–17.

12. Donald C. Clark, "Sexual Abuse in the Church: The Law Steps In," *Christian Century,* April 14, 1993, pp. 396–98.

13. Canice Connors, "Priests and Pedophilia: A Silence That Needs Breaking?" *America,* May 9, 1992, pp. 400–401; John Allan Loftus, "Question of Disillusionment: Sexual Abuse Among the Clergy," *America,* December 1, 1990, pp. 426–29.

14. Jim Castelli, "Abuse of Faith," *US Catholic,* September 1993, pp. 6–15; Canice Connors and Tim Unsworth "Abuse of Faith: How to Understand the Crime of Priestly Pedophilia," *US Catholic,* September 1993, pp. 6–15; Robert E. Burns, "Should All Priests Pay for the Sins of the Fathers?" *US Catholic,* December 1992, p. 2.

15. Peter Steinfels, "Needed: A Firm Purpose of Amendment," *Commonweal,* March 12, 1993, pp. 16–18.

16. Julie A. Wortman, "Pain May Overwhelm Exploited Victims," *Episcopal Life,* October 1991, p. 1; Julie A. Wortman, "Full Disclosure of Abuse Helps Parishes Heal," *Episcopal Life,* November 1991, p. 8; Julie A. Wortman and Ed Stannard, "Exploitation a Major Church Problem," *Episcopal Life,* September 1991, p. 1.

17. Jonathan Friendly, "Catholic Church Discussing Priests Who Abuse Children," *New York Times,* May 4, 1986, p. A26; Michael Harris, *Unholy Orders: Tragedy at Mount Cashel* (Toronto: Penguin, 1991), p. 259.

18. Berry, quoted in Bennetts, "Unholy Alliances," p. 227.

19. Peter Steinfels, "The Church Faces the Trespasses of Priests," *New York Times,* June 27, 1993.

20. See, for example, ibid.

21. Paul Wilkes, "Priests Who Prey," *New York Times,* September 26, 1992, p. A21.

22. Paul E. Dinter, "Celibacy and Its Discontents," *New York Times,* May 6. 1993, p. A27.

23. James MacLoughlin, "Just Following Orders: The Politics of Pedophilia," *National Catholic Reporter,* April 16, 1993, p. 15.

24. Elinor Burkett and Frank Bruni, *A Gospel of Shame* (New York: Viking, 1993).

25. Gaboury and Burkett, "The Secret of St. Mary's," p. 52.

26. Wilkes, "Unholy Acts," p. 68.

27. Vicki Quade, "Unholy Wars," *Human Rights,* fall 1992, pp. 18–21.

28. Ibid.

29. Sally Jessy Raphael television program, December 27, 1993.

30. Andrew Greeley, quoted in Peter Steinfels, "Inquiry in Chicago Breaks Silence on Sex Abuse by Catholic Priests," *New York Times,* February 24, 1992, p. A1.

31. Eugene C. Kennedy, "The See-no-problem, Hear-no-problem, Speak-no-problem Problem," *National Catholic Reporter,* March 19, 1993, p. 5.

32. The *Catholic League Newsletter* is a good source for such cartoon depictions, and the two 1989 examples from Phoenix are reproduced in that journal, vol. 16(10) (October 1989). The Oliphant cartoon described here was published in February 1994.

33. Jason Berry, *Lead Us Not into Temptation* (New York: Doubleday, 1992), p. 36.

34. Andrew Greeley, *Fall from Grace* (New York: G. P. Putnams, 1993), p. 116.

35. Ibid., p. 350; see below, chapter 9.

36. Greeley, *Fall from Grace,* pp. 48–49.

37. Ibid., p. 77.

38. Ibid., p. 117.

39. Ibid., p. 51.

40. Les J. Keyser and Barbara Keyser, *Hollywood and the Catholic Church* (Chicago: Loyola University Press, 1984); Philip Jenkins, "Beyond Reproach: Creating a Culture of Clergy Deviance," in Anson Shupe, ed., *White Collar Crime From The Pulpits,* forthcoming 1996.

41. Gregory D. Black, *Hollywood Censored: Morality Codes, Catholics and the Movies* (Cambridge: Cambridge University Press, 1994); James M. Skinner, *The Cross and the Cinema: The Legion of Decency and the National Catholic Office for Motion Pictures, 1933–1970* (Westport, Conn.: Praeger, 1993); Paul Blanshard, *American Freedom and Catholic Power* (Boston: Beacon Press, 1949), pp. 198–210.

42. "Notable Events in the Church in America During 1938," *Catholic Standard and Times* (Philadelphia) January 6, 1939, p. 5.

43. Uta Ranke-Heinemann, *Eunuchs for the Kingdom of God* (New York: Doubleday, 1991).

44. See, for example, Nick Tosches, *Power on Earth* (New York: Arbor House, 1986); Penny Lernoux, *In Banks We Trust* (New York: Doubleday, Anchor, 1984); David A. Yallop, *In God's Name* (New York: Bantam, 1984); Richard Hammer, *The Vatican Connection* (New York: Holt, Rinehart & Winston, 1982).

45. William Caunitz, *One Police Plaza* (novel published 1984; film released 1986).

46. John Gregory Dunne, *True Confessions* (New York: Dutton, 1977), p. 97.

47. Ibid., pp. 111–12.

48. Kennedy, "The See-no-problem, Hear-no-problem, Speak-no-problem Problem."

49. Wilkes, "Unholy Acts," p. 68.

50. George A. Kelly, *The Battle for the American Church* (New York: Doubleday, Image, 1981), p. 315.

51. George Seldes, *Lords of the Press* (New York: Blue Ribbon, 1941), pp. 34–35; Blanshard, *American Freedom and Catholic Power*, pp. 195–98; compare George Seldes, *The Catholic Crisis* (New York: J. Mesner, 1939).

52. "Catholic Campaign," *Time,* October 23, 1944, p. 59.

53. John Gunther, *Inside USA* (New York: Harper, 1951), p. 529.

54. Blanshard, *American Freedom and Catholic Power,* p. 195.

55. W. L. Marshall and Sylvia Barrett, *Criminal Neglect: Why Sex Offenders Go Free* (Toronto: Seal, 1992), p. 120.

56. Eugene C. Kennedy, *Cardinal Bernardin* (Chicago: Basic Books, 1989); Andrew Greeley, *Confessions of a Parish Priest: An Autobiography* (New York: Simon & Schuster, 1986), pp. 410–16.

57. Kennedy, *Cardinal Bernardin;* see below.

58. Kennedy, *Cardinal Bernardin.*

59. Charles M. Sennott, *Broken Covenant* (New York: Simon & Schuster, 1992), p. 431.

60. Ibid., pp. 353–54; 385–88.

61. Ibid., p. 395.

62. Berry, *Lead Us Not into Temptation*, p. 32 .

63. Burkett and Bruni, *A Gospel of Shame*, pp. 187–88.

64. Ibid., pp. 177–99.

65. Burkett and Bruni, *A Gospel of Shame*, pp. 191–92 .

66. Patrick Boyle, *Scout's Honor: Sexual Abuse in America's Most Trusted Institution* (Rocklin, Calif.: Prima, 1994), pp. 69–70.

67. Ibid., pp. 136–39.

68. Ibid., pp. 314–18.

69. Kennedy, *Cardinal Bernardin,* pp. 188–99.

70. Quoted in Boyle, *Scout's Honor,* p. 253.

71. Letter to *National Catholic Reporter,* July 19, 1985.

72. Arthur Jones, "Legal Actions Against Pedophile Priests Grow," *National Catholic Reporter,* June 7, 1985, pp. 4–6; Jason Berry, "Pedophile Priest: Study in Inept Church Response," *National Catholic Reporter,* June 7, 1985, p. 7.

73. "Pedophilia Problem Needs Tackling" *National Catholic Reporter,* June 7, 1985.

74. Barbara Blaine, "Abused by Priest, She Sought Healing Process," *National Catholic Reporter,* November 3, 1989.

75. *New York Times,* June 20, 1985.

76. *Time,* July 1, 1985.

77. CBS's *West 57th Street,* August 1986,

78. Carl M. Cannon, "Catholic Church Lax on Clergy in Child Sex Abuse Cases," *Philadelphia Inquirer,* January 4, 1988, p. A1.

79. Berry, *Lead Us Not into Temptation,* p. 287.

80. Quoted in A. W. Richard Sipe, *A Secret World: Sexuality and the Search for Celibacy* (New York: Brunner/Mazel, 1990), p. 165.

81. See, for example, Jim Cuddy, "Boys Story: How Trust of Priest Turned into Sexual Abuse," *Pittsburgh Press,* October 23, 1988, p. A1.

82. Richard Higgins, "Clergy Sexual Abuse: Dirty Secrets Come to Light," *Boston Globe,* May 11, 1990, p. 1; James L. Franklin, "Sex Abuse by Clergy Called Crisis for Churches," *Boston Globe,* July 17, 1991, p. 11; James L. Franklin, "Sexual Misconduct Seen as Serious Problem in Religion," *Boston Globe,* October 23, 1991, p. 24; James L. Franklin, "Churches Change Their Responses to Sex Abuse," *Boston Globe,* November 5, 1991, p.1.

83. Russell Chandler, "Sex Abuse Cases Rock the Clergy," *Los Angeles Times,* August 3, 1990, p. A1.

84. Berry, *Lead Us Not into Temptation,* p. 101.

85. Sipe, *A Secret World;* see Jason Berry, "Investigating Child Sexual Abuse in the Catholic Church," *IRE Journal,* January 1993, pp. 10–11; Jason Berry, "Listening to the Survivors: Voices of the People of God," *America,* November 13, 1993, pp. 4–9.

86. Greeley, *Confessions of a Parish Priest,* p. 476. Greeley also appeared as an expert on television programs highly critical of church policies, such as the 1994 "Sex and the Church: A House Divided," broadcast in the *Investigative Reports* series on the Arts and Entertainment network, October 21, 1994.

87. Quoted in Kennedy, *Cardinal Bernardin,* pp. 268–69.

88. Eugene C. Kennedy, "Seminary System Rates Quick Christian Burial," *National Catholic Reporter,* July 17, 1992, p. 6; Kennedy, "The See-no-problem, Hear-no-problem, Speak-no-problem Problem."

89. For Miller, see Burkett and Bruni, *A Gospel of Shame,* pp. 238–51. For Barbara Blaine, see Tim Unsworth, Catholics on the Edge (New York: Crossroad, 1995), pp. 64–76.

90. Bennetts, "Unholy Alliances"; see Mark E.Chopko, "Restoring Trust and Faith" *Human Rights,* fall 1992, pp. 22–24.

91. Steinfels, "Inquiry in Chicago Breaks Silence on Sex Abuse by Catholic Priests."

92. Harris , *Unholy Orders.*

93. Berry, *Lead Us Not into Temptation,* p. 320.

94. Compare Burkett and Bruni, *A Gospel of Shame,* pp. 106–10; Gaboury and Burkett, "The Secret of St. Mary's"; Cristine Clark, "Broken Vows," *Redbook,* November 1992, pp. 51–56. For Gaboury, see Burkett and Bruni, *A Gospel of Shame,* pp. 131–32, 249–50.

95. "NCCB Establishes Committee on Sexual Abuse," *Origins* (Catholic News Service) 23 (7) (1993): 104–11, at 106.

96. ABC's *Primetime Live,* July 2 and 23, 1992.

97. *60 Minutes,* March 21, 1993: Peter Steinfels, "Archbishop Concedes He Had Relationships with Three Women," *New York Times,* March 10, 1993, p. A12; Peter Steinfels, "Archbishop Is Resigning After Accusations of Sex," *New York Times*, March 20, 1993, p. A6.

98. Howard Kurtz, "A TV Station's Dirty Trick," *Washington Post,* June 12, 1993, p. C1.

99. "Sins of the Fathers," *Investigative Reports* special broadcast, Arts and Entertainment network, January 29, 1993.

100. "Fall from Grace," *CNN Presents* special, November 14, 1993.

101. Burkett and Bruni, *A Gospel of Shame*, p. 136.

102. Kathy Mellott, "Priest to Admit Sex with Boy," *Tribune-Democrat* (Johnstown, Pa.), February 3, 1994, 1; Kelly Kissel, "Lawyer Says Priest Will Admit to Some Illegal Sexual Acts," AP story in *Centre Daily Times* (State College, Pa.) February 3, 1994, p. A4; Tom Gibb, "Winner of Molestation Case Gets Justice But No Award," *Harrisburg Patriot News*, April 23, 1995, p. B5.

103. Broadcast May 16, 17, 18, 1994.

104. ABC's *20/20,* March 12, "Torn Between Two Loves."

105. Annie Murphy and Peter de Rosa, *Forbidden Fruit* (Boston: Little, Brown, 1993).

106. Compare Clyde H. Farnsworth, "Orphans of the 1950s, Telling of Abuse, Sue Quebec," *New York Times,* May 21, 1993, p. A3.

107. The film appeared on Home Box Office.

108. *N.Y.PD Blue,* May 17, 1994. On April 26, 1995, an episode of the NBC crime series *Law and Order* featured a character who was a former priest with a history of pedophilia.

109. David E. Brinkmoeller, "In the Face of Priest-Bashing," *Washington Post*, October 17, 1989, p. A27.

110. Charles M. Sennott, *Broken Covenant* (New York: Simon & Schuster, 1992), p. 372.

111. "Four Priests Linked to Sex Misdeeds," *New York Times,* April 2, 1993.

112. Quoted in Harris, *Unholy Orders,* p. 16.

113. "In New Mexico, Catholic Church Tries to Overcome Its Pain," *New York Times,* April 11, 1993, p. 1:15.

114. Fox Butterfield, "Silent Decades Ended, Dozens Accuse a Priest," *New York Times*, June 9, 1992, p. A18; Peter Steinfels, "Bishops Assail Press on Sex Charges," *New York Times,* November 16, 1993, p. A24.

115. Berry, *Lead Us Not into Temptation*, pp. 218–19.

116. Burkett and Bruni, *A Gospel of Shame*, p. 191.

117. Burns, "Should All Priests Pay for the Sins of the Fathers?"

118. "Priests and Sex," *Commonweal,* November 20, 1992, pp. 3–4.

119. Philip Jenkins, "Priests and Pedophiles? The Attack on the Catholic Church," in *Chronicles: A Magazine of American Culture*, December 1992, pp. 24–27.

Chapter 5: Pedophilia and Child Abuse

1. Philip Jenkins, *Using Murder: The Social Construction of Serial Homicide*, (Hawthorne, N.Y.: Aldine de Gruyter, 1994); Joel Best, ed., *Images of Issues* (Hawthorne, N.Y.: Aldine de Gruyter, 1989).

2. Joel Best, *Threatened Children* (Chicago: University of Chicago Press, 1990).

3. Quoted in Vicki Quade, "Unholy Wars," *Human Rights,* fall 1992, pp. 18–21.

4. A. W. Richard Sipe, *A Secret World: Sexuality and the Search for Celibacy* (New York: Brunner/Mazel, 1990); A.W. Richard Sipe, *Sex, Priests and Power: Anatomy of a Crisis* (New York: Brunner/Mazel, 1995).

5. Ibid.; A. W. Richard Sipe, "To Enable Healing," *National Catholic Reporter,* September 17, 1993, pp. 6–7; Leslie Bennetts, "Unholy Alliances," *Vanity Fair,* December 1991, pp. 224–78; Michael Harris, *Unholy Orders: Tragedy at Mount Cashel* (Toronto: Penguin, 1991), p. 259.

6. Carl M. Cannon, "Catholic Church Lax on Clergy in Child Sex Abuse Cases," *Philadelphia Inquirer,* January 4, 1988, p. A1.

7. Andrew Greeley, "Priestly Silence on Pedophilia," *New York Times,* March 13, 1992.

8. Bennetts, "Unholy Alliances."

9. Quoted by Rossetti and Lothstein in Stephen J. Rossetti, ed., *Slayer of the Soul: Child Sexual Abuse and the Catholic Church* (Mystic, Conn.: Twenty-Third Publications, 1990), p. 14.

10. John Boswell, *Christianity, Social Tolerance and Homosexuality* (Chicago: University of Chicago Press, 1980), pp. 28–30.

11. Harris, *Unholy Orders,* p. 16.

12. "USCC Pedophilia Statement," *Origins* (Catholic News Service) 17 (36) (1988): 624.

13. "Child Abuse Policy: Diocese of Salt Lake City," *Origins* (Catholic News Service) 20 (3) (1990): 42–44; "Sexual Abuse Policy: Diocese of Davenport," *Origins* (Catholic News Service) 20 (6) (1990): 93–94.

14. "Policy on Sexual Abuse by Priests: Los Angeles Archdiocese," *Origins* (Catholic News Service) 24 (5) (1994): 70–74, at 74.

15. Dennis Gaboury and Elinor Burkett, "The Secret of St. Mary's," *Rolling Stone,* November 11, 1993, p. 54.

16. Jason Berry, *Lead Us Not into Temptation* (New York: Doubleday, 1992), p. xix.

17. Ibid.

18. Jim Castelli, "Abuse of Faith," *US Catholic,* September 1993, pp. 6–15.

19. Andrew Greeley,"How Serious Is the Problem of Sexual Abuse by Clergy?" *America,* March 20/27, 1993, pp. 6–10; Julia Quinn Dempsey, John R. Gorman, John P. Madden, and Alphonse P. Spilly *The Cardinal's Commission on Clerical Sexual Misconduct with Minors: Report to Joseph Cardinal Bernardin, Archbishop of Chicago,* (Chicago: The Commission, 1992). Cited hereafter as *Cardinals' Commission.*

20. *Cardinal's Commission,* p. 22.

21. Andrew Greeley, "A View from the Priesthood," *Newsweek,* August 16, 1993, p. 45.

22. Thomas C. Fox, "Sex and Power Issues Expand Clergy-Lay Rift," *National Catholic Reporter,* November 13, 1992, pp. 17–19.

23. Peter Steinfels, "The Church Faces the Trespasses of Priests," *New York Times,* June 27, 1993, p. 4:1; Greeley,"How Serious Is the Problem of Sexual Abuse by Clergy?" p. 24. Richard N. Ostling,"The Secrets of St. Lawrence," *Time,* June 7, 1993, p. 44; Steinfels, "The Church Faces the Trespasses of Priests"; compare Sipe, "To Enable Healing"; Mary Crystal Cage, "Seminaries Review Screening of Applicants in Wake of Sex Scandals Involving Priests," *Chronicle of Higher Education,* July 28, 1993, pp. A29–30.

25. Castelli, "Abuse of Faith," p. 9; Canice Connors, "Priests and Pedophilia: A Silence That Needs Breaking?" *America,* May 9, 1992, pp. 400–401.

26. Rossetti and Lothstein, in Rossetti, *Slayer of the Soul,* pp. 16–17; emphasis in original.

27. *Cardinal's Commission,* p. 21; emphasis in original.

28. Fred Cohen, ed., *The Law of Deprivation of Liberty* (St Paul, Minn.: West, 1980), p. 663.

29. Cohen, *The Law of Deprivation of Liberty*; Nicholas N. Kittrie, *The Right to Be Different*, (Baltimore: Johns Hopkins University Press, 1971); Edwin Sutherland, "The Diffusion of Sex Psychopath Laws," *American Journal of Sociology* 56 (1950).

30. Cohen, *The Law of Deprivation of Liberty*, p. 704.

31. Kittrie, *The Right to be Different.*

32. Quoted in Cohen, *The Law of Deprivation of Liberty*, pp. 669–73.

33. Harry Elmer Barnes and Negley K. Teeters, *New Horizons in Criminology*, (3d, ed. Englewood Cliffs, N.J.: Prentice-Hall, 1959), p. 99.

34. Elmer H. Johnson, *Social Problems of Urban Man* (Homewood, Ill.: Dorsey Press, 1973), pp. 231–34.

35. S. Kirson Weinberg, *Incest Behavior* (Secaucus, N.J.: Citadel Press, 1955).

36. See chapter 7, below.

37. Susan Brownmiller, *Against Our Will* (London: Secker & Warburg, 1975), p. 281.

38. Diana E. H. Russell, *The Politics of Rape* (New York: Stein & Day, 1975); Diana E. H. Russell, *Sexual Exploitation, Rape, Child Sexual Abuse and Workplace Harassment* (Beverly Hills, Calif.: Sage, 1984); Florence Rush, "The Freudian Cover-Up," *Chrysalis* 1 (1977): 31–45; Florence Rush, *The Best-Kept Secret: Sexual Abuse of Children* (Englewood Cliffs, N.J.: Prentice-Hall, 1980).

39. Katie De Koster, ed., *Child Abuse: Opposing Viewpoints* (San Diego, Calif.: Greenhaven, 1994), p. 19.

40. Richard Wexler,*Wounded Innocents* (Amherst, N.Y.: Prometheus Books, 1990); John Crewdson, "Study Confirms Sexual Abuse Increase," *Chicago Tribune* article reprinted in *Centre Daily Times* (State College, Pa.), February 17, 1985, p. A6.

41. Quoted in Derrick Z. Jackson, "America Lags in Its Treatment of Children," *Boston Globe* column, reprinted in *Centre Daily Times*, (State College, Pa.), July 5. 1994, p. A4; my emphasis.

42. Frances Lear, "Letter," *New York Times,* February 14, 1993, "Book Review" sec.

43. David Finkelhor, *Sexually Victimized Children* (New York: Free Press, 1979); U.S. Department of Health, Education and Welfare, *Child Sexual Abuse, Incest, Assault and Sexual Exploitation* (Washington, D.C.: Government Printing Office, 1979); Jeanne M. Giovannoni and Rosina M. Becerra, *Defining Child Abuse* (New York: Free Press, 1979); Louise Armstrong, *Kiss Daddy Goodnight* (New York: Hawthorn, 1978); Sandra Butler, *Conspiracy of Silence: The Trauma of Incest* (New York: Bantam, 1978); Ann W. Burgess, A. N. Groth, L. L. Holmstrom, S. M. Sgroi, *Sexual Assault of Children and Adolescents* (Lexington, Mass.: Heath, 1978); Susan Forward, and Craig Buck, *Betrayal of Innocence: Incest and Its Devastation* (New York: Penguin, 1978); Lynda L. Holmstrom and Ann W. Burgess, *The Victims of Rape* (New York: Wiley, 1978); R. S. Kempe and C. Henry Kempe, *Child Abuse* (London: Fontana Books/Open University, 1978).

44. Ann W. Burgess, ed., *Rape and Sexual Assault: A Research Handbook* (New York: Garland, 1985); Ann W. Burgess and Marieanne Lindqvist Clark, *Child Pornography and Sex Rings* (Lexington, Mass.: Lexington Books, 1984).

45. David Finkelhor, *Child Sexual Abuse, New Theory and Research* (New York: Free Press, 1984); David Finkelhor, *The Dark Side of Families,* (Beverly Hills, Calif.: Sage, 1983.

46. Judith Lewis Herman, *Father-Daughter Incest* (Cambridge: Harvard University Press, 1981); Judith Lewis Herman, *Trauma and Recovery* (New York: Basic Books, 1992).

47. Roland Summit, "The Child Sexual Abuse Accommodation Syndrome," *Child Abuse and Neglect* 7 (1983): 177–93; Roland Summit, "Beyond Belief: The Reluctant Discovery of Incest," in Mary D. Pellauer, Barbara Chester, and Jane A. Boyajian, eds., *Sexual Assault and Abuse* (San Francisco: Harper & Row, 1987), pp. 172–97.

48. Patricia B. Mrazek and C. Henry Kempe, eds., *Sexually Abused Children and Their Families* (New York: Pergamon Press, 1981). See also Laura Lederer, ed., *Take Back the Night* (New York: Morrow, 1980); Rush, *The Best-Kept Secret*; J. Bulkley, *Child Sexual Abuse and the Law* (Washington D.C.: American Bar Association, 1981); Herman, *Father-Daughter Incest*; Rick Rubin and Greg Byerly, *Incest—The Last Taboo: An Annotated Bibliography* (New York: Garland, 1983); Russell, *Sexual Exploitation*; Diana E. H. Russell,*The Secret Trauma: Incest in the Lives of Girls and Women* (New York: Basic Books, 1986).

49. Richard R. Bootzin and Joan Ross Acocella, *Abnormal Psychology: Current Perspectives* (New York: Random House, 1984), p. 174.

50. Michelle Smith and Lawrence Pazder, *Michelle Remembers* (New York: Congdon & Lattes, 1980).

51. Jenkins, *Using Murder*; Best, *Threatened Children*; Paul Eberle and Shirley Eberle, *The Politics of Child Abuse* (Secaucus, N.J.: Lyle Stuart, 1986).

52. John Crewdson, *By Silence Betrayed: Sexual Abuse of Children in America* (New York: Little, Brown, 1988).

53. Jenkins, *Using Murder*; Paula Hawkins, *Children at Risk* (Bethesda, Md.: Adler & Adler, 1986); Kenneth Wooden, *The Children of Jonestown* (New York: McGraw-Hill, 1981).

54. Susan Rasky, "The Courts, the Law and Children's Rights," *New York Times*, March 24, 1985.

55. Russell, *Sexual Exploitation*; Russell, *The Secret Trauma*; compare Crewdson, *By Silence Betrayed*, pp. 24–33.

56. Quoted in Carol Tavris, "Beware the Incest Survivor Machine," *New York Times,* Book Review sec., January 3, 1993, p. 1; emphasis in original.

57. Brownmiller, *Against Our Will*, p. 282.

58. Patrick Boyle, *Scout's Honor: Sexual Abuse in America's Most Trusted Institution* (Rocklin, Calif.: Prima, 1994), p. 33.

59. Crewdson, *By Silence Betrayed*, p. 81.

60. W. L. Marshall and Sylvia Barrett, *Criminal Neglect: Why Sex Offenders Go Free* (Toronto: Seal, 1992), p. 108.

61. L. L. Constantine and F. M. Martinson, *Children and Sex: New Findings, New Perspectives* (Boston: Little, Brown, 1981).

62. Quoted in Cohen, *The Law of Deprivation of Liberty*, pp. 669–70.

63. Kempe and Kempe, *Child Abuse*, p. 55.

64. Stephen P. McCary and James Leslie McCary, *Human Sexuality*, (3d ed. Monterey, Calif.: Wadsworth, 1984), p. 226; my emphasis. Compare Constantine and Martinson, *Children and Sex*.

65. Jade C. Angelica, *A Moral Emergency: Breaking the Cycle of Child Sexual Abuse* (Kansas City, Mo.: Sheed & Ward, 1994); Mollie Brown, *Victim No More: Ministry to Survivors of Sexual Abuse* (Mystic, Conn.: Twenty-Third Publications, 1994); Tracy Hansen, *A Secret That's Never Been Told: Healing the Wounds of Childhood Sexual Abuse* (Mystic, Conn.: Twenty-Third Publications, 1994).

66. Cohen, *The Law of Deprivation of Liberty*; Kittrie, *The Right to Be Different*.

67. Sipe, *A Secret World,* pp. 182–83.

68. Quoted in "Settlement in Priest's Abuse Case Raises Question of Liability," *New York Times,* January 17, 1994. For the social context, see Peter Conrad and Joseph W. Schneider, *Deviance and Medicalization* (St Louis, Mo.: C. V. Mosby, 1980).

69. "More Suits Filed Against Ex-Priest," *New York Times,* July 26, 1992, p. 1:19.

70. Quoted in Rossetti, *Slayer of the Soul,* p. 3.

71. "Painful Pastoral Question: Sexual Abuse of Minors," *Origins* (Catholic News Service) 22 (10) (1992): 177–78.

72. Quoted in "Settlement in Priest's Abuse Case Raises Questions of Liability."

73. Andrew Greeley, "Priestly Silence on Pedophilia," *New York Times*, March 13, 1992, p. A31.

74. See, for example, Robert Lindsey, "Sexual Abuse of Children Draws Experts' Increasing Concern Nationwide," *New York Times*, April 4, 1984; Paul Eberle and Shirley Eberle, *Abuse of Innocence: The McMartin Preschool Trial* (Amherst, N.Y.: Prometheus Books, 1993).

75. "Give the Children a Chance," *National Catholic Reporter,* editorial, June 21, 1985, p. 11.

76. In Rossetti, *Slayer of the Soul*, p. 2.

77. John J. Dreese, "The Other Victims of Priest Pedophilia," *Commonweal,* April 22, 1994, pp. 11–14.

78. Peter Steinfels, "Giving Healing and Hope to Priests Who Molested," *New York Times*, October 12, 1992, p. A11.

79. Quoted in Peter Steinfels, "Policy is Issued on Investigating Abuse by Priests," *New York Times,* July 2, 1993, p. A1.

80. Peter Steinfels, "Inquiry in Chicago Breaks Silence on Sex Abuse by Catholic Priests," *New York Times*, February 24, 1992.

81. Fintan O'Toole, "Tracing Father Brendan's Forty Years of Child Abuse," *Irish Times,* October 8, 1994, p. A5; "Priest Sentenced to Jail for Four Years for Abusing Children," *Irish Times,* June 25, 1994, p. A1. This case was as significant for Ireland as the Gauthe case had been in the United States in arousing concern about the perceived menace of abuse by Catholic clergy. In 1994 controversy over the slow official response to the case led indirectly to the collapse of the government in the Republic of Ireland. In addition, publicity surrounding the case ensured that the media paid an unprecedented degree of attention to clerical scandals that hitherto would have been ignored. The sudden upsurge of sex cases produced an impression of a systemic crisis in the Irish church. Chris Moore, *Betrayal of Trust: The Father Brendan Smyth Affair and the Catholic Church* (Dublin, Ireland: Marino, 1995.)

82. Joan Chittister, "Priest Offenders and the Saga of the Paracletes," *National Catholic Reporter,* July 30, 1993.

83. Quoted in Elinor Burkett and Frank A. Bruni, *A Gospel of Shame (*New York: Viking, 1993), p. 41.

84. Connors, "Priests and Pedophilia"; Canice Connors, "The Moment After Suffering," *Commonweal,* October 21, 1994, pp. 14–17.

85. Compare L. M. Lothstein, "Can a Sexually Addicted Priest Be Returned to Ministry After Treatment?" *Catholic Lawyer* 34 (1991): 89–113.

86. Frank Valcour, "Treatment of Child Sex Abusers in the Church," in Rossetti *Slayer of the Soul*, p. 45.

87. Ibid. p. 45; Peter Steinfels, "Giving Healing and Hope to Priests Who Molested."

88. "Priest Held Liable for Civil Damages," *New York Times,* September 26, 1988. Other recent cases have involved as conditions of probation periods in residential facilities run by the Paraclete Order: see "Addenda," *National Catholic Reporter*, October 21, 1994, p. 4.

89. Berry, *Lead Us Not into Temptation*, p. 307.

90. Quoted in Harris, *Unholy Orders*, p.16.

91. Peter Steinfels, "O'Connor Orders Priests to Meetings on Sexual Conduct," *New York Times,* May 26, 1993, p. B1.

Chapter 6: Conflict in the Churches

1. Quoted in Angela Bonavoglia, "The Sacred Secret," *Ms.*, March–April 1992, pp. 40–46.

2. Paul Blanshard, *American Freedom and Catholic Power* (Boston: Beacon Press, 1949), p. 29.

3. Ibid.

4. Sydney E. Ahlstrom, *A Religious History of the American People* (New Haven:Yale University Press, 1972).

5. Penny Lernoux, *People of God* (New York: Viking, 1989).

6. Adrian Hastings, ed., *Modern Catholicism: Vatican II and After* (New York: Oxford University Press, 1991).

7. Peter Hebblethwaite, *The Runaway Church* (London: Collins, 1975); Peter Hebblethwaite, *The New Inquisition: Schillebeeckx and Küng* (London: Collins, Fount Paperbacks, 1980); Peter Hebblethwaite, *Synod Extraordinary* (New York: Doubleday, 1986).

8. Richard P. McBrien, *Report on the Church: Catholicism After Vatican II* (San Francisco: Harper, 1992); Mary Jo Leddy, Remi J. DeRoo, and Douglas Roche, *In the Eye of the Catholic Storm: The Church Since Vatican II* (Toronto: HarperCollins, 1992); John Seidler and Katherine Meyer, *Conflict and Change in the Catholic Church* (New Brunswick, N.J.: Rutgers University Press, 1989); George A. Kelly, *The Battle for the American Church* (New York: Doubleday, Image, 1981).

9. Eugene Kennedy and Victor Heckler, *The Catholic Priest in the United States: Psychological Investigations* (Washington D.C.: United States Catholic Conference, 1972).

10. Richard A. Schoenherr and Lawrence A. Young, *Full Pews and Empty Altars: Demographics of the Priest Shortage in United States Catholic Dioceses* (Madison: University of Wisconsin Press, 1994).

11. *Official Catholic Directory,* 1994.

12. Eric Eckholm, "Wellspring of Priests Dries, Forcing Parishes to Change," *New York Times,* May 30, 1994; Jason Berry, *Lead Us Not into Temptation* (New York: Doubleday, 1992), pp. 259–73.

13. Roger Finke and Rodney Stark, *The Churching of America, 1776–1990* (New Brunswick, N.J.: Rutgers University Press, 1992), p. 259.

14. Kenneth A. Briggs, *Holy Siege* (San Francisco: Harper, 1992); Lernoux, *People of God.*

15. Kelly, *The Battle for the American Church,* pp. 114–18.

16. Timothy A. Byrnes, *Catholic Bishops in American Politics* (Princeton: Princeton University Press, 1991); Eugene C. Kennedy, *Cardinal Bernardin* (Chicago: Basic Books, 1989); Lawrence Lader, *Politics, Power and the Church: The Catholic Crisis and Its Challenge to American Pluralism* (New York: Macmillan, 1987), p. 17. Blanshard, *American Freedom and Catholic Power,* pp. 61–62.

17. Dallas A. Blanchard, *The Anti-Abortion Movement and the Rise of the Religious Right* (New York: Twayne, 1994), pp. 61–62.

18. Briggs, *Holy Siege.*

19. Barbara Ferraro, Patricia Hussey, and Jane O'Reilly, *No Turning Back: Two Nuns' Battle with the Vatican over Women's Right to Choose* (New York: Poseidon Press, 1990).

20. Harvey Cox, *The Silencing of Leonardo Boff* (Oak Park, Ill.: Meyer-Stone Books, 1988); Hebblethwaite, *The New Inquisition;* Hebblethwaite, *Synod Extraordinary.*

21. Briggs, *Holy Siege,* p. 16.

22. Ari L. Goldman, "Catholics Are at Odds with Bishops," *New York Times,* June 19, 1992, p. A16; Ari L. Goldman, "Support Fading for Document about Women," *New York Times,* June 19, 1992, p. A16.

23. Dorothy Vidulich, "No Meeting Complete Without Protesters," *National Catholic Reporter,* December 4, 1992, p. 4.

24. David Crumm, "Bishops Face Abuse Victims, Gays and Women," *Centre Daily Times* (State College, Pa.), November 17, 1992, p. A3.

25. Berry, *Lead Us Not into Temptation,* pp. 183–89.

26. Troy D. Perry and Thomas L. P. Swicegood, *Don't Be Afraid Any More* (New York: St. Martin's Press, 1990); Jeannine Gramick, ed., *Homosexuality in the Priesthood and Religious Life* (New York: Crossroad, 1989); Enrique Rueda, *The Homosexual Network* (Old Greenwich, Conn.: Devin-Adair, 1982), pp. 362–70.

27. Gramick, *Homosexuality in the Priesthood and Religious Life;* Jeannine Gramick and Robert Nugent, *Building Bridges: Gay and Lesbian Reality and the Catholic Church* (Mystic, Conn.: Twenty-Third Publications, 1992).

28. James Ferry, *In the Courts of the Lord* (New York: Crossroad, 1994); Bernard Lynch, *A Priest on Trial* (London: Bloomsbury, 1993); James G. Wolf, ed., *Gay Priests* (San Francisco: Harper & Row, 1989); Rosemary Curb and Nancy Manahan, eds. *Lesbian Nuns: Breaking Silence* (Tallahassee: Naiad Press 1985); John J. McNeill, *The Church and the Homosexual* (Kansas City, Mo.: Sheed, Andrews & McMeel, 1976).

29. Patricia Nell Warren, *The Fancy Dancer* (New York: Morrow, 1976), p. 251.

30. Iris Murdoch, *Henry and Cato* (London: Chatto & Windus, 1976).

31. A. W. Richard Sipe, *A Secret World: Sexuality and the Search for Celibacy* (New York: Brunner/Mazel, 1990), p. 133.

32. Ibid. p. 107.

33. Quoted in Berry *Lead Us Not into Temptation*, p. 171.

34. Briggs, *Holy Siege.*

35. Robert Goss, *Jesus Acted Up: A Gay and Lesbian Manifesto* (San Francisco: Harper, 1994); John Leo, "The Gay Tide of Catholic Bashing," *U.S. News and World Report,* April 1, 1991.

36. Robert Dawson, "Act-Up Acts Out," *Commonweal,* July 14, 1990, pp. 476–77.

37. "Greeted with a Yawn," *Advocate,* September 21, 1993, p. 25.

38. Mary Jo Weaver and R. Scott Appleby, *Being Right: Conservative Catholics in America,* (Bloomington,: Indiana University Press, 1995); William D. Dinges and James Hitchcock, "Roman Catholic Traditionalism and Activist Conservatism in the United States," in Martin E. Marty and R. Scott Appleby, eds., *Fundamentalisms Observed* (Chicago: University of Chicago Press, 1994), 1: 66–141. The conservatives also dominated the *Catholic League Newsletter*, which combated anti-Catholic prejudice in the media.

39. Berry, *Lead Us Not into Temptation*, pp. 305–22

40. Enrique Rueda and Michael Schwartz, *Gays, AIDS and You* (Old Greenwich, Conn.: Devin-Adair, 1987); Michael Schwartz, *The Persistent Prejudice* (Huntington, Ind.: *Our Sunday Visitor,* 1984).

41. Rueda and Schwartz *Gays, AIDS and You*, pp. 61–65.

42. Ibid., p. 91.

43. Rueda and Schwartz, *Gays, AIDS and You*; Rueda, *The Homosexual Network.*

44. Rueda, *The Homosexual Network,* pp. 80–81, 176–79, 214–15, 545–46.

45. Lernoux *People of God,* pp. 175–76; Briggs, *Holy Siege,* p. 177.

46. Lernoux *People of God,* p. 176; Kennedy, *Cardinal Bernardin,* pp. 273–74.

47. Rueda, *The Homosexual Network,* pp. 317–23, 364.

48. Berry, *Lead Us Not into Temptation*, pp. 305–06.

49. Ibid., p. 306–20; "Statement on Priests and Child Abuse," *Origins* (Catholic News Service) 19 (24) (1989): 393–95.

50. Berry, *Lead Us Not into Temptation*, pp. 309–10, 317–18.

51. Ibid., p. 310.

52. Kennedy, *Cardinal Bernardin*, pp. 254–55, 284.

53. Elinor Burkett and Frank Bruni, *A Gospel of Shame*, (New York: Viking, 1993), p. 220.

54. Lynch *A Priest on Trial,* pp. 54–55; Lynch was acquitted.

55. In the A&E program "Sins of the Fathers," 1993, discussed in chapter 4, below: emphasis in original.

56. Quoted in Lader, *Politics, Power and the Church,* pp. 165–66.

57. Berry, *Lead Us Not into Temptation,* p. 367. Berry's political liberalism is suggested by writings such as his strongly pro-Clinton piece "Civil War on Values Stoops to Attack Dog Tactics," *National Catholic Reporter,* September 2, 1994.

58. Andrew Greeley, "Bishops Paralyzed over Heavily Gay Priesthood," *National Catholic Reporter,* November 10, 1989.

59. Rueda, *The Homosexual Network,* p. 96.

60. Berry, *Lead Us Not into Temptation,* p. 342.

61. David Margolick, "Facing Costly Abuse Suits, Diocese Turns to Parishioners," *New York Times,* December 22, 1993, p. A1; my emphasis.

62. Quoted in Berry, *Lead Us Not into Temptation,* pp. 285–86.

63. Annie Murphy and Peter de Rosa, *Forbidden Fruit* (Boston: Little, Brown, 1993); Terrance A. Sweency and Pamela Shoop Sweeney, *What God Hath Joined* (New York: Ballantine/Fawcett, 1993); Terrance A. Sweeney, *A Church Divided* (Buffalo, N.Y.: Prometheus Books, 1992); Michele Prince, *Mandatory Celibacy in the Catholic Church* (New Paradigm Books, 1992); Sipe, *A Secret World;* David Rice, *Shattered Vows: Priests Who Leave* (London: Michael Joseph, 1990).

64. Briggs, *Holy Siege,* p. 17. Tim Unsworth, *Catholics on the Edge* (New York: Crossroad, 1995).

65. Jason Berry, "Pedophile Priest: Study in Inept Church Response," *National Catholic Reporter,* June 7, 1985, p. 7; Berry, *Lead Us Not into Temptation,* p. 33.

66. A. W. Richard Sipe, "To Enable Healing," *National Catholic Reporter,* September 17, 1993, pp. 6–7; A. W. Richard Sipe, "Celibacy and Imagery: Horror Story in the Making," *National Catholic Reporter,* July 2, 1993, p. 5; William J. Freburger, "A Deeper Clerical Problem Than Sex," *National Catholic Reporter,* April 16, 1993, p. 17; Tim Unsworth, "Chicago Faces 'Lawyer Versus Pastor' Sex Abuse Response," *National Catholic Reporter,* December 6, 1991, p. 26; Tim Unsworth, "Church, State, Wrangle over Pedophilia Cases," *National Catholic Reporter,* September 25, 1992, p. 14; Tim Unsworth, "Clergy Suicides Tip of Depression Iceberg," *National Catholic Reporter,* October 1, 1993, pp. 13–14; Kenneth A. Briggs, "Size of Pedophilia Crisis More Obvious Than Causes," *National Catholic Reporter,* October 30, 1992, p. 22.

67. Eugene C. Kennedy, "The See-no-problem, Hear-no-problem, Speak-no-problem Problem," *National Catholic Reporter,* March 19, 1993, p. 5.

68. Thomas C. Fox, "Clergy Sex Abuse Survivors Break Silence," *National Catholic Reporter,* October 30, 1992, pp. 3–4; Thomas C. Fox, "Sex and Power Issues Expand Clergy-Lay Rift," *National Catholic Reporter,* November 13, 1992, pp. 17–19.

69. Thomas C. Fox and Jason Berry, "As Nation Discusses Pedophilia, Even Pope Admits It's a Problem," *National Catholic Reporter,* July 2, 1993, pp. 2–3.

70. Douglas Martin, "Feeling Slighted by Church Officials, New York Youth Sues over Abuse by His Priest," *New York Times,* February 24, 1993, p. B4.

71. *National Catholic Reporter,* March 19, 1993. For the newspaper's continued emphasis on the gravity of the sexual crisis within the church, see for example Arthur Jones, "Sexual Abuse by Priests: The Unrelenting Crisis," *National Catholic Reporter,* March 3, 1995, p. 6; Arthur Jones, "As Scandal Keeps Growing, Who is Accountable?" *National Catholic Reporter,* March 3, 1995, pp. 6–7; "Sex Abuse Scandal Erodes Church's Credibility," editorial, *National Catholic Reporter,* March 24, 1995, p. 24.

72. James MacLoughlin, "Just Following Orders: The Politics of Pedophilia," *National Catholic Reporter,* April 16, 1993, p. 15

73. Kennedy "The See-no-problem, Hear-no-problem, Speak-no-problem Problem."

74. Thomas C. Fox, "Sex and Power Issues Expand Clergy-Lay Rift"; "Chicago Sex-Abuse Policy Thoughtful and Firm," *National Catholic Reporter,* October 2, 1992, p. 24; Robert McClory, "Bernardin Issues Rigorous Pedophile Policy," *National Catholic Reporter,* October 2, 1992, p. 3.

75. Barb Fraze, "Canadian Bishops Move Vigorously on Sex Abuse Problem," *National Catholic Reporter,* July 2, 1993, p. 3.

76. Burkett and Bruni, *A Gospel of Shame*, p. 224; Fox, "Sex and Power Issues Expand Clergy-Lay Rift."

77. Fox, "Sex and Power Issues Expand Clergy-Lay Rift."

78. Michael A. Russo, *The Church, the Press and Abortion: Catholic Leadership and Public Communication* (Cambridge, Mass.: Joan Shorenstein Barone Center on the Press, Politics and Public Policy, 1991); David Shaw, "Abortion in America," *Los Angeles Times,* July 1–4, 1990. Conservative Catholic groups allege systemic media bias against the church: see, for example, S. Robert Lichter, Daniel Amundson, and Linda S. Lichter, *Media Coverage of the Catholic Church*, (Washington, D.C.: Center for Media and Public Affairs, 1991).

79. Andrew Greeley, "Why Do Catholics Stay in the Church? Because of the Stories," *New York Times Magazine*, July 10, 1994, p. 38.

80. Berry, *Lead Us Not into Temptation*, p. 366.

81. Jonathan Friendly, "Catholic Church Discussing Priests Who Abuse Children," *New York Times*, May 4, 1986, p. A26.

82. CNN program, "Fall from Grace," discussed in chapter 4 above.

83. Letter in *National Catholic Reporter*, April 16, 1993.

84. MacLoughlin, "Just Following Orders.

85. Harris, *Unholy Orders*, p. 18.

86. Burkett and Bruni, *A Gospel of Shame*, pp. 228–29.

87. Vicki Quade, "Unholy Wars," *Human Rights,* fall 1992, pp. 18–21.

88. Quoted in *National Catholic Reporter*, February 26, 1993, p. 5.

89. Compare Sweeney, *A Church Divided*; Prince, *Mandatory Celibacy in the Catholic Church;* Joseph H. Fichter, *Wives of Catholic Clergy* (Sheed & Ward, 1992).

90. Sipe, *Secret World*, pp. 159–87; Sipe, "To Enable Healing"; Sipe, "Celibacy and Imagery."

91. Fox, "Sex and Power Issues Expand Clergy-Lay Rift."

92. Richard N. Ostling, "Can a Priest Be a Husband?" *Time*, January 22, 1990, p. 72. Robert T. Zintl, "Big Gamble on the Priesthood," *Time* November 5,1990, pp. 83–84.

93. Kenneth L. Woodward, "The Sins of the Fathers," *Newsweek*, July 12, 1993, p. 57; Kenneth L. Woodward, "Sex and the Church," *Newsweek,* August 16, 1993, pp. 38–41.

94. "Should Priests Be Allowed to Marry?" *JET,* August 27, 1990, pp. 12–14.

95. Steve M. Klein, "The Roman Catholic Church's Married Priest Movement," *USA Today: The Magazine of the American Scene,* July 1992, pp. 52–53.

96. Lucretia B. Yaghjian, "Enabled for the Kingdom" *Commonweal,* July 12, 1991, pp. 430–31.

97. Mary Anne Huddleston, "Sex, Sense and the Celibate Priesthood," *America,* December 1, 1990, pp. 422–25.

98. "Celibacy Challenge," *Christian Century,* May 6, 1992, pp. 483–84.

99. Robert E. Burns, "Mind Your Own Celibacy," *US Catholic,* December 1990, p. 2; John Whelan, "What Married Clergy Say About Celibacy," *US Catholic,* August 1990, pp. 20–27. See also Richard A. Gardner, "Psychiatrist: How Possible Is Celibacy Today?" *National Catholic Reporter,* March 19, 1993, p. 9; Douglas W. Kmiec, "It's Time for the Church to Review Its Teaching on Priestly Celibacy," *Philadelphia Inquirer,* December 9, 1993; "Church Sex Cases

Raise Celibacy Issues," *Boston Globe*, May 30, 1992; "Eucharist, Not Celibacy, at Heart of the Church," *National Catholic Reporter,* January 18, 1991, p. 40; William R. Mackaye, "The Catholic Program: Is Celibacy Central?" *Christianity in Crisis,* April 8, 1991, pp. 126–28.

100. Compare Eugene C. Kennedy, "Seminary System Rates Quick Christian Burial," *National Catholic Reporter,* July 17, 1992, p. 6.

101. Richard N. Ostling, "The Secrets of St. Lawrence," *Time*, June 7, 1993, p. 44;

102. Berry, *Lead Us Not into Temptation*, p. 277.

103. Ibid.

104. Quoted in Leslie Bennetts "Unholy Alliances," *Vanity Fair,* December 1991, pp. 224–78, at 227.

105. Berry, *Lead Us Not into Temptation,* p. 191.

106. Ibid., 243–58.

107. Ibid., p. 265.

108. Ibid., p. 322.

109. Burkett and Bruni, *A Gospel of Shame*, p. 61.

110. Ibid., p. 49.

111. Ibid., p. 231.

112. Ibid., p. 232.

113. Ibid., p. 251.

114. Ibid., p. 234.

115. Andrew Greeley, "A View from the Priesthood," *Newsweek*, August 16, 1993, p. 45.

116. Stephen J. Rossetti, "Statistical Reflections on Priestly Celibacy," *America,* June 18, 1994, pp. 22–24; Burkett and Bruni, *A Gospel of Shame*, p. 216.

117. Rossetti, "Statistical Reflections on Priestly Celibacy," p. 23.

118. Quoted in Paul Wilkes, "Unholy Acts," *New Yorker,* June 7, 1993, p. 72.

119. Peter Steinfels, "Ancient Rock in Crosscurrents of Today," *New York Times,* May 29, 1994, p. 1:1; Ari L. Goldman, "Religion Notes: Sentiment for Married Priests," *New York Times*, June 13, 1992; Ari L. Goldman, "Catholics Are at Odds with Bishops," *New York Times*, June 19, 1992, p. A16; Arthur Jones, "Gallup Poll Results Unlikely to Please Vatican," *National Catholic Reporter,* July 3, 1992, p. 6.

120. Aric Press et al., "Priests and Abuse," *Newsweek,* August 16, 1993, pp. 42–44.

121. Reginald W. Bibby *Unknown Gods* (Toronto: Stoddart, 1993), pp. 68–77; Rae Corelli, "Rome's Rebels," *Macleans,* December 19, 1994, pp. 34–37; John Demont and Susanne Hiller, "Keeping the Faith," *Macleans,* December 19, 1994, p. 38.

122. D'Arcy Jenish, "Empty Pews, Angry Members," *Maclean's,* April 12, 1993, pp. 48–50. Other Catholic communities outside North America demonstrated a similar reaction to clerical sexual scandals. In Austria, for example, Cardinal Hans Hermann Groer resigned as head of the bishops' conference in 1995 following allegations of sexual involvement with seminarians in the 1970s. Over the following months, there was an upsurge of reformist petitions demanding, among other things, the abolition of mandatory celibacy, full equality for women within the structures of the church, the reduction of clerical privileges, and lay involvement in episcopal elections: Ingrid H. Schafer, "Like Luther, Austrians Demand Church Reform," *National Catholic Reporter*, June 16, 1995, p. 9. For comparable developments in contemporary Ireland, see Moore, *Betrayal of Trust: The Father Brendan Smyth Affair and the Catholic Church.*

Chapter 7: "Sins of the Fathers": The Feminist Response

1. W. L. Marshall and Sylvia Barrett, *Criminal Neglect: Why Sex Offenders Go Free* (Toronto: Seal, 1992), p. 122; my emphasis.

2. Wade Clark Roof, *A Generation of Seekers: The Spiritual Journeys of the Baby Boom Generation* (San Francisco: Harper, 1993), p. 223.

3. See above, chapter 5.

4. Susan Brownmiller, *Against Our Will* (London: Secker & Warburg, 1975).

5. Philip Jenkins, *Using Murder: The Social Construction of Serial Homicide* (Hawthorne, N.Y.: Aldine de Gruyter, 1994); Philip Jenkins, *Intimate Enemies: Moral Panics in Contemporary Great Britain* (Hawthorne, N.Y.: Aldine de Gruyter, 1992).

6. James Newton Poling, *The Abuse of Power: A Theological Problem* (Nashville, Tenn.: Abingdon Press, 1991), p. 148.

7. Roof, *A Generation of Seekers,* p. 233.

8. Barry A. Kosmin and Seymour P. Lachman, *One Nation Under God: Religion in Contemporary American Society* (New York: Harmony Books, 1993), pp. 10–11.

9. Kenneth L. Woodward, "Sex and the Church," *Newsweek,* August 16, 1993, pp. 38–41.

10. "Greeted with a Yawn," *Advocate,* September 21, 1993, p. 25.

11. Roof, *A Generation of Seekers,* p. 219; compare Annie Lally Milhaven, *The Inside Stories: Thirteen Valiant Women Challenging the Church* (Mystic, Conn.: Twenty-Third Publications, 1987).

12. Lawrence Lader, *Politics, Power and the Church: The Catholic Crisis and Its Challenge to American Pluralism* (New York: Macmillan, 1987).

13. This cartoon was originally published in the *San Antonio Express News*, and appeared in syndicated form on July 1, 1994. The *Catholic League Newsletter* (18[6] [July–August 1991]) published a selection of cartoons on the Thomas case; one, for example, depicted the new justice being hymned to the bench by a group of chanting nuns. The caption reads "Well, there goes *Roe v Wade*." A similar comment on the Thomas nomination by Pat Oliphant was regarded as egregiously anti-Catholic (ibid. 18[7] [September 1991]).

14. Mary Daly, *Beyond God the Father* (Boston: Beacon Press, 1973).

15. Rosemary Radford Ruether, *New Woman, New Earth: Sexist Ideologies and Human Liberation* (New York: Seabury Press, 1975); Rosemary Radford Ruether, *Gaia and God: An Ecofeminist Theory of Earth Healing* (San Francisco: Harper, 1992).

16. *National Catholic Reporter,* June 17, 1994.

17. Andrew Greeley, *The Catholic Myth* (New York: Collier, 1990), p. 228.

18. Mary Jo Weaver, *New Catholic Women: A Contemporary Challenge to Traditional Religious Authority* (San Francisco: Harper, 1985); Andrew Greeley and Mary G. Durkin, *Angry Catholic Women* (Chicago: Thomas More Press, 1984).

19. Michael J. Hunt, *College Catholics: A New Counterculture* (Paulist Press, 1993); Dirk Johnson, "Young Catholics Questioning Their Identity in the Church," *New York Times,* August 9, 1993, p. A1; Patrick McNamara, *Conscience First, Tradition Second: A Study of Young American Catholics* (Albany: SUNY Press, 1992).

20. Roof, *A Generation of Seekers,* p. 219.

21. Quoted in R. Gustav Niebuhr, "Image of God as 'He' Loses Its Sovereignty in America's Churches," *Wall Street Journal,* April 27, 1992, p. A1.

22. A. W. Richard Sipe, "Celibacy and Imagery: Horror Story in the Making," *National Catholic Reporter.* July 2, 1993, p. 5; compare Uta Ranke-Heinemann, *Eunuchs for the Kingdom of God*, (New York: Doubleday, 1991).

23. Quoted in Kenneth A. Briggs, *Holy Siege (*San Francisco: Harper, 1992), p. 46.

24. Cynthia Eller, *Living in the Lap of the Goddess: The Feminist Spirituality Movement in America* (New York: Crossroad, 1994); Ursula King, *Women and Spirituality: Voices of Protest and Promise* (University Park: Penn State Press 1993), pp. 177–97.

25. Eller, *Living in the Lap of the Goddess.*

26. Mary D. Pellauer, *Towards a Tradition of Feminist Theology* (Brooklyn, N.Y.: Carlson, 1991); Denise Lardner Carmody, *Feminism and Christianity: A Two-Way Reflection* (Nashville, Tenn.: Abingdon Press, 1982); Denise Lardner Carmody, *The Double Cross: Ordination, Abortion and Catholic Feminism* (New York: Crossroad, 1986); Denise Lardner Carmody, *The Good Alliance: Feminism, Religion and Education* (Lanham, Md.: University Press of America, 1991); Susan Nelson Dunfee, *Beyond Servanthood: Christianity and the Liberation of Women* (Lanham, Md.: University Press of America, 1988); Carolyn A. Osiek, *Beyond Anger: On Being a Feminist in the Church* (New York: Paulist Press, 1986).

27. Elizabeth Schüssler Fiorenza, *In Memory of Her* (New York: Crossroad, 1984); Elizabeth Schüssler Fiorenza, *Bread Not Stone: The Challenge of Feminist Biblical Interpretation* (Boston: Beacon Press, 1984); Elizabeth Schüssler Fiorenza, *Discipleship of Equals: A Critical Feminist Ekklesia-logy of Liberation* (New York: Crossroad, 1993).

28. Alan Cowell, "Pope Issues Censure of 'Nature Worship' by Some Feminists," *New York Times,* July 3, 1993, p. A1; Peter Steinfels, "Catholic Feminists Ask: Can We Remain Catholic?" *New York Times,* April 16, 1993, p. A19; Donna Steichen, *Ungodly Rage: The Hidden Face of Catholic Feminism* (San Francisco: Ignatius, 1991).

29. Peter Steinfels "Presbyterians Try to Resolve Long Dispute," *New York Times,* June 17, 1994, p. A24; Peter Steinfels, "Beliefs," *New York Times,* June 25, 1994, p. A12.

30. Peter Steinfels "Female Concept of God Is Shaking Protestants," *New York Times,* May 14, 1994, p. A28.

31. Joanne Carlson Brown and Carole R. Bohn, *Christianity, Patriarchy and Abuse: A Feminist Critique* (New York: Pilgrim, 1989), p. 90; for Harrison, see James R. Edwards, "Earthquake in the Mainline," *Christianity Today,* November 14, 1994, p. 40.

32. Marie M. Fortune, *Sexual Violence: The Unmentionable Sin* (New York: Pilgrim, 1983).

33. Pamela Cooper-White, *The Cry of Tamar: Violence Against Women and the Church's Response* (Minneapolis: Augsburg Fortress, 1995); Elizabeth Schüssler Fiorenza and M. Shawn Copeland, eds., *Violence Against Women,* special volume 1 of *Concilium* (New York: Orbis, 1994); Emilie Buchwald, Pamela R. Fletcher, and Martha Roth, eds., *Transforming a Rape Culture* (Minneapolis: Milkweed Editions, 1993); Annie Imbens and Ineke Jonker, *Christianity and Incest* (Minneapolis: Augsburg Fortress, 1991); Mary D. Pellauer, Barbara Chester, and Jane A. Boyajian, eds., *Sexual Assault and Abuse* (San Francisco: Harper & Row, 1987).

34. Pellauer, Chester, and Boyajian, *Sexual Assault and Abuse,* p. 56.

35. Rosemary Radford Ruether, *Women-Church: Theology and Practice of Feminist Liturgical Communities* (San Francisco: Harper, 1985), p. 129.

36. Ibid., pp. 153–58.

37. Ibid., pp. 151–52.

38. Ibid., p. 152.

39. Pellauer, Chester, and Boyajian, *Sexual Assault and Abuse*, pp. 223–47.

40. Ruether, *Women-Church*, p. 41. Compare Brown and Bohn, *Christianity, Patriarchy and Abuse,* p. 37; A. W. Richard Sipe, *A Secret World: Sexuality and the Search for Celibacy* (New York: Brunner/Mazel, 1990), pp. 30–31.

42. Ruether in Brown and Bohn, *Christianity, Patriarchy and Abuse,* p. 39.

43. Matthew Fox, *The Coming of the Cosmic Christ* (San Francisco: Harper & Row, 1988), pp. 181–82.

44. Brown and Bohn, *Christianity, Patriarchy and Abuse.*

45. Ibid., p. 2.

46. Ibid., p. 51.

47. *Episcopal Life,* October 1991, p. 1.

48. Poling, *The Abuse of Power,* p. 169. Compare David R. Blumenthal, *Facing the Abusing God: A Theology of Protest* (Westminster, Tenn.: John Knox Press, 1993); Phyllis Trible, *Texts of Terror: Literary-Feminist Readings of Biblical Narratives* (Philadelphia: Fortress, 1984).

49. Brown and Bohn, *Christianity, Patriarchy and Abuse,* p. 27.

50. Ibid., p. 70.

51. Dawn Gibeau, "Link-Up Gains Momentum on Road to Healing," *National Catholic Reporter,* August 26, 1994, p. 3.

52. Quoted in "NCCB Establishes Committee on Sexual Abuse," *Origins* (Catholic News Service) 23 (7) (1993): 104–11, at 107.

53 David Hechler, "Sins of the Father," *McCall's,* September 1993, pp. 113–19+.

54. Angela Bonavoglia, "The Sacred Secret," *Ms.,* March–April 1992, pp. 40–46.

55. Leslie Bennetts, "Unholy Alliances," *Vanity Fair,* December 1991, pp. 224–78.

56. Cristine Clark, "Broken Vows," *Redbook,* November 1992, pp. 51–56.

57. Bonavoglia, "The Sacred Secret."

58. Susan Armstrong, "Sexual Abuse of Women and Girls by Clergy," *Canadian Women Studies* 11(4) (Summer 1991).

59. James A. Sparks, Robert O. Ray, and Donald C. Houts, "Sexual Misconduct in Ministry," *Congregations,* November–December 1992, pp. 3–8; Peter Rutter, *Sex in the Forbidden Zone: When Men in Power—Therapists, Doctors, Clergy, Teachers and Others—Betray Women's Trust* (Los Angeles: J. P. Tarcher, 1989).

60. See, for example, Pellauer, Chester, and Boyajian, *Sexual Assault and Abuse,* pp. 209–18.

61. Pamela Cooper-White, "Soul-Stealing: Power Relations in Pastoral Sexual Abuse," *Christian Century,* February 20, 1991, pp. 146–49.

62. Marie M. Fortune, "How the Church Should Imitate the Navy," *Christian Century,* August 26–September 2, 1992, pp. 765–66.

63. Ann-Janine Morey, "Blaming Women for the Sexually Abusive Male Pastor," *Christian Century,* October 5, 1988, pp. 866–69.

64. Marie M. Fortune, "Is Nothing Sacred? The Betrayal of the Ministerial or Teaching Relationship," *Journal of Feminist Studies in Religion* 10(1) (1994): 17–24; Celia Allison Hahn, "Inhabiting Our Longing," *Congregations,* November–December 1992, pp. 9–13.

65. Marie M. Fortune, *Is Nothing Sacred? When Sex Invades the Pastoral Relationship* (San Francisco: Harper & Row, 1989).

66. Ibid., p. 72.

67. Ibid., p. 124.

68. Ibid.

69. Fortune, "How the Church Should Imitate the Navy."

70. Kenneth L. Woodward and Patricia King, "When a Pastor Turns Seducer," *Newsweek,* August 28, 1989; Lloyd Rediger, *Ministry and Sexuality* (Minneapolis: Fortress Press, 1990).

71. Bonavoglia, "The Sacred Secret," p. 41, my emphasis; Tanya Barrientos, "In Ministry, Dealing with Temptations of the Flesh," *Philadelphia Inquirer* Magazine section, March 22, 1995, p. H1.

72. "Policy on Sexual Abuse by Priests: Los Angeles Archdiocese" *Origins* (Catholic News Service) 24 (5) (1994): 70–74, at 74; compare Don Gonsiorek, ed., *Breach of Trust: Sexual Exploitation by Health Care Professionals and Clergy* (Thousand Oaks, Calif.: Sage, 1995).

73. James Ferry, *In the Courts of the Lord* (New York: Crossroad, 1994); Bryan V. Hillis, *Can Two Walk Together Unless They Be Agreed? American Religious Schisms in the 1970s* (Brooklyn, N.Y.: Carlson, 1991); Berry, *Lead Us Not into Temptation,* p. 198.

74. Virginia Culver, "Insurance Warning Issued," *Denver Post,* January 4, 1992, p. B6. Virginia Culver, "Church Facing Second Trial," *Denver Post,* January 22, 1994, p. B3. Virginia Culver, "Church Abuse Serious," *Denver Post,* May 16, 1994, p. B1.

75. "Churches Should Focus on Abuse of Clergy As Well," editorial, *Denver Post* May 13, 1994, p. B10.

76. Peter Steinfels, "Beliefs," *New York Times,* June 25, 1994, p. A12.

77. See, for example, John Shelby Spong, *Rescuing the Bible from Fundamentalism* (San Francisco: Harper, 1991); John Shelby Spong, *Born of a Woman* (San Francisco: Harper, 1992).

78. For women in the Episcopal church, see Catherine M. Prelinger, ed., *Episcopal Women: Gender, Spirituality and Commitment in an American Mainline Denomination* (New York: Oxford University Press, 1992); Mary Sudman Donovan, *Women Priests in the Episcopal Church* (Cincinnati: Forward Movement, 1988).

79. Julie A.Wortman, "Pain May Overwhelm Exploited Victims," *Episcopal Life,* October 1991, p. 1; Julie A.Wortman, "Full Disclosure of Abuse Helps Parishes Heal," *Episcopal Life,* November 1991, p. 8. The pervasive rhetoric of abuse found its way into other church scandals that at least on first appearance had nothing to do with sexual misconduct. In 1995 the Episcopal church accused a former national treasurer of embezzling some two million dollars. The accused woman blamed her actions on stress caused by the climate of "pain, abuse and powerlessness" from which she suffered in the denomination, and which had led her to block actions from her memory: "Ex-Treasurer Blames Theft on Job Stress," *Christianity Today,* June 19, 1995, p. 46; Ed Stannard, "Prosecution of Cooke Appears Unlikely," *Episcopal Life,* June 1995, p. 1.

80. James L. Franklin, "Sex Abuse by Clergy Called Crisis for Churches," *Boston Globe,* July 17, 1991, pp. 11.

81. Nan Cobbey, "Clergy Discipline Canons Fairer to Victim, Accuser," *Episcopal Life,* October 1994, p. 14; David Skidmore, "Proposal Recommends Standards in Sexual Misconduct Cases," *Episcopal Life,* July 1994, p. 9.

Chapter 8: The Legal Environment

1. Walter K. Olson, *The Litigation Explosion* (New York: Dutton, 1991).

2. Christopher Farrell,"An Avalanche of Lawsuits Descends on Insurers," *Business Week,* April 11, 1988, pp. 60–61.

3. Olson, *The Litigation Explosion*, p. 169.

4. Peter W. Huber, *Liability: The Legal Revolution and Its Consequences* (New York: Basic Books, 1988).

5. Olson, *The Litigation Explosion*, p. 157.

6. Ibid., pp. 23–24.

7. Huber, *Liability*, p. 77; Peter W. Huber, *Galileo's Revenge: Junk Science in the Courtroom* (New York: Basic Books, 1991).

8. Richard Perez-Peña,"US Juries Grow Tougher on Plaintiffs in Lawsuits," *New York Times,* June 17, 1994, p. A1; Ben Gose, "Lawsuit Feeding Frenzy," *Chronicle of Higher Education,* August 17, 1994, p. 27.

9. A. W. Richard Sipe, *A Secret World: Sexuality and the Search for Celibacy* (New York: Brunner/Mazel, 1990), p. 163. For the growing sensitivity in these years about sexual misconduct by doctors and therapists, see John C. Gonsiorek, ed., *Breach of Trust: Sexual Exploitation by Health Care Professionals and Clergy* (Thousand Oaks, Calif.: Sage, 1995).

10. Jeffrey Warren Scott, *State Mandatory Reporting of Child and Elder Abuse: A Challenge to the Privacy of Penitential Communications* (Ph.D. diss., Baylor University, 1991);

Ronald K. Ballis, "Child Abuse Reporting Requirements: Liabilities and Immunities for Clergy," *Journal of Pastoral Care* 44(3) (1990); Alexander D. Hill, "A Current Church-State Battleground," *Journal of Church and State* 32(4) (1990); Raymond C. O'Brien, "Pedophilia: The Legal Predicament of Clergy," *Journal of Contemporary Health Law and Policy* 4 (1988): 91–154; Marie M. Fortune, "Confidentiality and Mandatory Reporting: A False Dilemma?" *Christian Century*, June 18, 1986, pp. 582–83.

11. Jeffrey Warren Scott, "Confidentiality and Child Abuse: Church and State Collide," *Christian Century*, February 19, 1986, pp. 174–75; Scott, *State Mandatory Reporting of Child and Elder Abuse.*

12. Raymond C. O'Brien and Michael T. Flannery, "The Pending Gauntlet to Free Exercise: Mandating That Clergy Report Child Abuse," *Loyola of Los Angeles Law Review* 25(1) (1991).

13. Paul Blanshard, *American Freedom and Catholic Power* (Boston: Beacon Press, 1949), p. 54, citing Canon 2341; William G. McLoughlin, *Rhode Island: A History* (New York: Norton, 1986), pp. 186–88.

14. Angela Bonavoglia, "The Sacred Secret," *Ms.*, March–April 1992, pp. 40–46; see chapter 3 above, for the Schwartz case.

15. "Brief History: Handling Child Sex Abuse Claims," *Origins* (Catholic News Service) 23 (38) (1994): 666–70.

16. Patrick Boyle, *Scout's Honor: Sexual Abuse in America's Most Trusted Institution* (Rocklin, Calif.: Prima, 1994).

17. Jason Berry, *Lead Us Not into Temptation* (New York: Doubleday, 1992); Ari L. Goldman, "Three Cases Challenge Privacy of Talks with Clergy," *New York Times*, August 27, 1985.

18. "Priest Held Liable for Civil Damages" *New York Times,* September 26, 1988.

19. Vicki Quade, "Unholy Wars," *Human Rights,* fall 1992, pp. 18–21.

20. Howard Chua-Eoan, "After the Fall," *Time,* May 9, 1994, pp. 56–58; Arthur Gross Schaefer, "Combatting Clergy Sexual Misconduct," *Risk Management,* May 1, 1994; Julie Gannon Shoop, "Suffer the Little Children: Lawsuits Target Churches for Sex Abuse by Clergy," *Trial,* February 1993, pp. 11–13; "When the Shepherd Preys on the Flock: Clergy Sexual Exploitation and the Search for Solutions," *Florida State University Law Review* 19 (2) (1991): 499– .

21. Berry, *Lead Us Not into Temptation,* pp. 371–73.

22. Andrew Greeley, "But Father, They're Priests!" *Critic* 47(2) (1992): 1–3; Richard N. Ostling, "The Secrets of St. Lawrence," *Time*, June 7, 1993, p. 44.

23. Berry, *Lead Us Not into Temptation,* pp. 372–73.

24. Lawrence Lader, *Politics, Power and the Church: The Catholic Crisis and Its Challenge to American Pluralism* (New York: Macmillan, 1987), p. 101.

25. Ibid. For Milwaukee, see Leslie Wirpsa, "Weakland Profiles Diocese as Economic Force," *National Catholic Reporter,* October 21, 1994, p. 5.

26. Peter Steinfels, "Camden Diocese Settles Sexual Abuse Cases," *New York Times*, January 12, 1994, p. B5.

27. Dennis Gaboury and Elinor Burkett, "The Secret of St. Mary's," *Rolling Stone*, November 11, 1993, p. 54.

28. Art Babych, "Price of Canada Scandals Hits $23 Million," *National Catholic Reporter,* July 2, 1993, p. 6; Art Babych, "Former Students Sue Order for $40 Million," *National Catholic Reporter,* September 16, 1994, p. 6; "Addenda," *National Catholic Reporter,* October 7, 1994, p. 5

29. Lawrence I. Shulruff, "His Specialty: Sex Abuse Suits Against Priests," *New York Times,* June 25, 1993, p. B16.

30. Quade, "Unholy Wars."

31. Ibid.; Douglas Martin, "Feeling Slighted by Church Officials, New York Youth Sues over Abuse by His Priest," *New York Times,* February 24, 1993, p. B4.

32. Huber, *Liability,* 76.

33. "Lawsuit by Priest Charges Sex Abuse," *New York Times,* June 11, 1993, p. A17; Patricia Lefevere, "Racketeering Statutes Cited in Sex Lawsuit," *National Catholic Reporter,* July 2, 1993, pp. 5 6; "Three Settle Sex Suit Against Two Priests," *New York Times,* October 13, 1993; Maureen Graham and Larry Lewis, "Sex Abuse Suit Claims Cover-Up by Bishops," *Philadelphia Inquirer,* November 1, 1994; Patricia Lefevere, "Lawsuit Alleges Church Covered up Sex Abuse," *National Catholic Reporter,* November 11, 1994, p. 4; "Bishop McHugh Vows to Fight Abuse Charges," *National Catholic Reporter,* November 18, 1994. Allegations of wide-ranging clerical conspiracies were also made elsewhere, for example, in Northern California: see Don Lattin, "Lawsuit Accuses Catholic Leaders," *San Francisco Chronicle,* January 27, 1995, p. C11.

34. Federal RICO provisions are found in 18 U.S.C. ss. 1961–1968. The 1994 Camden suit was based on New Jersey's RICO statutes.

35. "Letter After Charges Involving Local Priest," *Origins* (Catholic News Service) 23 (7) (1993): 111–12.

36. John W. Kennedy, "$1.75 million Paid to Abuse Victims," *Christianity Today,* June 20, 1994, p. 56.

37. This case was *Broderick v. King's Way Church*; see Donald C. Clark, "Sexual Abuse in the Church: The Law Steps In," *Christian Century* April 14, 1993, pp. 396–98.

38. James M. Wall, "There Ought to Be a Law," *Christian Century,* May 4, 1994, pp. 454–60.

39. Maureen Graham and Larry Lewis, "Sex Abuse Suit Claims Cover-Up by Bishops," *Philadelphia Inquirer,* November 1, 1994; Douglas W. Kmiec, "It's Time for the Church to Review Its Teaching on Priestly Celibacy," *Philadelphia Inquirer,* December 9, 1993.

40. "Settlement in Priest's Abuse Case Raises Question of Liability," *New York Times,* January 17, 1994; Demetria Martinez, "Priests' Treatment Facility Rocked by Suits" *National Catholic Reporter,* February 26, 1993, p. 5.

41. "Statement on Therapy for Pedophilia," *Origins* (Catholic News Service) 22 (16) (1992): 284.

42. Elinor Burkett and Frank Bruni, *A Gospel of Shame* (New York: Viking, 1993), pp. 126–27.

43. Demetria Martinez, "Diocese Sells Retreat in Sex Abuse Bailout," *National Catholic Reporter,* September 30, 1994, p. 3; David Margolick, "Facing Costly Abuse Suits, Diocese Turns to Parishioners," *New York Times,* December 22, 1993, p. A1.

44. "Settlement in Priest's Abuse Case Raises Question of Liability" (*New York Times*).

45. Perez-Peña,"US Juries Grow Tougher on Plaintiffs in Lawsuits."

46. Compare Milo Geyelin, "Cross Purposes: The Catholic Church Struggles with Suits over Sexual Abuse," *Wall Street Journal,* November 24, 1993, p. A1.

47. In the television program "Sins of the Fathers," 1993; see chapter 4, above. Critics termed a legislative attempt to limit payment in clergy malpractice suits as "The Pedophile Protection Act of 1995": see "Santa Fe Church Officials Back Bill to Limit Child Abuse Suits," *National Catholic Reporter,* March 10, 1995, p. 7.

48. Cheryl Lavin, "Lost Sanctuary: Accusing a Priest of Sex Abuse, a Family Battles Church and State," *Chicago Tribune,* September 13, 1992, p. 5:1.

49. Andrew Greeley, *Fall from Grace* (New York: G. P. Putnams, 1993), pp. 90–94, 142–45.

50. Berry, *Lead Us Not into Temptation,* pp. 334–60.

51. Berry, *Lead Us Not into Temptation*, p. 341, but see below.

52. The *60 Minutes* program was entitled "I Solemnly Swear"; cf. Thomas C. Fox and Jason Berry, "As Nation Discusses Pedophilia, Even Pope Admits It's a Problem," *National Catholic Reporter,* July 2, 1993, pp. 2–3.

53. Peter Steinfels, "O'Connor Orders Priests to Meetings on Sexual Conduct," *New York Times*, May 26, 1993.

54. Julia Quinn Dempsey, John R. Gorman, John P. Madden, and Alphonse P. Spilly, *The Cardinal's Commission on Clerical Sexual Misconduct with Minors: Report to Joseph Cardinal Bernardin, Archbishop of Chicago* (Chicago: The Commission, 1992), pp. 21–22.

55. "Priest, Principal Cleared of Charges," *National Catholic Reporter,* July 15, 1994. There were other cases in which juries utterly rejected allegations of priestly abuse. See for example Allen Lengel, "Jury Rejects Sex Charge Against Capuchins," *Detroit News*, March 29, 1995, p. B1.

56. Steinfels, "O'Connor Orders Priests to Meetings on Sexual Conduct."

57. Gaboury and Burkett, "The Secret of St. Mary's," p. 84.

58. Farrell,"An Avalanche of Lawsuits Descends on Insurers." "Archdiocese of Milwaukee Sues Insurers on Sexual Abuse Claims," *New York Times*, December 27, 1994.

59. Margolick, "Facing Costly Abuse Suits, Diocese Turns to Parishioners."

60. "Insurers Sue Diocese over Molestation Case," *New York Times,* August 20, 1992, p. A25.

61. "Malone Asks Diocesan Workers to Sign Sex Abuse Affidavits," *National Catholic Reporter,* March 25, 1994.

62. David Skidmore, "Parishes Face Limits to Insuring for Sex Abuse," *Episcopal Life,* April 1993, pp. 1, 7.

63. Jim Borgman, cartoon, *Cincinnati Inquirer*, March 1994; reprinted in *New York Times*.

Chapter 9: Defending Therapy

1. Quoted in Susan Brownmiller, *Against Our Will* (London: Secker & Warburg, 1975), p. 369.

2. Jeffrey M. Masson, *The Assault on Truth: Freud's Suppression of the Seduction Theory* (New York: Farrar Straus Giroux, 1984); Florence Rush, "The Freudian Cover-Up," *Chrysalis* 1 (1977): 31–45.

3. Quoted in Gail S. Goodman et al., "The Child Witness," special issue of *Journal of Social Issues* 40 (2) (1984): 2.

4. Ellen Gray, *Unequal Justice: The Prosecution of Child Sexual Abuse* (New York: Free Press, 1993); Billie Wright Dziech and C. B. Schudson, *On Trial: America's Courts and Their Treatment of Sexually Abused Children*, 2d ed., (Boston: Beacon Press, 1991).

5. Nancy Walker Perry and Lawrence W. Wrightsman, *The Child Witness: Legal Issues and Dilemmas* (Newbury Park, Calif.: Sage, 1991); Stephen J. Ceci, Michael P. Toglia, and David F. Ross *Children's Eyewitness Memory* (New York: Springer-Verlag, 1987).

6. Lucy S. McGough, *Child Witnesses: Fragile Voices in the American Legal System* (New Haven: Yale University Press, 1994); Maria S. Zaragosa et al., *Memory and Testimony in the Child Witness* (Thousand Oaks, Calif.: Sage, 1994).

7. "Prosecuting Child Abuse," special issue, *Prosecutors' Perspective* (American Prosecutors Research Institute, Alexandria, Va.) 2(1) (January 1988); Debra Whitcomb, *Prosecution of Child Sexual Abuse: Innovations in Practice* (U.S. Department of Justice, National Institute of Justice) (Washington, D.C.: Government Printing Office, 1985); Debra Whitcomb, "Prosecuting Child Sexual Abuse: New Approaches," *NIJ Reports*, no. 197. (May 1986); Debra

Whitcomb, Elizabeth R. Shapiro, and Lindsey D. Stellwagen, *When the Victim Is a Child: Issues for Judges and Prosecutors*, NCJ 97664 (U.S. Department of Justice, National Institute of Justice) (Washington, D.C.: Government Printing Office, 1985).

8. Roland Summit, "The Child Sexual Abuse Accommodation Syndrome," *Child Abuse and Neglect* 7 (1983): 177–93.

9. James F. Richardson, Joel Best, and David Bromley, eds, *The Satanism Scare* (Hawthorne, N.Y.: Aldine de Gruyter, 1991).

10. Paul Eberle and Shirley Eberle, *The Politics of Child Abuse* (Secaucus, N.J.: Lyle Stuart, 1986); Paul Eberle and Shirley Eberle, *Abuse of Innocence: The McMartin Preschool Trial* (Amherst, N.Y.: Prometheus Books, 1993); Mark Sauer and Jim Okerblom, "Trial by Therapy," *National Review*, September 6, 1993, pp. 30–39.

11. Valerie Sinason, ed., *Treating Survivors of Satanist Abuse: An Invisible Trauma* (London: Routledge, 1994); Gail Carr Feldman, *Lessons in Evil, Lessons from the Light* (New York: Dell, 1994); Linda Blood, *The New Satanists* (New York: Warner, 1994); "Cult Abuse of Children: Witch Hunt or Reality?" special issue *Journal of Psychohistory*, spring 1994; Stephen A. Kent, "Deviant Scripturalism and Ritual Satanic Abuse," *Religion* 23(1993): 229–41; David K. Sakheim and Susan E. Devine, *Out of Darkness: Exploring Satanism and Ritual Abuse* (New York: Lexington Books, 1992); "Satanic Ritual Abuse: The Current State of Knowledge," special issue, *Journal of Psychology and Theology* 20 (3) (1992); Torey L. Hayden, *Ghost Girl: The True Story of a Child in Peril and the Teacher who Saved Her* (Boston: Little, Brown, 1991).

12. A. S. Ross, "Blame It on the Devil," *Redbook*, June 1994, pp. 86–89+; Jeffrey Victor, *Satanic Panic* (Chicago: Open Court, 1993); Philip Jenkins, *Intimate Enemies: Moral Panics in Contemporary Great Britain* (Hawthorne, N.Y.: Aldine de Gruyter, 1992); Philip Jenkins and Daniel Maier-Katkin, "Protecting the Victims of Child Sexual Abuse: A Case for Caution," *Prison Journal* 68(2) (1988): 25–35.

13. Lawrence Wright, "Reporter's Notebook: Remembering Satan," *New Yorker*, May 17 and 24, 1993; Lawrence Wright, *Remembering Satan* (New York: Knopf, 1994).

14. Elizabeth S. Rose, "Surviving the Unbelievable: Cult Ritual Abuse," *Ms.*, January 1993, pp. 40–45; Leslie Bennetts, "Nightmares on Main Street," *Vanity Fair*, June 1993, pp. 42–62; Daniel Goleman, "Proof Lacking for Ritual Abuse by Satanists," *New York Times*, October 31, 1994, p. A13.

15. Lenore Terr, *Unchained Memories: True Stories of Traumatic Memories Lost and Found* (New York: Basic Books 1994); Judith Lewis Herman, *Trauma and Recovery* (New York: Basic Books, 1992).

16. Michael D. Yapko, *Suggestions of Abuse: True and False Memories of Childhood Sexual Trauma* (New York: Simon & Schuster, 1994); Daniel Goleman, "Childhood Trauma: Memory or Invention?" *New York Times*, July 21, 1992, p. C1; Daniel Goleman, "Studies Reveal Suggestibility of Very Young as Witnesses," *New York Times*, June 11, 1993, p. A1; Bruce Bower, "Sudden Recall," *Science News*, September 18, 1993, pp. 184–86.

17. Ellen Bass and Laura Davis, *The Courage to Heal* (New York: HarperCollins, 1988).

18. Ibid., quoted in Carol Tavris, "Beware the Incest Survivor Machine" *New York Times*, January 3, 1993, Book Review sec., p. 1+.

19. Quoted in Tavris, "Beware the Incest Survivor Machine."

20. Harry N. MacLean, *Once upon a Time* (New York: HarperCollins, 1993); "Courts Begin to Respect Memory of Child Abuse," *New York Times*, January 8, 1991, p. A17.

21. Carol Lynn Mithers, "Incest and the Law," *New York Times Magazine* October 21, 1990, p. 44+; Thomas J. Lueck, "Sharing Horrors of Childhood Sexual Abuse, Three Join Legal Debate," *New York Times*, May 5, 1992, p. B1.

22. Jason Berry, *Lead Us Not into Temptation* (New York: Doubleday, 1992), p. 263.

23. Ellen K. Coughlin, "Recollections of Childhood Abuse," *Chronicle of Higher Education*, January 27, 1995, p. A8; Mark Pendergast, *Victims of Memory: Incest Accusations and Shattered Lives* (Upper Access, 1995); Elizabeth Loftus and Katherine Ketcham, *The Myth of Repressed Memory: False Memories and Allegations of Sexual Abuse* (New York: St. Martin's Press, 1994); Elizabeth Loftus and Laura A. Rosenwald, "Buried Memories, Shattered Lives," *ABA Journal,* November 1993, 70–72 ; Richard Ofshe and Ethan Watters, *Making Monsters: False Memories, Psychotherapy and Sexual Hysteria* (New York: Scribner's, 1994); Ethan Watters, "The Devil in Mr. Ingram," *Mother Jones*, July–August 1991, pp. 30–33+.

24. John Mack, *Abduction: Human Encounters with Aliens* (New York: Scribners, 1994) .

25. Wendy Kaminer, *I'm Dysfunctional, You're Dysfunctional: The Recovery Movement and Other Self-Help Fashions* (Greenwich, Conn.: Addison-Wesley, 1992) .

26. David Rieff, "Victims All: Recovery, Co-dependency and the Art of Blaming Somebody Else," *Harper's,* October 1991, pp. 49–56.

27. Stuart A. Kirk and Herb Kutchins, *The Selling of DSM* (Hawthorne, N.Y.: Aldine de Gruyter, 1992).

28. See, for example, Carol Tannehill, "Recovery Movement a Cultural Phenomenon," syndicated Knight-Ridder article in *Centre Daily Times (*State College, Pa.), August 2, 1992, p. E1; Darrell Sifford, "When a Parent Is Wrongly Accused of Sexual Abuse," syndicated Knight-Ridder article in *Centre Daily Times* (State College, Pa.), December 26, 1991; Darrell Sifford, "Therapists Blast New Sex Abuse Industry," syndicated Knight-Ridder article in *Centre Daily Times* (State College, Pa.), January 9, 1992, p. C1; Darrell Sifford, "Not Everyone with Problems Has Been Sexually Abused," syndicated *Philadelphia Inquirer* article in *Centre Daily Times* (State College, Pa.), February 16, 1992, p. E7; Darrell Sifford, "Claims of Parental Abuse Can Be Wrong, Damaging," syndicated Knight-Ridder article in *Centre Daily Times* (State College, Pa.), February 23, 1992; Sharony Andrews, "Experts Clash over Abuse Advice," syndicated Knight-Ridder article in *Centre Daily Times* (State College, Pa.), April 12, 1992, p. E6.

29. Tavris, "Beware the Incest Survivor Machine."

30. *Time,* October 28, 1991.

31. Leon Jaroff, "Lies of the Mind," *Time,* November 29, 1993, pp. 52–59.

32. *Newsweek,* April 19, 1993.

33. *60 Minutes*, April 10, 1994; Michaels's case was also reported sympathetically in CBS's *48 Hours*, May 5, 1993.

34. *60 Minutes*, April 17, 1994.

35. *Frontline,* May 7, 1991; July 17, 1993 .

36. ABC *Primetime Live,* January 7, 1993; CNN, August 1, 1993.

37. Goleman, "Studies Reveal Suggestibility of Very Young as Witnesses."

38. ABC's *20/20*, October 22, 1993 .

39. Loftus and Ketcham, *The Myth of Repressed Memory*; Ofshe and Watters, *Making Monsters*; Wright, *Remembering Satan* .

40. "My Family, Forgive Me," *20/20*, July 22, 1994; compare John Taylor, "The Lost Daughter," *Esquire,* March 1994, pp. 76–87.

41. Quoted in Katie De Koster, ed., *Child Abuse: Opposing Viewpoints* (San Diego, Calif: Greenhaven, 1994), p. 76.

42. Berke Breathed's *Outland,* May 1, 1994.

43. Jane Gross, "Suit Asks, Does Memory Therapy Heal or Harm?" *New York Times*, April 8, 1994, p. A1.

44. Susan Chira, "Sex Abuse: The Coil of Truth and Memory," *New York Times*, December 5, 1993, p. 4:3.

45. John E. B. Myers, ed., *The Backlash: Child Protection under Fire* (Thousand Oaks, Calif.: Sage, 1994); Frances Lear, letter, *New York Times Book Review,* February 14, 1993, Book Review sec.; compare Rose, "Surviving the Unbelievable."

46. "Cult Abuse of Children: Witch Hunt or Reality?" special issue, *Journal of Psychohistory,* spring 1994.

47. Fox Butterfield, "Silent Decades Ended, Dozens Accuse a Priest," *New York Times,* June 9, 1992, p. A18.

48. Goleman, "Childhood Trauma."

49. Butterfield, "Silent Decades Ended, Dozens Accuse a Priest."

50. Quoted in Fox Butterfield, "Diocese Reaches Settlement With 68 Who Accuse Priest of Sexual Abuse," *New York Times,* December 4, 1992, p. A22.

51. Dennis Gaboury and Elinor Burkett, "The Secret of St. Mary's," *Rolling Stone,* November 11, 1993, p. 49. It might be asked whether the litany of confusion and personal misfortunes described here was significantly longer or graver than that of any comparable baby-boom cohort not subject to the abuse described.

52. "Former Catholic Priest Sentenced to 18 to 20 Years for Sex Crimes," *New York Times,* December 7, 1993, p. A22.

53. Elinor Burkett and Frank Bruni, *A Gospel of Shame* (New York: Viking, 1993), p. 103.

54. Thomas C. Fox, "Clergy Sex Abuse Survivors Break Silence," *National Catholic Reporter,* October 30, 1992, pp. 3–4.

55. Ibid.

56. Goleman, "Childhood Trauma"; Chira, "Sex Abuse."

57. Leslie Bennetts, "Unholy Alliances," *Vanity Fair,* December 1991, pp. 224–78; Bennetts, "Nightmares on Main Street."

58. "Every Parent's Nightmare," *Maclean's,* June 22, 1992, pp. 24–25.

59. Andrew Greeley, *Fall from Grace* (New York: G. P. Putnams, 1993), pp. 163–64.

60. Ibid., p. 164 and afterword.

61. Ibid., pp. 195–202.

62. Berry, *Lead Us Not into Temptation,* p. 158.

63. Martha Woodall, "Conference Focussing on Abuse by Priests," *Philadelphia Inquirer,* May 22, 1993, p. B1.

64. Jeanne Miller, *Assault on Innocence* (Albuquerque: B&K Publishers, 1988; originally published under the pseudonym Hilary Stiles.

65. Burkett and Bruni, *A Gospel of Shame,* pp. 237–51; Berry, *Lead Us Not into Temptation,* p. 305; Jerry Thornton, "Cleric Abuse Group to Share Information," *Chicago Tribune,* November 4, 1991, p. 2C:3.

66. "Every Parent's Nightmare" (*Maclean's*).

67. Arthur Jones, "Ecumenism, Sex Abuse, Top CTSA Agenda," *National Catholic Reporter,* July 2, 1993, p. 4.

68. Dawn Gibeau, "Link-Up Gains Momentum on Road to Healing," *National Catholic Reporter,* August 26, 1994, p. 3; "Bishop's Apology Welcome Response to Abuse Victims," *National Catholic Reporter,* August 26, 1994, p. 20.

69. Jason Berry, "Listening to the Survivors: Voices of the People of God," *America,* November 13, 1993, pp. 4–9.

70. Sally Jessy Raphael television show, December 27, 1993 .

71. This was broadcast in June 1994 in the HBO series *Lifestories: Families in Crisis,* in the episode "Betrayed: The Calvin Mire Story."

72. Fox, "Clergy Sex Abuse Survivors Break Silence."

73. Thomas C. Fox, "Accuser's Counsel a Critic of Bernardin," *National Catholic Reporter,* December 3, 1993, p. 6.

74. Sidney Callahan, "Memory Can Play Tricks," *Commonweal,* December 17, 1993, pp. 6–7.

75. Gross, "Suit Asks, Does Memory Therapy Heal or Harm?"

76. Ibid.

77. Reprinted in *New York Times,* November 21, 1993.

78. *Doonesbury,* April 1994.

79. *Doonesbury,* February 1994 .

Chapter 10: Meanings and Directions

1. Joel Best, *Threatened Children* (Chicago: University of Chicago Press, 1990), pp. 65–66.

2. Charles J. Sykes, *A Nation of Victims* (New York: St Martin's Press, 1992); David Rieff, "Victims All: Recovery, Co-dependency and the Art of Blaming Somebody Else," *Harper's,* October 1991, pp. 49–56.

3. George A. Kelly, *The Battle for the American Church* (New York: Doubleday, Image, 1981), p. 315.

4. Roger Finke and Rodney Stark *The Churching of America, 1776–1990* (New Brunswick, N.J.: Rutgers University Press, 1992), pp. 40–46.

5. Ibid., pp. 255–74.

6. Ibid., p. 264 .

7. Jason Berry, *Lead Us Not into Temptation* (New York: Doubleday, 1992), p. xxi.

8. Lawrence Lader, *Politics, Power and the Church: The Catholic Crisis and Its Challenge to American Pluralism* (New York: Macmillan, 1987), p. 11.

9. Berry, *Lead Us Not into Temptation*, pp. 191–92; Andrew Greeley, *The Catholic Myth* (New York: Collier, 1990).

10. Steve Bruce, "Puritan Perverts: Notes on Accusation," *Sociological Review,* n.s., 33 (1985): 47–63.

11. Thomas Robbins, *Cults, Converts and Charisma* (Newbury Park, Calif.: Sage, 1991).

12. Bruce, "Puritan Perverts," p. 56.

13. Andrew Greeley, "Priestly Silence on Pedophilia," *New York Times*, March 13, 1992, p. A31.

14. Peter Steinfels, "Beliefs", *New York Times,* June 25, 1994, p. A12.

15. Supported by texts such as Matt. 18:15–22; 1 Cor. 6:1–7.

16. Robert Wuthnow, *Sharing the Journey* (New York: Free Press, 1994); Wade Clark Roof, *A Generation of Seekers: The Spiritual Journeys of the Baby Boom Generation* (San Francisco: Harper, 1993).

17. Warren Bird, "The Great Small Group Takeover," *Christianity Today,* February 7 1994, pp. 25–29.

18. Roof, *A Generation of Seekers,* pp. 214–15.

19. Peter W. Huber, *Liability: The Legal Revolution and Its Consequences* (New York: Basic Books, 1988), pp. 77, 183.

20. Stephen J. Rossetti, ed., *Slayer of the Soul: Child Sexual Abuse and the Catholic Church* (Mystic, Conn.: Twenty-Third Publications, 1990), pp. 45–66.

21. Julia Quinn Dempsey, John R. Groman, John P. Madden, and Alphonse P. Spilly, *The Cardinal's Commission on Clerical Sexual Misconduct with Minors: Report to Joseph Cardinal Bernardin, Archbishop of Chicago* (Chicago: The Commission, 1992), pp. 38–39.

22. Jim Bowman, "Is Male Headship Linked to Spousal Abuse?" *Christianity Today,* June 20, 1994, p. 62.

23. John Boswell, *Christianity, Social Tolerance and Homosexuality* (Chicago: University of Chicago Press, 1980); John Boswell, *Same-Sex Unions in Pre-Modern Europe* (New York: Villard Books, 1994).

24. Andrew Greeley, in Berry, *Lead Us Not into Temptation*, p. xiii.

25. Douglas Martin, "Feeling Slighted by Church Officials, New York Youth Sues over Abuse by His Priest," *New York Times,* February 24, 1993, p. B4.

26. Thomas T. McAvoy, *The Great Crisis in American Catholic History, 1895–1900* (Chicago: Regnery, 1957); compare Robert D. Cross, *The Emergence of Liberal Catholicism in America* (Chicago: Quadrangle, 1968).

27. Elinor Burkett and Frank Bruni *A Gospel of Shame* (New York: Viking, 1993), p. 219.

28. Peter Berger and Thomas Luckman *The Social Construction of Reality* (New York: Doubleday, Anchor, 1967), p. 149.

29. "Policy on Sexual Abuse by Priests: Los Angeles Archdiocese" *Origins* (Catholic News Service) 24 (5) (1994), p. 70.

30. Reginald W. Bibby, *Unknown Gods* (Toronto: Stoddart, 1993), p. 208.

31. Richard P. McBrien, "Celibacy, Priest Shortage, Plot May Thicken," *National Catholic Reporter,* July 30, 1993, p. 20.

32. Erich Goode and Nachman Ben-Yehuda, *Moral Panics* (Oxford: Blackwells, 1994).

33. Stuart Hall et al., *Policing the Crisis (* London: Routledge, 1978); all emphases in the original.

34. Stan Cohen, *Folk Devils and Moral Panics: The Creation of the Mods and Rockers* (Oxford: Blackwells, 1972), p. 28.

35. The changing nature of audience receptivity is usefully discussed in James R. Andrews, *The Practice of Rhetorical Criticism* (New York: Macmillan, 1983).

Index

Leyva, Tony, 10–11, 38, 52
Liability, legal. *See* Legal environment
Liberation theology, 96, 98, 116
Lindsey, Hal, 31
Linkup. *See* VOCAL (Victims of Clergy Abuse
    Linkup)
Litigation. *See* Legal environment
Los Angeles, Calif., archdiocese of, 35, 80, 122,
    128
Louisiana. *See* Cinel, Dino; Gauthe, Gilbert
Luddy, Francis, 70, 72
Lutherans, 22–23, 51, 118
Lutz, Robert, 135–36
Lynch, Bernard, 103

McBrien, Richard, 109
McCann, David, 47
McCutcheon, Peter, 35, 128
McMartin preschool, child abuse case at, 31, 90,
    141–42, 144, 155
McNeill, John, 98, 100
Mann Act, 131
Manning, Paul, 75
Manson, Charles, 58
Maria Monk, 26, 31
Martin, Malachi, 103
Maryland, abuse cases in, 35, 45, 146. *See also*
    Baltimore, Md.; St. Luke's Institute, Suitland,
    Md.; Washington, D.C., archdiocese of
Massachusetts, 45, 61, 128, 182n109. *See also*
    Boston, Mass.; Law, Bernard (Cardinal);
    Manning, Paul, Porter, James; Worcester,
    Mass., diocese of
Mayer, Robert, 11, 41–42
Media, 53–76. *See also* Cinema; Press; Television
    news and documentary programs
Memories, recovered, 18, 142–52, 199n79. *See
    also* Ritual child abuse; Therapy and therapists
Methodists, 9–10, 118, 122
Michaels, Kelly, 144–45, 148
Michigan, 12, 51. *See also* Detroit, Mich.
Miller, Jeanne, 40–43, 48, 50, 67–69, 106, 120,
    135, 150. *See also* VOCAL (Victims of Clergy
    Abuse Linkup)
Milwaukee, Wisc., 48, 103, 129, 150. *See also*
    Weakland, Rembert
Minneapolis, Minn., 117
Minnesota, 39, 130, 143, 150–52. *See also*
    Adamson, Thomas; Anderson, Jeffrey;
    Minneapolis, Minn.; Porter, James
Mire, Calvin, 151, 205n71
Moral panics, 169–71
Morley, Pat, 102–3
Mount Cashel. *See* Newfoundland, abuse cases in
Mouton, Ray, 35–38, 108

Movies. *See* Cinema; Television movies
Mowat, Anton, 45
Ms. 54, 120–21, 145
Multiple personality disorder, 86. *See also*
    Memories, recovered
Murdoch, Iris, 59
Murdoch, Rupert, 63

National Catholic Reporter. See Press, *National
    Catholic Reporter*
National Catholic Welfare Conference, 96, 99
National Conference of Catholic Bishops
    (NCCB), 37, 40, 42, 44, 50, 98–99, 128,
    131, 151
National Lampoon, 31
Nativism, 22, 31, 105
"New Age" religion, 116–17, 160
Newark, N.J., archdiocese of, 34
Newfoundland, abuse cases in, 38–40, 44, 54, 61,
    71–73, 79, 109, 149
New Jersey, 47. *See also* Camden, N.J., diocese
    of; Newark, N.J., archdiocese of
New Mexico, 46, 134. *See also* Porter, James;
    Sanchez, Roberto; Santa Fe, N.Mex.,
    archdiocese of; Servants of the Paraclete
New Orleans, La., 51. *See also* Cinel, Dino
New religious movements, 158–59, 161, 182n100
News media. *See* Press; Television news and
    documentary programs
Newspapers. *See* Press
New York, archdiocese of, 31, 44, 73, 93, 101,
    103, 129. *See also* Calabrese, Daniel; Lynch,
    Bernard; O'Connor, John (Cardinal); Pipala,
    Edward
New York City, 22. *See also* New York,
    archdiocese of; Press; Ritter, Bruce
New York state, 44, 52
Nova Scotia, 79
Novels. *See* Fiction
Nuns, 24–26, 48, 61, 97–99, 116, 175n20

Oakeley, Edmund, 34, 128
O'Brien, Thomas, 57
O'Connell, William, 35–36, 64
O'Connor, John (Cardinal), 44, 59, 91, 135
O'Malley, Jack, 49
Ontario, 40, 47, 48, 130, 149–50
Ordination of women. *See* Women, ordination of,
    as priests

Papacy, 19, 22, 27, 30, 66, 99, 109. *See also* John
    Paul I, Pope; John Paul II, Pope; Roman
    Catholic church
Paraclete, House of the. *See* Servants of the
    Paraclete